"The Thernstroms painstakingly review possible reasons for this [racial] academic gap.... The biggest obstacle of all may be our collective unwillingness to acknowledge the racial gap in the first place.... The Thernstroms mean to bring that secret out in the open. And thank goodness for that.... We can only hope that their analysis, coming on the eve of the fiftieth anniversary of *Brown* v. *Board of Education*, will help lead the way toward what that court decision aimed to bring about, equal opportunity for every American child."

—Clint Bolick, *The Wall Street Journal*

"[Abigail Thernstrom and Stephan Thernstrom of Harvard] are also the authors of the best book on race relations—*America in Black and White*—so there are high expectations for this new book. *No Excuses* lives up to those expectations. If you read just one book about American education all year, this should be the book."

—Thomas Sowell, Hoover Institution, Stanford University

"This book, [Abigail and Stephan Thernstrom's] manifesto, is one of the most valuable guides to saving American schools I have ever read."

—Jay Mathews, *Woodrow Wilson Quarterly*

"*No Excuses* is destined to become one of the most discussed . . . books on the nation's crisis in education in quite some time.... [It] asks the tough questions, takes a hard look at the numbers, and comes up with carefully considered, admittedly imperfect solutions to one of our society's most urgent concerns."

—Andrew Wolf, *New York Sun*

"An important, bracing, and deeply conscientious book. *[No Excuses]* is a combination of cool scholarship and passionate caring."

—Jay Nordlinger, *National Review*

"An absolutely brilliant analysis of what ails American education today.... This learned and deeply humane book shines a spotlight on [failing schools] and points the way to a better future."

—Mona Charen, *Jewish World Review*

"*No Excuses* is in large part a devastating indictment, laden with statistics, case studies, and powerful analysis, of how disastrously our educational system has failed black students.... Abby and Steve Thernstrom [are] perhaps the nation's most careful and candid scholars on what their book calls 'the main source of ongoing racial inequality [and] the central civil-rights issue of our time: our failure to provide first-class education for black and Hispanic students, in both cities and suburbs.' "

—Stuart Taylor, Jr., *National Journal*

"A damning account of how the public schools fail black students. . . . One cannot read the Thernstroms' book without wondering: Where are the civil-rights marches protesting the public schools?"

—Rich Lowry, *New York Post*

"If current education-reform efforts fizzle, we'll need a strong 'Plan B' to follow immediately. A good place to start is with the lessons from *No Excuses*."

—Matt Rosenberg, *The Seattle Times*

"A comprehensive and informed effort to explore the racial gap in education and what can be done about it."

—Nathan Glazer, *The New Republic*

"This important new book by the Thernstroms, who also wrote *America in Black and White*, will be widely noted and much discussed in education circles."

—Justin Torres, *Education Gadfly*

"*No Excuses* assembles an impressive array of evidence to demonstrate that the 'typical' (in the statistical sense) black or Hispanic child in the U.S. enters school behind, and stays behind. . . . What makes the Thernstroms' contribution distinctive and valuable is that they also identify a path forward, a way to begin tackling what they aptly call 'the most important civil-rights issue of our time.'"

—Leslie Lenkowsky, *Commentary*

"Meticulously documented and powerfully written."

—Kim Marshall, *The Boston Globe*

"Abigail and Stephan Thernstrom have once again written a book that goes to the heart of an important issue. *No Excuses* is a timely, well-documented analysis of the achievement gap in education. It provides the information that will bring us closer to understanding and addressing one of the most urgent problems in our society."

—Diane Ravitch, author, *The Language Police*

"*No Excuses: Closing the Racial Gap in Learning* is the most important civil rights book in a generation. And one of the most encouraging. . . . The uncannily insightful authors of the encyclopedic *America in Black and White*, perhaps the definitive work on race and race relations in contemporary America, take an unflinching look at the problem, the reasons therefore, and proven and potential remedies. This is not a book for the merely well-intentioned. This is a book about *results*."

—Peter Kirasanow, *Engage*

ALSO BY ABIGAIL THERNSTROM AND STEPHAN THERNSTROM

America in Black and White: One Nation, Indivisible
Beyond the Color Line: New Perspectives on Race and Ethnicity
in America (editors)

BOOKS BY ABIGAIL THERNSTROM

Whose Votes Count?: Affirmative Action and Minority Voting Rights
A Democracy Reader: Classic and Modern Speeches, Essays, Poems,
Declarations and Documents on Freedom and Human Rights Worldwide
(with Diane Ravitch)
School Choice in Massachusetts

BOOKS BY STEPHAN THERNSTROM

Poverty and Progress: Social Mobility in a 19th-Century City
Nineteenth-Century Cities: Essays in the New Urban History
(edited with Richard Sennett)
Poverty, Politics, and Planning in the New Boston: The Origins of ABCD
The Other Bostonians:
Poverty and Progress in the American Metropolis 1880–1970
Harvard Encyclopedia of American Ethnic Groups (editor)
A History of the American People
Our Changing Population (with Richard Gill and Nathan Glazer)

NoExcuses

Closing the Racial Gap in Learning

Abigail Thernstrom and Stephan Thernstrom

Simon & Schuster Paperbacks
New York   London   Toronto   Sydney

SIMON & SCHUSTER PAPERBACKS
Rockefeller Center
1230 Avenue of the Americas
New York, NY 10020

First Simon & Schuster Paperbacks edition 2004

SIMON & SCHUSTER PAPERBACKS and colophon are registered trademarks
of Simon & Schuster, Inc.

For information regarding special discounts for bulk purchases,
please contact Simon & Schuster Special Sales at
1-800-456-6798 or business@simonandschuster.com

Designed by Karolina Harris

Manufactured in the United States of America

10   9   8   7   6   5   4   3   2   1

The Library of Congress has catalogued the hardcover edition as follows:
Thernstrom, Abigail M., 1936–
No excuses : closing the racial gap in learning /
Abigail Thernstrom and Stephan Thernstrom.
p.   cm.
Includes bibliographical references and index.
1. Minority students—United States.   2. Academic
achievement—United States.   3. Educational equalization—
United States.   4. Education—Social aspects—United States.
I. Thernstrom, Stephan.   II. Title.
LC3731.T455   2003
371.829'00973—dc21   2003054439

ISBN 0-7432-0446-8
0-7432-6522-X (Pbk)

Acknowledgments

We don't know any authors who write books alone. In our case, we are deeply indebted to the institutions and foundations that supported us, to a great collection of research assistants, to a handful of friends and colleagues who read the final manuscript, and to educators and educational scholars too numerous to name who were willing to talk and keep talking as we struggled with ideas.

Abigail Thernstrom has been a senior fellow at the Manhattan Institute for Policy Research since 1993, and MI's support has been indispensable in writing this book. Lawrence Mone, Manhattan Institute's president, has turned a small organization into a large and thriving home for scholars working on public policy, and we are enormously grateful for his unwavering commitment to this project. We thank, as well, the generosity of the John M. Olin Foundation and the Earhart Foundation, both of which contributed substantially to the funding of the book.

Since 1999, Stephan Thernstrom has also been a senior fellow at the Manhattan Institute, and that association has meant support for both research assistants and research-related travel. He took sabbatical leave from Harvard in 1998–1999, and Harvard University and the John M. Olin foundation made that break from teaching possible.

Cornelia Davidson was a gift to us from the Earhart Foundation. Twice a week for three and a half years, she kept the almost overwhelming flow of information on education in order, chased down stories and facts on the Web and elsewhere, and served as a wonderful sounding board and critic, prompting us on many occasions to revise arguments. Kevin Amer, Thomas Koelbl, Michael Shumsky, and David Weinfeld—all of them either undergraduates or taking time out between college and law school—were splendid research assistants at one time or another. They, too, not only worked on substantive issues but gave us terrific feedback. Michael Dotsikas of the Manhattan Institute provided invaluable help with the preparation of the graphs.

At the point at which we had a complete draft of the manuscript, Norman Atkins, Douglas Besharov, Rafe Esquith, Michael Feinberg, Tom Fortmann, Bill Guenther, David Levin, Brett Peiser, James Peyser, Diane Ravitch, Ricky Silberman, and Grant Ujifusa read some or all of it carefully. For his detailed critique of many substantive points, we are particularly indebted to Bill Guenther, who as president of Mass Insight has been deeply involved in education in Massachusetts for many years. Our son, Sam, read the manuscript once for substance, prompting important revisions, and then, in a break between jobs, provided extraordinary line editing. Our daughter, Melanie, doesn't edit our books, but she enriches our life in a multitude of other ways.

Finally, Glen Hartley and Lynn Chu, Writers' Representatives, have been our long-standing, wonderful literary agents, and Bob Bender is the perfect Simon & Schuster editor. We thank all three profusely.

                                                    Abigail Thernstrom
                                                    Stephan Thernstrom
                                           Lexington, Massachusetts

To Thomas Sowell
for his pioneering scholarship and unflagging courage

Contents

List of Figures

Nine: Racial Isolation

Ten: Teacher Quality

Twelve: Raising the Bar

Introduction

There's nothing the school can do.
Latisha Robinson, a black eighth-grader in Elk Grove, California

You've got to have to want to do better.
Kiarra Gibson, her classmate[1]

The student body of Cedarbrook Middle School in a Philadelphia suburb is one-third black, two-thirds white. The town has a very low poverty rate, good schools, and a long-established black middle class. But an eighth-grade advanced algebra class that a reporter visited in June 2001 contained not a single black student. The class in which the teacher was explaining that the 2 in 21 stands for 20, however, was 100 percent black. A few black students were taking accelerated English, but no whites were sitting in the English class that was learning to identify verbs.[2]

The Cedarbrook picture is by no means unique. It is all too familiar, and even worse in the big-city schools that most black and Hispanic youngsters attend. This is an American tragedy and a national emergency for which there are no good excuses.

The racial gap in academic achievement is an educational crisis, but it is also the main source of ongoing racial inequality. And racial inequality is America's great unfinished business, the wound that remains unhealed. Thus, this is a book about education, but it also addresses the central civil rights issue of our time: our failure to provide first-class education for black and Hispanic students, in both cities and suburbs.

The black high school graduation rate has more than doubled since 1960. And blacks attend college at a rate that is higher than it was for whites just two decades ago.[3] But the good news ends there. The gap in academic achievement that we see today is actually worse than it was fifteen years ago. In the 1970s and through most of the 1980s, it was closing, but around 1988 it began to widen, with no turnaround in sight.

Today, at age 17 the typical black or Hispanic student is scoring less well on the nation's most reliable tests than at least 80 percent of his or her white classmates. In five of the seven subjects tested by the National Assessment of Educational Progress (NAEP), a majority of black students perform in the lowest category—Below Basic. The result: By twelfth grade, African Americans are typically four years behind white and Asian students, while Hispanics are doing only a tad better than black students. These students are finishing high school with a junior high education.

Students who have equal skills and knowledge will have roughly equal earnings. That was not always true, but it is today. Schooling has become the key to racial equality. No wonder that Robert Moses, a luminous figure in the civil rights revolution of the 1960s, is convinced that "the absence of math literacy in urban and rural communities throughout this country is an issue as urgent as the lack of registered Black voters in Mississippi was in 1961." Algebra, he believes, is "the gatekeeper of citizenship."[4]

Literacy, too, is a "gatekeeper," and the deadline for learning is alarmingly early. "For many students . . . the die is cast by eighth grade. Students without the appropriate math and reading skills by that grade are unlikely to acquire them by the end of high school . . . ," a U.S. Department of Education study has concluded.[5]

Race has famously been called the "American dilemma." But since the mid-1960s, racial equality has also been an American project. An astonishing, peaceful revolution in the status of blacks and the state of race relations has transformed the country. And yet too few Americans have recognized and acknowledged the stubborn inequalities that only better schools can address.

Even civil rights groups have long averted their gaze from the disquieting reality. "You can have a hunch that black students are not doing as well, but some of this was surprising," A. V. Fleming, president of the Urban League in Fort Wayne, Indiana, said, as the picture of low black achievement began to emerge in the late 1990s.[6] In Elk Grove, California, an affluent suburb of Sacramento, black parents were shocked, angry, and in tears when they learned of the low test scores of their kids. "People know that this is an important issue, and they don't know how to talk about it," said Philip Moore, the principal of the local middle school, who is black himself.

For too long, the racial gap in academic performance was treated not only by civil rights leaders, but by the media, and even by scholars, as a dirty secret—something to whisper about behind closed doors. As if it were racist to say we have a problem: Black and Hispanic kids, on average, are not doing well in school.

Suddenly, however, this shamefully ignored issue has moved to the front and center of the education stage. In part, the new attention is simply a response to an altered economic reality. A half century ago, an eighth-grade dropout could get a secure and quite well-paid job at the Ford Motor Company or U.S. Steel. Today, the Honda plant in Ohio does not hire people who cannot pass a test of basic mathematical skills.

Demographic change, too, has forced Americans to pay attention to an educational and racial catastrophe in their midst. Fifty years ago, Hispanic children were no more than 2 percent of the school population. Today, a third of all American students are black or Latino.[7] In California, Louisiana, Mississippi, New Mexico, and Texas white schoolchildren have become a numerical minority. These numbers, in themselves, drive home the urgency of educating all children.

The unprecedented sense of urgency is unmistakable in No Child Left Behind (NCLB), the 2001 version of the nation's omnibus 1965 Elementary and Secondary Education Act. The central aim of the revised statute, as its preamble states boldly, is "to close the achievement gap . . . so that no child is left behind." Closing the gap is the core purpose of the legislation—and the test of its eventual success.

Thus, the act requires all states to test children in grades 3–8 and report scores broken down by race, ethnicity, and other demographic characteristics associated with educational disadvantage. Each group must show significant annual progress. Affluent districts will no longer be able to coast along, hiding their lower-performing black and Hispanic students in overall averages that make their schools look good. A bucket of very cold water has been poured on educators—and particularly those who have been quite complacent. NCLB has been an overdue attention-getter. At a well-attended national meeting on education in September 2002, the audience was asked to name the most important new policy requirement in No Child Left Behind; closing the racial and ethnic achievement gap was the clear winner.[8]

Indifference to minority children who arrive in kindergarten already behind and continue to flounder is no longer an option for schools. The problem has been acknowledged—and thus must now be addressed. Racial equality will remain a dream as long as blacks and Hispanics learn less in school than whites and Asians. If black youngsters remain second-class students, they will be second-class citizens—a racially identifiable and enduring group of have-nots.

Certain assumptions and arguments run through this book. We list some of the most important here as a guide to our readers, with references to the chapters in which they first appear.

• Before we discuss remedies, we must outline the problem (which we do in Chapter 1). Only if the full magnitude of the racial gap is understood will Americans begin to appreciate the need for a radical rethinking of what counts today as school reform. The racial gap is not an IQ story; this is not a book about innate intelligence. The bad news that we discuss simply means we must work harder and smarter at delivering better education.

• Test scores matter (Chapter 2 argues). They tell us precisely what we need to know if we have any hope of reforming education and closing the racial gap in academic achievement. Good tests measure the knowledge and skills that demanding jobs and college courses require. When black and Latino students leave high school barely knowing how to read, their future— and that of the nation—is in jeopardy. Our sense of danger and moral outrage should be particularly strong when so many of these students are African Americans—members of a group that suffered the brutality of slavery, legally enforced segregation, and racial exclusion.

• Terrific schools that serve highly disadvantaged minority kids do exist. There just aren't enough of them. (We take a very close look at some of them in Chapters 3 and 4). These schools are not waiting until the day social and economic disparities disappear. "No Excuses" is their relentless message. Every student is expected to work hard to acquire the skills and knowledge that tests measure. These are schools with great leaders and great teachers who have high academic and behavioral standards, and the schools provide nonstop learning through longer school days, weeks, and years.

• These schools also aim to transform the culture of their students—as that culture affects academic achievement (we argue in Chapter 4). "We are fighting a battle involving skills and values," David Levin, founder of the KIPP Academy in the South Bronx, New York, has explained. This is a fight that all good schools must engage in. Those we came to admire set social norms that create effective learning environments. Students learn to speak politely to the principal, teachers, and strangers; they learn to dress neatly, to arrive at school on time, to pay attention in class, finish homework, and never waste time. Teachers work hard to instill the desire, discipline, and dedication—the will to succeed—that will enable disadvantaged youth to climb the American ladder of opportunity. These are essential ingredients in the definition of effective education for high-need kids.

• When it comes to academic success, members of some ethnic and racial groups are culturally luckier than others. "Culture" is a loose and slippery term, and we do not use it to imply a fixed set of group traits, but rather values, attitudes, and skills that are shaped and reshaped by environment. Asians (at whom we look in Chapter 5) are typically more deeply engaged in academic work than their peers, cut classes less often, and enroll in Advanced Placement courses at triple the white rate. The explanation: family expectations. These relative newcomers belong to the group that has most intensely embraced the traditional American work ethic. But their story contains good news: Hard work is a culturally transferable trait. Their success can be replicated. Culture matters, but it is also open to change.

• Family messages don't always mesh well with the objectives of schools. The Hispanics who are flooding into American schools today (the subject of Chapter 6) are very much like Italian immigrants circa 1910. For those Italian peasants, school was not a high priority; they expected their children to take a job as soon as possible. But over the generations, academic success rose in importance; time had a salutary effect. Hispanics are also making real gains over generations—gains obscured by a continuing influx of new immigrants. There are thus historical and demographic reasons why so many Latino children are not faring well academically. Those reasons do not let schools off the hook; they can do better. Some cultures are academically advantageous, but neither poverty nor culture is educational destiny.

• Black academic underachievement (the subject of Chapter 7) has deep historical roots. The first signs of underachievement appear very early in the life of black children, and although scholars have not been able to pinpoint the precise reasons, they can identify some of the risk factors that seem to be limiting their intellectual development. Among them: low birth weight, single-parent households, and birth to a very young mother. African-American children not only arrive in school less academically prepared; they also tend to be less ready to conform to behavioral demands. They watch an extraordinary amount of television—essential to belonging to the peer culture, they say. The process of connecting black children to the world of academic achievement isn't easy in the best of educational settings. But the good schools we describe in Chapters 3 and 4 show that it can be done. Not without fundamental change in American public education, however.

• Greater school funding could be put to good use; racially integrated schools are desirable; and teacher quality is a real problem in too many schools—particularly in those serving the children who most need an excellent education. But the usual reasons given for the racial achievement gap—a shortage of money, racial isolation, markedly worse teachers by the usual criteria of education school credentials, and the like—do not in fact explain the skills and knowledge gap between the average Asian or white student and the typical black or Hispanic youngster. (This is the argument we make in

Chapters 8, 9, and 10.) It does not cost more to raise academic and behavioral standards, and money, per se, is no panacea. Additional funding poured into the existing system will not solve the problem of underachieving black and Hispanic students. Schools are not becoming "resegregated"; they cannot, in any case, magically become racially balanced given existing residential patterns. Most important, what matters in a school is not the racial mix but the academic culture and the quality of the teachers, which is not likely to improve unless the rules governing hiring, firing, and salaries, as well as working conditions, are changed.

• Since 1965, the federal government has poured money into Title I and Head Start in an effort to close the poverty—and, indirectly, the racial—gap in academic achievement. The returns have been crushingly disappointing (the subject of Chapter 11). Head Start remains the right idea; whether it can be translated into a truly effective program remains uncertain. In 2001 the secretary of education described Title I as a $125 billion program with "virtually nothing to show for it."[9] When the provision was first being debated in 1965, Senator Robert F. Kennedy turned to the U.S. commissioner of education and said: "Look, I want to change this bill because it doesn't have any way of measuring those damn educators like you. . . ."[10] Kennedy got his way only on paper. Measuring schools by student results goes against the grain of the traditional educational culture, but the newest revision of Title I—in 2001—insists on it. It's a long-overdue change. Student results are the educational bottom line.

• Starting in the late 1980s, a movement for testing, standards, and accountability began to sweep the states, and in January 2002, the president signed into law the 2001 No Child Left Behind Act. (Chapter 12 reviews this history.) Closing the racial gap is its central aim. Will mandatory testing, scores broken down by race and ethnicity, an insistence on "adequate yearly progress," and various sanctions for poor performance finally level the academic playing field? If the record of two model states, Texas and North Carolina, is any measure, the prospects are not good. The much-celebrated efforts in those two states did improve the knowledge and skills of all students, but the racial gap did not narrow. White scores went up and black scores went up, but the difference between them remained about as wide. Closing that gap is the acid test of educational reform.

• Americans are educational reformers, but in fact little has changed despite much activity, particularly in the last quarter century. That's not surprising. "Reformers" have had limited appetite for true reform, and, in any case, the roadblocks to fundamental change are formidable. (Chapter 13 reviews those obstacles.) The teaching profession does not reward imaginative, ambitious, competitive innovators. Big-city superintendents, as well as principals, operate in a straitjacket. The politics of school reform often have little to do with kids. Most important, the enormous power of teachers unions stops almost all real change in its tracks. No Child Left Behind was envisioned as a means of circumventing these obstacles to reform. It contains promising steps in the right direction, but closing the racial gap in academic achievement will demand more. It is no accident that the revolutionary schools we describe in Chapters 3 and 4 are outside the traditional public system. These are schools that students, parents, and staff have chosen, and choice is integral to their success. The forces of opposition to more school choice are powerful; on the other hand, the lure of charter schools and perhaps vouchers may prove irresistible if No Child Left Behind fails to close the racial gap in academic achievement, as we predict it will.

In its call for drastic action to overcome a national crisis, this is a book with a tough message. That message is directed not only to schools, but also to students and their families. In our epigraph, Latisha Robinson is wrong, but her classmate Kiarra Gibson is right. In fact, schools can do much to close the racial gap; students, however, have to do their part: coming to school on time, attending every class, listening with their full attention, burning the midnight oil.

A letter to *The New York Times* in June 2002 asked: "Why bother to learn in school if there is no advantage, no opportunity after, and nobody cares?"[11] No advantage? No opportunity? Today? It's a familiar but misguided and dangerous claim—particularly dangerous when delivered to school-age kids making often irrevocable decisions about who they are and where they're going. Pessimism is a self-fulfilling prophecy.

The best schools deliver quite a different message. At North Star Academy in Newark, New Jersey, the students in the morning circle often chant answers—with claps and stomps and fists held high—to a series of questions posed by one of the codirectors: Why are you here? To get an education. And what will you have to do? Work! Hard! Work, work, work hard! Work! Hard! Work, work, work hard! And what will you need? Self-discipline Why? To be the master of my own destiny!

You *can* become the master of your own destiny: It's the most important message that schools like North Star deliver. A sixth-grader defined success "as having the freedom to decide what you want to do in life instead of someone choosing your path, because when someone chooses your path, you're going to get something probably that you don't want."[12]

For too many years, too few black and Hispanic youngsters—particularly those in urban public schools—have acquired the skills to choose their own path. It is time to bring an end to that heartbreaking story. But a new beginning will require radical change in America's schools. Our hope, in writing this book, is to do our small part in turning that vision into an idea whose time has come.

1 The Problem

One: Left Behind

When I see those gaps, my heart goes out to the kids. They are our future.
I wonder what's going wrong.
Demetra Skinner, teacher, Hambrick Middle School, Aldine, Texas[1]

"Are you in the right class?" Roderick Sleet's teacher asked on the first day of an honors class in a Fort Wayne, Indiana, high school.[2] It was a terrible question, for which there was no good excuse, but a black student in a demanding course had evidently caught her by surprise. In schools across the country, there are too few black students in honors classes, and too many floundering even in the elementary years. At the Bull Run Elementary School in Fairfax County, Virginia, the fifth- and sixth-graders in a gifted program study geometry and, in the spring of 2002, were reading *To Kill a Mockingbird*. There were no black or Hispanic students in the class.[3]

This heartbreaking picture reinforces one of America's worst racial stereotypes: Blacks just aren't book-smart. As the Introduction made plain, black and Hispanic children are typically academic underachievers, but innate intelligence is not the explanation. In a wonderful Los Angeles class about which we will talk much in Chapters 3 and 4, Latino and Asian children are doing equally well, even though Asian-American children are usually the academic stars. Great teaching makes a huge difference—with all kids.

Before we discuss remedies, however, we must outline the problem. Only if its full magnitude is understood will Americans grasp the need for a radical rethinking of what counts today as educational reform. The shocking facts are a wake-up call. Another generation of black children is drifting through school without acquiring essential skills and knowledge. Hispanic children are not faring much better, and for neither group is there a comforting trend in the direction of progress. Although the current president has put educational reform at the top of his domestic agenda, complacency abounds. We ignore the plight of these youngsters at our peril. As these children fare, so fares the nation.

The Four-Year Skills Gap

This is a book about the racial gap in academic achievement, but how do we actually know how much students are learning? The best evidence comes from the National Assessment of Educational Progress (NAEP), often called "the nation's report card." Created by Congress in 1969, NAEP regularly tests nationally representative samples of American elementary and secondary school students in the fourth, eighth, and twelfth grades (or sometimes at ages 9, 13, and 17).[4]

The NAEP results consistently show a frightening gap between the basic academic skills of the average African-American or Latino student and those of the typical white or Asian American.[5] By twelfth grade, on average, black students are four years behind those who are white or Asian. Hispanics don't do much better.

It is important to remember that in every group, of course, some students do well in school, while others flounder. There are plenty of low-performing whites. In fact, they outnumber African Americans and Hispanics, since whites are still more than 60 percent of the nation's schoolchildren, while blacks and Latinos are a little less than one-third together. Nevertheless, it's important to look at group averages, not simply absolute numbers. If blacks have an exceptionally high poverty rate and few have incomes above the national average, that is obviously a cause for social concern. So too with disparities in educational performance.

Since the numbers we discuss in this chapter and later are deeply depressing, the reader should remember that they are not measurements of fixed, innate traits that are independent of the environment and cannot be changed. If we thought that, we would not have written this book. The measurements that are the foundation of this work register how well or badly groups of young people are developing the intellectual skills that are essential to doing well in America today and tomorrow. Only by recognizing the severity of the problem can we begin to think about possible remedies. The racial gap in academic achievement is a problem that can be solved; there is a way, if we have the will.

A small thought experiment perhaps illuminates the seriousness of the gap today, however. To function well in our postindustrial, information-based economy, students at the end of high school should be able to read complex material, write reasonably well, and demonstrate a mastery of precalculus math. Imagine that you are an employer considering two job applicants, one with a high school diploma, the other a dropout at the end of eighth grade. Unless the job requires only pure brawn, an employer will seldom find the choice between the two candidates difficult.

The employer hiring the typical black high school graduate (or the college that admits the average black student) is, in effect, choosing a youngster who has made it only through eighth grade. He or she will have a high school diploma, but not the skills that should come with it. This shocking fact is plain from Figure 1-1, which displays the results of the most recent NAEP tests in four core subjects.[6] Figure 1-1 reveals that blacks nearing the end of their high school education perform a little worse than white eighth-graders in both reading and U.S. history, and a lot worse in math and geography. In math and geography, indeed, they know no more than whites in the seventh grade.[7]

Hispanics do only a little better than African Americans. In reading and U.S. history, their NAEP scores in their senior year of high school are a few points above those of whites in eighth grade. In math and geography, they are a few points lower.

Asians, by contrast, perform about the same as whites, despite the fact

Figure 1-1. The Four-Year Gap: How Black and Hispanic High School Seniors Perform Compared to Whites and Asians in the 8th Grade

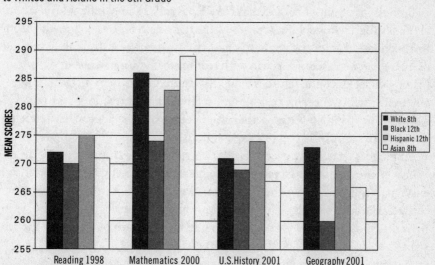

Source: National Assessment for Educational Progress Data Tool.

that they are a nonwhite racial group. They fall a bit below the white average in history and geography, but are a bit ahead in mathematics.

"Below Basic"

Looking at the average black or Hispanic student as compared to the average white or Asian student yields these depressing results. There is another way of judging the magnitude of the racial gap in academic achievement.[8] The NAEP assessments report not only average scores for each racial or ethnic group; they also place each individual test-taker in one of four different "achievement levels." The bottom is labeled Below Basic, which is reserved for students unable to display even "partial mastery of prerequisite knowledge and skills that are fundamental for proficient work" at their grade. Those who have only a partial mastery are at the Basic level. To rate as Proficient, the next step up, students must give a "solid academic performance," demonstrating "competency over challenging subject matter." Advanced, the highest achievement level, is reserved for a performance that is "superior."[9]

An alarmingly high proportion of *all* American students, the NAEP results show, are leaving high school today with academic skills that are Below Basic. In reading and writing, it is nearly one-quarter of all students. In geography, math, and civics, it is about a third. A dismaying 47 percent of all students ranked Below Basic in the 2000 science assessment. Worse yet, in American history the figure in 2001 was 57 percent.

Some experts have charged that NAEP has set its achievement levels unrealistically high.[10] Possibly so. Certainly, the definition of "Basic" does not seem to be consistent across subjects, since less than a quarter of students at the end of high school are Below Basic in both reading and writing, while in American history and science the figure is roughly 50 percent. Is the typical student really that much weaker in history and science than in reading and writing? Maybe. But it is also possible that the experts who decided what students should know simply had higher expectations in some subjects than in others.

This controversy, however, has little bearing on the issue that concerns us. Whether the standards in particular subjects err in being too tough or too easy, within each subject they are applied in precisely the same way across the racial and ethnic spectrum. The question is how racial groups compare in their distribution at the four achievement levels. Figure 1-2 provides the answer.

It shows that the proportion of white students who have not acquired even Basic skills by twelfth grade is around one-fifth in most subjects, and it ex-

Figure 1-2. Percentage of 12th-Graders Scoring "Below Basic" on the Most Recent NAEP Assessments

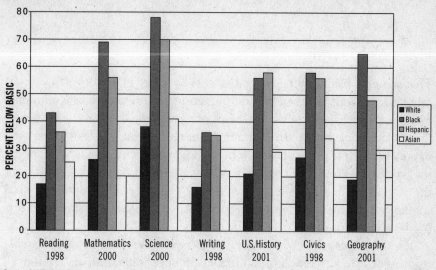

Source: NAEP Data Tool.

ceeds one-third only in science. Asian-American pupils did about the same as whites, though it is somewhat surprising that significantly more of them fell into the Below Basic level in science.

The figures for whites and Asians are worrisome. But the rather disappointing scores of many whites and Asians look good when compared with those of blacks and Hispanics. Only in writing is the proportion of African Americans lacking the most basic skills less than 40 percent. In five of the seven subjects tested, a majority of black students perform Below Basic. In math, the figure is almost seven out of ten, in science more than three out of four. These are shocking numbers. A majority of black students do not have even a "partial" mastery of the "fundamental" knowledge and skills expected of students in the twelfth grade. In most subjects, but particularly in math and science, Hispanic students at the end of high school do somewhat better than their black classmates, but they, too, are far behind their white and Asian peers.

Employers who seek to hire young people who are literate and numerate will thus be hard pressed to find non-Asian minority applicants who qualify. Approximately two-thirds of black and Hispanic students do not enter the workplace immediately, but go on to college, and a great many are clearly entering higher education unprepared for true college-level work—work that as-

sumes a basic mastery of high school material. That is a subject to which we
will return in the next chapter.

High Achievers

That so many black and Hispanic students have had at least twelve years of
schooling without developing even the most fundamental skills is alarming.
The news is no happier when we switch our gaze from those at the bottom to
those who are at the top. In 1990, the National Education Goals Panel set a
national objective that every student become proficient in basic subjects by
the year 2000. We didn't come close to meeting that objective by 2000, but
the 2001 No Child Left Behind legislation reaffirmed that aim—universal
"proficiency." Thus, it is important to ask who is meeting that standard? Figure 1-3 gives the answers.

The criteria developed by NAEP's experts, we see again, vary considerably
from subject to subject. A much higher proportion of students are judged
Proficient or Advanced in reading, for example, than in mathematics or science. But within each subject, the differences between whites and Asians, on
the one hand, and blacks and Hispanics on the other hand, are huge.

Nearly half of all whites and close to 40 percent of Asians in the twelfth

Figure 1-3. Percentage of 12th-Graders Rated as "Proficient" or "Advanced" on the Most
Recent NAEP Assessments

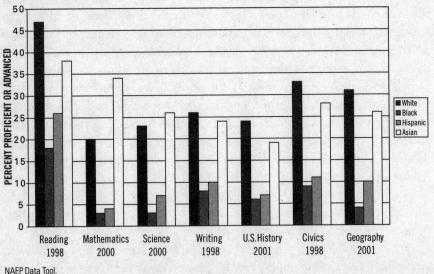

NAEP Data Tool.

grade rank in the top two categories in reading, while less than a fifth of blacks and a quarter of Hispanics achieve that level. In science and math, a mere 3 percent of black students were able to display more than a "partial mastery" of the "knowledge and skills that are fundamental for proficient work" at the twelfth-grade level, in contrast to seven to ten times as many whites and Asians. Hispanics performed only a bit better than blacks in each of these subjects.

The disparities are even greater if we look only at the elite within the elite—at the very small group of students whose performance is rated as Advanced. These are the academic stars whose records will catch the eye of admissions officers at Ivy League or comparably competitive schools. For all groups, the numbers are small. Only the top 3.4 percent of white students and 3.0 percent of Asian Americans score at the Advanced level in science. But for African Americans, the figure is just 0.1 percent. The black-white disparity is thus 34 to 1, and the Asian-black disparity 30 to 1. In math, only 0.2 percent of black students are Advanced; the figure for whites is 11 times higher and for Asians 37 times higher.[11] Hispanic students are but a shade ahead of blacks in the proportion of high performers in every subject. Again, these are very sobering figures, suggesting a state of emergency. With so few blacks and Hispanics with superb academic skills by the end of high school, the pool of those destined to become part of the American professional and business elite is very small.

These glaring disparities shape educational policy in the K–12 years and beyond. They drive the widespread and controversial use of racial double standards in admissions to selective colleges and universities. If black and Hispanic applicants to highly competitive schools were judged by the same academic standards as whites and Asians, the number accepted in the immediate future would be very low—much lower than it is today. As it is, glaring racial double standards are needed in order to get a freshman class that is as much as 6 or 7 percent black at schools like Wesleyan and the University of Michigan. The demand for academically highly accomplished black and Hispanic students is much greater than the current supply.[12]

Narrowing or Widening?

Is the gap getting narrower or is it widening? That obviously matters. But the answer depends upon the baseline one starts from.

Blacks have made tremendous educational gains since the days of Jim Crow, when roughly 80 percent of African Americans grew up in the South, where they were legally required to attend segregated schools. Not only were these schools generally mediocre; most did not go beyond eight grades because white officials assumed that African Americans needed nothing more than a primary school education. Even where further schooling was available, impoverished African-American teenagers were under pressure to find work.

Thus, in 1950, only 24 percent of blacks aged 25–29 had completed high school, less than half the rate for whites.[13] The average black person in that age group had spent 3.5 fewer years in school than the typical white; in the segregated South it was 3.8 years.[14] Moreover, given what we know about the quality of the Jim Crow schools, the racial gap in actual knowledge was undoubtedly much larger than the number of years in school suggests.

Today, a large majority of blacks and whites graduate from high school, although it should be noted that some scholars contend that the official estimates are much too optimistic.[15] But there is no disagreement over the huge skills gap that remains. Equal years spent in school do not mean equal skills and knowledge acquired. Have the disparities at least lessened over time, however?

We can't answer the question for the years prior to the 1970s. But Figures 1-4, 1-5, and 1-6 indicate how well black and Hispanic students at the end of high school have done on the reading, mathematics, and science tests since then. The figures are for 17-year-olds rather than high school seniors, because they rely on what is called the Trend NAEP studies, which collect data by age group rather than grade level. (The Trend NAEP is an exam that is designed explicitly for the purpose of tracking changes in scores since the 1970s, which demands continuity in the contents of the assessment.)

The graphs show where the average black or Hispanic student stands in the white percentile distribution. (Asian scores are not available over this period.) If there were no racial gap at all, then the averages for both groups (in each subject in each year) would fall at the 50 percent mark. The average reading score, for instance, for all groups would be the same, such that the white average (the 50 percent line, half below and half above) would also be the black and Hispanic average. Figures 1-4, 1-5, and 1-6 would have a straight line running across the top.

In fact, the typical black and Hispanic student does not come anywhere near the 50th percentile on any of these tests, and only once (in reading in 1990) did the Latino average reach as high as the 30th percentile. Most of the time, the average students in these groups are below the 20th percentile, which means they are scoring less well than at least 80 percent of their white classmates. They are clustered, in other words, at the bottom of the white distribution.

Black progress since the 1970s has been most impressive in reading, but, as Figure 1-4 shows, even that picture is very mixed. In 1975, for obvious historical reasons, black students at the end of high school were appallingly far behind whites, ranking in only the 10th percentile on average. Just one out of ten African Americans could read as well as the typical white. Over the latter part of the 1970s, black reading scores were flat, but in the 1980s, they did move strongly upward. By 1988, black 17-year-olds had reached the 28th percentile. That was still far behind the average white student, but the rate of progress was impressive and heartening. If the trend had continued, the gap in reading skill would have closed within a generation or so. That might seem an extraordinarily slow and frustrating rate of change, but it would have been far better than what actually happened.

Nineteen eighty-eight, as it turned out, was the high-water mark, for reasons we do not know. Over the next eleven years, the rank of black students plunged by 10 percentile points, and although it rebounded a bit, African Americans in 1999 scored in the 23rd percentile, little better than in 1984. That means that 77 percent of white students today read better than the average black student. And, conversely, only 23 percent of black students read as well as or better than the average white.

When it comes to mathematics and science—so important in today's economy—the picture is even bleaker. In 1978, as Figure 1-5 indicates, the aver-

Figure 1-4. Trends in the Reading Gap: Percentile Rank of the Average Black and Hispanic 17-Year-Old, 1975–1999

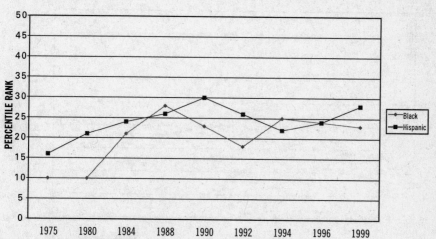

Source: NAEP Data Tool. The rank of black and Hispanic students in the white distribution was determined by calculating how far their mean scores were below those of whites in standard deviation units, and then converting the standard deviations to percentiles.

age black student was at the 13th percentile in math, behind seven out of eight whites. By 1990, African Americans had moved up to the 24th percentile—encouraging progress. But over the 1990s the average black math score fell dramatically, and in 1999 it was at the 14th percentile, a statistically insignificant one point ahead of what it had been twenty-one years before. Over the past two decades, no sustained progress has been made. During a period in which school class size has dropped and spending has gone up—particularly that directed toward the least advantaged—black performance in math has slid back to its 1978 level.

The science scores reveal less both in the way of initial progress and of subsequent regression, as Figure 1-6 shows. The picture is utterly dismal from beginning to end. In 1977, the average black student was in the 8th percentile, behind 92 percent of all whites. Black scores improved modestly over the next few years, reaching a peak at the 14th percentile in 1986. But then they slipped. In 1999, the average African-American youngster knew less science than 90 percent of white students.

In sum, we have indeed made some progress in narrowing the black-white gap in reading, but in the five tests given since 1988 the trend has been backward, not forward. In math and science, the gap has been huge and pretty much constant for an even longer period. Civil rights organizations frequently and rightly bemoan the scarcity of African-American engineers,

Figure 1-5. Trends in the Mathematics Gap: Percentile Rank of the Average Black and Hispanic 17-Year-Old, 1978–1999

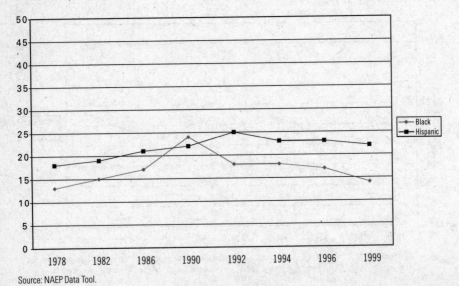

Source: NAEP Data Tool.

Figure 1-6. Trends in the Science Gap: Percentile Rank of the Average Black and Hispanic 17-Year-Old, 1977–1999

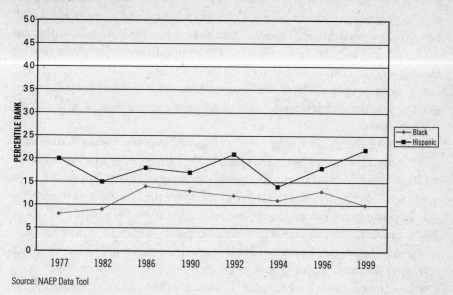

Source: NAEP Data Tool

physicians, Silicon Valley computer whizzes, and the like. But when we see how little math and science African Americans typically know at the end of high school, we see the source of the problem. Too few are ready for the rigorous math and science education that such professions demand.

In 1999, 29 percent of all white students had NAEP math scores as good as those of black students at the 95th percentile for black test-takers—the top 5 percent. That is, only 5 percent of blacks could demonstrate the understanding of math that more than a quarter of whites had. The numbers in science were even worse. Thirty-six percent of whites scored as high as blacks at the 95th percentile of the black distribution; the top 5 percent among blacks in math are competing against more than a third of all white students. A dismal picture altogether.

Hispanics

We have less information about the educational achievement of Americans of Hispanic background, because "Hispanic" wasn't even a U.S. Census category before 1970. But this we know: In 1960, the typical Mexican-American adult living in the United States had just 6.4 years of schooling, compared to

11.0 years for native-born whites. The figure for Puerto Ricans was 7.5 years, and for Cuban Americans 8.4 years.[16] Overall, Latinos were about as far behind non-Hispanic whites in years of school completed as were blacks, although for a very different reason. Many were born in countries without a strong system of public education, and migrated to the United States after leaving school. Thus, in the years for which we have no data, the gap in academic skills between whites and various Latino groups was probably even greater than the differences in years of schooling would suggest, as it was for African Americans.

The NAEP data on the academic skills of Hispanics begin in the mid-1970s. Overall, Latino 17-year-olds performed a little better than blacks on almost all these tests—by an average of 4 percentile points in reading, 5 in math, and 7 in science. But the trend in scores for the two groups is quite similar. In reading, considerable progress was made from 1975 to 1990, but the 1990s saw a bit of slippage—reversing progress—although it was less dramatic than for blacks. In math, Latino scores rose moderately over the 1980s and then declined slightly. In science, in 1999, Hispanics were just 2 percentile points above where they had been more than two decades earlier.

Left Behind

The average black and Hispanic student at the end of high school has academic skills that are at about the eighth-grade level; in fact, on most of the NAEP tests, the majority of black students in twelfth grade have scores Below Basic, while those of Hispanics look only slightly better. At the end of their secondary school education, too many non-Asian minority students lack even "partial mastery of prerequisite knowledge and skills that are fundamental for proficient work," and too few fall in the Proficient and Advanced NAEP categories.

No wonder then, that when Harvard economist Ronald F. Ferguson surveyed middle and high school pupils in fifteen affluent school districts, he found that 48 percent of the black students reported that they "completely" understood the teacher's lesson just "half the time or less." That was almost double the figure for whites (27 percent).[17]

Ferguson also asked these students whether they understood "very well" only "half or less of what they read for school," and got an equally dismal result. Fifty-five percent of the African-American students felt that they did not understand "very well" what they were assigned to read at least half of the time, again nearly double the rate for whites (30 percent). By the time these black youngsters had left elementary school, they had fallen tragically behind, and in the more academically demanding schools in the well-off districts that Ferguson was studying, they found themselves sitting in classes and doing homework that too often bewildered them.

Black students were of course even further behind a quarter century ago, when NAEP data first became available. But the modest progress that occurred during the 1980s has largely come to an end, and there are some indications that the racial gap is widening. In 1999, with just one exception (Hispanics in science), the average scores for both groups in all three subjects was either worse than it had been in 1990 or much the same.

Thus, the record of the recent past offers no grounds for complacency. Time alone will not heal these wounds. Nor will the usual educational strategies—smaller classes, more money, standards, testing, accountability, and so forth. We are certainly not opposed to additional funding for schools, but the dollars must be used wisely. And we are not opposed to smaller classes, although we do not see reducing class size as the best use of scarce dollars. We see standards, testing, and accountability as important but insufficient steps in the right direction. Down the road—in later chapters—we will talk about these and other related topics. In the meantime, suffice it to say that bad news means we must work harder and smarter at delivering better education. This is not a problem beyond America's ability to solve.

Two: Tests Matter

*I am an honors student, you know what I mean? Like, I obviously know what I'm
doing if I can still maintain that grade point average, you know, do all . . .
I just don't test well.*
Erin Sawyer, high school junior in Scottsdale, Arizona[1]

If you think test scores are overrated, let me ask: Are good jobs overrated?
Rod Paige, U.S. secretary of education[2]

Mayra Marquez, 17, is a junior at the Burncoat High School in Worcester, Massachusetts. She wants to be a pediatrician, she says. But her grades
haven't been great, and in order to graduate from high school she must pass
the statewide MCAS exam—the Massachusetts Comprehensive Assessment
System tenth-grade test. MCAS, *The Boston Globe* reports, is an "intimidat-
ing obstacle [that] stands between Mayra and her dream." But it's not clear,
the *Globe*'s story continues, that Mayra herself can be held responsible for
her MCAS score. Her poorly educated mother "isn't much help with homework. Single and 32, she has an active social life, and Mayra is often left to
care for her two younger half-sisters when her mother is out with a boyfriend.
Sometimes mother and daughter argue over who gets to go out on a date."
The previous year, her mother had spent seven weeks in prison, and her best
friend had been murdered.[3]

It is certainly tempting to let Mayra off the hook. Doing well in school is
not easy for a student so distracted by her life at home. And yet it is not the
statewide test, which assesses basic academic competence, that stands between Mayra and her dream of becoming a pediatrician. Without the skills
that the MCAS tests, she cannot make it through college, medical school, and
medical board exams.

As we have seen, the NAEP scores indicate that black and Hispanic
students, on average, are not acquiring the skills and knowledge necessary

to thrive in school and in the workplace. Every assessment tells the same story.

But how important are those results? "There is no standardized test for tolerance," the education writer for *The New York Times* wrote in late 1999.[4] True. Intolerant people—and those with a multitude of other character flaws—can test well. But that is not an argument for regarding test scores as meaningless and misguided. In fact, test results tell us precisely what we need to know if we are to have any hope of refashioning instruction to bring the performance of black and Hispanic students up to the level of Asians and whites. It is precisely for that reason that annual testing in grades 3–8 has been built into No Child Left Behind (NCLB), the federal legislation passed in 2001 that is the latest revision of the omnibus 1965 Elementary and Secondary Education Act.

A False Dichotomy

Federal legislation, however, will not end the debate over testing; No Child Left Behind has not magically changed minds. Confronted with the evidence of a glaring racial gap in skills that raises uncomfortable questions about the educational system, some educators, parents, and students have responded by attacking the tests themselves. Blaming the messenger, or at least denying the validity of the message, is far easier than figuring out how to deal with the problem that the test scores have identified.

Deborah Meier, much-celebrated as the founder of the Central Park East schools in New York, has condemned standardized tests as failing to "measure the only important qualities of a well-educated person." "Life scores [not math scores] based on living" should be the educator's concern, she has written.[5] Theodore Sizer, former dean of the Harvard Graduate School of Education, is also opposed to the entire standards-based educational package. "The myriad, detailed and mandatory state 'curriculum frameworks,' of whatever scholarly brilliance, are attacks on intellectual freedom," he has said. " 'High stakes' tests arising from these curricula compound the felony."[6] Statewide tests force "scripted journeys, where there is no room for whimsical discoveries and unexpected learnings," Jonathan Kozol, a well-known writer on education, has declared. For Kozol, standardizing testing of students evokes memories of "another social order not so long ago that regimented all its children . . . to march with pedagogic uniformity, efficiency, and every competence one can conceive—except for independent will— right into Poland, Austria, and France, and World War II."[7]

Meier, Sizer, and Kozol have many supporters, including (it seems) most members of the faculty at the leading graduate schools of education. But opponents of standards-based testing are fighting a battle that has already been lost—at least for the moment. The commonsense idea that schools should be held accountable for providing a grounding in core subjects, and that it is necessary to measure what students have actually learned by means of good assessments, has gained wide public support. Americans reject the idea that our schools should foster the "intellectual freedom" to remain ignorant of basic educational skills. Thus, NCLB, with its tough mandatory annual testing requirements, passed Congress with overwhelming bipartisan support in 2001. Even Monty Neill, the executive director of FairTest, perhaps the most important of the antitesting voices, has admitted that "there's absolutely no surprise that when asked if they want some standardized testing, the majority of people say yes."[8]

Indeed, the polls do indicate high levels of support, in principle, for both standards and tests. Public Agenda is a nonpartisan, nonprofit, widely respected public opinion research organization. In September 2000, it found that only 11 percent of parents thought "schools today place far too much emphasis on standardized test scores." Seventy-one percent supported "testing students at a young age . . . because struggling students can be identified and helped." Fifty-five percent said there was "nothing wrong" with teaching to the test, since it measured "important skills and knowledge."[9] In a national survey commissioned by the Business Roundtable a month earlier, 65 percent of parents and 70 percent of the general public said students should "pass statewide tests before they can graduate from high school." Those percentages went up when people were told the students "could take the tests several times."[10] The surveys did not break down their results by race, but a Public Agenda poll in the winter of 1997–1998 found that 78 percent of black parents agreed that testing "calls attention to a problem that needs to be solved."[11]

As these parents seem to understand, test opponents who worry about an indifference to "life scores" and about "scripted journeys" are presenting a false dichotomy. Those who have knowledge and skills are better prepared to live life well. And fresh thinking about, say, the Civil War depends on a grounding in facts. Indeed, the study of history does not begin to be interesting until the student has mastered the basic terrain. Ron Rude, the superintendent of public schools in Plains, Montana, has written that he hated the high school history teacher "who immersed us daily in a long list of facts and names from the past." But some years later he found himself in what was then West Germany. "I spent time," he wrote, wandering through medieval castles, Romanesque and Gothic cathedrals, 17th-century bishops' residences, and villages still rebuilding from the ravages of the World Wars. I stood in the ruined Nuremberg amphitheater where Adolf Hitler once inflamed his followers, and I felt the weight of history that place represented. . . . And history became fascinating. . . . I discovered then that, despite his indefensible methods, my high school teacher had taught me a smattering of European history that enabled me to understand what I was seeing and to learn more. I had a knowledge base, minuscule though it was, and I had finally grown up enough to do my part.[12]

He was in the military at the time, surrounded by GIs indifferent to the historical story through which they were wandering. How much richer Rude's life was! Ignorance of "facts and names from the past" impoverished the experience of those around him.

Racial Bias

The tests are not only worthless, but racially biased, some critics charge. Thus, in his widely noticed 1999 book *Standardized Minds: The High Price of America's Testing Culture and What We Can Do to Change It,* Peter Sacks argued that testing is "abusive," "inaccurate," "meaningless," and "a highly effective means of social control." Even worse, it is discriminatory: When schools use tests to separate students into easier and harder classes, they practice "what amounts to the academic lynching of children of color." Sacks calls the statewide tests in Texas "state-sanctioned punishment of . . . poor and minority school-children."[13]

Others use less lurid language but share Sack's basic concern. Gary Orfield, codirector of Harvard University's Civil Rights Project, considers high-stakes testing "reckless." "If we take kids who are getting a bad education and coming from a situation of social crisis and then make them unemployable in the process," he maintains, "we are not helping them or their communities." Such tests, he alleges, "have a very large cost for people who are politically powerless."[14] Assessments raise dropout rates and "leave poor children and children of color further behind," FairTest's executive director has charged.[15] "Biased cultural assumptions," the organization asserts, are inevitably built into standardized tests.[16] Although the National Association of State Boards of Education does not condemn all high-stakes assessments, it has warned that they can "spell trouble in terms of equity, since . . . students in high poverty areas and many minority students tend to score lower."[17]

The nation's major civil rights organizations have had a history of opposing standardized tests, and some—but not all—continue to do so. The Mexican American Legal Defense and Educational Fund (MALDEF) filed suit against the State of Texas in 1997, arguing that TAAS (Texas Assessment of Academic Skills), the statewide exam that all students must pass in order to graduate from high school, was discriminatory. But the federal district court ruled against the plaintiffs.[18] In 1998, the Texas NAACP tried unsuccessfully to persuade the U.S. Department of Education that relying on the TAAS test as a graduation requirement was discriminatory. By 2001, however, the NAACP had softened its opposition. The organization's "Call To Action," in which it outlined its views on educational access for minority children, referred to testing only in a murky paragraph that expressed the organization's concern that "the standards-based school reform movement is shaped effectively to serve fairly the needs of minority communities."[19]

The Lawyers' Committee for Civil Rights Under Law of the Boston Bar Association is, as we write, a party to a suit in Massachusetts against MCAS, but neither the National Urban League nor the NAACP Legal Defense and Education Fund joined in. The Urban League and other major civil rights groups are political organizations with constituents to whom they have to answer—unlike Orfield, FairTest, or even MALDEF and the Lawyers' Committee, whose litigation is not membership-funded. The constituents of the grassroots groups include many parents who want their children better educated, and believe that testing appears to drive better instruction. MALDEF, in its 1997 suit, claimed to speak for Texas Hispanics, but subsequent survey data suggested that almost 60 percent of Latino voters favored the TAAS graduation requirement, even though 40 percent thought that the test was biased.[20] A majority of these parents worried about the achievement of their children.

The Texas parents who believed testing bias was a problem were concerned undoubtedly about how well their kids would do. But bias, properly defined, has to mean something more than mere disparate impact—black and Hispanic students typically scoring lower than students who are white or Asian. If we define unbiased tests as those that reveal no racial differences at all in educational achievement, no one has yet managed to invent one. Note that by the standards of simple disparate impact, the SAT mathematical reasoning test is strongly biased against whites and in favor of Asians, whose average scores are higher than those of any other group.[21] No one makes that argument because disparities alone, almost everyone understands, do not prove that a test is discriminatory.[22]

The more sophisticated point, frequently made, is that racially and ethnically disparate test results register misleading news—news that is inaccurate rather than simply unwelcome. Testing critics often say, for instance, that black students actually know more than the tests reveal. These critics point to the work of Stanford psychologist Claude M. Steele, who argues that black students suffer from "stereotype vulnerability," the fear that doing badly on exams like the SAT will reinforce the pernicious racial stereotype of intellectual inferiority.[23] Such anxiety, particularly on the part of black students who care about academic success, leads them to underperform on tests, Steele says. He has run a series of experiments involving black Stanford undergraduates, and his aim is to explain the lower grades and graduation rates of black students at elite colleges.

The theory, however, is impossible to square with what we know about the link between SAT scores and college performance. Black college students at schools like Stanford don't do better in their courses than their SATs would predict, they actually do worse. Their grades are disappointing relative to their scores, even though a college GPA is not the result of a single test and often includes courses with grades entirely dependent upon term papers.[24]

Equally important, the NAEP assessments are not high-stakes tests; they are no-stakes tests. No grades or scores are given to the individuals who take them, or to their schools or school districts. With no consequences attached to the results, black students should logically perform much like whites and Asians if anxiety were, in fact, a main reason for the relatively low SAT scores of non-Asian minorities. In any case, if all African-American students, starting in the early grades, are truly worrying about the academic reputation of the group and testing badly—a proposition for which there is no evidence— surely ignoring the scores is no solution. All youngsters need to get to the point of doing well on tests—starting early. Those who don't will find themselves handicapped in life, whether they're taking a police academy exam or medical boards. Tests aren't going away.

Some argue that tests underestimate the academic strength of black students for a different reason: "content bias." The students are asked the wrong questions—questions that are slanted and unfair. But how can a statewide math test be racially biased? Tests that assess vocabulary and reading skills pose a more complicated question, since some black students come from homes in which "black English" rather than standard English is spoken. However, students who hope to do well in American society need to know standard English well, at least by the end of their high school years. The NAEP tests for twelfth grade thus assess a needed skill. In addition, words that might appear culturally biased aren't necessarily the ones that black children find hard, a careful review of the literature by Harvard sociologist Christopher

Jencks concludes. Nor do these children have particular difficulty with questions on a test that presume familiarity with "white" or "middle class" culture.[25]

Bias has long been a concern on the part of testing companies, and all carefully screen their assessments to eliminate any questions that might have a racial or gender bias—defined as questions on which African Americans or Hispanics or females do consistently worse than on similar questions of the same degree of difficulty. FairTest argues that stripping NAEP and other assessments of "offensive words" and using "statistical bias-reduction techniques" are inadequate because they "cannot detect underlying bias in the test's form or content."[26] The bias is there even if you can't find it. But if we cannot detect bias, how do we know it exists?

Why Not Portfolios?

Maybe, however, NAEP and other tests that reveal severe black and Hispanic underperformance don't tell the whole story. Perhaps other forms of assessment give a more accurate picture and suggest that non-Asian minority students in fact have the skills and knowledge to do well in college and the workplace. Why stress test scores so heavily?

The war over testing, we noted earlier, has been substantially won; standards-based tests (of some sort) are federally mandated in the No Child Left Behind Act. The National Education Association (NEA), the larger of the nation's two teachers unions, resisted this change until the very end of the battle, urging that parents should have the right to veto the testing of their children.[27] Despite the power of the union within the Democratic Party, it lost that fight; Senator Ted Kennedy was a leading sponsor of the legislation. Nevertheless, the argument continues over the precise nature of the tests, who should take them, and how much weight should be attached to the scores.

Despite the strong public support for testing that we described above, it is far from unqualified. A 2001 survey by the Business Roundtable found that a large majority of Americans were opposed to relying solely on tests to determine high school graduation, and 80 percent believed that some students don't show what they know on standardized assessments.[28]

In Massachusetts, the Department of Education originally planned to have student MCAS scores recorded on high school transcripts; a public outcry forced a retreat.[29] Educational authorities in Massachusetts, along with most parents, have been steadfast in their belief that students lacking basic academic skills should not receive a high school diploma. But they shied away from the plan to make the distinctions between those with higher and lower MCAS scores part of permanent student records.

Unable to stop the drive for standards-based assessments, the NEA now calls for what it terms "smarter testing"—judging students by portfolios they submit and other "multiple indicators of success."[30] The "multiple indicators" that NEA and others are pushing may be of use for some purposes, but they are inevitably inadequate as complete measures of acquired academic skills. Take the question of portfolios, the most frequently cited form of alternative or supplemental assessment. Theodore Sizer, one of the testing opponents quoted above, has described what portfolios—demonstrating true academic "understanding"—should look like. Imagine a high school senior having taken a course entitled "What is slavery, and why might a caged bird sing?" he says. That student "might put together a portfolio of images of slavery from the different perspectives of others—the slaves and the enslavers—in the past."[31] And upon that portfolio, the student's academic accomplishments would be assessed.

Such a portfolio might be a valuable part of a course, supplementing other information about a student's skills and knowledge. But it is not a substitute for a good history test, and falls far short of an adequate high school exit exam. The portfolio Sizer describes would not assess a student's true mastery of the subject of slavery. What does the student understand about the Missouri Compromise, the Kansas-Nebraska Act, the formation of the Republican Party, the Dred Scott decision, the evolution of Lincoln's views on slavery, and so forth? And, moving beyond the issue of slavery, we should also expect an understanding of such subjects as the great debates at the Philadelphia Convention, the Bill of Rights, and the causes of World War II. In education, "less is more," Sizer writes. He worries about "an effort merely to cover content."[32] In reality, no good education "merely" covers content. But too many classes in elementary and secondary schools have been very short on substance. "Less" has simply been less.

Teachers are already free to ask their students to prepare portfolios in classes, and to give them whatever weight they choose in the grading process. Colleges are free to accept such portfolios and drop the requirement to submit SAT or ACT scores—as a few have done. But no state can entirely rely on portfolios to judge whether students have earned a high school diploma—or mastered the skills needed to enter the workforce or pursue higher education. Among the nation's passionate proponents of portfolios, perhaps no one was more prominent than Vermont's former education commissioner Richard P. Mills. By 1995, however, when he was hired as New York's education commissioner, he had become a convert to the state's tough Regents exams.[33] The Vermont program had not been a success.

Portfolios are not a testing program. No one has ever developed clear criteria for grading them; the standards are inevitably very subjective. Standardized tests can be carefully screened to avoid racial or other biases, but portfolios are open to great abuse. Thus, when the NEA calls for so-called "smarter tests" like portfolios, it is really objecting to the basic idea that all students must be able to display a certain measurable level of competence in the basic subjects.

Whether students have reached that level of competence cannot be left solely to the judgment of the 3 million teachers currently working in the nation's schools. That is why the No Child Left Behind Act (and those who drive reform in the states) insist that standards-based tests rather than classroom grades must be used in assessing the performance of students and schools. Grades tend to cluster at the high end and are thus unreliable. A 2001 national survey of teenagers found that 61 percent received no grade lower than a B on their last report card.[34] And 41 percent of students who take the SATs currently have grade-point averages in the A– to A+ range.[35]

We need to know how much American students in general are learning, and we especially need data on the progress of youngsters belonging to racial, ethnic, and income groups that have traditionally moved through school learning too little. Without solid information, we will never close the gap. As Education Secretary Rod Paige has said, there is a very easy way to make group differences disappear: Just get rid of the tests. But "the worst thing that could happen to disadvantaged students is not to have the gap visible."[36] An invisible problem is never addressed.

Getting In and Dropping Out

"The thing is, we're learning that school is more important than I guess a lot of kids think," seventh-grader Jasmine Travis-Mills told a *Boston Globe* reporter in September 2001. Jasmine participated in a summer residential program aimed at catching struggling students before it's too late.[37]

Let's hope Jasmine does not forget the lesson she learned over the summer, because school is indeed very important. How much Jasmine learns, and the test scores that reflect her skills and knowledge, have long-term implications—in college and on the job. It would be nice to believe that the slate is wiped clean when a student graduates—that it's a new day, a new beginning.

Alas, that is not the case. The kids who have fallen behind generally stay behind. It is hard to catch up.

Contrary to what most people think, there is now hardly any racial gap in rates of college attendance, as the last chapter noted. Not all colleges are equally academically demanding; many are community colleges and most are basically nonselective. Nevertheless, it is remarkable that black students are about as likely to enroll as whites, and Hispanics only slightly less so.

In the sample of 1988 eighth-graders in the National Education Longitudinal Study (NELS) who were followed until 2000, when the students were in their late twenties, an identical 76.5 percent of whites and of blacks had gone on to some form of postsecondary education, and the figure for Latinos was almost 70 percent (Figure 2-1).[38] These findings may be too optimistic. Other sources suggest a black-white difference in college attendance rates of 10 to 15 points, and a Hispanic-white gap of about 25 points. But these are still surprisingly small gaps when you consider the higher poverty rate, the much lower proportion of children with highly educated parents, and the poor high school grade records and test scores of so many black and Latino students.[39]

The doors to colleges are open, even to those with extremely weak academic records. The problem is not getting in but staying and graduating. Three-quarters of the whites in the NELS sample entered college, but little more than a third (36 percent) managed to earn a four-year degree. For blacks and Hispanics, though, the dropoff from the start of their freshman year to a diploma was far greater. Three out of four African Americans entered college, but only one in six finished. The dropoff for Hispanics was almost as large; 70 percent began higher education, but just 15 percent obtained a bachelor's degree.

The extraordinarily high black and Hispanic dropout rate is no mystery. Students who leave high school with skills at the eighth- or ninth-grade level can't keep up in colleges that are not geared to teaching students what they should have learned in high school.

In the summer of 2001, six African-American teenagers spoke to the Portland, Oregon, school board. They were all seemingly successful graduates of Jefferson High School—students who made the school feel proud. Jonica Henderson, whose high school transcript contained a lot of A's, went to Dillard University in New Orleans and received her first F. "That shot my dreams down because I thought Jefferson had prepared me," she said. Her classmates told exactly the same story: A's in high school, but F's at college. No one should have been surprised. As a Portland educator noted, kids at troubled high schools with B+ grade-point averages often got a combined verbal and quantitative SAT score below 800.[40] To ignore such a dismal score

Figure 2-1. Education Attained by the 1988 8th-Graders in the National Education Longitudinal Study Sample, 2000

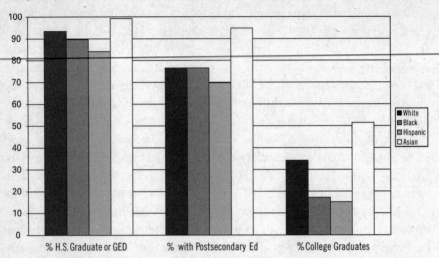

Source: National Center for Education Statistics, *Coming of Age in the 1990s: The Eighth-Grade Class of 1988 12 Years Later.* NCES 2002-321 (Washington, D.C.: U.S. Department of Education, 2002), 14, 21.

is to condemn the students to a shock in college from which many never re-cover. The appallingly high black and Hispanic dropout rate would seem to be the result.

An analysis of white and black youths who graduated from high school in the 1970s and 1980s shows clearly which students are likely to make it through college. Those who did well on standardized reading and math tests went on to succeed in college. Because black students were typically less well prepared academically, they had a much harder time surviving the four years. The study delivered some good news, however. White and black students with similar high school test scores had the same college dropout rates. No racial difference.[41] Close the gap in the early years, in other words, and black and Hispanic kids will be on the road to success. Precisely the same conclu-sion emerged from a massive study of students beginning college in 1995–1996 and traced for six years thereafter. Those with weak high school records and poor SAT scores were only half as likely to earn a college diploma as their better-prepared classmates, and disproportionate numbers of blacks and Hispanics had inadequate preparation.[42]

Many of the black and Hispanic students who do go on to college end up taking remedial classes. At the California State University system, reserved for students with grades in the top third of the state's high school graduates, no less than two-thirds of all black freshmen who started in the 2000–2001 academic year had to take a remedial course in English, double the rate for whites. Even worse, a staggering 78 percent of entering black students required remedial classes in math, while the white rate was 36 percent. Some 62 percent of Mexican Americans needed remedial work in English and 55 percent in math.[43]

A majority of the black and Hispanic students entering the Cal State system still need, in effect, a high school education. (And about a third of whites as well, it must be remembered.) Most of the students who enter college with this handicap—whatever their race or ethnicity—are not able to catch up with their more academically prepared peers. In a sample of 1982 high school graduates, 69 percent of those who took only regular classes earned their diplomas; for those assigned to a remedial reading course, however, the figure dropped to just 39 percent.[44] If the observations of one Cal State professor who teaches remedial math are accurate, that is not surprising. "Many students enter our university with mathematical proficiency below the fifth grade level," he reports. They don't know their times tables. "The majority do not have proficiency in simple calculations involving fractions and decimals."[45]

Colleges have no magic formula to overcome a dozen years of inadequate education. Young men and women who enter college with basic skills at a level that might be expected of a good junior high school student find it very tough to keep up, and most fall by the wayside. As Christopher Jencks notes, "by the time students are old enough to apply to college, their minds have developed in particular ways: some neural paths have grown strong and others have atrophied." Although "the mental differences among seventeen-year-olds do not completely determine their future, neither are they easy to change."[46]

There is only one solution to this problem: More black and Hispanic students must graduate from high school having acquired the skills and knowledge that college work demands. College dropouts—with a few notable exceptions like Bill Gates and Michael Dell—do not become high earners. They certainly do not enter the professions that require more schooling, such as medicine or law.

Adult Literacy Differences

The problem of a skills gap is not confined to the K–12 years. Whites and blacks with the same number of years of formal schooling are not necessarily equally educated. The best evidence comes from the National Adult Literacy

Survey conducted by the National Center for Education Statistics. This study administered brief tests of "prose literacy" and "quantitative literacy" to a large national sample of American adults in 1992.[47] The results revealed huge racial differences. The lowest level in "prose literacy" was defined as being unable to "make low-level inferences based on what they read and to compare or contrast information that can easily be found in [a] text." By that definition, two out of five black adults—two and a half times the figure for whites—were either functionally illiterate or close to it. In "quantitative literacy" almost half of African Americans were on the bottom level, compared to about one-seventh of whites.[48] Functional illiteracy was even more common among Hispanics.

These raw differences, though, do not take schooling into account. It would be logical to think that they would be eliminated, or at least greatly reduced, if we only compared whites, blacks, and Latinos who had had roughly the same amount of education. Logical, but quite wrong. Figures 2-2 and 2-3 do precisely this, showing prose and quantitative literacy scores at different educational levels—for adults without a high school diploma, for those who completed twelfth grade, and so forth.

The results of the National Adult Literacy Survey are dismaying. The average black college graduate, Figure 2-2 indicates, is no more adept at reading prose than the typical white who attended college only briefly, leaving before receiving even a two-year degree. Even worse, Figure 2-3 shows that the

Figure 2-2. Adult Prose Literacy by Years of Education Completed, 1992

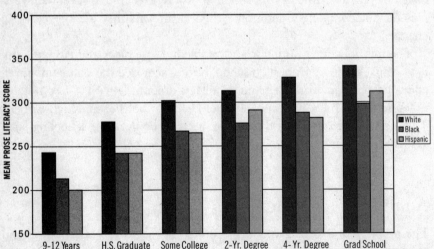

Source: National Center for Education Statistics, *Adult Literacy In America: A First Look at the Results of the National Adult Literacy Survey* (Washington, D.C.: U.S. Government Printing Office, 1993), 127.

Figure 2-3. Adult Quantitative Literacy by Years of Education Completed, 1992

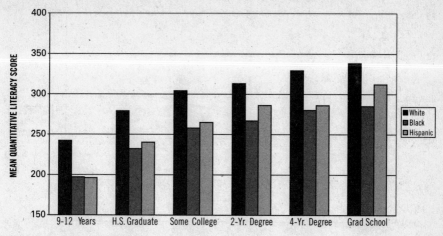

Source: *Adult Literacy in America*, 127.

quantitative skills of the average black with a bachelor's degree are no stronger than those of whites who only graduated from high school and did not attend college—a four-year gap. As of 1992, at least, African Americans who had done graduate work did not read prose as well as whites with only a year or so of college, and their quantitative scores were only a few points above those of whites who had no higher education at all. The pattern for Hispanics closely resembles that for blacks, though Latinos tend to have modestly higher levels of quantitative literacy.

Education Pays Off

The racial gap in skills and knowledge complicates a familiar point. Most people understand that those who stay in school generally earn more. This was always true to some extent, but what economists call "the returns to education" have increased sharply in recent years. Group differences in educational achievement thus matter more than they ever did.

The striking relationship between income and schooling is clear in Figure 2-4, which relates the annual incomes of Americans age twenty-five and older to the number of years of school they have completed. Those who left school before ninth grade earn only about a third as much as those who completed a bachelor's degree. Walk up the educational ladder, and with each step earnings rise. Thus, the fact that whites have more schooling than blacks or Hispanics is a major source of the racial gap in income.

Figure 2-4. Median Annual Income by Years of School Completed, 1999

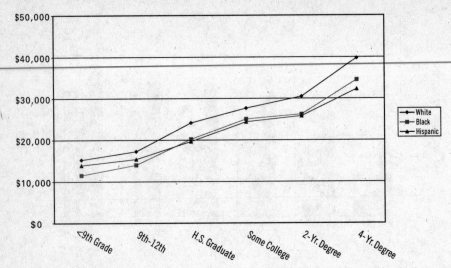

Source: Current Population Survey, March 2000, "Educational Attainment—People 25 Years Old and Over, by Total Money Earnings in 1999," Table PINC-03, www.hhes-info@census.gov.

But more years in school is not the whole story, Figure 2-4 also reveals. At each educational level, whites earn somewhat more than blacks and Hispanics with seemingly equal schooling. Among those with fewer than nine years of education, Latino incomes were 9 percent below those of whites and black incomes 24 percent below. White college graduates earned 15 percent more than African Americans with a college diploma and 23 percent more than comparably well-educated Hispanics.

This looks like proof of discrimination in the labor market, and some social scientists have attempted to calculate "the cost" of being black on the assumption that differences in earnings with equal amounts of schooling must mean racial bias.[49] In fact, the lower earnings of non-Asian minorities reflect a number of factors, the most important of which is the racial gap in skills and knowledge.[50] Years of school completed is a very crude indicator of what people actually know, as should be clear by now. High school graduates, for instance, are not all equally well educated, and disparities in acquired knowledge and skills strongly affect earnings.

A number of sophisticated studies demonstrate clearly that whites and blacks who are truly equally educated are equal earners. Income differences are eliminated. (Less work has been done on Hispanic earnings, but the same logic applies to their case.) George Farkas and Keven Vicknair looked at the 1991 earnings of white and black men aged 26–33. When their education levels were held constant in the traditional way (years of school completed), African Americans earned 19 percent less than comparably educated whites. But when the yardstick was how well these men performed on tests of basic skills in reading and mathematics, blacks actually earned 9 percent more.[51]

Thus, the seemingly terrible numbers on black underperformance in school actually contains some heartening news. The racial differences in basic academic skills—which NAEP and other tests so clearly reveal—are the most important source of racial differences in earnings and incomes. If schools, parents, and students can work together to narrow substantially the racial gap in academic skills, black earnings should look very much like those of whites and Asians.

Test Scores Matter

Particularly in affluent communities—in towns like Scarsdale, New York, and Cambridge, Massachusetts—it is fashionable to scoff at the vulgarity of "teaching to the test." "While high-stakes testing may seem great on paper, the reality is that rigorous standardized testing measures only one thing: how well students take tests," Gretchen Hoff, a Cambridge activist, wrote *The New York Times* in December 1999. "Rather than teaching students to take tests, we should be teaching them to think," she went on.[52]

Ms. Hoff presents a false dichotomy, we've argued above; students need to learn basic math skills and how to think mathematically. There is a seamless web between the two, and a really good test assesses both. If students are truly being taught "to think," they should be able to demonstrate the quality of their thinking in a test situation.

The MCAS tests and similar assessments are not biased against any group. It is a regrettable but inescapable fact that the results indicate that some groups are not learning as much as they should and could. That fact can't be wished away. Down the road, these students will also have a harder time meeting the demands of skilled jobs and college courses. It is impossible to protect those with poor skills and limited knowledge from the consequences of their academic underperformance. They live in a world in which people will be sorted on the basis of their literacy and numeracy. Low test scores, as early as third grade, are a flashing yellow light: they warn the students, their families, and their schools that more effort is needed. A high school senior with the reading comprehension of an eighth-grader is a student facing a bleak economic future. That is a reality our society has been ignoring for too many years.

In short, test scores matter. They tell us what students, educators, parents, and the general public need to hear. When students leave high school barely knowing how to read, their future—and that of the nation—is in jeopardy. Our sense of danger and moral outrage should be particularly great when those students are non-Asian minorities. A decent society does not turn a blind eye to such racial and ethnic inequality.

2 Great Teaching

Three:
Building Academic Skills

If I had 25 percent of my products fail, I'd be out of business.
Louis Gerstner, CEO of IBM

Well, if you could guarantee me the quality of the raw material that [we] get, then you could criticize us. We're working with the reality of dysfunctional families, the reality of poverty.
Bob Parks, school board member, Broward County, Florida[1]

No Excuses. That is the message that superb schools deliver to their students. And that is the message that schools (and school board members) need to hear. Sure, some kids are easier to teach than others. But dysfunctional families and poverty are no excuse for widespread, chronic educational failure.

Scattered across the American landscape are what some call "break-the-mold" schools—high-poverty public schools with students who score well on statewide tests. There aren't many of them, and all are atypical within their own districts. Nevertheless, their record of success suggests that truly radical educational innovation can change the lives of inner-city students, whatever their race or ethnicity. The goal is thus clear. But how to get there? The road is littered with obstacles.

We focus on a handful of remarkable schools, and on one stand-alone classroom within an otherwise undistinguished school. We chose these particular examples of fabulous education only because they came to our attention and we visited them.[2] The single classroom is that of Rafe Esquith, who has been teaching fifth grade at the Hobart Boulevard Elementary School in central Los Angeles since 1985. The schools are in a variety of cities.

We describe the KIPP Academy in the South Bronx in New York in exceptional detail because we came to know it best. KIPP began as one school in a Houston barrio, but a year later one of its directors, David Levin, created an offshoot in New York. Today, there is a network of KIPP academies—fifteen in the 2002–2003 academic year, with another nineteen expected to open in the summer of 2003. KIPP's founders, David Levin and Michael Feinberg, learned much from Esquith, whom they met in 1993 when they were just starting out. The other schools we visited derived their inspiration from a variety of sources, but all are similar to KIPP in some fundamental respects. The formula for these terrific schools is not a mystery.

In our search for great schools, we saw a number of schools that did not make it into our narrative, although they, too, were excellent. To describe them, we fear, would exhaust the reader's patience. Some we do not discuss because they are outside the public school system. They include the Reverend Floyd H. Flake's Allen Christian School in Queens, New York, and the Chad School in Newark, New Jersey. We confined ourselves to public schools because 90 percent of American children today attend them. It seemed worthwhile to demonstrate that it is possible to have public schools that are spectacularly good—at least if they are charter schools, as our prize examples are.

Norman Atkins is the cofounder and executive director of the North Star Academy in Newark, New Jersey. "Wandering through hundreds of classrooms, I'd often wondered whether you could capture within the public sector the magic of the small, mission-driven private schools I'd seen in Harlem and the Lower East Side," he has written.[3] It is, of course, the Big Question: Working within the regular public school system, is it possible to capture that "magic"? For reasons we will discuss at length in a subsequent chapter, all of the successful schools we describe are or became charter schools. That is, they are public schools of a new and special type. They are largely independent of district control, generally able to hire nonunion teachers, and have considerable discretionary power over their budgets. No one tells them which textbooks to buy or how to organize their instructional day.

Esquith's fifth grade is a classroom within a regular public school, and thus an exception. But he has managed to create the freedom that charter schools enjoy by running, in effect, a one-room schoolhouse with little connection to the rest of the school, which contains a dozen other fifth-grade classrooms. A combination of amazing teaching skills, sheer obstinacy, the luck of extraordinary national attention, and money for his program (from a variety of outside sources) explains his unique freedom.

The KIPP academies are small middle schools—grades 5–8—and we found ourselves most interested in the problem of educating inner-city students in those transition years—the years in which "kids really fall off the page or get it together," as one of North Star's codirectors has put it.[4] Arguably, those are also the last years in which youngsters can surely catch up academically. Even the best of teachers find working with ninth-graders who have second-grade math skills extremely difficult. None of the high schools we visited had come up with a way to teach algebra to students who do not know arithmetic. And none knew how to involve already disengaged parents in their children's academic life.

Pockets of Superb Education

The Hobart Elementary School in central Los Angeles, where Rafe Esquith teaches, is an inner-city educational factory, serving 2,400 students in grades K–5. Its drab stucco buildings are scattered across an expanse of concrete surrounded by a high, protective chain-link fence—essential in a neighborhood of gangs, drugs, and violence. Esquith's class is half Hispanic, half Korean. But a high percentage from both groups come from single-parent, impoverished households with a multitude of too-familiar problems.

Korean children typically do well in school; black and Latino kids generally come to school much more educationally disadvantaged. But the Korean students in Esquith's class are mostly from low-income, often single-parent families, and Koreans in other Hobart classes are not high achievers. The principles Esquith has developed work equally well with his Asian and his Latino pupils. And they work equally well with the black and Hispanic students at the KIPP academies, which continue to view Esquith as a source of educational wisdom and inspiration.

KIPP is an acronym for Knowledge Is Power Program. The South Bronx KIPP—with approximately 250 black and Hispanic students—is in one of the city's worst high-poverty neighborhoods. Its four grades (5–8) occupy the top floor of a regular public school that draws from the same local population and gets academically shameful results. Houston's original KIPP Academy (there is now another) has 340 students, almost all low-income second-generation Latino. The school has added a ninth grade for those who need an extra year before entering a competitive high school. KIPP DC: KEY Academy started with a fifth grade in the fall of 2001, and is adding one grade a year. It draws most of its students from Anacostia, a very low-income African-American area of Washington. All three are now charter schools, but KIPP-Bronx was a regular public school for its first five years, until the fall of 2000.

North Star also started as a small middle school but has been slowly adding the high school years as well. Located in the heart of downtown Newark, its student body is 85 percent black, 0 percent white. Its students typically come into fifth grade with scores on the statewide exam even lower than the district average. With one exception, the demographic profile of all the schools we describe is much the same as that of the KIPP academies and North Star. The one exception is the South Boston Harbor Academy, a majority of whose students are low-income and white. But in the summer of 2002 SBHA opened a sister school—the Edward W. Brooke Charter School—that is 70 percent African American and 24 percent Hispanic. It basically replicates SBHA.

The children at these schools are playing catch-up with their more advantaged peers. They need and get more instructional time than regular public schools—at KIPP, an additional 67 percent. Students arrive at 7:25 A.M. (earlier if they want breakfast), and leave at 5:00 P.M. During the regular academic year, there are half-day Saturday classes, and school is in session for three weeks during the summer. More hours mean more chance to learn; and less time to run into trouble in the neighborhood.

The school day for students at Newark's North Star Academy also runs an extra hour, and the academic year is eleven months. At the Amistad Academy in New Haven, Connecticut, the day starts at 7:45 and ends at 5:00, which translates into three hours of extra instruction every day. The school year has been lengthened by two weeks, and the academy runs a summer school for those who need extra help. Almost all the schools we describe added hours to the day and days to the year. The conventional schools may offer after-school programs of one sort or another, but those programs are what Atkins calls "mop-up duty"—an attempt to compensate for "what schools are not doing."[5]

The Hobart Elementary School runs from 7:58 A.M. to 2:58 P.M., but Esquith opens his classroom doors at 6:30 every morning, and most students are working by 7:00. He also has a program of after-school activities that keeps the students who want to stay until 6:00. He gives guitar lessons at recess and lunchtime for those who wish to remain in the room. Saturday mornings he works with some of his former students in grades 6–10 on algebra, Shakespeare, and SAT preparation. Saturday afternoons, it's back to music. During the sixteen weeks of scheduled vacation, his students continue to come to class, although their regular classroom is occupied by another class—one of the costs of Los Angeles's staggered school year. Esquith meets them in the auditorium, in the library, on benches outside if necessary. Or he takes them on trips (financed by donations) to Washington, D.C., South Dakota, and elsewhere.

He also keeps in close touch with his students after they leave his class, and his activities for his "alumni" serve both to keep them on track and to provide his fifth-graders with role models. In addition to his Saturday morning classes, he takes these older students on white-water rafting trips, to the Oregon Shakespeare Festival, to Europe, and on tours of two dozen leading colleges and universities.

Like Esquith, the charter schools all raise extra money, but they use it in different ways. North Star's public funding is about 10 percent lower than that of other Newark public schools, but the directors don't want private donations used for the operating budget. The additional money goes to capital projects. Even with private contributions, KIPP-Bronx is still short-changed by regular New York Public Schools standards. Nevertheless, the creative budgetary decisions allow the school to pay teachers about 20 percent more than their colleagues in the city's regular public schools.

Schools That "Cream"?

Not all minority students in the inner city are alike, of course. Some are more academically promising than others. Some have parents who place a particularly high value on education. Do the schools we so admire cream? Are the schools getting unrepresentative academic results because their students are not representative of the neighborhoods from which they draw?

With one exception, none of the schools selects students on the basis of test scores, grades, or recommendations. It is true that, in theory, Rafe Esquith's kids are part of a "gifted" program, although the school's definition of "gifted" means he has, in fact, a mixture of academically talented and struggling youngsters. There are about ten such "gifted" classes at Hobart, and the others do not yield remotely comparable results. Some of these schools, like the Amistead Academy in New Haven and the KIPP academies, simply select their students by a lottery.

At almost all the schools we celebrate, though, there is an application process that tends to—and is intended to—discourage families unlikely to cooperate with the school. Indeed, one of the five pillars upon which the KIPP schools rest is "choice and commitment." Students, their parents, and the faculty of a KIPP academy "have made a choice to be at the school," the literature reads. "No one is assigned or forced to attend these schools." Choice entails commitment—a commitment that not every parent and student is willing to make. And thus KIPP and other schools of choice are, in this minimal sense, self-selective. Families interested in KIPP must be willing to come in for initial interviews, and to sign on to a rigorous program that includes long days, a long year, and summer school, as well as a strict behavioral code.

Parents attracted to North Star come to an open house, where Norman

Atkins, the cofounder, gives them a "very negative sell," as he describes it.[6] The school is not for them, he says, if they want to take the family on vacation in July, if they don't like school uniforms, if two hours of homework a night seems excessive. If they still find North Star appealing, they watch a simulated school day on a Saturday and can pick up an application. Students are picked randomly from the applicant pool. Among the schools we refer to in the pages below, only the Frederick Douglass Academy in Harlem looks at test scores and other indices of academic and personal strength in admitting students.

The commitment that KIPP demands is spelled out in contracts that set expectations and are signed by teachers, parents, and students. Students must agree, for instance, to "always work, think, and behave in the best way [they] know how and . . . do whatever it takes for [them] and [their] fellow students to learn." They must promise to attend school faithfully, do their homework, and "behave so as to protect the safety, interests, and rights of all individuals in the classroom." And they must understand that they are "responsible for [their] own behavior." The contract parents sign is similar, but includes provisions on helping their "child in the best way we know how" and making themselves available to their children and the school. They, too, must agree that the ultimate responsibility for the "behavior and actions" of their child lies with the family.

North Star parents are urged to sign a voluntary "Covenant" that includes such items as: "We will make certain that our child attends school every day, except in cases of illness or another legitimate reason," and "We will check our child's homework each night and provide quiet time and space for the work to be completed." At South Boston Harbor Academy (SBHA) and most of the other successful schools we visited, there were similar agreements, although many parents inevitably fail to keep their end of the bargain. In running SBHA, the biggest surprise, the principal told us, was the lack of parental support for the high standards; parents often took their children out of school for an appointment or family vacation or made excuses for inexcusable absences.

And yet, with almost no exceptions, the children who violate the terms, or whose parents do, are not expelled.[7] Norman Atkins stated the problem well: "There is always," he said, "in good schools serving inner-city populations, a tension between rigor and rescue." North Star can stick to the letter of its law and toss a recalcitrant student out, but where will he or she go?

Nevertheless, the fact that these are schools of choice is not incidental to their success.[8] "Most of what we do here, if it's not reinforced at home, becomes incredibly challenging," one North Star staff member said to a doctoral candidate writing a dissertation on the school.[9] Others at North Star, KIPP, and elsewhere have echoed the sentiment. Families that choose a school have at least, on paper, committed themselves to supporting the academic program. And schools of choice gain leverage from the simple fact that students who come willingly can be told, you have another option: Return to a school where fights are common, kids talk in class and curse teachers, and no one does any homework. But, remember, since the students at these schools learn little, their future is dim.

"This school is all about choice," James Verrilli, cofounder of North Star, noted in his opening remarks to students on their first day a few years back. "See that back door? See any locks on it? Is this a prison? Am I forcing you to be here? . . . If you cannot live by our rules, if you cannot adapt to this place, I can show you the back door." Norman Atkins, that same day, delivered much the same message: "We have 479 students, 479 students, who want to be sitting where you're sitting, who wish deep down that they had your seat. And you got it. So if you're not making the most of your experience here—if you're not working to your absolute top potential, if you're not going home, running home to do your homework every night, if you're not respecting your teachers and each other with all your energy—some of the other kids would like your spot."[10]

That is precisely the message, of course, that no regular public school delivers. An urban principal whose school we visited told us that she was sending her own children to parochial schools. She wanted a school that could impose limits, with consequences for those who refused to abide by them. Why couldn't she do that, herself, in the school she runs? we asked. "I'm powerless," she answered. The students are stuck with the school and the school is stuck with them.

Great Schools and Great Teaching

The walls of all KIPP academies are plastered with messages, some of which originated many years ago in Rafe Esquith's class. "There Are No Shortcuts." "Be Nice!!! Work Hard!!!" "No Excuses." In the gym at KIPP-Houston, the students can read these mottoes—painted on the floor—as they play sports. Civility, hard work, high standards, and superb teaching are the not-so-secret formula that gets the results reflected in the high test scores that Esquith's students and KIPPsters (as they're called) earn.

All of the schools we describe do splendidly on statewide assessments. For instance, at the KIPP Academy New York in 2000, 66 percent of the students in math and 55 percent in reading had scores above grade level by New York State standards. In District 7, in which KIPP is located and from which it draws all its students, only 9 percent in math and 16 percent in reading were above grade level. For the city as a whole, the figures were 34 percent in math, 23 percent in reading. At New Haven's Amistad Academy, where 66 percent of the students are African-American and 33 percent are Latino, the eighth-graders way outpaced the Connecticut "index scores" by which achievement is reported. On eighth-grade math, the New Haven city average score for black students in 2002 was 38.9; for the state as a whole it was 44.3; but for Amistad it was an amazing 73.6. The school's reading score was even higher, although the contrast with the city and state was slightly less dramatic.

Newark's North Star has a student body that is entirely low-income African American. On the 2002 Proficiency Assessment, 77.8 percent of the students passed English Language Arts, while the figure for the neighborhood schools was 32.1 percent and for Newark as a whole 40 percent. North Star's math passing rate was 58.4 percent in contrast to 20.4 percent for the neighborhood and 27.1 percent for the city. Every excellent school we describe in this chapter and the next had a record of extraordinary achievement.[11]

Great teaching is central to this success. The high quality of the instruction was evident in almost every classroom we visited. In part, the right people were hired; in part, talent is nurtured; and in part, the teachers are freed up to teach. "The administrative headaches are gone. The lunch duty is gone. The paperwork is gone. Teachers are in the school a very long day, but we build in a minimum of two and a quarter hours of lesson planning time," KIPP's David Levin explained to a Massachusetts audience in October 2000.[12]

Many schools, especially in big cities, have neither good principals nor a critical mass of excellent teachers. In one urban high school we visited, a young and promising (but inexperienced) teacher told us: "The principal never comes to my floor, never works with the teachers. We have one member of the staff who plays sitcom videos in her classroom until she hears that the accreditation team or other visitors are coming around." This new teacher wanted some guidance, but her principal was apparently either incapable of providing useful assistance or indifferent to the quality of the teaching in general. At another school, the principal himself recalled his experience as a beginning teacher. His former principal never left his office; he didn't know that "I was working, whereas the other teachers were not." Perhaps he didn't care to find out because he could do nothing to reward the most diligent teachers or to penalize slackers.

An urban superintendent to whom we talked lamented the teachers who "look for any kind of excuse for saying, 'We can't do it.'" One excellent teacher we encountered noted the "many teachers [who] look at teaching as just a job" and are frequently absent, while another spoke of how few applied for teaching positions that required extra hours and extra effort. Moreover, teachers who are rate-busters—who come in early, stay late, go the extra miles with students who need their help—find themselves ostracized by others on the staff and are the subject of ugly retaliation. For instance, we interviewed a Teach for America graduate who took a job in Los Angeles, worked nonstop for his kids, and left the school after a year. "What are you trying to do?" other staff members asked. "Make us look bad?" Esquith has survived at Hobart in part by ignoring the hostility of colleagues who resent his extraordinary dedication—and success.

Many teachers are in fact trying hard and want to succeed. But they need help—more professional training, mentoring, and collegial advice. They are well intentioned, but they aren't teachers, effectively communicating skills and knowledge to their students. In one school at which we spent a day, the students in a fifth-grade history class were filling in a time line on the blackboard. Go back two hundred years, the teacher said; what is the date? The students offered answers: 1982? 1922? 1898? 1902? Finally, one young man did come up with the correct year, and the teacher left it at that, leaving the rest of the class in the dark as to how he arrived at it.

In that same school, a fourth-grade math class, broken into small "learning groups," was supposed to be filling in worksheets on fractions. In fact, the students didn't know enough to tackle the problems, and the teacher was sitting with just one cluster of students, and thus couldn't teach fractions to the whole class. The "learning" groups were chatting about the things that ten-year-olds, left to their own devices, find interesting: the classmate who dressed "funny," the television program most had watched the night before, and other math-irrelevant topics. Such scenes are familiar to anyone who visits schools frequently. Weak pedagogical skills are often the least of the problem. Even at schools with a reputation for excellence, we found teachers who did not know the difference between "it's" and "its," or who were teaching math without a real grasp of the subject.

Unlike those that are charters, the regular public schools generally have to settle for any teacher the central office sends them. A teacher may be completely wrong for a school with an opening, but with sufficient seniority, that teacher will have a right to that job if he or she wants it. (More on that subject in a later chapter.) Charter schools are free to hire whom they want, and the great schools we describe all look hard for potentially fabulous teachers. But the pickings are inevitably slim.

When North Star started, the cofounders posted openings at graduate schools of education, advertised widely, participated in regional job fairs, and sent letters to more than 1,500 Teach for America graduates. They sifted through about 400 applications, came up with a few that sparked their interest, interviewed those few, and watched them teach. They assembled a potential team of teachers, who spent the summer of 1997 (before the school opened) introducing themselves, sharing ideas, and even working together on an Outward Bound–like excursion.[13] KIPP and other schools also engage in a national search for terrific teachers who will buy into their distinctive educational vision. None of these schools is inundated with untapped talent.

"The principal is the key variable in a school," Joseph Viteritti, a scholar who has long been studying education, has noted.[14] First-rate principals are great instructional leaders—often in the classrooms, directing a continuous process of professional development, turning promising teachers into members of a superb team. Most often, as the Amistad Academy literature notes, classrooms are "isolated and idiosyncratic . . . inspired by the styles of particular teachers." Not at the charter schools we admired. North Star's summer teamwork continues in the school year. These are schools in which the staff meets together constantly, reviewing the progress of individual students, thinking out loud about problems that baffle them.

In *The Teaching Gap*, James W. Stigler and James Hiebert describe Japan's "continuous process of school-based professional development" for teachers. As one aspect of that process, the teachers engage in "lesson study." For long periods of time, groups of teachers work on improving the classroom presentation of a single topic—say, subtraction and borrowing. Minute details are discussed: the problem with which the lesson should begin, the exact wording and numbers to be used, the various strategies that students might suggest in struggling with the problem, the questions teachers should ask, the organization of the chalkboard, and so forth.

Eventually, a planned lesson emerges, with one teacher chosen to test it with students. The group prepares the material, stages a dress rehearsal, and then all the participants watch the actual class. That class is followed by further discussion—a review of what worked and the difficulties that at least some students faced, suggesting a need for revision. When the revised lesson is ready, the entire school faculty comes to observe another group member present the new version to a different class. Then another faculty meeting follows, after which the findings might be written up and shared with the larger Japanese educational community.[15]

In most American schools, there is nothing remotely equivalent to the Japanese "lesson study." Teachers get "professional development" credits (towards a salary increase) by taking courses that may have nothing to do with what they teach. The quality of these courses may be low and their messages inconsistent. Moreover, instructors may have nothing to say about the nitty-gritty of teaching. "I've never been to a professional development meeting where you're asked to share your own reflections on what works and what doesn't work in your classroom," a Massachusetts history teacher told a *Boston Globe* reporter in July 2002. He was running a four-week summer program on VideoPaper Builder, software that enables teachers to share ideas by producing and circulating best-practices videos. "I think it will create a feeling of community that a lot of teachers don't currently feel," an eighth-grade science teacher said.[16]

New educational programs like VideoPaper Builder, as well as James Stigler's LessonLab, are small signs of a dawning recognition that the absence of teamwork among teachers affects learning. Statewide standards and testing also appear to be encouraging a new interest in some minimum sharing of ideas. At most public schools, however, teachers remain isolated in their classrooms; isolation is deeply engrained in the educational culture. At the good charter schools we observed, on the other hand, the faculty is engaged in a collaborative process that bears some relation to the Japanese practice. Teachers meet, they watch each other, they discuss strategies, and see themselves as a team dedicated to finding the best way to reach their students—a collective responsibility. Moreover, the principals never sit in their office shuffling papers. They are both teachers and instructional leaders—coaching teachers, helping them plan lessons to reach all children, and so forth.

Working as a close-knit team is time-consuming. KIPP-Bronx devotes an entire week to professional development before the students arrive each year. The staff reviews instructional issues, as well as classroom management, the organization of blackboards (so that every teacher's looks the same), the planning of lessons. Throughout the year, the teachers receive nonstop feedback.

At KIPP, the long days are further extended by its rule that all members of the staff must keep cell phones on at all hours. Those phones have 800 numbers so that students can dial for help at any time. They can call with homework questions; they can call when they or their families are in trouble; and they do so frequently. At none of the schools does the pay cover all the overtime. "We do it for the kids. We sacrifice and do what we have to do to get the kids where they need to be academically," a fifth-grade teacher at North Star tells a reporter.[17] "If you want to be here," Atkins tells the students on the first day of school, "we will be here for you . . . when the sun comes up and when the sun goes down. We'll be thinking about you when we're home at night and on our weekends and all the time; we will put all of our life and all of our energy into this school for you. We will care for you, we will hold you up."[18]

Teachers who will put all of their life and energy into educating inner-city kids: it's an extraordinary commitment, made by extraordinary people. Most of these schools have been started by young idealists who view inner-city teaching as a calling. James Verrilli, cofounder of North Star, talks about "service to the poor" as "rooted in my drive for social justice and my spirituality." He joined the Jesuit Volunteer Corp after college and worked in New York as a tenant organizer. His colleague, Norman Atkins, also came to the school after working in a philanthropic organization dedicated to helping families in low-income neighborhoods.[19] David Levin and Michael Feinberg came out of Teach for America determined to transform the lives of urban children—to "reach the so-called unreachable children," Levin told us.

This level of commitment raises two depressing questions: Would these schools have the same success if their staffs weren't, as it were, running for sainthood? And if good schools require this level of idealism and energy—this sense of the job as (in effect) a religious calling—how many can there be? Rescuing urban kids on a massive scale can't depend on finding hundreds of thousands of David Levins and Rafe Esquiths, a subject to which we will return in later chapters.

The Academic Day

"Kids have too much free time in our country and we're paying for that," Esquith is convinced. Since Hobart is a regular public school, his students need not show up early or stay for Shakespeare and other after-school activities. But most do. "I have a definite point of view," he says. "Kids need to work much harder than they've been working, much longer than they've been working, and with much more discipline than they've been working." It is the philosophy that runs through every great school we saw.

At KIPP, all fifth-grade students get double reading and double math classes. "We don't do anything that doesn't improve reading, writing, and math skills," David Levin notes. The school has only one major extracurricular activity: music. Every child plays an instrument, and there is a school orchestra. Otherwise, almost the entire day is devoted to learning core subjects.

That day is long, as we've already noted, and every minute is regarded as precious. The contrast with regular public schools is marked. Public schools normally waste the most astonishing amount of potential instructional time—getting seated in a classroom, finding the right notebook, waiting for a teacher who is working with other kids, marking time while someone yaks over a public address system, winding down for a vacation, winding up from a vacation, making holiday decorations for days, attending assemblies of no instructional use, munching on a snack in the classroom, cruising the halls for one reason or another, and so forth.

At one urban public high school, we sat in a forty-minute English class bifurcated by a twenty-minute lunch break. The students wandered in at the start of the class, finally got settled, had about ten minutes of instruction, and then bolted for the door for lunch. Eventually, they dribbled back in, but the number of minutes spent actually learning was ridiculously small. Protecting instructional time in the charter schools is not always easy. On a day we happened to be with him, David Levin spent many hours attempting to persuade the district's central office that his youngsters should not waste valuable minutes going to and from the cafeteria—down four flights of stairs—in order to have their midmorning snacks.

At good schools, the day is organized for nonstop learning, and the children generally go home with hefty homework assignments. Again, the contrast with regular public schools is stark. Our homework policy "depends on the child's learning style and home life," one urban principal told us. Another said that homework was not assigned because his high school students would refuse to do it. At a Los Angeles elementary school, a teacher begged his students to put aside "some" time for study. At other schools we visited, students went home with work, but if they failed to complete it, they had second, third, and fourth chances to find time before the end of the year.

At KIPP, those who don't get their work done stay "Wall Street" hours, as KIPP calls them. They remain in school, working late, like brokers on Wall Street. At North Star, Amistad, and South Boston Harbor Academy, those who don't do their homework stay an extra hour to get help. Chronic offenders are assigned to a daily "Homework Club" that they must attend until the problem is solved.

Order in the Classroom

There is no learning without order in the classroom. Parents know it; teachers know it; school administrators know it. And yet the classrooms, the hallways, the lunch rooms, and the bathrooms in the typical urban school are most often unruly, sometimes dangerous.[20] "At their old school [students] weren't protected," Norman Atkins says. "Kids' heads were being shoved down toilets and books were getting thrown out windows, and teachers, whom they were supposed to respect, were getting punched. Weird stuff was happening that made it feel like the Wild West and not like a comfortable, safe place."[21]

Serious violent crimes, even in Newark schools, are relatively rare; never-theless, students in majority-minority schools are more than sixteen times as likely to report incidents of robbery than their peers in overwhelmingly white schools.[22] In a 1997 survey, California students were asked to name "the most important problem" facing their local school; 32 percent said "crime/gangs/violence/drugs."[23]

Just plain disorder, incivility, and disobedience should have been added to the list. Beepers going off, provocative clothing, desks turned over, yammer-ing, singing, rude remarks to teachers, marijuana sold in bathrooms, graffiti that suggests trouble brewing: this is not the sort of stuff that gets picked up in surveys of school violence. But there is plenty of anecdotal evidence that suggests it's all too real. Undercover police and metal detectors most often keep guns and knives out of school, but such measures do not stop everyday chaos.

In the academic year 1989–1990, *New York Newsday*'s education reporter, Emily Sachar, took a job teaching eighth-grade mathematics at the Walt Whitman Intermediate School in Brooklyn, New York. Many kids, she dis-covered, had never been taught how to sit still, how to control what they said, how to behave.[24] Her students called her "cuntface," told her to "fuck off," spat in her face, played radios during class, and threw chairs at one another. Even if a majority wanted to learn, a small group of troublemakers could turn the room upside down in minutes.[25] Sachar's story was hardly unique. In 1997, a new and frustrated Los Angeles high school teacher described her job as "nine-tenths policeman, one-tenth educational."[26] A parent participating in a Public Agenda focus group in the winter of 1997–1998 reported visiting a Cleveland middle school. "I didn't want to go in," she said. "The school was a madhouse; it was filthy. Who's in control here? The kids?" she asked rhetori-cally.[27]

A school that is a "madhouse" is one in which most students are not learn-ing much. "Serious and non-serious offenses [are] negatively related to gains in achievement," an Educational Testing Service study concluded in Octo-ber 1998.[28] That finding would not surprise the parents who responded to a 1998 Public Agenda survey. Ninety-three percent of black parents and 97 per-cent of those who were white thought it "absolutely essential" that schools "be free from weapons, drugs, and gangs." Eighty-two percent of blacks and 87 percent of whites were equally adamant about making "sure that students behave themselves in class and on the school grounds."[29]

The students hardest hit by disorder in the schools are of course those whose educational needs are the greatest. And thus every good school we saw put order high on its list of priorities—a topic to which we will return in the next chapter. There are clear rules about fighting, cursing, graffiti, trash, running in the hallways, shouting, eating in classrooms, dress (including jewelry), and demeanor toward teachers and other students.

At KIPP-Houston, students who break the rules—by failing to do the homework, showing disrespect toward an adult, visiting the bathroom without permission—go to "the porch"; they go to classes, but they wear their KIPP shirts inside out and cannot talk to or eat with their classmates. They become, in other words, social isolates, separated from their all-important peer group. Other schools too, have a zero tolerance policy toward disciplinary infractions. As Brett Peiser, the principal of South Boston Harbor Academy, puts it: "We have eliminated warnings. A real connection is made between actions and consequences." It is perhaps the single most important message that a school can deliver to youngsters—particularly those who grow up in chaotic homes and neighborhoods.

At KIPP, the disciplined atmosphere allows large classes, reducing the number of teachers on the payroll, with the result that discretionary funds are available for other purposes. "Class size is not an issue if teachers know how to manage kids," Levin notes. We watched him "manage" a math class one day, with a principal from another school at our side. "This class has forty-five students in it, and they are all learning!" the principal gasped. Not only learning, but having fun doing so—or so it seemed from the level of enthusiastic participation. All eyes were on Levin at all times, and a multitude of eager, excited hands went up whenever he asked them a question.

High Expectations

The long hours that Esquith and his kids put in are in part devoted to reading and then producing a Shakespeare play, the after-school activity for which he is most famous. His "Hobart Shakespeareans" (as the kids are called) have performed with Britain's Royal Shakespeare Company, and have, in effect, been adopted by a well-known British actor, Sir Ian McKellen, who flies in to see them perform. In 1999, they were also selected by Sir Peter Hall to perform in his Los Angeles production of *A Midsummer Night's Dream.*

Why Shakespeare? Esquith loves the plays himself, and decided there was no better way to teach English to children whose first language is either Spanish or Korean. Esquith appreciates that the Bard "tackles the big issues—love, violence, jealousy, comedy, and humorous situations . . . in a language that nobody has ever duplicated."

To watch his class read and analyze a Shakespeare play is an amazing experience. "We go over everything word by word, explaining every conflict, every bit of symbolism," he says, and indeed he does. Esquith chose *King Lear* for his 9- and 10-year-olds to perform in the spring of 2001. "Who's the smartest in the play?" Esquith asks his class. "The fool," one student answers. "But Kent is smart, too," Esquith responds. And what about "bedlam beggars"? What does that mean? There are fifty-five students in the room, some from other classes who come only for Shakespeare. Almost everyone is following along totally enraptured. "Should you stop at the end of all the lines?" The students agree that you shouldn't. "Why does Shakespeare talk of "roaring voices?" Hands go up with each question.

In the spring, his young Shakespeareans, wearing regular clothes except for "Will Power" T-shirts, put on eight performances in the classroom. One of us saw the final production of *King Lear*—an unforgettable experience. Why the classroom setting? "A real stage and costumes are showbiz," Esquith explains. "This is about education." And because he adds music, played and sung by the students, everyone has a chance to participate—not only the members of his class, but students from other fourth and fifth grades who wanted to become part of the production.

Although Shakespeare is a voluntary after-school activity that includes students from other Hobart classrooms, all of Esquith's students are exposed to a great deal of other literature during regular school hours. Esquith has his students read books out loud—books that are too hard for fifth-graders to tackle on their own. *Tom Sawyer, Huckleberry Finn, Native Son, Great Expectations*, and Esquith's favorite, Harper Lee's *To Kill a Mockingbird*, are on the list. South Boston Harbor Academy Charter School expects incoming fifth-graders to read three books in the summer before they arrive; among the choices: *The Magician's Nephew* by C. S. Lewis and *Charlie and the Chocolate Factory* by Roald Dahl. The school starts each day with fifteen minutes of silent reading by everyone—including teachers. Surely, there's nothing unusual about exposing children to good books, one might think. But, in fact, in many schools we have seen, students almost never read. One urban high school English class we visited had managed in the course of the entire year to get through Elie Wiesel's *Night* and half of Richard Wright's *Black Boy*. "Will you finish *Black Boy* at home?" we asked one of the students. It has a wonderful ending, we noted. No, he said; he didn't like to read. At other schools, teachers told us that they "suggested" perhaps students might try reading books on weekends.

"High expectations" are a current educational buzzword, with much hand-wringing about just how high those expectations can be for black and Hispanic children in poverty. There is no hand-wringing in Esquith's class or at any of the superb schools we visited. All of KIPP's eighth-graders have completed a two-year high school–level Algebra I class by the time they graduate. Part of the secret is a lack of the usual educational ambivalence about the need to memorize basic mathematical facts and strategies for solving problems. Levin himself teaches math, and he turns, for instance, the speed with which kids can accurately run through the times tables into a competition, the object of which is to beat his own time. To watch him explain to new fifth-graders (with minimum preparation for the academic demands of KIPP) how to tell which of two numbers is the larger is to see a level of sophistication in illuminating the structure of math that is very rare.

The teachers set academic expectations, and they work hard to get their students to internalize those expectations. The day we visited Amistad, the kids were chanting: "People, people, can't you see? Education is the key. People, people, don't you know? College is where we will go." (North Star has almost the identical chant.) All the schools we admired offered various rewards for academic performance, about which we will say more in the next chapter. Such rewards, publicly labeling some students as more academically accomplished than others, make many public school teachers nervous on grounds of equity. At a Los Angeles elementary school we visited, every month one student was recognized from each classroom. But the teachers, we were told, "don't get specific about the criteria." In other words, recognition was arbitrary, and the students fail to learn a crucial lesson: Schools and employers generally reward hard and good work.

KIPP's sixth-graders are expected to spell such words as *audible, audience, confidential, hyperbole, hypertension,* and *pianist.* (Rich vocabularies open literary doors). In Houston, on a day we visited, an eighth-grade English class was engaged in a close textual analysis of *The Lord of the Flies.* Later that day in a "thinking skills" class, Michael Feinberg, the principal, led a sophisticated discussion of the federal highway program, the power of Congress over interstate transportation, and the political pressures behind appropriation decisions.

We watched seventh-grade history students at Newark's North Star playing a game visually traveling across a map of Europe with countries and cities differently colored but unidentified by name. Start at Berlin, travel 500 miles east, drop straight south, through one country to the next. Where are you? Almost all hands went up; the student called on had the right answer.

Esquith's fifth-graders play mental mathematical games—no pencil and paper allowed. Take the total IQ of everyone on the board of education ("It's zero!" he says with a twinkle); add 8; multiply by 7; subtract 5; divide by 17. In a flash the students hold up tiles with the number 3 on it. Take the number of holes on a golf course, add the number of years in a decade, add the number of weeks in a fortnight, add 19, and take the square root. Up come the number 7 tiles with amazing speed. These are inner-city kids, but Esquith does not ask "inner-city" questions; he wants them to know what a golf course looks like.

Esquith pushes the kids hard, and believes "facts are good." But there's nothing grim about his class. (We saw kids at lunchtime shouting, "Let's skip lunch," so they could keep working.) He plays games with history, geography, and literature as well. Who campaigned in support of the ratification of the Constitution? Who was the ruler of England during the Revolutionary War? Who was the British prime minister during the French and Indian War? Name the country directly east of Libya. Name the country north of the Sudan. Name the country south of Libya with four letters. How many states border the Pacific Ocean? (A trick question since they might forget Hawaii and Alaska.) Five states border the Gulf of Mexico; what are they? Let's see how many Shakespeare plays we can name. He goes around the room, and almost all hands are raised.

Against the Educational Grain

Although North Star students perform mock trials, engage in formal debates, and write stories, letters, poems, skits, and essays, they are also expected to spell correctly, and know English grammar, as well as the times tables and basic mathematical algorithms. In a class that we watched, the teacher was rapidly firing square root questions. The square root of 81 is? Students called on to answer rose from their chairs and gave the answer, loud and clear, standing tall. (An education in public speaking as well as math.) In other classes, students memorize poems and speeches. Fifth-graders must know the elements of the periodic table; sixth-graders can explain the process of DNA replication.[30] At South Boston Harbor Academy, the incoming fifth-graders are expected to learn the multiplication tables before they start school and are orally and randomly tested on a Times Table Day that culminates with a "Times Table Off" when champions compete for accuracy and speed.

"Students must master a core set of basic academic skills . . . ," the SBHA brochure reads. "Students cannot understand algebra without knowing their times tables. Students cannot discuss historical events without knowing the basic historical facts surrounding those events. . . . Students cannot write a five-paragraph essay after reading a work of literature without knowing the rules of spelling, punctuation, and capitalization." Common sense? Alas, no. It's an educational philosophy squarely against that which prevails in many public schools.

A solid education clearly involves both skills and understanding; the two are inseparable. But even at schools with good reputations, we found principals and teachers opposed, for instance, to correcting spelling; they did not want to limit the youngsters' ability to express themselves, they said. Teachers put essays and other student material full of errors on the classroom wall. In one school we visited, the students' New Year's resolutions were up: "This is my anther personal improvement promise will also listen to more music . . ." "I promises I am going to . . ." "The promise is to do my home work reason is because don't want to fail."

The ambivalence about gaining mastery over "a core set of basic academic skills," E. D. Hirsch, Jr., founder of the Core Knowledge network of schools, and others have argued, has a particularly pernicious impact on low-income minority children who are more likely to have weak teachers and less likely to have someone at home to correct "anther," and garbled syntax, and mangled math in homework. The impact on low-income minority children is particularly worrisome with respect to math, a subject on which black students do particularly badly on the NAEP tests. The white-black gap is much larger in math than in reading. Our central focus in the pages that follow is thus on math education.

For a century now, an intense debate—some would say, a war—has raged over what to teach and how to teach it.[31] In the battle over math, on one side are what E. D. Hirsch, Jr. has called the "romantics"—educational progressives who pursue John Dewey's child-centered, active learning to the near-exclusion of computational skills. In its purest form, "progressivism" views the teacher as a facilitator—"a guide on the side and not a sage on the stage"—who helps students construct their own answers to problems. The acquisition of skills occurs naturally through discussion, collaboration, and discovery.

In fact, Dewey would probably have deplored such misuse of his theories, which (critics charge) results in students who end up as math cripples. We ourselves have watched math tutors in Massachusetts public schools struggling with perfectly intelligent students who haven't memorized the multiplication tables and thus cannot grasp factoring polynomials.

On the other side of the conflict are those who believe in teacher-led instruction and careful attention to mathematical substance, including the standard algorithms of arithmetic—the rules for doing long division, and so forth. They charge that the influential 1989 "standards" issued by the National Council of Teachers of Mathematics (NCTM), although subsequently revised, were not really standards at all. They stated *how* a child should be taught, but not *what* he or she should learn.

No state embraced the "progressive" approach to math instruction more enthusiastically than California. The results were disastrous. On the 1996 NAEP math assessment, California's fourth-graders scored below those in forty other states, just a shade ahead of Mississippi. And the proportion of freshmen at a campus of California State University who needed to take remedial math jumped from 23 percent in 1989 to 54 percent by 1997.[32] In the spring of 2000, Los Angeles mayor Richard Riordan signed on to the statement of almost two hundred university mathematicians and scholars who were dismayed when the federal government endorsed programs such as "Connected Mathematics," which entirely omits the topic of division of fractions in the grade 6–8 curriculum.[33]

California became the extreme example, but in New York City, Texas, Arizona, Virginia, Michigan, and elsewhere, parents have organized to fight "fuzzy math" or "rain forest math," as it has been variously called.[34] In New York, the parents charged teachers with asking for answers that were only estimates (which NCTM in 1989 had endorsed for the early grades), rather than precise computations, and with spending months counting coins and solving equations that had been dumbed down to include only easy numbers.[35]

New York parents are "scared that their kids are not going to be competitive," one of the leaders of the movement protesting "constructivist" math has said.[36] The concern may sound like that of an overanxious parent, but at least some prominent educators do invite worry. They are relentlessly hostile to schooling that seems hierarchical, elitist, and thus inequitable.

Lee V. Stiff, president of NCTM, testified before the Massachusetts Board of Education in 2000. "Traditional mathematics," he said, "is the mathematics of exclusion. . . . Some students should not be given access to high-quality mathematics that lead to heightened opportunities while other students are relegated to traveling slower or different pathways to reach the same goals."[37] Stiff seemed to imply that no students should be taking AP calculus because not all students are equally prepared (or interested). If he meant only to say that equity concerns should prompt higher, not lower, standards—for all children—then we agree, of course.

That is certainly a conviction central to the schools that we have described in this chapter. No "soft bigotry of low expectations," as Governor George W. Bush put the point in his 2000 campaign for the presidency. And to the extent to which these schools have taken sides in the polarizing and education-ally counterproductive curriculum wars (involving reading as well as math), they tend to fall into the learn-the-time-tables camp, much to the dismay of their detractors.

The commitment to teaching all students how to add fractions, where to find Paris on a map, how to spell "receive," who wrote the Federalist Papers, and which constitutional amendment protects Americans against "unreason-able searches and seizures" is called "traditional" education. But in fact "tradi-tional" is a bit of a misnomer in describing a school like KIPP, where the emphasis on such skills and knowledge is combined with what one reporter has called a style that is "fast-paced, funny, and edgy."[38]

To the best of our knowledge, no one has actually counted the number of teachers who stop students from using standard methods to solve problems. And no one knows the number of teachers who have discarded phonics-based instruction in reading in favor of the "whole language" approach—an-other favorite "reform." But, in the course of our travels, we were struck by the distinctiveness of the charter schools we visited. With their stress on basic arithmetic skills, paving the way to algebra by eighth grade, and their general belief that "facts are good," they are clearly outside the educational main-stream. They have, indeed, captured "the magic of the small, mission-driven private schools" of which Norm Atkins had dreamed.

Building Academic Skills

"Without an education, these children are slaves to the world they live in. With real learning, there's no end to what they might do," Gregory Hodge, the principal at the Frederick Douglass Academy in Harlem, has said.[39] "Real learning" is not what goes on in too many schools. The days are too short, the year is too short, instructional time is wasted, the classrooms are chaotic, the academic expectations are woefully low, basic skills are not taught, intellectu-ally sophisticated and stimulating material is not offered, tests are viewed as antithetical to education, and equity and excellence are seen as incom-patible.

Is that too harsh a judgment? Perhaps, but the difference between the schools we have described in this chapter and the typical urban school we have visited is like night and day. High-poverty and high-minority schools that perform well "abound throughout the United States," Douglas Reeves, an educational consultant, has said. High achievement doesn't require "heroic, individualistic teachers. These are ordinary people doing regular teaching jobs, but with more focus on academic standards and assessment than you regularly see."[40] We wish that were so. In our search for great schools in difficult settings, we found the pickings slim. And those we did find were little islands of true heroism.

That does not have to be the case. Many teachers have the potential to reach even the seemingly unreachable students. But many also need help to do so, and they need a more expansive definition of education. Building academic skills is only part of their job. Eugene Williams, Sr., spent thirteen years in the D.C. public schools as a teacher, an assistant principal, and a director of an "academic enhancement" program. "I have been in classrooms where students essentially dared the teacher to teach," he has said. "And I have seen good teachers eventually succumb to the defiance."[41]

That should never happen. Where defiance is the norm and teachers succumb, something is wrong with the culture of the school. Manners and civility are missing from the curriculum. Students haven't learned disciplined work habits, and they are not acquiring a sense of personal responsibility for their own future. Teachers have failed to communicate the excitement and importance of learning, and the link between hard work and a rewarding life.

Schools need to teach the core subjects well. But math classes that teach only math will not succeed in educating students who need much, much more. And that is the subject to which we next turn.

Four: Not by Math Alone

*Brandon and Bobby and Princess and Shukuha and Latorsha and Montreal,
children who were nine and ten years old . . . told me . . . how fervently they
wished night after night that their mothers would win the lottery so that they could
move to the "serberbs," convinced it would all be better there, kids who had simply
grown tired of hitting the tarmac of the playground every time a gun went off.*
Jonathan Coleman, *Long Way to Go*[1]

*The idea is . . . [to] make the kids feel as if the world is theirs, that there's nothing to
be afraid of, nothing that will oppress them, that the world is something they can own.*
Norman Atkins, cofounder of the North Star Academy[2]

The students at North Star (who have won the admissions lottery) have, in
effect, won the lottery of which the children who talked to Jonathan Coleman dreamed. No, their moms didn't guess the numbers that would magically transport them to the "serberbs." Something much more important has
happened. They've been given the chance to acquire the knowledge and
skills to never return to the playgrounds where the guns go off. What Brandon and Bobby and Princess and Shukuha and Latorsha and Montreal need
to hear is the message of North Star and other wonderful schools: Stick with
us, and "the world is something [you] can own."

Stick with us—for more than just math. KIPP, North Star, and other successful schools aim to transform the culture of their students—as it affects academic achievement. The Web site of the Amistad Academy in New Haven
contains a section called "Pillars of 'Harder and Smarter' Instruction." "Behavior," it explains, "should be thought of in the same way as academics—it
must be taught. Effective behavioral instruction, like effective academic instruction, must be modeled, practiced, and reinforced."[3] "Are we conservative here?" Gregory Hodge, the head of the Frederick Douglass Academy asks
us rhetorically. "Of course we are. We teach middle-class values like responsibility."

Setting Social Norms

In 1997, the College Board organized a "National Task Force on Minority High Achievement." The group consisted of representatives of mainstream civil rights groups, and the College Board itself tends to stick to very safe ground. And yet its report, *Reaching the Top*, which was released in October 1999, courageously placed considerable stress on the culture of the home, drawing a sharp contrast between East Asians and non-Asian minorities.[4]

Reaching the Top described the problem of underachievement as emerging "very early" in a child's life, and it referred to the "cultural attributes of home, community, and school," talking at length about the views toward school and hard work that Asian parents transmit to their children. "East Asian American high school and college students . . . spend much more time on their studies outside of school and are more likely to be part of academically oriented peer groups." In addition, "East Asian parents are more likely than Whites to train their children to believe success is based on effort rather than innate ability," and thus they instill in their children the values of hard work, "diligence, thoroughness, and self-discipline."[5] It was a point that Laurence Steinberg, in *Beyond the Classroom*, had made three years earlier. "In terms of school achievement," his study found, "it is more advantageous to be Asian than to be wealthy, to have nondivorced parents, or to have a mother who is able to stay at home full-time."[6]

"Culture" is a loose and slippery term that has been used in a great many different ways. It is sometimes taken to mean a fixed set of group traits that are passed on from generation to generation, an inheritance that is fairly impervious to changes in the social environment.

This is not how we use the term. In arguing that the cultures of racial and ethnic groups strongly influence the educational performance of youths, we are simply saying that children first develop values, attitudes, and skills as a result of their experience in the families that raised them. But those values, attitudes, and skills continue to be shaped by children's interaction with their peers, teachers, neighbors, and other aspects of their environment. In part, a common American culture influences American children in general. But some cultural patterns vary with social class or region. And some vary systematically along racial and ethnic lines. These differences are not identical to those that could have been identified a century or two centuries ago. The cultures of these racial and ethnic groups have altered as a result of changes in the social environment, and they will continue to change in the future. Good schools can become an enormously important element in that environment.

One further comment about what we mean by "culture." It is in part group differences in values. But it is also, as sociologist George Farkas has argued, "a tool kit of *skills,* the means by which strategies of action are constructed." Low-income parents, he notes, value education, stable marriages, steady jobs, and other "middle class" objectives. But they differ in the "culturally-shaped skills, habits, and styles" that facilitate the realization of those aspirations.[7] The College Board endorsed the Farkas argument that counterproductive "culturally-shaped skills, habits and styles" were a key source of the poor academic performance of some groups. What should schools do? Except for its advocacy of after-school and other supplementary educational programs, *Reaching the Top* skirted the question

None of the schools we mentioned in the previous chapter skirts the issue, however. Indeed, they confront it head-on. The habits of "diligence, thoroughness, and self-discipline" are precisely those they try to instill, a daunting task in dealing with inner-city youth. KIPP's South Bronx black and Hispanic students all reside in a neighborhood in which, as the school's literature puts it, "illiteracy, drug abuse, broken homes, gangs, and juvenile crime" are rampant. This is equally true of the other schools we describe.

"We are fighting a battle involving skills and values," David Levin notes. "We are not afraid to set social norms." In effect, he has adopted political scientist James Q. Wilson's "broken windows" theory and applied it to schools. To ignore one piece of trash on the floor ("I hate trash," Levin remarked on our first visit to the school), one shirt improperly tucked in, one fight between kids, one bit of foul language, would send a disastrous no-one-cares message. And thus, at KIPP, the staff responds to every sign of disorder—however slight. The result: Even in the lunchroom, students talk quietly and need the supervision of only one staff member.

At North Star a few years back, a student had penciled what a reporter called a "rather benign four-letter word" on a hallway wall. The cofounder, James Verrilli, called an emergency meeting of the student body. "Somebody here does not belong with the rest of us. Somebody here wants to live amidst trash," he shouted.[8] Making a big deal over small infractions prevents larger problems from happening. The same point is made in the South Boston Harbor Academy brochure. "SBHA addresses each and every incident of inappropriate behavior, fostering in students the real connection between actions and consequences," it reads.

Chaos and violence disrupt learning, a point discussed in the previous chapter. But these schools aim for something more than a safe and orderly environment. "Teachers need to teach ethics, morals, and responsibility to the kids. Those are the things I think are lacking in our curriculum," famed teacher Jaime Escalante said in a 1993 interview. "We need . . . to develop the simple concept of responsibility in our kids."[9]

At North Star, students pledge to abide by the "Core Values of Community—Caring, Respect, Responsibility, and Justice." "Amistad Academy will graduate students who can do well—and who will do good," the school's program statement states. "We really wanted these kids to understand what it means to be a citizen of a society," Dacia Toll, the director, adds.[10] Amistad students are expected to demonstrate consistent adherence to the norms embodied in REACH: Respect, Enthusiasm, Achievement, Citizenship, and Hard Work.

Both schools start their mornings with all the students gathered together in a circle. Individual students step forward to apologize to the group when a core value has been violated, when behavioral expectations have not been met—including the expectation of arriving at school on time. The apologies are a recognition that students who have failed to take their responsibilities seriously have chosen to do so. Those who meet expectations have also made a choice, and that choice is rewarded in a variety of ways. They are given priority status when students are chosen for a cross-country skiing trip or for a scholarship to a summer camp. The middle-school class of students with the best attendance each month gets to order lunch from a downtown restaurant of its choice.

Respect for teachers is a prerequisite for a disciplined and focused academic environment. At the schools we admire, a bright line is drawn between teachers and students; teachers are friendly, but they are not the students' friends and (with the exception of Esquith) are called by their last names. Indeed, at KIPP DC: KEY Academy the principal, Susan Schaeffler, recalls having to tell a mother that her daughter needed a mom, not a pal. Mothering means setting behavioral standards.

Students at these schools learn to speak politely to teachers and the principal, as well as to strangers. It's another invaluable skill. In a seventh-grade class we watched at Amistad, students said "Thank you" as the teacher handed out worksheets, and she replied, "You're welcome." At North Star, we found ourselves shaking the hands of a stream of students who told us their names, looked us in the eye, smiled, and welcomed us to their school. At many of the schools we visited, youngsters brought in extra chairs on which we could sit to watch a class. Rafe Esquith has his youngsters write individual thank-you notes to visitors.

A 1992 survey of a representative sample of the metropolitan Detroit population found that young unemployed blacks failed to grasp the importance of dress and appearance to potential employers.[11] Those are not skills overlooked at the schools we celebrate. KIPP's education in "self-discipline" includes learning how to dress for success, how to sit in a classroom chair (no heads on desks), the importance of looking directly at the person to whom you are talking, and the point of standing when greeting someone.

KIPP has a dress code, although there aren't uniforms. That code includes closed shoes, shirts with sleeves, skirts to the knees, no big earrings or other jewelry, no tight clothing, and belts for the boys. At most of the other schools, though, students did wear uniforms—green shirts tucked in, khaki pants or skirts, dark shoes (no sneakers) at North Star, for instance. At none of the schools were students allowed to use clothes as a means of self-expression; no baggy pants with waists dropped to hip level, no untied shoes, no revealing shirts or blouses.

Students at both KIPP and North Star spend the beginning of the fifth grade (their first year) learning the school's code of behavior. At all these schools, teachers are role models; they, too, dress professionally and are invariably courteous. All the principals at our favorite schools know the name of every student. David Levin is not alone in never walking by a kid without saying hello. Civility and decorum permeate these schools. "Who are you to set behavioral standards?" Levin has been asked. "I'm the boss," he replies.[12] Understanding who's in charge (in any school and most jobs) is also integral to a good education.

Esquith, as the lone teacher in a contained classroom, doesn't need a dress code, but he does expect perfect behavior. A student from another teacher's class comes to his early morning math lessons. "Everything is noisy and rude in my classroom," the boy says. Esquith takes his kids to concerts, ballgames, and restaurants. Before they go, they learn to sit quietly at the concert, and to clap at the right time. Their presence at a restaurant never disturbs the other patrons; they talk quietly. "Teachers can't say at the last minute [before a field trip], I want you to be on your best behavior," Esquith explains. "By then, it's too late." "Best behavior" takes practice.

Disciplined Work Habits

Visit any classroom in any school, and it's immediately clear whether or not students are engaged in learning. In schools with a culture of work, no one is slouching in a seat, staring into space, doodling, eating, whispering to classmates, fixing a friend's hair, wandering around the room, or coming and going in the middle of class. Teachers are teaching; chaos is not an ever-present threat.

Disciplined behavior and disciplined work go hand-in-hand. "Oh, Steven, you weren't listening? Sorry to bother you," Esquith said to a student who couldn't answer a question because his attention had wandered. Esquith was delivering two simultaneous messages: zero tolerance for inattention, and civility works better than anger. Total attention, diligence, and thoroughness are also expected when the students participate in sports. On one of our visits, Esquith was teaching volleyball. For two months, his class practiced handling the ball and moving properly, but without any net in place. Students play the actual game when they're ready to do so well. Good athletes, they learn, pay meticulous attention to their craft; excellence in every endeavor requires discipline.

At KIPP students chant rules in unison:

> We "slant" at all times.
> We listen carefully at all times.
> We follow the teachers' instructions.
> We answer when given the signal.
> We stay focused to save time.
> We will always be nice and work hard.

"Slant" is an acronym for: Sit up. Listen. Ask and answer questions. Nod your head so people know you are listening and understanding. Track your speaker by keeping your eyes on whoever is talking.

KIPPsters learn to avoid wasting work time by walking down halls rapidly and quietly in orderly lines, and sitting in their classroom seats immediately. They are taught small habits that make a big difference—like using a finger on their left hand to keep track of their place in a book while the right hand is raised to ask a question. They learn to organize their pencils, notebooks, and assignment sheets; six rules for notebook organization are spelled out in a handout. "God wants you to be organized, whatever God you believe in," Levin tells a class. At Houston's KIPP, the students pick up worksheets containing math, logic, and word problems as they walk into school; they do them in their spare minutes in the day. "If you're off the bus, you're working," Mike Feinberg, the director, says.[13]

What Will My Friends Think?

Ronald Ferguson, who has been studying middle-class black students in Shaker Heights and elsewhere, has found that 21 percent of black males in the lower track in school say, "I didn't try as hard as I could in school because I worried about what my friends might think." He also notes the "misguided love" of many teachers who "are a little too sympathetic . . . [letting] the black kids in elementary school get away with more, just relax, doze off in class, or not pay much attention."[14]

Teachers whose definition of "love" is letting kids doze off should be fired. Or not hired to begin with, although only charter schools are truly free to pick their staff and fire those who don't work out. Good teachers aren't tempted by racial double standards in judging academic work. But they also know that nurturing an alternative peer culture in which high academic achievement earns respect is essential.[15]

In the Detroit survey, young blacks (both employed and unemployed) underestimated the degree to which employers expected those whom they hired to be a "team player."[16] Esquith has created a supportive and nurturing community within his classroom. "Who has a compliment to give someone today?" he frequently asks. "We're a team," a KIPP teacher says. "Everyone ready? We wait until they are." To an incoming group of fifth-graders, Levin explains: A team is a family. We don't make fun of teammates. If you make other students feel bad, they won't concentrate in class. They'll be thinking about how to get back at you. And that will make you feel terrible, and around and around it will go. At the end of the year, that's what you will have spent your time on. But there will be no questions on the state test about being mean. "You are all KIPPsters," he concludes. "We're only worried about everyone moving ahead together." The stress on teamwork is a strategy to alter both behavioral norms and the academic culture. The student who can't spell a word is letting the "family" down. The youngster who thinks schoolwork is nerdy can't be part of the team.

Who wants to be left off a team? Other schools, too, nurture a sense of belonging to a special (and academically serious) group. The morning circles at North Star and Amistad are a daily reminder of the students' membership in a culture so different from the one to which many of their neighborhood peers belong. "Why are you here?" a teacher asks in a "call-response" chant that students run through in the morning circle. "To get an education," the students reply. "And what will you have to do?" Part of the students' response: "Take care of each other!" Teammates "take care of each other," and take care of their special place—which the school becomes.

At North Star and KIPP, we noticed students picking up trash when they saw it; they viewed the school as their second home. They are expected to wipe their own lunch tables clean. Rafe Esquith's fifth-graders constantly scrub the tables, sweep the floor, and put things away, making the place look orderly. They don't need to be asked to do so; it's a routine part of their magic life in his one-room schoolhouse. And it's inseparable from the habit of hard academic work to which the "team" becomes committed.

Wages and Property

Levin is "trying to break a complicated cycle" (as he puts it) in which the kids who start behind stay behind. In effect, the school is the employer they will later encounter. There are weekly paychecks in KIPP dollars that reflect such qualities as attendance, promptness, organization and neatness, hard work, behavior outside of class, and the respect given other "teammates." Checks are given out on Mondays, must be cosigned by parents, and can be used to purchase school supplies and other items in the KIPP store. Those whose paychecks maintain a certain average are eligible for trips to places like Utah, California, and Washington, D.C.

In the real world, irresponsible decisions can be costly. At the KIPP DC: KEY Academy one of the students broke a window. Either the school pays for it or your mother pays and she can't afford it, Susan Schaeffler, the principal, told the student. She offered a deal: double dollars on the student's paycheck, but everything he earned would go toward replacing the window. At every KIPP Academy, the connection between hard work, good behavior, and rewards in life is very clear.

Grades don't figure into the KIPP Bronx paychecks, but there are plenty of rewards for academic accomplishment: a Wall of Honor in the hallway, award assemblies, "students of the week" listed on the classroom walls, along with "Homework Champs" and "Reading Champs" and samples of excellent written work.

Esquith, too, has a complicated system of points, awards, and paychecks. In class, students lose more points by giving a wrong answer than they gain by a correct one; he wants them to think before speaking. Trips to D.C., California's Muir Woods, Philadelphia, the Oregon Shakespeare Festival, and elsewhere have long been integral to the education he offers; they reward mature behavior. A role in a Shakespearean production is also earned, in part by a willingness to spend countless hours working on the play, putting the classroom in order after hours, and so forth.

Paychecks in Esquith's class—unlike those at KIPP—reflect both academic and other work, as well as behavior. Every student in his class has a job, some more demanding and better paying than others. For instance, the attendance monitor, who keeps track of student absences, earns less than the janitors, who are responsible for keeping the room spotless. Students have checking accounts, with the amounts recorded in ledgers by bankers, hired for their reliability. On top of their regular pay, students earn money by getting a perfect score on a test, having perfect attendance for a month, coming to school for the 7:30 A.M. math class, joining the orchestra, or staying after school for Shakespeare. On the other hand, they are fined for being late to school, having a messy desk, and breaking other classroom rules. Once a month, there is an auction in which the students bid on such items as pens, calculators, and chess sets.

Property, as well, is bought and sold at Esquith's auctions. Classroom seats are real estate—with some locations worth more than others. The students pay rent, but if they have earned and saved enough, they can buy their seat as a condo. In fact, they can buy other students' seats, at which point rent is paid to them. (The kids know that if they are profligate and can't pay rent, they could be "homeless" and find themselves sitting on the floor, although we saw everyone safely in their chairs.) All students pay income taxes, and seat-owners pay a property tax as well. "This is like Monopoly," one youngster notes. To which Esquith answered, "Buddy, this is real life." His kids are learning the rules of the American game—which they can choose to join or reject.

Other schools attempt to acculturate the students to the larger world they will be entering in a variety of ways. At Amistad, for instance, every student participates in the school's "microsociety." Some students own their own "businesses," and there is a student-run bank, newspaper, museum, police force, court system, and legislature. The teachers pick the managers, but the managers choose the employees who apply for the jobs and are paid in Amistad dollars. Students who interview poorly (mumbling, failing to ask questions, and so forth) are not likely to be hired, and may end up in the ranks of the unemployed, with no income. If they've already been lawyers in the sixth and seventh grades, these children learn to think, "I can be a lawyer," Dacia Toll, the director, notes.[17]

The Ladder of Opportunity

A variety of messages is intertwined in the education we have been describing.

In a KIPP phonics class, the teacher asks, "What room is this?" The students chant the answer. "This is the room that has the kids who want to learn to read more books to make a better tomorrow." "We are giving the kids the skills and confidence to take them to someplace better," David Levin says.

"Someplace better": the world of opportunity that awaits them if they are ready to take advantage of it. Getting ready is the point of working so hard. "Good things happen," Levin says, letting the students finish the sentence, "when you do the right thing." He goes on: "You never know when good things are going to happen. You want to be in a situation in which nothing is ever denied you."

On one of our visits to the KIPP Academy New York Levin has extra tickets to a Yankees game. They go to the students with the highest paycheck averages—the students who have met the behavioral demands of KIPP. And while grades aren't part of the mix, hard work (essential to learning) is. In a "Thinking Skills" class, Levin rhetorically asks, "Why do you have to finish work at home that you didn't finish here?" The answer: "You want knowledge." KIPP, it's important to recall, stands for "Knowledge Is Power Program." Knowledge provides the power to get you to that better place.

Rafe Esquith, the KIPP academies, North Star, Amistad, and other schools, in a multitude of ways, remind the students what they're striving for. "Where are you headed?" a North Star teacher asks the students in the morning circle. "College!" they answer, pointing upward. North Star and KIPP name classrooms after various colleges. "Every day, starting in fifth grade, we heard about college, college, college," a KIPP alumnus remembers.[18] Esquith has long had college banners from elite schools decorating his walls, with the names of his students admitted to them underneath. When he takes his kids on trips, they stay at good hotels and eat at good restaurants. "I want to show them what they're working for," he explains. "In our neighborhood, you look outside your window and you see burned buildings," one of his students has remarked. But, she went on, he "teaches us that there is more to life than just [what's] outside the window."[19]

The schools we saw are helping their students get ready for a life beyond the burned buildings, but they can't do the job for them. The students must take responsibility for their own lives. "We do everything we can to help, but we place the burden on them to get the job done," Gregory Hodge, the principal at the Frederick Douglass Academy in Harlem, explains.[20] "You've got to be ready in life," Levin tells his KIPPsters. "We will help you get ready; that's what we're trying to do." "My job is to open a lot of doors for these kids," Esquith says. "Their job is to choose which ones to walk through." They make choices, and choices have consequences. "It's not my job to save your souls," he tells his class. "It's my job to give you an opportunity to save your own soul."

It's an optimistic message about America, and about the rules that govern social mobility—the climb out of poverty to greater affluence. "There Are No

Shortcuts" on the road to success, although doors are open for those determined to walk through them. Neither KIPP nor Esquith promises a rose garden—a future in which race and ethnicity will not matter. But the opportunities outweigh the barriers, they suggest; skills and persistence will pay off.[21]

In any case, barriers too easily become an excuse for failure. In May 2001, *The New York Times* quoted a Massachusetts teacher, James Bougas, on the subject of the statewide testing to which he objected. "Low scores," he said, "can reflect family hardship, not lack of effort or teaching."[22] That is a very different philosophy from that which informs KIPP. "You live in a world in which things are often not fair," Levin tells a sixth-grade class. But the road to success is not paved with excuses. Or second chances.

At all the schools we admired, if a student goofs off or violates the rules of behavior, there are predictable and immediate consequences. No sob stories could persuade Levin to let a student go to the Yankee game unless he or she had earned a ticket. "You can't argue your way into privilege," Levin tells the sixth-graders. "You've got to earn it step-by-step." A disruptive student asks Esquith, "Can we talk about it?" "No," he replies without hesitation. A young girl is not listening to a classmate reading *King Lear*. "Tomorrow if you're not listening, what's going to happen?" he asks. "I'll have to leave," she whispers. "Yes, and how long will you be outside? The rest of the year, yes." They know he means it.

There are plenty of middle-class kids who need to hear the same message, but, as with inadequate instruction in math and other core subjects, when schools fall down on their job, those who suffer most are the students who arrive with the least. Much is made of the fact that more affluent children have parents who read to them, and start school with larger vocabularies and a knowledge of numbers, letters, and colors. Those from low-income families certainly need help in beginning to acquire academic skills at an early age. But arguably the more difficult job is to teach "desire, discipline, and dedication," the watchwords painted in red and blue letters on sidewalks throughout Houston's KIPP. The students need to believe, just for starters, that indeed they can go "someplace better."

"We want students who, when we say, run through that wall, will run because they believe something is good on the other side," Levin tells a group of goofing-off students. "Fire, trust, the will to succeed, is what we want to see. If you have that fire, it should show every day." It's hard to find that "fire" in many youngsters in any school—whatever its demographic profile. Analyzing a survey of 20,000 teenagers in nine high schools in 1987–1990, Laurence Steinberg found widespread disengagement from academic work.[23] But, again, the consequences are particularly severe for those students who do not come to school with the "tool kit" of "culturally-shaped skills, habits, and styles" they need to succeed.

Protégés of Ellison

The effort to put disadvantaged youngsters on the traditional ladder of social mobility has another component, never explicitly articulated. Both Esquith and KIPP—but not every school we visited to the same degree—introduce their students (black, Hispanic, and Korean) to great writing, great music, and great documents. The Declaration of Independence, the words to "God Bless America," "My Country 'tis of Thee," and quotations from Henry David Thoreau and Oliver Wendell Holmes, Jr.—as well as Michael Jordan and others—decorate the walls in the KIPP academies in Houston and New York. Esquith's class is known as "The Hobart Shakespeareans," but on one of our visits the students were reading *Huckleberry Finn* out loud, and on another, *Animal Farm*. The class discussion, as they read along, had everyone (nine- and ten-year olds) mesmerized.

Esquith and KIPP are guiding their students down the road that Ralph Ellison walked almost seven decades ago. "In Macon County, Alabama," Ellison wrote in 1963, "I read Marx, Freud, T. S. Eliot, Pound, Gertrude Stein and Hemingway. Books which seldom, if ever, mentioned Negroes were to release me from whatever 'segregated' idea I might have had of my human possibilities. I was freed not by propagandists . . . but by composers, novelists, and poets who spoke to me of more interesting and freer ways of life."[24]

Even in the Jim Crow South, Ellison thought of himself as a writer and an American. "The values of my own people are neither 'white' nor 'black'; they are American," he wrote.[25] That is not how most educators think about black and Hispanic youngsters, it appears. They offer minority children a " 'segregated' idea" of their potential.

A majority of both black and Hispanic adults in the nation wants schools to "promote a common culture."[26] And yet many of the schools we saw—some we liked and many we did not—stressed racially linked cultural differences. Students were kept on a very heavy diet of literary and historical material that stressed America's moral failings and the importance of racial identity. Their walls were decorated exclusively with pictures of African Americans, Malcolm X being most popular. Posters featured "African Americans in the Arts," alleged African sayings, Michael Jordan, Paul Robeson, and some quite obscure figures such as the first African-American woman to receive an international pilot's license. In one school, classrooms were given Kwanzaa names. At another, students recited "A Pledge for African People" that runs, in part: "We are an African People. . . . We will struggle to resurrect and unify our homeland; we will raise many children for our nation. . . . We will be free and self-determining; we are an African People."[27]

What, precisely, is the "homeland" or the "nation" to which this pledge referred? "I am as American as any," the well-known writer Richard Rodriguez has said.[28] African Americans—with the exception of recent immigrants— are *more* American than most of the nation's residents; unlike Rodriguez's, their families go back centuries. "We feel that for too long our history was not told. They see whites on television," one principal said to us. "They want to read about issues relevant to them," another argued.

Fair enough. Until roughly the early 1970s, American history was mainly white history. It is also true that many black children remain too racially isolated; whites are strangers in their daily life. But too heavy a dose of African-American history and literature arguably reinforces the isolation. Perhaps the very fact of racial isolation makes the stress on black history and literature particularly "relevant," but Ellison's view is worth remembering. In the brutally segregated South, he could never forget that he was black. He was also an avid reader of black literature. And yet it wasn't mainly black writing that spoke to him "of more interesting and freer ways of life." In fact, his discovery of T. S. Eliot's poem "The Wasteland" was the intellectual turning point that sent him on the road to becoming a writer.[29]

There are magnificent books whose authors are not white, and of course all students should be exposed to them. Ellison's own masterpiece, *Invisible Man,* is an obvious example. It's not *black* literature; it's American literature—about the black experience that is so central to the nation's history. "The price of being a brown author is that one cannot be shelved near those one has loved. The price is segregation," Richard Rodriguez has said. You are "shelved south of the border with the other writers who write about growing up Puerto Rican, and that's your section and you are so far away from James Baldwin, the writer who so influenced you when you were growing up."[30]

This is not an easy issue, however. Color has something to do with most people's sense of identity—more or less, depending on the individual and the particular racial or ethnic group. But where, precisely, is the line between what Ellison called "propaganda" (and Rodriguez calls "segregation") and material on Hispanic history, for instance, that is perhaps especially inspirational for Hispanic kids? Particularly for black students, there is still no escape from racial identity. In the morning circle at North Star, three students beat West African–style drums. And yet that did not seem like "propaganda" to us, in part because the central message of the school is so very clear. Racial identity is not destiny.

The notion of race-as-destiny, Ellison argued, stifles the development of individuality and nurtures "that feverish industry dedicated to telling Negroes who and what they are"—an industry that "can usually be counted upon to deprive both humanity and culture of their complexity."[31] The "industry" to which he referred was created by both blacks and whites.

"If white society has tried to do anything to us," he noted in the 1970s, "it has tried to keep us from being individuals"—to deprive blacks of the understanding that "individuality is still operative beyond the racial structuring of American society."[32] The best classes that we saw try to teach children the lessons that Ellison had to figure out in terrible racial circumstances. The extraordinary amount of time their students spend in school, the serious academic demands made upon them, and what they read are all aimed, in part, at helping students define themselves as individuals and Americans in a society rich with opportunity.

If these students come to think of themselves as unique, free to choose their identity, to emphasize their racial and ethnic group ties as much or little as they wish, and if they come to understand that they belong in the country in which they live, they will have an excellent chance of going far if they acquire solid skills. This is not a truth confined to racial and ethnic minorities. The traditional ticket to social mobility in America has been the ability of individuals to define themselves apart from the group (as defined by social class, geographical location, and a variety of other indicators) into which they were born.

Culture Matters

"One of the kids asked me how I define freedom. And I told him that freedom is the power to choose to make a change in the right direction," Jaime Escalante has said.[33] But that freedom to choose requires both academic skills and an understanding of what the writer Jonathan Rauch once called "Main Street Codes"—the "rules for public behavior," the social norms that most Americans understand.[34]

Freeman A. Hrabowski III, the president of the University of Maryland-Baltimore County, is nationally known for his work with black students. "Unless we have some interventions in settings where you have large numbers of poor people, poor children will not rise to the top," he said in an April 2002 interview. "[We must] give them the support to get the values they need. . . .

I'm talking about values like hard work, respect for authority and willingness to listen to teachers. Many parents don't know how important these things are."[35]

Many schools don't understand their importance, either, although KIPP, North Star, the South Boston Harbor Academy, and others we have described certainly do. It's a point, however, not often articulated. It makes most people astonishingly nervous. Aren't these "white" values that President Hrabowski (black, himself) is pushing?

No. And Hrabowski is not the only black voice making that clear. In the summer of 2002, the Boston headquarters of Verizon was host to a dozen interns from Dorchester High School, where 70 percent of the students are African American and 25 percent are Hispanic. The summer interns came (in the words of a *Boston Globe* reporter) "sporting the styles and languages of school hallways and street corner hangouts." But they heard some tough talk from Karen Hinds, a West Indian immigrant who went to Dorchester High herself.

If you're interested in good jobs, you "have to know how to speak proper English," she admonished. Ignore those who say you are "acting white" or "sucking up," she went on. Your large hoop earrings, hip-hop styles, and inner-city walk have to go—when you're in the workplace, that is. Hinds's message was reinforced by an African-American attorney from a prestigious law firm. "I don't think it is unreasonable to expect that you know how to speak with correct grammar when you walk into my office," Harry Daniels said to the assembled teenagers.[36]

It isn't a message that goes down well with everyone. In 1998, a school board member in majority-black Prince George's County, Maryland, suggested that teachers should correct the English of their students. Asked about the issue, the chairman of the English Department at the University of Illinois, Urbana-Champaign, responded: "Does the school board want [students] to start sounding less black?"[37]

"If you know how to do your job, it shouldn't matter what you look like or how you talk," said Kiara Robinson, one of the students at the Verizon meeting. "I don't think it's fair." In fact, it's not "fair" to students when schools fail to teach the rules of success—including standard English and the dress code of most well-paying jobs.[38] "The greatest problem now facing African-Americans is their isolation from the tacit norms of the dominant culture, and this is true of all classes," the sociologist Orlando Patterson has written.[39]

The best schools understand that fundamental point and work hard to address the question; most schools do not, however. Students need to acquire the culture of success. That process of cultural acquisition has been easier for members of some racial and ethnic groups than for others—the topic that we will explore in greater depth in the next three chapters. Asian immigrants, for instance, generally arrive in this country with a "tool kit" that gives them an advantage in their drive for education and prosperity in their adopted country. Group cultures matter.

3 Culture Matters

Five: Asians

Every day [our parents] tell us: "Obey your teachers. Do your schoolwork. Stay out of trouble. You're there to learn, not to fight. Keep trying harder. Keep pushing yourself. Do your homework. After you have done that, you can watch TV."
Sikh immigrant students in a California high school[1]

Culture matters—that which informs a school, and that which students bring to a school. "Talking about cultural influences on achievement makes Americans uncomfortable. . . . But cultures differ in many ways, including academic orientation," former *New York Times* education columnist Richard Rothstein has written. "Nobody knows a good way to discuss this. . . ."[2]

True enough. And yet group cultural differences, which are the subject of this and the next two chapters, are certainly no secret. "Sometimes my friends say, 'Can I borrow your notes?' They want them because I'm Asian and they assume I'm really smart," Karissa Yee, a freshman at San Francisco's Lowell High School, told a reporter.[3] But raw intelligence, we will argue, is not the story. The Sikh immigrant students quoted in the epigraph had it right: In large part, Asian students typically do well in school because their parents insist upon it, and they feel obliged to comply with their parents' wishes. "In Chinese culture, parents don't listen to children," said Iris Leung, a San Francisco parent. "They say, 'Do this now.' And kids do. . . . People in America say, 'You should be a friend to your kid.' But, I don't know how to do that. That's not Chinese culture. It's American."[4]

Parents who say, "Obey your teachers," "Do your schoolwork," "Keep trying harder," and kids who actually follow parental orders: what an advantage when it comes to academic achievement! Not all Asian parents and their children fit the stereotype, of course, and Asian Americans are not actually one "group." The label is a construct that obscures vital cultural differences among Koreans, Chinese, and other "Asian" ethnic groups.[5] Yet, with respect to academic achievement, they have a common profile.

In the literature on education, writers often refer to the gap in academic achievement between "minorities" and whites. In fact, it is non-Asian minorities who generally have such worrisome NAEP, SAT, and other standardized test scores. This is a vital distinction, too often overlooked.

Indeed, those who overlook it miss two crucial points: Impoverished Asian students at inferior inner-city schools outperform their black and Hispanic classmates. Same schools, same teachers, different results. Second, these "students of color" actually do better, on average, than whites. In certain respects, white students are academically inferior to Asian students. On some math tests, for instance, the white-Asian gap is larger than the black-white gap.

How can that be the case in an allegedly racist society? Julian Weissglass, director of the National Coalition for Equity in Education and a professor of education at the University of California, Santa Barbara, has an explanation. "The processes of racism and internalized racism help explain why some Asian-American groups outperform blacks, Latinos, and Native Americans," he has written. "Although Asian-Americans experience racism, they do not usually get stereotyped as less intelligent than whites, so they internalize and transfer messages about themselves that are different from those of blacks, Latinos, and Native Americans."[6]

It is, of course, a neat trick to "experience racism" and yet escape being stereotyped as inferior; the two usually go hand-in-hand. In fact, Asian-American academic success has nothing to do with racism. And it has nothing to do with the power of whites to determine the status of groups, as Weissglass implies. Asian children typically do extraordinarily well in school for one reason: family culture—the culture that has a Chinese mother expressing bewilderment at the idea that she should be her child's "friend."

That explanation, however, offers grounds for optimism: Parental pressure to work extraordinarily hard in school—which is the typical Asian story—is a culturally transferable trait. You don't have to be Asian to put the time into conquering algebra.

Remarkable Academic Success

Stare at the list of valedictorians in the Boston public high schools, and almost every June it is the same story. Remarkable numbers of Asian students, most often first-generation immigrants, take the prize. Look as well at the data on racial and ethnic enrollment in New York City's elite public schools, Bronx Science and Stuyvesant. Asian Americans are a shade less than 10 percent of the city's population, but they win roughly half of the coveted seats in these competitive schools.

The picture is much the same at the highly selective institutions of higher education: The Asian presence is striking. Roughly 4 percent of Americans today are of Asian background. And yet Asian Americans made up 27 percent of the 2000–2001 freshman class at MIT, 25 percent at Stanford, 24 percent at Cal Tech, 19 percent at the University of Pennsylvania, 18 percent at Columbia, 17 percent at Harvard, 15 percent at both Brown and Yale, 12 percent at Duke and Princeton.[7] At these schools, Asian Americans have from a minimum of three to as much as seven times their proportional share of places.[8]

These are striking examples, but Asian Americans are also faring much better than whites by a broader measure. They are far more likely to graduate from college—a startling fact. In 2000, a majority (54 percent) of Asian Americans ages 25–29 had a bachelor's degree or more, as compared with just a third (34 percent) of whites.[9] The 20-point Asian-white graduation rate gap is even larger than the 16-point black-white gap.

The Asian success story in graduate education is equally impressive. For example, Asian-American students now make up one-fifth of all the medical students in the United States, five times their share of the population as a whole.[10] Given the enormous prestige and high income of doctors, this is a stunning achievement. Asian Americans have begun to enter the legal profession in large numbers as well. In 1989–1990, they accounted for 2.9 percent of law school enrollments, just about their share of the total population at the time; ten years later the proportion was more than double that (6.3 percent).[11] The trend is especially evident at the leading law schools. Asians currently account for 10 to 20 percent of the law students at Harvard, Yale, Stanford, Columbia, NYU, Cornell, Northwestern, Berkeley, UCLA, and the University of Southern California.[12]

In discussing the educational successes of Asian Americans, unfortunately we cannot depend much upon the results of the National Assessment of Educational Progress, the key source of evidence upon which much of this book is based. Asian Americans are a very small percentage of the population, and thus the number of Asian students included in the typical NAEP assessment is tiny—two-to-three hundred out of several thousand tested. In fact, on some recent assessments (on, for example, the 2000 fourth-grade math and science tests), no scores were reported for Asian-American students; the investigators lacked confidence that the results were accurate enough to disseminate.[13] Even when NAEP data for Asian students are available, they are based on such a small number of cases as to limit their usefulness. Differ-

ences between Asian and other youths need to be very large to reach statistical significance—of sufficient magnitude to ensure that the estimated figure
is not simply the result of chance variation.

Compounding this difficulty is the fact that most of the NAEP figures
available include Pacific Islanders as part of the Asian group, even though
they come from quite different cultural backgrounds, and including their
scores pulls the Asian average down appreciably. On the few assessments in
which separate scores are reported for Asians and for Pacific Islanders
(Samoans, Tongans, and Hawaiian natives, for example), Pacific Islanders
typically score 15 to 20 points below other Asians. Despite these limitations,
however, it is abundantly clear from the NAEP evidence that Asian-
American students perform dramatically better than their black and Hispanic
classmates—so dramatically better as to rule out the possibility of sampling
error.

A key question about Asian-American academic achievement in the K–12
years cannot be fully resolved with the NAEP evidence. How does the Asian
performance compare with that of whites? Asians have a very large advantage in rates of admission to selective colleges, in college graduation, and in
enrollments in medical school, law school, and Ph.D. programs. But if we had
only the NAEP results to go on, we would conclude that white and Asian
schoolchildren perform at about the same average level. In almost all recent
assessments of students in grades 4, 8, and 12, no statistically significant differences between white and Asian students showed up. The one exception is
in math at the high school level. Asian-American twelfth-graders outscored
whites by an average of about ten points on the four mathematics assessments conducted between 1990 and 2000.[14]

We can obtain a more accurate picture of how Asian and white students
compare by shifting our focus to high achievers—students whose academic
records qualify them for admission to selective colleges and universities.
Some striking evidence comes from California, home to more than a third of
the Asian-American population of the United States. Admission to a campus
of the University of California, the best state university system in the country, is guaranteed to state residents who rank in the top eighth of their high
school graduating class. Grades are the primary criterion, but SAT scores are
also considered in determining the list of students who are "UC-eligible."

Who qualifies for the University of California? Figure 5-1 supplies the answer for 1999, the most recent year for which data are available, and it is quite
striking.[15] No one who has read the earlier chapters of this book will be surprised to discover that both blacks and Hispanics are hugely underrepresented. Less than 3 percent of African-American and under 4 percent of

Latino high school graduates rank in the top 12.5 percent. Whites do far better, but the important point is that they are not proportionally overrepresented among the "UC-eligibles." It turns out that 12.4 percent of them score in the top 12.5 percent. The only group of overachievers is Asian Americans, nearly one-third of whom meet the requirements for admission. Asian students are a remarkable 2.5 times more likely than their white classmates to qualify for admission to the University of California. They make up 10 percent of the state's population, but almost half of the student body at the state's two flagship schools, Berkeley and UCLA.

Evidence from the nation as a whole that confirms the California picture is available from the SAT examinations conducted by the College Board. Students who take the SAT are not representative of their age group, of course. Only the college-bound take the test, but the results are good indicators of the relative accomplishments of different groups of students.

In 1999, when Asian Americans were just 4.2 percent of all students of the age at which the SATs are taken, they accounted for almost 8 percent of the students who actually took the exams, itself a sign of academic ambition, because SATs are used only for admissions at selective colleges and universities (see Figure 5-2). Furthermore, 11 percent of the students who scored in the very top bracket (750–800) of the basic SAT I verbal reasoning test, and a stunning 25 percent of all those doing that well in mathematical reasoning were Asian. In the more specialized SAT II subject tests, Asians had, at the

Figure 5-1. Percentage of Members of Various Racial Groups Who Qualified for Admission to the University of California, 1999 High School Graduates

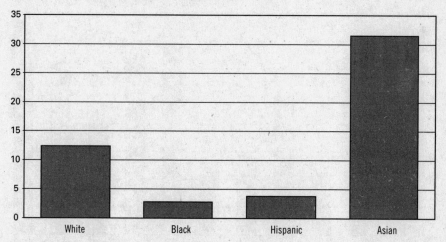

Source: Calculated from data given in Emory Curtis, "Another View: We Need Radical Changes in K–3 School," *Ethnic News Watch*, March 9, 2000.

least, triple their share of top scores in writing and in history, five times their proportional share in biology, and about *eight* times their share in both SAT II math tests, in chemistry, and in physics.

These remarkable racial disparities are far larger than most of the differences one ever finds between whites and blacks or whites and Hispanics.

In short, immigrants from Asia and American-born citizens whose ancestry can be traced back to Asia are generally succeeding spectacularly in our schools today. This is true despite the fact that, as we said earlier, they are actually a very diverse group that is artificially lumped together.

Is It Just Social Class?

Perhaps the school success of Asian Americans is no mystery. We know that recent Asian immigrants to the United States tend to be more highly educated than the average American, have somewhat better jobs, and somewhat higher incomes. Since those factors are associated with the success of children in school, it might be that they are sufficient to explain the pattern we have described. In an article entitled "The Secret to Those High Asian Test Scores: Affluent, Well Educated Daddies, Mommies, Too" one educational writer has recently claimed that this is all there is to it.[16] The author, Gerald

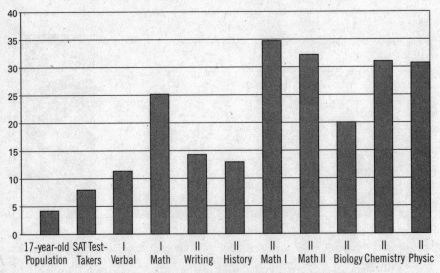

Figure 5-2. Asian Americans as Percentage of All 17-Year-Olds, of All Students Taking the SAT, and of Those Scoring 750 or Better on the SAT I and Various SAT II Tests, 1999

Source: College Entrance Examination Board, *1999 National Ethnic/Sex Data*, unpublished report, unpaginated.

W. Bracey, argues that the Asian academic success story is entirely reducible to what he calls the "mundane" facts of parental socioeconomic status.

Bracey mentions two bits of evidence. First, he notes that Asian parents have higher average incomes than whites and are more often college graduates. True enough, but the question is whether their children's advantage in school simply mirrors their parents' advantage in income and education. In fact, Asian adults in California, for instance, are not notably more likely as whites to be in the highest educational and income bracket. Their children, however, are two and a half times as likely to have academic records that qualify them for admission to the University of California.

In addition, Bracey argues, Asian scores are highest for children from high-income or highly educated households. Again, true, but children from better-educated, higher-income families in all groups tend to test better than those lower on the socioeconomic scale. It does not necessarily follow that all group differences are the result of social class.

Much scholarly literature suggests otherwise. Asian students outperform others when the influence of social-class differences is eliminated from the equation. Laurence Steinberg studied 20,000 students in nine high schools in California and Wisconsin in the 1987–1990 school years. He found that Asian Americans did notably better than whites, just as whites did much better than black or Hispanic students, even when differences in social-class background were taken into account. The contrast between Asian and non-Asian students, Steinberg discovered, was sharper than that between poor and affluent children, between those with two parents and those with only one, and between any other groups defined along economic or demographic lines—remarkable findings.[17]

The point is apparent in Figures 5-3 and 5-4, which show SAT scores from 1999 broken down by family income and parental education. Within each family income category except the very lowest one, Asian students outperform whites by an average of 40 points on the math SATs. (To judge the significance of this difference, note that it amounts to more than one-third of the black-white gap of 106 points on this test.) Considering parental education (rather than income) and comparing white and Asian youths, a huge gap is also left unexplained. The average difference between the two groups when parental education is held constant is 35 points. Asian children whose parents never finished high school score 48 points higher than whites from similarly uneducated families. And Asians with parents who had earned graduate degrees outperform white students from comparable homes by 42 points.

Asians do not have the same advantage on SAT verbals (Figure 5-4). Among families in the income brackets below $60,000, whites do better, al-

Figure 5-3. Mean SAT I Mathematics Scores for White and Asian Students, 1999, by Family Income and Parental Education

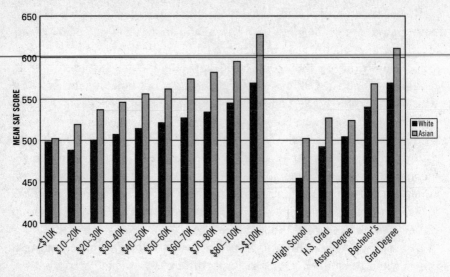

Source: College Board, *1999 National Ethic/Sex Data.*

though it is important to note that the size of that advantage diminishes steadily as incomes rise, and is reversed at $60,000 and above. The pattern with respect to parental education is similar, although whites retain a slight advantage even among families in which the parents have graduate degrees.

That math and verbal scores display different patterns is predictable; most Asian students grow up in homes in which English is not the main language. Many of those from families in the lower income brackets in particular are recent immigrants who had part of their schooling in another country. Nearly 40 percent of the Asian students who took the SATs in 1999 said that English was not their first language, and another third reported growing up bilingual. The one-quarter of all Asian students who learned English as their first language scored 41 points higher on the verbal SAT than their peers who did not. If we could exclude children whose first language was not English from the tabulations, it is probable that Asians would outperform whites even on the verbal test, though perhaps not by the same large margin as in mathematics.

Hard Courses and Homework

If social class is not the explanation for the remarkable academic record of Asian-American students, perhaps, on average, they are simply more intelligent—endowed with greater innate ability to do the kinds of things that

Figure 5-4. Mean SAT I Verbal Scores for White and Asian Students by Family Income and Education, 1999

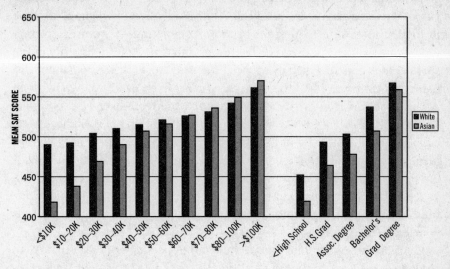

Source: College Board, *1999 National Ethnic/Sex Data.*

teachers demand. Some people certainly think that. Education writer Gerald Bracey tells of a principal from Brooklyn who "once joked that when he was a kid, all of the students knew that Jewish kids had a 'smart gene.' Now, he said, the students in this same Brooklyn neighborhood know with equal certainty that the smart gene resides in Asian brains."[18]

The assumption that differences in IQ are primarily genetic rather than environmental is one that we reject, and the scanty evidence available does not sustain the argument that Asian students are born with a "smart gene."[19] They simply care more about academic success. They are much more engaged in school than their peers, Laurence Steinberg found in his survey of 20,000 high school kids. They cut classes less often and reported higher levels of attention and concentration during class. In the priority they place on school, "Asian students outscore all other groups by a wide margin."[20] They spent only about half as much time as other students hanging out with friends, were less likely to hold part-time jobs, and less likely to devote large blocks of their time to extracurricular activities.[21]

Asian Americans are also far more likely to enroll in the most academically demanding courses. The clearest evidence is from enrollment patterns in Advanced Placement courses, classes that are supposed to be at the introductory college level, and indeed count for credit at many colleges and universities. With high grades on a number of AP exams, you can enter Harvard College, for example, with sophomore standing. Figure 5-5 shows the racial distribution of students who took the AP exams in 2001, expressed as an index that compares the share of the group in the total high school population to its share of AP exam-takers. White students, 64 percent of all those in high school, were 65 percent of those completing AP courses, so their index is just a shade above 100. There was only a tiny racial disparity in the share of such courses taken by whites. Proportionate to their population, Hispanics, by contrast, were little more than half as likely as whites to have done AP work, and African Americans only about a quarter as likely.

These glaring black-white and Hispanic-white differences will have been expected by anyone who has read the preceding pages. But it is surely surprising that the difference between whites and Asians is of an equivalent order of magnitude. Asian-American high school students complete Advanced Placement courses at triple the white rate. Whites are strikingly behind Asians in their commitment to taking the most academically rigorous courses.

Contrary to popular mythology, these differences do not mean that Asian students are always toiling away at their books while their non-Asian classmates are sitting with eyes glazed before the television set. Students taking NAEP tests are asked how much television they typically watch on a school day, and the results are surprising (Figure 5-6). In the fourth, eighth, and twelfth grades, Asians are as likely or even more likely than whites to watch

Figure 5-5. The Asian Advantage in Advanced Placement, 2001

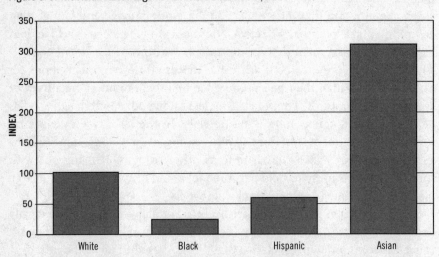

Source: College Board, "Participation in AP: Minority Students," available on the College Board web site, www.collegeboard.com. The index is calculated by dividing a racial group's share of AP enrollments by its share of the total high school population. It equals 100 when the proportion of students in a group taking the AP exams matches its share of high school enrollments.

four or more hours of television daily. In the fourth grade, a slightly higher proportion of Asian students watches no more than an hour a day, but in the eighth grade the two groups are indistinguishable, and in the twelfth grade a modestly higher proportion of whites watches little television. Television-watching, it appears, is ubiquitous among American children whatever their race.

Whether Asian students separate television from schoolwork, doing the latter first, or follow the pattern of many of their peers and watch and work simultaneously is not a question the NAEP data can answer. But Steinberg found that Asian-American high schoolers spent twice as much time on homework as their non-Asian peers. NAEP also asks students (in lower grades, too) how much time they devote to doing homework on a typical school day, and Asian responses are distinctive (Figure 5-7).

Not very much homework is assigned to American fourth-graders in general; less than a fifth do more than an hour's worth per day. Asian students, however, are somewhat more likely than others to do at least an hour, and they are also less likely to report that they either had no homework or didn't bother to do it.

By eighth grade, these differences sharpen. Only a quarter of white students in middle school spend more than an hour daily on schoolwork, but half of all Asian-American children do so. By the twelfth grade, the difference is even starker. Less than a quarter of whites, but 53 percent of Asians, report

Figure 5-6. Percentages of Students Watching Television Four or More Hours or No More than One Hour on School Days, 1998–2000

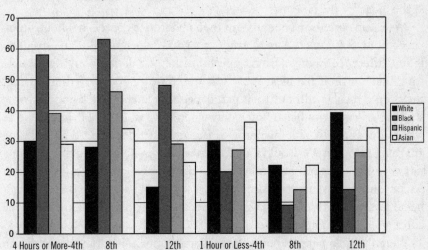

Source: NAEP Data Tool. Figures given are the average of responses to the 1998 reading and 2000 math assessments.

Figure 5-7. Percentages of Students Doing More than an Hour of Homework per Day or None at All in the 4th, 8th, and 12th Grades, 1998–2000

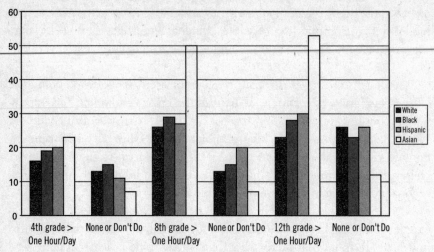

Source: NAEP Data Tool. Figures are the average of responses to the 1998 reading and 2000 math assessments.

doing over an hour of homework every day. Twenty-six percent of whites versus a mere 12 percent of Asians say that they either have no homework or don't do it. Asian-American youths study a lot more, and spend fewer of their after-school hours on sports or part-time jobs.

Asian-American students, it is clear, are more deeply engaged in school than their peers, but why? Here we are back to the question of parents, raised at the outset of the chapter.

American parents in general want their children to do well in school, Steinberg found; few deny the importance of a good education. But an intriguing group difference emerged from a question asking students about the "trouble threshold" in their families. What was the lowest grade they thought that they could receive without their parents getting angry? Black and Hispanic students got into trouble at home only when their grades fell below C−. For whites it was a full grade higher, B−. But Asian students felt that receiving anything below an A− would incur parental wrath—suggesting that our quotation in the epigraph at the beginning of this chapter tells a larger story. Asian youths were successful, Steinberg writes, "not because of their stronger belief in the payoff for doing well, but because they have greater fear of the consequences of not doing well."[22]

Weren't Asian parents being unrealistic in demanding that their children always get A's? Many Asian youths, they must have understood, are merely average or below average in their abilities. But Steinberg made a fascinating discovery: Asian parents and their children had a set of distinctive attitudes. They did not think in terms of innate ability. Nor did they see luck or teacher biases as playing a part in their grades. Academic success or failure did not (in their view) depend upon things "outside their personal control."[23] They believed instead that their academic performance depended almost entirely on how hard they worked; their performance was within their control. A grade below an A was evidence of insufficient effort.

The basic reason why Asian-American students today are outperforming American whites in school is somewhat ironic, as Steinberg notes. The children of immigrants are typically beating the competition because they are the true descendants of Benjamin Franklin. These American newcomers are the group that has most intensely embraced the traditional American work ethic.

Americanization and Achievement

Although we draw heavily on Steinberg's study to support our argument about the cultural sources of Asian-American achievement, he gives a twist to the analysis that we believe is wrong. Immigrant culture in general, he contends, produces children who have an exceptional drive to succeed in school. Americanization has a "high cost." "The longer a student's family has lived in this country, the worse the youngster's school performance. . . ."[24] Sociologists who advance what has been called the "new second generation" theory make a similar claim. Immigrants, according to this analysis, are naively optimistic about opportunities in their adopted home. Their American-born children, though, experience the bitter realities of racism and class oppression, with the result that they disengage from school.[25]

This generalization applies to Hispanics as well as Asians, Steinberg argues. This is a dubious claim that we will address in the next chapter. Here the issue is whether foreign-born Asian immigrant children perform better in school than their native-born peers, and whether native-born Asians whose parents were also born in the United States do less well than either the first or second generation.

Steinberg presents no statistical evidence to support his claim that school achievement declines with greater exposure to American society. He studied nine California and Wisconsin high schools, and it seems unlikely that his samples included enough native-born Asian children of native-born parents to draw any meaningful conclusions. The massive immigration of Asians occurred only after 1965, when immigration law was substantially overhauled. Only 12 percent of Asian students in American schools today have two native-born parents. A quarter of these students were born abroad, and 62 percent are the American-born children of immigrants.[26] It is too early to tell how the third generation of the group will fare.

The best available evidence on the declining achievement question comes from the National Educational Longitudinal Study (NELS) of students who were high school seniors in 1992 (Figure 5-8). The Asian sample did not include enough students from families that were themselves born in the United States; NELS thus contains no reliable estimates of school performance over three or more generations. But the contrast between immigrants and the second-generation is clear and reveals a pattern quite the opposite of that which Steinberg describes as typical.[27]

Asian-American students born in the United States and exposed their entire lives to the allegedly negative influence of American culture consistently outperformed their immigrant counterparts. Over a third of second-generation Asians ranked in the top quartile nationally on the reading test used in the study, double the proportion for the foreign-born immigrant students. Only 12 percent of second-generation Asians were in the bottom quartile in reading, while the proportion of immigrants struggling with English was twice as large. In math, even Asian immigrants were above the national

Figure 5-8. Proportion of Foreign-Born and U.S.-Born Asian-American 12th-Graders Scoring in the Top and Bottom Quarters on Reading and Math Tests, 1992

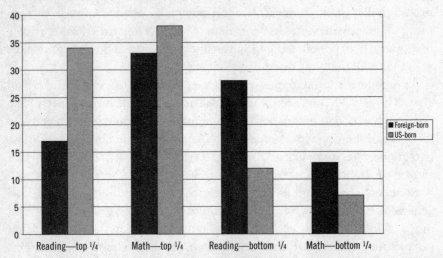

Source: Heather Kim, *Diversity Among Asian American High School Students* (Princeton, N.J.: Educational Testing Service, 1997), 21.

average, with about a third in the top quartile and only 13 percent in the bottom quartile. But American-born Asians did even better.

Direct evidence about the academic achievement of Asians whose parents
were at least second-generation is thus lacking in the studies we found, but
data from the 1990 Census throw some light on the issue. The United States
took in substantial numbers of immigrants from China and Japan in the nine-
teenth and early twentieth centuries; both migrations were abruptly cut off
by discriminatory immigration laws thereafter. Few Chinese entered the
country after the Chinese Exclusion Act of 1882. Japanese immigration
peaked in the first decade of the twentieth century and was sharply reduced
by the 1907 Gentleman's Agreement and cut off altogether by a change in
immigration law in 1924. If Steinberg is right about the debilitating effect of
Americanization, we could expect the descendants of Chinese immigrants to
be doing pretty badly in school after more than a century of exposure to
American culture. The Japanese should be faring nearly as poorly, after several decades in the country.

To see if this is true, we can examine the educational achievement of native-born Chinese and Japanese aged 25 or more in 1990, people who were
born before the 1965 immigration reform that opened the door wide to Asian
newcomers.[28] Given the timing of immigration restriction, the Japanese in
this category must almost all have been at least third-generation Americans,
and the Chinese were from families whose roots often went back four or five
generations.

In fact, Figure 5-9 shows that the 1990 educational achievements of the
Asian group with the longest exposure to Americanizing pressures—the Chinese—were spectacular. Half of them were college graduates, two and a half
times the national average. They were about twice as likely to have earned
master's degrees, doctorates, or professional degrees in fields like law and
medicine. Indeed, the Chinese record in education compares very favorably
with that of native-born persons of Russian parentage, a predominantly Jewish group that ranks at the very top of the educational ladder. Chinese youths
were just as likely to graduate from college as Russians, and not far behind
them in the proportion earning advanced degrees.

The Japanese have had fewer generations of exposure to American life
than the Chinese, and on measures of academic achievement did not do as
well as the more "Americanized" group. They still ranked far above the national average, however. Both these points are contrary to what Steinberg's
theory would predict.

The remarkable academic success of Asian Americans today, this evidence
suggests, cannot be the result of transitory immigrant cultural values that are

Figure 5-9. Educational Attainment of the Total Population and of Native-Born Americans of Chinese, Japanese, and Russian Ancestry, 1990

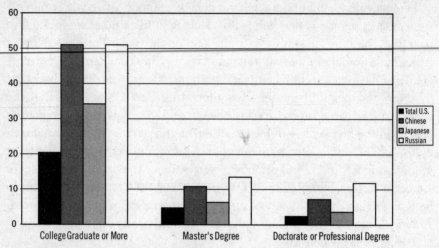

Source: Calculated from U.S. Bureau of the Census, 1990 Census of the Population, *Asian and Pacific Islanders in the United States,* 1990 CP-3-5 (Washington, D.C.: U.S. Government Printing Office, 1993), table 3, and *Ancestry of the Population in the United States,* 1990 CP-3-2 (Washington, D.C.: U.S. Government Printing Office, 1993), table 3.

doomed to disappear in the course of assimilation to American culture. That success is the product of cultural attitudes that various Asian groups brought with them and transmitted from generation to generation over a very long time. The closest historical parallel is with East European Jews, who have also experienced rapid Americanization in the century since their arrival on American shores without losing their extraordinary drive for educational excellence.[29]

Looking into the Future

The story of Asian-American success in school is obviously extraordinary. They are a tiny minority (roughly 4 percent of the American population) but a big presence in all highly selective schools. In many respects, they do far better academically than whites. Even taking social class—family education and income—into account, they outperform members of all other groups.

The explanation is no mystery. They typically care more about academic success, and are more deeply engaged in their schoolwork than their non-Asian classmates. They take Advanced Placement courses at triple the white rate. They have embraced the American work ethic with life-or-death fervor. Their parents expect nothing less.

The history of Chinese and Japanese immigrants who came in the nine-teenth and early twentieth century suggests this commitment to succeeding through school has not waned over time. On the other hand, we cannot be certain that the past will repeat itself. Earlier generations probably attended American public schools that were better than most today. If the quality of academic instruction has declined in recent decades, then the process of as-similation will have a different impact. The intellectual performance of stu-dents even from groups with a strong cultural predisposition toward academic success may slip.

Furthermore, Chinese and Japanese were almost the only Asians who ar-rived before World War II, and intense prejudice in that era isolated them from the dominant culture in many respects. That isolation facilitated the transmission of their distinctive cultural attitudes from generation to genera-tion, particularly because intermarriage between Asians and whites was very rare at the time.

By now, of course, Koreans, Filipinos, Indians, Pakistanis, Vietnamese, Cambodians, and others have joined the earlier groups, and intermarriage rates are very high. This argument, however, would apply equally to Jews. Anti-Semitism has declined sharply, and Jewish-Gentile intermarriages are very common. And yet Jewish educational achievement has not visibly de-clined. If Asian Americans—recently arrived and long here—show as much commitment to the preservation of this aspect of their cultural heritage as have Jews, their educational success should continue long into the future.

Asian-American families have successfully transmitted to their children a culture conducive to high academic achievement. Families from other groups with very different histories also deliver cultural messages to their off-spring. When we turn to the education of Hispanic Americans, we will see that these messages do not always mesh so well with the objectives of the school.

Six: Hispanics

Stupid is he who makes his children better than himself.
Italian proverb[1]

You ought to be embarrassed. Twenty-three years old and without a job.
Paternal reprimand of a Mexican-American student at East Los Angeles College, who
subsequently dropped out to become a welder like his father[2]

Lf Asians are the Jews of contemporary America, Hispanics are the Italians.[3] A century ago, immigrant children from the south of Italy attended the same big-city schools as East European Jews, but they responded to those schools quite differently. Jews were the model students; Italians were the problem students. Their enrollment rate was lower than that for children from other groups; they were truant more often; their grades were poorer; they were much more likely to be held back a grade and to drop out of school as soon as they reached the age at which they were legally free to do so.

Italians tended to be problem students partly because most of their parents were peasants with little formal education themselves. At the time of the mass migration, Italian law only required children to attend school for three years, and in much of the underdeveloped southern part of the nation, even that minimal requirement was often not enforced.[4] Because so many Italian immigrants were uneducated and unskilled, they were confined to poorly paid laboring jobs, and their children were under great pressure to leave school to work and help out.

Italians were also slower than many of their immigrant contemporaries to commit themselves to a permanent life in America. Well over half returned home after a short residence in the United States, and many—"birds of passage," they were called at the time—shuttled back and forth between the two nations. They were slower than other groups to take out American citizenship, and a high proportion did not speak English.[5] These factors, too, made it less likely that their children would accept the values of American schools and focus their energies on academic pursuits.

Even taking such circumstances into account, the Italian experience in school was distinctive.[6] Group culture matters for school performance, George Farkas has observed, because "parental skills, habits, and styles determine the very early cognitive skills of their children, and these influence the child's habits and styles via his/her estimation of the success they can expect from hard effort at tasks that both require and increase cognitive skill."[7] Italian culture did not place a high priority on developing the intellectual skills of their children; success in school was not viewed as the key to success in later life. Early entry into the workforce was more important.

Large-scale immigration from Italy came to an end in the 1920s, as a result of changes in American immigration law designed to stem the flow of newcomers from southern and eastern Europe. With fewer new Italian immigrants, cultural ties to the old country became weaker, and Italian Americans gradually assimilated to American society. Over time, the culture immigrants brought with them increasingly faded, and their children began to do better in school. Italian immigrants arriving in the first quarter of the twentieth century had almost four fewer years of schooling than white Anglo-Saxon Protestants—WASPs. Their American-born children cut the gap in half, to 1.7 years of school. By the third generation, according to data compiled in the 1970s, Italians had actually moved slightly ahead of WASPs, with an average of 13.4 years of school completed.[8]

The cultural characteristics of Italians that held their children back in school were not permanent barriers to advancement. But it took generations for those barriers to erode fully. Indeed, the low value placed on education for females in Italian-American families still had a discernible impact on the third and fourth generations as late as the 1970s. By then, Italian males had a slightly higher college graduation rate than their WASP counterparts. But WASP females then were 48 percent more likely to have completed college than Italian-American women.[9]

Parallel Experiences

Today, the parallel between the earlier experience of Italian immigrants and that of Hispanics is strong. Many of the problems affecting the school performance of Latino children are rooted in their immigration background, in their movement back and forth across the border, and in the specific cultural characteristics of the families who choose to migrate. As with the Italians many decades earlier, however, time has had a salutary effect. In recent years, Hispanics have made far more educational progress than is usually assumed. At present, they are moving ahead at roughly the Italian pace in the second quarter of the twentieth century, although the Latino-white gap will be eliminated only if this process continues for decades to come. How many decades? The answer depends in great part on immigration patterns—whether Hispanics continue to pour across the border, reinforcing old-country culture.

"Hispanics" are not a single ethnic group, but an ethnic category, an umbrella label that was first employed in the U.S. Census of 1970. The term embraces roughly two dozen national origin groups that have little in common beyond the fact that they originated in countries in the Western Hemisphere that once were part of the Spanish empire and that have remained predominantly Spanish-speaking since then. Puerto Ricans are quite different from Venezuelans, and Cubans are different from both. The conclusion of an exhaustive demographic study, *The Hispanic Population of the United States* (1987), warns that "it is impossible to speak of a single, unified 'Hispanic population' in any strict sense of the term." To treat Hispanics as a single population "risks overlooking differences that are so great that such an approach becomes virtually meaningless," the authors add.[10]

We are stuck with the label, however, because most often that is how the relevant educational data have been tabulated. Fortunately, figures on Hispanics are not a meaningless average of two dozen groups of roughly equal size. Almost two out of three Hispanics living in the U.S. today derive from just one Latin American country—Mexico.[11] Figures for Hispanics in general will at least be reasonable estimates of what is true for Mexican Americans, because the group is so large that it dominates the averages. When data are available for Mexicans specifically, we do focus on them.

The educational story for Hispanics, as for Asians—and Italians earlier—is inextricably bound up with immigration. Many writers and activists, though, willfully ignore immigration, and insist that the key fact about Hispanic children is that they are nonwhite, and that many are "trapped in a caste-like minority status." One sociologist alleges that they react to their "exclusion and subordination with resentment" directed against the "oppressive authority" of the schools.[12] Deeply ingrained American racism, it is claimed, dooms these children to second-class status in school, and in the job market down the road.

In fact, most Latinos today do not regard themselves as nonwhite, as "people of color."[13] But in any event, immigration is the dominant force shaping Hispanic America today, not race. Some Americans of Mexican origin have

very deep roots in the United States and are far removed from the immigration experience. Their ancestors were living in the Southwest before 1848,
when it became part of the United States as a result of war with Mexico. But
only about 50,000 Mexican nationals stayed on in the area after the United
States acquired it. Just a tiny fraction of the more than 20 million people of
Mexican ancestry living in the U.S. today are descendants of those early settlers. The vast majority are themselves immigrants or the descendants of immigrants who arrived after the Mexican Revolution broke out in 1910.[14]

From the nineteenth century down to today, Mexicans have been the
largest single Hispanic immigrant group. They made the journey to the
United States by land, not by boat, and that powerfully affected where they
settled and the level of economic opportunity available to them. Unlike Italians and almost all other European groups, they were not transplanted into
the diverse and dynamic economies of New York, Philadelphia, and other
East Coast seaports.

Instead, they settled in the region closest to the Mexican border, the
Southwest, where the only jobs for which they qualified were unskilled, low-
wage positions in agriculture, mining, and service industries. Two-thirds of
the Mexican population at the time was illiterate, and the proportion was
even higher among immigrants.[15] Many could find no work except as migra-
tory farm laborers, and they went wherever there were crops to plant or har-
vest. Their children thus bounced from school to school, or—even
worse—were not enrolled at all if their family's stay was expected to be short.
In addition, fairly young children could pick fruit and pull up weeds, making
a contribution to the family's low and irregular income that seemed more important than their schooling.[16] These adverse conditions were exacerbated by
the widespread racial prejudice that darker-skinned Mexicans encountered.

As a result, the Mexican-American community lagged far behind the national norm in its educational development. As late as 1960, the average Mexican American who was at least twenty-five years old and lived in the
Southwest had just over seven years of schooling, as compared with twelve
years for non-Hispanic whites. Even African Americans in that region had
more education than Mexicans—almost two years more.[17]

These figures are misleading, though. Because they mix together Mexicans of different generations, they conceal important evidence of progress
over time. In 1960, second-generation Mexican Americans had nearly four
more years of schooling than their immigrant parents.[18] Those additional
four years were their ticket to better jobs in the economically booming Sunbelt states. Between 1950 and 1970, the proportion of men of Mexican ancestry who were employed as farm laborers plunged from 28 percent to 10

percent, and the fraction who were white-collar workers or skilled craftsmen jumped from 24 to 39 percent.[19] Mexicans were moving up—just as Italians and other European newcomers had done in earlier decades.

Interrupted Progress

The parallel between Italians and Mexicans is imperfect, however. Large-scale immigration from Italy came to an end in the 1920s, never resumed, and the Italian case became one more example of the classic American story of upward mobility from generation to generation. The proportion of the group that was foreign-born declined steadily. With each passing year, more Italian Americans were second- and third-generation, and thus had more education and access to better jobs.

Mexican Americans were on this same path, but in the 1970s legal immigration from Mexico accelerated to unprecedented levels. It averaged a mere 30,000 a year in the 1950s. By the 1970s, however, it was running at 64,000 a year, by the 1980s 165,000 a year, and by the 1990s, 225,000 a year, almost eight times the level of the 1950s. For the past two decades, Mexico has been by far the most important source of legal immigration to the United States, accounting for about a quarter of all newcomers. And these figures do not count the unknown but undoubtedly very large numbers of illegal immigrants, a large majority of whom come from Mexico.[20]

Figures from a 2001 Gallup poll for Hispanics as a whole—a group that includes Colombians, Ecuadorians, and so forth—underscore the magnitude of this very recent immigration. They indicated that 47 percent of Hispanics had been born abroad and another 27 percent were American-born but had foreign-born parents. Of the immigrant Hispanics, six out of ten had arrived only within the past twenty years.[21]

Although the children of earlier Mexican immigrants have made educational and economic progress, the huge and continuing influx of uneducated and unskilled immigrants—legal and illegal—has obscured those earlier intergenerational gains. When A. J. Jaffe, Ruth M. Cullen, and Thomas D. Boswell wrote their sophisticated 1980 study, *The Changing Demography of Spanish Americans*, the latest available data was the 1970 census. Impressed by the evidence of progress, they predicted that "within a generation or two [Hispanics] would be almost indistinguishable from the general U.S. population."[22]

Jaffe and his colleagues sounded a prescient note of caution about the possible impact of immigration, however. The "constant influx of migrants from Mexico" would serve to "keep the Spanish language alive" and would "continue to reintroduce elements of the Mexican culture to the Mexican American population." Those Mexicans who were assimilating to the broader culture would be "replaced by immigrants who bring in the traditional values and characteristics."[23] In particular, the authors warned, a big jump in the number of immigrants with very little schooling by American standards would pose major problems for the schools that had to educate their children.[24]

That very big jump has occurred. Data on Mexican-American schoolchildren specifically are not available on this point, but figures for Hispanics as a whole are a reasonable proxy. Latino children now account for one-sixth of total enrollments in K–12 education, a proportion that has nearly tripled in just the past twenty-five years.[25] In California, Texas, Arizona, and New Mexico, the figure ranges from a third to half of all elementary and secondary school enrollments.[26] In 1999, only a little over a third (35 percent) of Hispanic pupils were native-born of native-born parentage. A sixth were foreign-born themselves, the remaining half were second-generation newcomers, the American-born children of Latinos born abroad.[27] Two out of three Latino children thus reside with parents who were born in another country.

These Latino immigrant families are uneducated and unskilled for the most part, and it is the presence of so many Hispanic newcomers that explains why the economic situation of Hispanics as a group is comparable to that of African Americans. Hispanic immigrants are twice as likely as native-born Hispanics to have incomes below the poverty line. The longer Latinos live in the U.S., the better their jobs and the higher their average incomes.[28] But this crucial fact is obscured by the continuing influx of unskilled newcomers, who depress the overall position of the group.

Hispanic immigrants in general and Mexicans in particular also stand out in another way. They seem to be much more ambivalent than European or Asian immigrants about making a permanent commitment to living in the United States, and are thus more resistant to assimilation. They tend to be sojourners, not settlers—"birds of passage" like their Italian predecessors a century ago. A great many, of course, live a short distance from the Mexican border—in Southern California, South Texas, Arizona, or New Mexico. Even those farther away geographically remain psychologically closer to their mother country than do most other immigrants.

The clearest indication is that they are far less likely to take out American citizenship. In 1997, 53 percent of all European-born immigrants had become naturalized citizens, and 44 percent of those born in Asia. But the overall figure for immigrants from Latin America was only 24 percent, and for those from Mexico it was a staggeringly low 15 percent.[29] Like other newcomers, they come to America to better their lot economically. Far more than others, though, they seem to see the move as a temporary pragmatic choice, and they keep alive the option of returning to the country they still consider "home."

 In addition, their attachment to the Spanish language is particularly intense. Latino children, we shall see later in this chapter, are slower than others to become fluent in English, a fact with very important implications for their adjustment to the schools of an English-speaking country.

Latino Educational Achievement

The new wave of Hispanic immigration has profoundly affected the education of Latino children. The Asian-American school population has an even higher share of first- or second-generation Americans, to be sure. But, given the number of affluent, highly educated, and educationally oriented Asian immigrants, the presence of so many recent arrivals does not exert a similar drag on the educational performance of the group.

Thus, when scholars and other observers see so many Latino students struggling in school, in diagnosing the problem they should first ask: How many of their families are newcomers? Most current discussions of Hispanic education blithely ignore the question.

For example, in 2000 the President's Advisory Commission on Educational Excellence for Hispanic Americans issued an eighty-page report, *Creating the Will*. Astonishingly, the word "immigrant" appeared just once in this document, buried away in an appendix.[30] With that sole exception, the data presented in the report were meaningless averages that lumped together newly arrived immigrants with Hispanic families long resident in the United States.

The report complained that "the low high school completion rate for Latinos has not changed substantially in several years," citing a high school graduation rate of "only 63 percent" for Hispanics versus 90 percent for whites and 81 percent for blacks.[31] Fully 37 percent of Latinos were thus allegedly high school dropouts. This was intended to back up the commission's generalization that "in the United States, public education has not worked for Hispanic children."[32]

These figures are grossly misleading. The rate of high school graduation, used in the study is merely the proportion of 16–24-year-olds who had completed high school, and the numbers are greatly distorted by immigration. Many Hispanics aged 16–24 came to the United States only *after* they had completed their education in Mexico or Guatemala or Colombia at the age of

13 or 14. And they took jobs as soon as they arrived in this country. Such youths had never set foot in any school in the United States. If any educational institutions had "not worked" for them, they were the schools in the country in which these young people were born—not those in America.

More recent figures, for 2000, indicate that the overall Hispanic high school dropout rate is indeed high—28 percent (Figure 6-1), though substantially lower than the 37 percent reported in *Creating the Will*. But that number is meaningless, because it averages two populations with radically different experiences. The President's Commission could easily have found data that compared foreign-born children to those born in this country but was oblivious to the importance of that distinction. In fact, 44 percent of foreign-born Hispanic youths fail to complete high school, but only 15 percent of those born here are dropouts.[33] The latter figure is no different than that for African Americans and only a few points higher than that for non-Hispanic whites. It would be even better, of course, if every native-born Hispanic managed to graduate from high school. But the fact is that six out of seven do, not a mere 63 percent.

A recent study of Mexican-American educational and economic progress based on Current Population Surveys for 1996–1999 further illuminates the crucial significance of immigration (see Figure 6-2). Adults born in Mexico

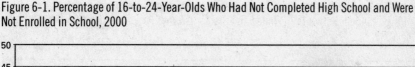

Figure 6-1. Percentage of 16-to-24-Year-Olds Who Had Not Completed High School and Were Not Enrolled in School, 2000

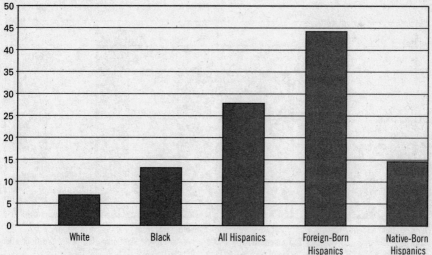

Source: National Center for Education Statistics, *Dropout Rates in the United States: 2000*, NCES 2002-114 (Washington, D.C.: U.S. Department of Education, 2002), 13.

had an average of little more than eight years of school. Although some scholars have argued that the Americanization of immigrants results in declining
educational attainment, in fact American-born children of Mexican immigrants average nearly twelve years of school—an immense difference. Only
14 percent of the immigrants in the sample had attended college; for their native-born children the figure was 40 percent.[34] Had there not been a massive
immigration of Latinos to the United States in the past three decades, the col-
lege-attendance rate of the group as a whole would be dramatically higher
than it actually is.

One of the limitations of this study is that the figures cover a wide age
range. Some members of the sample only left school in the 1990s, but older
ones did so decades earlier, and their experience does not necessarily reflect
the current pattern. A better gauge of the educational achievement of
Latinos in recent years may be obtained from the National Education Longitudinal Study of 1988 (NELS), which examined students who were eighth-
graders in 1988 and followed them until the year 2000, when they were about
twenty-five years old.

Racial differences in rates of high school graduation, the study found,
were surprisingly small; Hispanics did lag behind whites, but only by about
the same amount as whites lagged behind Asians.[35] Add in the students who

Figure 6-2. Average Number of Years of School Completed for Mexican Americans, by
Generation, and for Native-Born Whites and Blacks of Native Parentage, Ages 25–59,
1996–1999

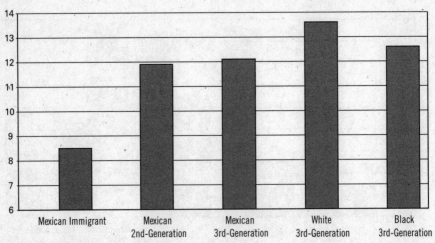

Source: Jeffrey Grogger and Stephen J. Trejo, *Falling Behind or Moving Up? The Intergenerational Progress of Mexican Americans*
(San Francisco: Public Policy Institute of California, 2002), 12. To make the pattern clearer, we have averaged the figures for men and
women, and for recent versus earlier immigrants.

did not graduate with their high school class but earned alternative certification by passing the General Educational Development (GED) exam, and the differences were smaller still. Including students with equivalency certificates, 93 percent of whites and 85 percent of Hispanics are completing high school today. And some of the Hispanics in the sample were born abroad. If it had been possible to isolate U.S.-born Latinos, it is likely that the high school graduation rate for Hispanics would be even higher.

Equally striking, whites and blacks in this study attended college at precisely the same rate—76.5 percent—and the rate for Hispanics was only 7 percentage points lower. If you think that 7 points is large enough to be worrisome, note that the gap between whites and Asians in college attendance was 18 points. The white-Asian gap is more than double the Hispanic-white gap.

It's clear that Latinos have made enormous educational progress within the past generation. Years of school completed strongly influence long-run earnings, we noted in Chapter 2. As recently as 1970, native-born Mexican Americans aged 25 or more had spent an average of just 9.2 years in school. That was 4 years more than their immigrant parents, but it was also 3 years below the figure for non-Hispanic whites, a glaring gap. The typical white adult three decades ago had a high school diploma; the typical second-generation Mexican had dropped out at the end of the eighth grade.[36] If we take 1970 as our point of comparison, the racial differences in high school graduation depicted in the NELS study that tracked a group of students a few years later—from 1988 to 2000—look small. Latinos have come a very long way in a very short time.

The really serious gap in education is not at the point of transition from junior high to high school or even at the transition from high school to college. Latinos are not very far behind others in their rates of college entry. But, like blacks, they are much less successful in remaining in college long enough to earn a degree. Just 15 percent of the Latino eighth-graders of 1988 had obtained a four-year college degree by 2000, about the same proportion as for blacks and only half of that for whites. Close to half of all whites who start college earn their bachelor's degree, but less than a quarter of Hispanics and blacks do so.

The high college dropout rate of Hispanics is not surprising, given the low level of academic skill Latinos demonstrate on the NAEP assessments. In recent decades, America's colleges and universities have made enormous efforts to attract applicants from "underrepresented minority" groups, but none has found a formula that allowed them to overcome the glaring gap in levels of academic achievement that exist at the end of high school.

Since, as we have seen earlier, Latino children typically perform only slightly better than African Americans, it is no wonder that they are equally likely to flounder in college and leave without a degree.

Additional evidence about the depressing effect of immigration upon Latino achievement is available from the NAEP assessments. Laurence Steinberg and others argue that Hispanic children born abroad outperform their native-born classmates, whose scores decline as they become Americanized, as we noted in the previous chapter. In other words, the longer these children live in America, the worse they do in school; they acquire the rotten work habits of other nonimmigrant classmates. In fact, the opposite is the case, Figure 6-3 reveals. Latino immigrant children lag behind those who are second-generation or more by an average of 14 points—at least a full grade—on each test. (The data are for 1992 because that was the last year in which NAEP collected information about the country of birth of students taking the test.)

NAEP evidence (not given in Figure 6-3) also makes it possible to see how the test scores of Hispanic immigrant children vary with the number of years their families have lived in the United States. Those data show the same positive gains from greater exposure to American society, and the differences would be even sharper if NAEP tested all students who are classified as Limited English Proficient (LEP).[37] Thus, the average NAEP scores for Hispanics are about as low as those for blacks, but only because the presence of so many low-scoring immigrant children pulls them down.

Figure 6-3. Reading and Math Scores of Immigrant and U.S.-Born Hispanic Children, 1992

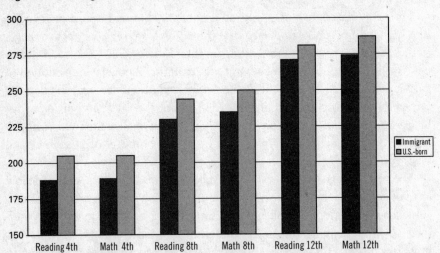

Source: NAEP Data Tool. It is unfortunate that NAEP dropped the place-of-birth question after 1992, so that more recent information on the issue is not available.

The crucial role of immigration in depressing average Latino educational achievement is also evident from the results of a study of Hispanics in Southern California during the 1980s. Over that ten-year period, the proportion of American-born Latino heads of households who had no more than a high school education declined 14 percent, the fraction who had attended college jumped 32 percent, and the proportion with a college diploma rose 27 percent. These impressive gains, though, were hard to discern in figures for all Hispanics because in 1990 more than two-thirds of Southern California Latino householders were foreign-born, and four out of five of these immigrants had lived in the United States for fewer than twenty years.[38]

Learning English

Acquiring the ability to function well in English is a challenge that immigrants from any non-English-speaking country must meet. The poor educational performance of Latino immigrant children has much to do with the fact that they have been far less successful in doing so than their Asian peers. A 1995 study found that 55 percent of Mexican-born children of school age—twice the Asian percentage—did not speak English "very well." (Figure 6-4) More than four out of ten students from other Hispanic groups had a similar language handicap. This is evidence based on reports by the household mem-

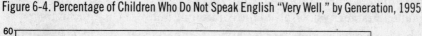

Figure 6-4. Percentage of Children Who Do Not Speak English "Very Well," by Generation, 1995

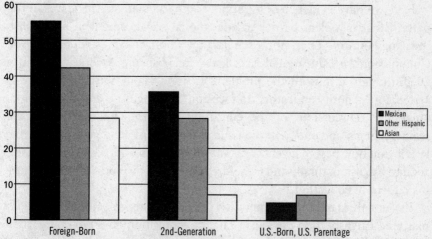

Source: Jorge Ruiz-de-Velasco and Michael Fix, *Overlooked and Underserved: Immigrant Students in U.S. Secondary Schools.* (Washington, D.C.: Urban Institute, 2000), 25.

ber who fills out the questionnaire, and the estimates undoubtedly err on the low side. Parents who think that their children speak English "very well" are often mistaken.

At the time of the 1995 survey, many of these foreign-born children had only recently arrived, and it is hardly surprising that their English was limited. But many American-born Hispanic children also have difficulty communicating in English. The survey found that over a third of all second-generation Mexican-American students could not use English very well, and the percentage was almost as high for other Hispanics. By contrast, a mere 7 percent of second-generation Asian students were still struggling with the language. Latinos are taking three generations to reach the same level of English competence that Asians attain by the second generation. In part, the limited education of many Hispanic parents explains the difference, but the figures may also reflect their propensity to work in unskilled jobs that don't require a knowledge of English. Clearly, the difference has something to do with the sojourner status of the group as well. If Mexican parents are more determined than other immigrants to keep alive their non-English mother tongue, and are more doubtful that they will be living in the United States for the rest of their lives, it seems plausible to expect that their children will not embrace English as enthusiastically as other immigrant youths.

The 1990 Census supports the survey's findings. It identified 1.5 million Hispanic children aged 5–17 who were unable to speak English "very well"; two-thirds of them, nearly a million children, were American-born.[39] Similar data from the 2000 Census have not yet been released, but the number is undoubtedly larger by now, given the continuing influx of Hispanic immigrants.

Here we have evidence of a Latino, and particularly a Mexican, cultural pattern that is a clear barrier to educational advancement in an English-speaking country. The Latino scholars on whom the President's Advisory Commission on Educational Excellence for Hispanic Americans relied in 2000, though, dismissed the problem. It was entirely misguided, they asserted, for "majority educators" to focus on "the linguistic deficits" of Latino children.[40] "Discussions of the education of these children," they complained, "begin and end with the issue of the English language, or how they lack it, and how best to give it to them." And yet, "in U.S. society all children acquire English naturally and therefore English acquisition should not be the main focus of education."

If over a third of second-generation Mexican-American students have not mastered English, then obviously English acquisition does not come "naturally." Needless to say, reading and writing fluency matters not only in school, but is the ticket to economic mobility. Those who speak only a foreign tongue generally remain at the margins of the American economy.[41] There is a reason why schools like KIPP and North Star spend so much time on reading: It is the key to learning in general.

It is thus undeniable that the linguistic handicap from which so many Hispanic students suffer has devastating consequences for their educational achievement. The glaring contrast between Asians and Latinos on this count is surely one reason that Asians are so much more successful in school. A study of 1980 Census data found that 75 percent of those Mexican immigrant children who spoke English "poorly," and 83 percent of those who did not speak it at all, left high school without a diploma. Even among Mexicans born in the United States, 48 percent of those who spoke English poorly and 63 percent of those who knew only Spanish, dropped out before graduation.[42] More than two decades have passed since this evidence was collected, but there is every reason to believe that the same holds true today.

Language skills in English remain a problem for Hispanics even beyond the second generation. Some scholars have worried that native-born Latinos with native-born parents—from the third or higher generation—do not do notably better educationally than those from the second generation. The data from Figure 6-2 above showed that Mexican Americans made far more impressive educational progress from the first to the second than from the second to the third or higher generations.[43] The most likely explanation is that even after two full generations of residence in the United States, Latinos are less likely than other groups to have made the transition to speaking English in the home. An analysis of 1990 Census data reveals that 90 to 95 percent of third-generation children (ages 6–15) from various Asian groups speak only English at home, but only 64 percent of Mexican third-generation youths do so.[44] And for third-generation Mexican children living with a parent who spoke a language other than English, just 43 percent spoke only English at home themselves, again far below the Asian figure.

On the 1970 Census, the distinctiveness of the Mexican pattern stood out even more sharply. Well over 90 percent of third-generation Americans of European origins reported English as their mother tongue in 1970, as compared with a mere 26 percent of Mexicans.[45]

The unusually strong attachment of Hispanics to the language of their original homeland is in part a function of the huge numbers of Spanish-speakers living in the United States and of their strong concentration in certain areas. Serbian immigrants living in New York can find few places outside the home in which they can function speaking only Serbian, while Mexicans in Los Angeles and Cubans in Miami can do almost everything they wish in Spanish.

Nevertheless, relying upon Spanish and using English only when it is absolutely necessary is a cultural choice. It is a choice that Hispanics are free to make, of course. But it is one that may have a serious cost in limiting the ability of their children to function at a high level in educational institutions that function in English.

Bilingual Education

Hispanic children often spend many school years sitting in classes taught not in English but in Spanish. This may be another reason why they fail to become proficient in English. "Bilingual education" programs were created three decades ago to improve the educational opportunities of students who had difficulty functioning in regular classrooms taught in English. Whether they have had that effect has become a hotly debated question.

The term "bilingual education" has been loosely applied to a wide variety of efforts to assist pupils from non-English-speaking homes, but the controversy centers on self-contained, segregated classrooms in which students are taught in their home language. In some of these classes (no one knows how many) the teachers have a weak command of English themselves. (The term "bilingual" can thus be very misleading.) And in a substantial number of schools (although, again, no one has an exact count), students remain in these classes more or less indefinitely, since they do not learn enough English to transition out of them.

For more than two decades, critics have raised questions about these classrooms, but until recently the issue remained outside the political arena. In 1998, however, a large majority of the California electorate approved Proposition 227, which mandated the end to bilingual classes (unless parents specifically asked for them) and their replacement with "structured immersion," which means special classes for Spanish-speaking children but taught mostly in English. Almost a third of the nation's Hispanic population lives in California, and this surprising victory for bilingual education opponents was bound to have a ripple effect. A similar ban was enacted in Arizona in 2000 and in Massachusetts in 2002.

Although bilingual education is theoretically open to all language-minority children (unless their numbers are too small to justify separate classes), in practice it is a program serving Latinos almost exclusively. Christine Rossell's authoritative study of California found that Latino children were alone in receiving bilingual education in the strict sense of the term. That is, they alone sat in classes in which instruction in English was regarded as a supplement, taught for as little as an hour a day. By contrast, Chinese immigrant children in the state's so-called "bilingual" classes were taught mainly in English, with instruction in Chinese only as additional enrichment.[46]

The literature on bilingual education is substantial. Is it the best method of instruction for Limited English Proficient children? Rossell's survey of all of the published literature as of 1996 yielded a strongly negative verdict.[47] Her more recent monograph on California before and after 227 also reaches negative conclusions, but her findings are somewhat tentative because of limitations inherent in the evidence. Opponents of the initiative who predicted that an end to bilingual education would have a disastrous impact on Hispanic schoolchildren were clearly wrong, she concludes. In both reading and math, Latino students in regular classrooms scored slightly higher than those exposed to bilingual education. Dropping the bilingual programs was thus a net benefit, not a loss.

The benefit was modest, however. Rossell found that the passage of Proposition 227 did not produce the soaring test scores anticipated by the sharpest critics of bilingual education. In part, the modest impact of the initiative was due to the limited number of classes in which Spanish had been almost the sole language of instruction. In the 1997–1998 school year, for example, only one-third of the million-plus Hispanic students in California categorized as English Learners were in classes taught mainly in Spanish.[48] Thus even the complete elimination of all such classes would not dramatically elevate the overall score of Hispanics as a group. In addition, the criteria for placement in bilingual education, Rossell shows, guaranteed that the program would include mostly students whose academic performance was weak, and likely to remain weak, whatever the method of instruction.[49]

Perhaps things will look a lot better a few years hence. Major gains from English immersion and rapid mainstreaming of the children who once were typically exposed to several years of bilingual education may be gradual and cumulative. In the meantime—until those definitive results are in—it seems safe to say that bilingual education appears "on average, the least effective approach to educating English Learners" when judged strictly as a program to improve the academic skill of students on tests in English.[50] Since it also costs more than the alternatives, and has the further negative consequence of segregating Hispanic children—keeping them ethnically isolated—the case for abandoning it is strong.

Cultural Maintenance

Neither bilingual education nor its elimination is the panacea its supporters and critics have envisioned. Why, then, does the issue stir such passion?

Home-language classes for immigrant children are only partly an educational question. Bilingual education originated in the culture wars that erupted in the late 1960s, and classes taught in the students' home language were not seen as just one possible educational strategy that should be tried out and evaluated by test-score results. They were conceived as a means of preserving immigrant cultures from the inroads of Americanization—an instrument for the maintenance of separate group identities.

The presence of many residents who spoke languages other than English was nothing new in American history, of course. In the opening decades of the twentieth century, the country had one of the largest Italian-speaking populations in the world. Likewise with German, Polish, Yiddish, and a host of other languages. But few Americans at the time drew the conclusion that the public schools should be segregated along linguistic lines, with separate classes to protect the language and culture of each group from the influence of the larger society. Most Americans assumed that a complex modern democratic society could not function without a lingua franca, and that the common tongue of their adopted country was obviously English. To deny immigrant children the most important tool they needed if they were to take advantage of America's abundant opportunities was a profound disservice, they believed.

This is a view that went out of fashion and has now come back. Students with limited English need some help, almost everyone believes, and indeed it is against the law to let them sink or swim. Moreover, families should be free to speak their native tongue at home and maintain the traditions of the old country. But there is a growing consensus that children must learn America's "common tongue," as well as American history and culture. The well-being of the nation and of its individual citizens depend on both.

The less settled question is the content of instruction in American history and the role of schools in cultural maintenance. Should schools assume that their language-minority children (whose families have freely chosen to become American residents) appropriately and permanently belong to another culture? The Hispanic experts at the Harvard Graduate School of Education contend that Latino students would be much better off if their schools provided them with more in the way of "culturally appropriate educational experiences."[51] This is a widely held view in education circles.

What constitutes the "culturally appropriate educational experiences" that the Harvard scholars urge? Immigrants from Cuba, Mexico, Puerto Rico, the Dominican Republic, Argentina, and other Spanish-speaking countries hardly share a common culture. Moreover, "nonwhite" is not a cultural category, although it is often treated as such. At one solidly black and Hispanic school we visited, a teacher had put up a poster depicting an American Indian with a feather headdress, smoking a peace pipe. It featured "The Indian Ten Commandments": "Treat the Earth and all that dwell thereon with respect," "Work together for the benefit of all Mankind," "Dedicate a share of your efforts to the greater good," and so forth. Aside from the absurd notion that Indians were ever one people who subscribed to such "Commandments," what was the connection to the Hispanic and black students in the school? One might think that the Declaration of Independence—with its ringing phrases about the "self-evident" truth "that all men are created equal . . . endowed . . . with certain unalienable rights," and governments "deriving their just powers from the consent of the governed"—would be more culturally appropriate in educating American newcomers, as well as those whose ancestors arrived on slave ships centuries ago.

Two Hispanic educators complain that schools are too remote from the families of the students they serve, and assert that when "parent and community . . . are in control, the results are ultimately superior," because "continuity with the intellectual and social climate of the home is of paramount importance if the school is to help children develop and foster their intellectual and social growth."[52] No one believes that parents should be shoved aside, or that the "intellectual and social climate of the home" should be disparaged. The values of the home can be maintained—at home, and in after-school programs. But the public schools have a different role: connecting students to the world of academic accomplishment, putting them on the ladder of economic opportunity, and introducing them to the history, culture, and institutions of the nation in which they live.

There is potentially, of course, some tension between respect for the culture of the home and stressing the importance of academic achievement to which not all cultures are equally committed. The Harvard Graduate School of Education experts referred to above have conducted research that purports to show that the culture of Mexican immigrants does not interfere significantly with their educational achievement. In a volume titled *Transformations*, they report on a study of middle school students in a Mexican city that has sent many immigrants to the United States. These students, they found, had much more positive attitudes about school than both the Mexican immigrant and the Anglo children they examined in a similar survey in Southern California. Mexican culture values education even more than

American culture does, they conclude. Living in the United States, according to them, destroys the healthy educational attitudes that Mexican immigrants bring with them.

The middle school students in Mexico that they studied, however, did not resemble the typical immigrant youngster with blue-collar or agrarian working-class parents. The average age of these students was 15.7 years, in a society in which children typically leave school at age 13.[53] Even more striking, every member of the student sample planned to attend college, again wildly atypical of ordinary Mexican working families—and of Mexican immigrants to the United States.[54] The authors studied the wrong people; their investigation tells us nothing about the cultural attitudes toward schooling that actual Mexican immigrants bring with them.

In *Transformations* and a more recent volume, *Children of Immigration,* the authors also make much of surveys of Mexican and other immigrant parents and their children that display very widespread support for such platitudes as "school is important to get ahead."[55] It is hard to take this very seriously when we recall Laurence Steinberg's work on high school students in California and Wisconsin, discussed in some detail in the previous chapter. There were huge differences when students were asked about the "trouble threshold" in their family—how low a grade they could get without getting into trouble with their parents. Steinberg's concrete question seems far more illuminating than the abstract one about the importance of an education.

Nor do the authors cite any surveys that probe such questions as that of the trade-off between earning wages immediately and deferring full-time work until the completion of college or a postgraduate program. One of the two epigraphs at the start of this chapter involves a Mexican father who persuaded his son that, at age twenty-three, he ought to be working rather than staying in college. We have not found any systematic survey data to indicate that this anecdote is typical. But there is much evidence that suggests the culture that Asian immigrants bring with them is very strongly oriented toward academic excellence, while that of Mexicans—like the Italians before them— is not. And those cultural differences inevitably have an impact on academic performance, most notably on newcomers.

Schools Can Do Better

One should think of Hispanics as the Italians of a century ago, we have argued. Italian parents were often peasants with very little education themselves, and they were slower than many other immigrant groups to learn

English and acquire citizenship. These cultural characteristics were not permanent barriers to advancement, but it took generations for them to erode.

The Italian-Hispanic analogy is strong—up to a point. Italian immigration was cut off in the mid-1920s, but large numbers of Latinos continue to arrive every year. These newcomers obscure the very real gains that have been made by those who came earlier—a widely ignored point. The longer Hispanic families stay in America, the better their children do in school. Success, however, depends on acquiring English, and if schools hope to connect these students to the world of academic achievement, they also need to introduce them to the history, culture, and institutions of their adopted country.

There are historical and demographic reasons why so many Latino children are not faring well academically. Those reasons do not let schools off the hook. They can do better with their Latino students; in Rafe Esquith's class, by the end of the year the reading and math skills of his Latino youngsters are on a par with those of their Asian classmates. Great teaching makes the difference. Some cultures are academically advantageous; none should defeat students or their schools.

Seven: Blacks

I believe a lot of African American students choose to fail. That doesn't change our determination to help them succeed.
A. Jack Rumbaugh, principal of Shaker Heights High School[1]

I watched them do their jobs and there was no magic there, just work.
African-American author Debra J. Dickerson on what it took to become an Air Force officer[2]

In 1980, just shy of her twenty-first birthday, Debra J. Dickerson joined the U.S. Air Force. She was, as she describes herself, "a clinically depressed, college dropout, binge-eating insomniac who literally wished she were dead." She had grown up in the St. Louis ghetto—a world in which "people dropped out of school, used drugs, committed crimes, and, of course there was the never-ending tide of illegitimate babies."[3] But she was smart, she liked to read books, and she was determined to succeed. When she joined the Air Force, little did she know, she writes, "that from day one I would be pushed, cajoled, praised, and punished into high achievement."[4]

This chapter contains a painful discussion of the sources of black underachievement in school. Our focus is on the present, and yet clearly the problem has deep historical roots. Black culture, we argue, has much to do with the racial gap in academic achievement. John McWhorter, a professor of linguistics at the University of California, Berkeley, has observed that "what one sees in black students is less a refusal to contribute any effort than a sad tendency for their efforts to stop before the finish line. This tendency stems not from laziness or inferior mental power, but from a brake exerted on them by a cultural inheritance that schoolwork is more a pit stop than a place to live."[5] Harvard sociologist Orlando Patterson argues in a similar vein that the explanation of the glaring racial gap in educational performance cannot be attributed to genetic differences between the races or to social-class differences. "In a nutshell," he said, it is "culture."[6]

The "cultural inheritance" of African Americans today is the product of a very long history of racial oppression—centuries of slavery, followed by disfranchisement, legally mandated segregation, and subordination in the Jim Crow South and intense racial prejudice in the North.[7] Slaves were, of course, denied the opportunity to learn to read and write; even a little learning might have inspired a dangerous thirst for freedom. After emancipation, black people displayed a strong hunger for education, but the southern states responded only grudgingly, by creating separate and grossly inferior all-black schools. It was very difficult for African Americans to get much education, and when they entered the world of work, determination in school paid off very little. Most jobs that required the skills that were learned in school were closed to black people.

We live in a radically different world today. Even before the civil rights revolution of the 1960s, the educational opportunities available to black children were expanding and good jobs were beginning to open up to educated African Americans. That trend has accelerated in the decades since. As we saw in Chapter 2, black and white workers with the same level of math and literary skills now have incomes that are about the same. But the cultures of groups are shaped by historical memories and are slow to adjust to new realities. Such is the case with African-American culture today as it relates to education, we believe.

In reviewing the data on academic achievement, we do not intend to convey a pessimistic message. As Chapters 3 and 4 make plain, determined schools and hardworking students can make a great difference. Neither poverty nor culture is educational destiny. Black children can be "pushed, cajoled, praised, and punished into high achievement." What happened to Debra Dickerson in the military can happen to other black youngsters in their local schools. But not unless the schools themselves change.

Something Wrong in Suburbia

"Why are you talking about race when the issue is social class?" a distinguished educator asked us at a conference some years back. Class is certainly a less painful topic, but, unfortunately, it is only part of the story. Black children from well-off families, as well as those who are disadvantaged, tend to do poorly in school. And that fact makes our hearts sink.

The most famous example of something-wrong-in-suburbia is that of Shaker Heights, Ohio. The painful disparity between the academic performance of black and white students in that affluent Cleveland suburb first surfaced in the

national media in 1998 when Michael Fletcher of *The Washington Post* wrote
an article appropriately entitled "A Good-School, Bad-Grade Mystery."[8]

Very few residents of Shaker Heights have incomes below the poverty
line; very few are high school dropouts. Most are college graduates. A third
of the residents are African American, and they, too, are generally well-
educated homeowners with middle-class jobs, though they do fall somewhat
below their white neighbors in average educational and income levels.[9]

The community is strongly committed to racial integration, and school attendance zone lines have been carefully drawn to ensure that each school reflects the overall racial mix in the community. Per pupil spending is roughly
$10,000 a year, 50 percent above the national average. Tutors and mentors
work with struggling students starting in kindergarten, and after-school,
weekend, and summer academies offer additional help. Teachers and administrators are strongly committed to improving the performance of black students, and have devoted a great deal of attention to discussions of how to do
it. Shaker Heights was a founding member of the Minority Student Achievement Network, along with Cambridge, Massachusetts; Berkeley, California;
Madison, Wisconsin; and about a dozen other affluent and liberal communities. Its specific aim is to improve the academic performance of minority students, particularly African Americans.[10]

And yet all is not well in Shaker Heights. There is no racial gap in the high
school's very high graduation rate (98 percent), but the good news begins and
ends there. By every other measure of academic performance, African-
American students are woefully far behind whites. For example, Shaker
Heights makes every effort to get black students to take the most demanding
honors or AP courses; students are not tracked into more or less challenging
courses on the basis of test scores or their previous performance in class. But
students cannot be forced to accept the challenge. Only 30 percent of
African Americans take any AP or honors courses at all, as compared with 87
percent of whites.[11] Only one of nine black students chooses to take half or
more of their classes at this level, but six out of ten whites do so.

These radical differences in course-taking patterns are reflected in the disparate results glaringly apparent on Ohio's statewide proficiency tests in
basic subjects. In the 1999–2000 academic year, more than two-thirds of the
city's black twelfth-graders failed one or more of the state tests, as compared
with just one-sixth of whites (Figure 7-1).[12] More than half of all Shaker
Heights whites passed the proficiency tests with honors. For blacks, the figure was an astonishingly low 4 percent. That 4 percent was no higher than
the statewide average for African Americans, despite the fact that the income
and educational levels of black families in Shaker Heights were far above

those for blacks in Ohio as a whole, and their children were attending integrated schools that were regarded as among the best in the state.

The middle-class black community of Shaker Heights is obviously not typical of black America today. But it is not wildly atypical either, contrary to what many think, thanks to our understandable but excessive preoccupation with black poverty in the inner city. Although it is not well known, more than a third of black Americans today live in a suburb—well below the white figure of 56 percent, but more than double the black proportion in 1970.[13] And some 31 percent of blacks live in households that took in $50,000 or more in 2000. Again, this is well below the white proportion (55 percent), but is more than double the proportion of blacks earning that much (in constant dollars) just a generation ago.[14] The rise of a black suburban middle class is a striking recent development, and Shaker Heights illustrates its implications for the large problem that concerns us here. If there is something wrong in Shaker Heights, the fruits of upward mobility for African Americans may not be as sweet as we would hope.

The black-white test score gap even in affluent, suburban settings is exceedingly painful and disconcerting, and it's tempting to run for more comfortable ground. In September 2001, *The Washington Post* carried a long feature article entitled "Pupils' Poverty Drives Achievement Gap."[15] "The achievement gap that divides America's schoolchildren has usually been defined in racial terms," the reporters wrote, but "recent research" has demon-

Figure 7-1. Black-White Differences in Enrollment in AP or Honors Courses and in Performance on State Proficiency Tests, Shaker Heights 12th-Graders, 1999–2000

Source: Web site of the Ohio Department of Education, www.ode.state.oh.us.

strated that "economic status is far more accurate than race in projecting who will do well on tests."

Would that it were true. The "recent research" to which the authors refer was in part their own examination of student records in Maryland's affluent suburban Montgomery County. But they failed to provide any details of their analysis, leaving the reader without a clue as to how they disentangled the impact of poverty from that of race. The article also relied heavily on Richard Kahlenberg's book *All Together Now*, which argues that it is primarily poverty that puts children at educational risk—a problem that is compounded when low-income children are isolated from their middle-class peers.[16] However, Kahlenberg, too, fails to offer solid quantitative analysis that controls simultaneously for the effects of social class and race; thus he does not demonstrate the primacy of class in explaining academic performance. Race and class are closely intertwined; Kahlenberg did not pull them apart in order to judge their relative importance.

Class and Race

This is not to say, however, that family income is irrelevant to school performance. Clearly, that's not the case. Children from low-income homes do come to school with a real disadvantage. So, too, do those whose parents do not have much education, an influence many studies have shown to be even more powerful than family income. Although poor academic performance of black students in prosperous communities like Shaker Heights adds a puzzling complication to the story, it should not obscure that basic point.

Black students are far more likely than whites to grow up in disadvantaged circumstances. Figure 7-2 summarizes some of the evidence. A third of all black children but only one-tenth of white children live in families with incomes below the poverty line.[17] More than half of all white families had incomes exceeding $50,000 in 1999, compared to just over 30 percent for African Americans. Those are indeed big group differences.

Black children are less likely to come from affluent homes, and their parents are generally much less well educated. As Figure 7-2 indicates, 20 percent of the mothers of black school-age children today never completed high school, as compared with a mere 7 percent of white mothers. At the other end of the educational spectrum, nearly 60 percent of white mothers attended some college; the percentage for blacks is 43. Furthermore, a fact not included in Figure 7-2, white women are twice as likely as African-American women to have stayed four years and received a college degree.

Figure 7-2. Black-White Differences in Family Socioeconomic Status, 1999–2000

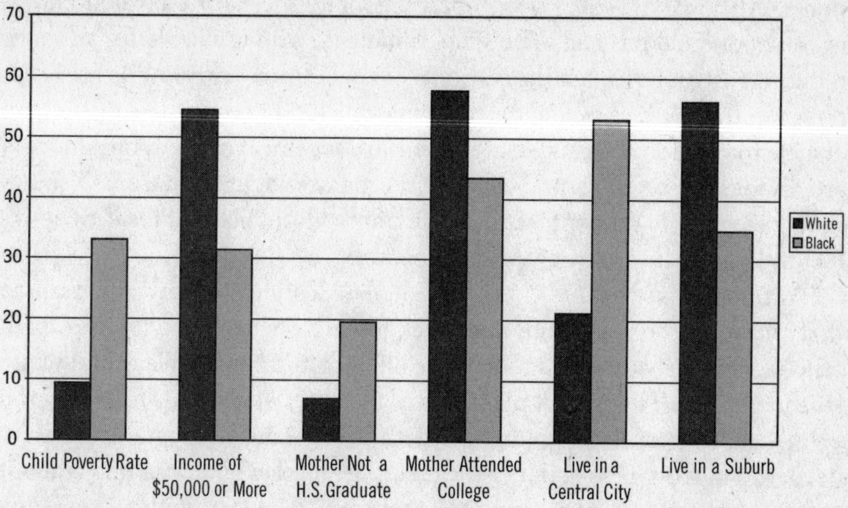

Source: Poverty, family income, and residential data from U.S. Bureau of the Census, *The Black Population in the United States: March 2000*, PPL-142 (Washington, D.C.: U.S. Government Printing Office, 2001). Educational attainment of mothers of children 6–18 in 1999 from National Center for Education Statistics, *The Condition of Education 2000*, NCES 2000–062 (Washington, D.C.: U.S. Department of Education, 2000), 124.

Where you live is another indicator of social status. And place of residence is particularly important when the subject is education, since suburban schools are generally assumed to be better than those in urban districts. Today, barely a fifth of whites live in central cities, as compared with a clear majority of blacks. Conversely, as mentioned earlier, close to 60 percent of whites are suburban dwellers, versus only 34 percent of African Americans. These racial disparities are very large and could explain much of the racial gap in achievement.

Black students are more likely than whites to grow up economically disadvantaged. But are black children generally learning less than their white peers because so many are stuck in urban schools and grow up in families with lower incomes and less education?

To answer that question, we must look at similar families and ask: Are there still racial and ethnic differences in skills and knowledge? Do black and white children whose parents have some college education score pretty much alike on the authoritative NAEP tests? Is Shaker Heights unusual? Do black students from affluent families generally do well in school? If so, money, not race, is the real story.

In attempting to disentangle race and social status—and establish the importance of each for academic performance—we rely on data that are not ideal. Nevertheless, they allow us to make a beginning at answering the question. NAEP asks students how much schooling the most educated parent in the household has had. The schools indicate who is eligible for a free or reduced-cost lunch (under the National School Lunch Program)—a proxy for poverty often used as well in determining which schools within a district are eligible for Title I funds aimed at helping low-income children. And students are also identified as central-city or suburban residents. Figure 7–3 shows how these factors—parental education, poverty, and place of residence—affect the black-white gap in NAEP test scores.

Turning first to the question of parental education, it is logical to assume that the test scores of white and black children whose parents were high school dropouts would be much more alike than those for black and white kids in general. The overall picture, it seems very likely, is distorted by the greater number of black youngsters with poorly educated parents. And indeed, to a modest degree, that is the case. The black-white racial gap is about one-third smaller when we compare, as it were, apples to apples—kids similarly educationally disadvantaged by having no parent who graduated from high school.

Figure 7-3. How the Racial Gap in Reading and Math Scores in Grades 4, 8, and 12 Is Altered by Controls for Parental Education, Place of Residence, and Eligibility for Federal Lunch Program, 1998–2000

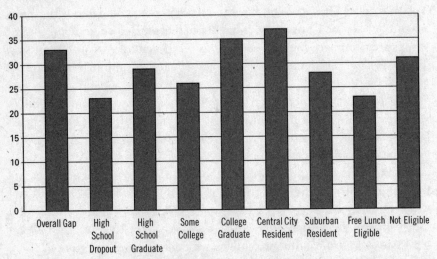

Source: NAEP Data Tool. The first column on the left reveals the size of the point gap between black and white students. The others show how much the gap is changed by looking only at black and white students whose parents shared some social characteristic, such as being a high school graduate or a suburban resident. Figures are averages of reading and math scores for students at the three grade levels tested in the 1998 reading and the 2000 math assessments. Parental education is only available for 8th- and 12th-graders. The question was not asked of 4th-graders, because it was thought that too many would not be able to answer correctly.

But a one-third reduction in the racial gap in academic performance does not begin to wipe it out. Black students whose parents had little education do considerably worse than similarly disadvantaged white kids on the NAEP tests. Suppose for a moment that all black and white parents were high school dropouts. The average African-American student in the twelfth grade would still be nearly three years behind the average white youngster. The current overall gap of four years would have shrunk significantly. Yet despite the shared disadvantage of poorly educated parents, the racial difference in test scores would remain dismayingly large.

As we climb the educational ladder in Figure 7–3, parental education explains even less of the black-white gap. It reduces the gap by only one-eighth among parents with just a high school diploma, and by one-fifth among those with some college but no bachelor's degree. That is, looking at kids with parents who did finish high school but went no further, the racial gap is only a bit smaller than it is for all black and white students, from every social class. The advantage of having at least one parent with some college education is quite modest, too.

Most alarmingly, perhaps, if we isolate the children of college graduates, the gap actually increases by about 6 percent. The disparity in academic performance between black and white children of highly educated parents is actually larger than it is for the whole student population. If all black and all white parents were college graduates, the racial gap would be even greater than it is now. The average NAEP score for black students would be higher than it is, of course; the children of highly educated parents do better in general than those whose parents have less schooling. But, just as black scores rise with parental education, so do those of whites—to an even greater degree, Figure 7–3 suggests.

This pattern, it should be noted, differs strikingly from that revealed in a similar analysis of the Hispanic-white gap. Looking only at students whose parents were high school dropouts cuts the black-white gap by a third, but it reduces the Hispanic-white gap by 57 percent. Across all educational categories, restricting comparisons to children with similarly educated parents makes twice as much difference for Latinos as for African Americans. Rising educational levels are a central ingredient in the story of Hispanic assimilation, and the more education the parents obtain, the better their children do in school. Black children, by contrast, derive much less of an educational advantage from what their parents have achieved in school.

Figure 7–3 also looks at the impact of residence on NAEP scores. As it makes apparent, although suburban schools are viewed as dramatically better than those in the inner city, the type of community in which a child lives has surprisingly little impact on the racial gap in educational achievement. Comparing just suburban kids—white versus black—hardly changes the basic picture.[18] The racial gap between relatively affluent students living outside the central cities is smaller than that which divides blacks and whites in general, but only marginally so—just 15 percent smaller than the overall gap. Suburban Shaker Heights, it turns out, is no anomaly. And looking only at students living in central cities makes the gap widen slightly.

Needless to say, these are very disconcerting numbers. The overall racial gap in academic skills and knowledge, it is widely believed, has a clear explanation: The majority of African-American students are stuck in inferior big-city schools. But the data in Figure 7–3 suggest a more sobering conclusion: Increased movement of black families into suburban communities—as desirable as that is—will not solve the problem of black academic underperformance. It's not that black kids in suburbia don't do better than their urban peers. They do. But suburban whites also outperform urban whites, and the gap—the difference in scores between the two racial groups—remains almost unchanged.

Poverty—by the measure of eligibility for a free or reduced-price lunch—matters somewhat more than place of residence. Black and white low-income students have academic skills that are more alike than those of blacks and whites in suburbia. As Figure 7–3 shows, the racial gap for kids covered by the federal school lunch program is about one-third smaller than the national one. This finding closely matches that of Meredith Phillips's study of the racial gap among eighth-graders, which discovered that the racial difference in academic performance shrank 34 percent among families who were in the bottom fifth of the income distribution.[19]

In Figure 7–3, we use three indicators of social status: parental education, residence, and free lunch eligibility. As we suggested earlier, they are not entirely satisfactory as measures of social and economic well-being. The categories are crude and fail to capture all the differences that might have an impact on school performance. Students eligible for school lunch assistance, for instance, come from families across a wide economic spectrum, with incomes ranging from below $10,000 a year to over $30,000 a year. On average, black children who qualify for the program come from families suffering deeper poverty than that experienced by their white classmates whose lunch is also subsidized. Likewise, white parents who are high school dropouts may have had more years in school than black parents who left before finishing the twelfth grade. Within each category, in other words, there may be important racial differences that the data conceal.

Thus, it would have been too much to expect, in comparing white and black suburban kids, for instance, that we would find no racial gap. White families in suburbia probably have higher incomes, on average, than their black neighbors. And suburban towns differ in both their racial and their social class composition. One suburban community is not necessarily identical to another. Nevertheless, if those who argue that social class drives academic performance are right, we should have seen a dramatic narrowing of the racial gap in comparing families with similar social and economic status. If poverty is all-important, then white and black kids who qualify for the federal school lunch program should have pretty similar NAEP scores. In fact, parental education, place of residence, and income all have some impact on academic skills, but less than one might expect—or than many assume.

The rather small effects of holding these various socioeconomic factors constant might still add up to something impressive if they were entirely independent of each other, so that we could add the effects together. If, for example, we could say that poverty accounted for 40 percent of the difference, parental education another 35 percent, and the city-suburb variable another 15 percent, little would be left that was attributable to race per se. But these are not distinct variables that can be added up; they overlap. Poor people, that is, are also highly likely to have little education and to live in a central city. The data available to us were not in a form to permit an analysis that would reveal exactly how great the overlap is, but a number of sophisticated studies of the black-white achievement gap have found that controlling for all the standard measures of socioeconomic status together cuts the black-white gap by only about one-third.[20] After taking full account of racial differences in poverty rates, parental education, and place of residence, roughly two-thirds of the troubling racial gap remains unexplained.

The measures of social background that we have been able to make use of, it must be underscored, are crude. They all pertain to the current status of families. But it could be that black children from college-educated families are less successful in school than their white counterparts, for example, because their parents were less likely than white parents to have grown up in a middle-class home themselves. People who have just arrived in the middle class may have cultural orientations and tastes different from those of people born into it, and their family culture could affect how their children adjust to the demands of school. Furthermore, current income is not the same thing as wealth—the total assets of the family. Although black middle-class families have reasonably high current incomes, they still lag well behind whites in wealth, partly because they are much less likely to inherit substantial assets.[21] A more refined measure of social class that took into account the socioeconomic status of grandparents as well as parents and that included information about wealth would doubtless narrow some of the differences that we have attributed to race. But we doubt that it would eliminate them altogether.

Preschoolers

The racial gap in academic achievement appears very early in life—a fact that we have not touched upon in earlier chapters. The earliest NAEP assessments are for fourth-graders or students at age 9. But clear racial differences in levels of intellectual development are evident by the time children first set foot in school. Schools can do a good job or a bad job of teaching their students, but those students do not enter kindergarten as interchangeable blank slates.

Researchers at the National Center for Education Statistics (NCES) have closely examined a representative sample of 22,000 pupils enrolled in kindergarten in the 1998–1999 school year. Since the children were tested shortly after they first arrived, the racial disparities found in the study clearly predated school.[22] As Figure 7–4 indicates, from a third to half of black and Hispanic pupils entered kindergarten already testing in the bottom quarter of students in reading, math, and general knowledge. Only about a sixth of whites scored that low. The picture in the top quarter was a mirror image. From 30 to 40 percent of whites were in the highest achievement group, but the percentage for blacks and Hispanics was less than half the white figure. About the only encouraging thing that can be said about these results is that previous studies of children of the same age revealed even more glaring racial gaps.

A follow-up study tested the same children at the end of first grade, after they had completed close to two full years of school, and the results showed discouragingly little change in the black-white gap. In math, it remained the same, and in reading it actually increased a bit.[23] The Hispanic-white gap, by contrast, did narrow significantly, from 5 to 3 points in reading (on a scale averaging 50) and from 6 to 4 points in math. The explanation may be that some of the Latino deficit apparent at the start of kindergarten reflected their family's recent arrival in the U.S.; two years later, they had learned English and had become more Americanized.[24] The difference between black and white children, unfortunately, was more intractable.

Other tests of children at about this age have revealed even sharper racial differences. For example, black five- and six-year-olds in the Children of the National Longitudinal Survey of Youth (hereafter referred to as the Youth Study) in the years 1986–1992 scored a full standard deviation below their

Figure 7-4. Percentage Scoring in the Bottom and Top Quartiles on Tests of Reading, Mathematics, and General Knowledge, Kindergarten Class of 1998–1999

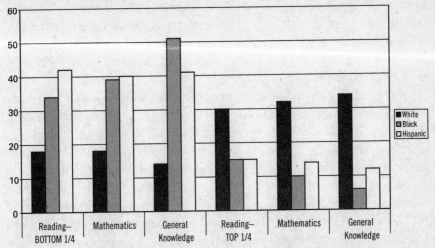

Source: National Center for Education Statistics, *America's Kindergartners: Findings from the Early Childhood Longitudinal Study, Kindergarten Class of 1998–99, Fall 1998,* NCES 2000-070 (Washington, D.C.: U.S. Department of Education, 2000), 18–19.

white peers on the Peabody Picture Vocabulary Test, a standard gauge of intellectual development for children before the age at which they can read. A difference of one standard deviation means that half of all black children were in the bottom sixth of the white distribution, and that only one-sixth of African Americans performed as well as or better than the average white child.[25]

Something about the lives of these children before they entered school shaped their intellectual development. More than three decades ago, assistant secretary of labor Daniel Patrick Moynihan raised the question of black family culture in a report that caused such a storm that scholars shied away from the topic for decades thereafter.[26] Although the "Moynihan Report" focused specifically on the proliferation of black female-headed households, it raised the larger question of the role of family culture as an obstacle holding back African Americans. After being ignored for too long, the cultural issue is now receiving renewed attention. The College Board's 1999 "National Task Force on Minority High Achievement" report, many of the papers in the Jencks and Phillips volume, *The Black-White Test Score Gap,* and scholars such as Orlando Patterson and John McWhorter have all begun the necessary exploration.[27]

Sociologist David Armor has examined data in the Youth Study sample of children born in the 1980s, the most comprehensive investigation of child de-

velopment ever undertaken in the United States. Armor asks which environmental or cultural factors most influence racial differences in average levels
of cognitive development.[28] He finds, for example, that low-birth-weight babies (those weighing less than 5 pounds) tend to lag behind others in their intellectual development. In the Youth Study, the rate of such births was twice
as high among black as among white mothers (11 percent versus 5 percent),
with Hispanics close to the white rate.[29]

A more important and far more common risk factor for children is living
with just one parent. This is the issue that the Moynihan Report first brought
to the fore. The firestorm of controversy it provoked has by now died down,
and there is something close to a scholarly consensus. Today most social
scientists agree that growing up in a single-parent, female-headed family "is
almost always associated with lower educational attainment and more behavioral and psychological problems."[30] Those behavioral and psychological
problems, the data indicate, include getting into trouble both in school and
with the law, dropping out of school, and early pregnancy, as well as depressed academic performance.

We can expect large racial differences in all of these things, because racial
differences in family structure are huge. Currently, only 37 percent of black
children live with two parents, as compared with 77 percent of whites, 65 percent of Hispanics, and 81 percent of Asian Americans.[31]

Even these dramatically contrasting figures do not convey the full magnitude of the difference two-parent homes make for child-rearing because
black families tend to be somewhat larger on average than white ones. These
two facts together mean that the ratio of children to parents is uniquely high
for African Americans: roughly three children per parent, as compared with
one child per parent for whites. And, in turn, that means black children necessarily receive less individual parental attention.

Armor's analysis of the Youth Study reveals that being born to a very
young mother (age 18 or less) is another risk factor with a strong negative impact on cognitive skills. Over a third of black mothers bear their first child at
that early age—two-and-a-half times the proportion among whites, and about
50 percent above the figure for Hispanics.

Some of these racial differences are obviously related to economic circumstances. But the higher incidence of poverty among blacks is not the whole
story. Income levels do not explain the higher incidence of teenage pregnan-
cies and the prevalence of black female-headed households.[32] Clearly, if
poverty is only part of the problem, then rising incomes among black families
are likely to be only a partial solution, as the story of Shaker Heights and other
affluent suburbs suggests.

Parenting Practices

Differences in parenting practices that reflect group culture are also important influences on the intellectual growth of children—*the* important influence, Christopher Jencks and Meredith Phillips argue in their authoritative
volume *The Black-White Test Score Gap.* "Changes in parenting practices,"
they conclude,

> might do more to reduce the black-white test score gap than changes in par-
> ents' educational attainment or income. . . . Cognitive disparities between
> black and white preschool children are currently so large that it is hard to
> imagine how schools alone could eliminate them. . . . Changing the way
> parents deal with their children may be the single most important thing we
> can do to improve children's cognitive skills.[33]

This is a tough and startling message from two liberal scholars. Jencks and
Phillips suggest that social scientists who seek to understand the racial gap
must take a close look at "the way family members and friends interact with
one another and the outside world"; "how much parents talk to their children,
deal with their children's questions, how they react when their child learns or
fails to learn something"; and "cultural and psychological differences."[34]

The Youth Study did in fact send investigators into homes and created a
HOME scale (Home Observation for Measurement of the Environment) that
ranked families in terms of both the cognitive stimulation and the emotional
support they provided their children. Cognitive stimulation was measured by
noting, for example, the number of children's books in the home, the fre-
quency with which a parent read to a child, how much effort was made to
teach the alphabet, numbers, and colors and to visit parks, museums, and
stores. Emotional support, obviously a more subjective concept, was determined by observations of mother-child interactions. Expressions of physical
affection for the child, patient attention to a child's questions, and discipline
by means other than physical punishment all contributed to a high score.

The judgments that were made by these undoubtedly middle-class and
probably mostly white "experts," it must be admitted, are not like gauging
temperature in a chemistry experiment. The HOME scale itself is surely not
an infallible guide as to who is a good parent and who is not, and the ratings of
individual parents were made on the basis of a relatively brief home visit, not
close observation over a prolonged period. Even a far more intensive examination of these families might well not unlock the mysteries of how they
function. Social science can reveal important social patterns, but it cannot

fully explain human behavior. Nevertheless, the scale has been shown to be "an important predictor of children's test performance," and it is valid for at least that limited purpose.[35]

Measurements of cognitive stimulation and emotional support revealed pronounced racial differences (Figure 7-5). Black and Hispanic parents scored respectively 9 and 10 points below the white average (on a scale in which 100 was the overall average) in the extent to which their homes provided cognitive stimulation to young children. The home environment of the typical white child was, in this sense, much more of a school than that of the black or Hispanic child.[36]

In terms of emotional support, the black-white gap was an even larger 12 points. It is striking, though, that the Hispanic-white gap was just 4 points. The low educational level of many Latino mothers and their lack of English skills made them unable to provide any more cognitive stimulation than black mothers. But they did give more in the way of emotional support than most black mothers, probably because the latter were more often raising children entirely on their own, leaving them less able to attend to the emotional needs of each child.

Of course, some of these differences in family environments are related to socioeconomic differences between the races. Black women are less likely than whites to be college graduates, for example, and less likely to have a fam-

Figure 7-5. Cognitive-Stimulation and Emotional-Support Scores of Parents of Children Aged 3 to 9, 1986–1994

Source: David J. Armor, *Maximizing Intelligence* (New Brunswick, N.J.: Transaction Books, 2003), 119.

ily income that is above average. And yet "black-white differences in parenting practices persist after controlling for measured socioeconomic status," Meredith Phillips found in an intricate and high-powered statistical analysis. She went on to suggest that "the relative importance that mothers place on many child-oriented activities and skills may be related to group identity or membership."[37]

Powerful additional evidence that confirms David Armor's analysis of Youth Study data is available from the NCES study of pupils entering kindergarten in 1998. Using these data, economists Roland Fryer and Steven Levitt have shown that the black-white gap in reading and math skills among those students largely disappears when just a few factors are controlled.[38] First, they find that parental education, occupation, and income have a strong influence. Second, the child's weight at birth and the age of its mother contributed substantially to the gap, as Armor had demonstrated earlier. Both low birth weight and having a very young mother slow cognitive development, and black children are more likely to have both of these strikes against them.

The data available in this survey unfortunately did not include a HOME scale or other evaluation of the quality of parenting. But one simple indicator may have captured much of what such detailed evidence would have shown—namely, the number of children's books in the home. The average white kindergartner in the study had ninety-three books, the average black child less than half that many. We doubt that the sheer number of books available to a child itself has a huge influence per se; a program providing every black preschooler an additional fifty books would likely accomplish very little. The point instead is that this parental choice is a good measure of broader differences related to the world of learning, differences that stand out very sharply on the HOME scale.

Behavioral Differences Among Kindergartners

These are some of the main reasons why black, and to some extent Hispanic, children are well behind their white and Asian classmates in cognitive skills when they first arrive at kindergarten. They may also help to explain why such children tend to be less well prepared to adjust to the behavioral demands of school. The 1998 kindergarten survey asked teachers three questions about their students: whether they persisted at the tasks assigned to them, whether they were eager to learn new things, and whether they regularly paid attention in class. Marked racial differences showed up in the responses to all three questions. Black children showed less persistence at school tasks, appeared less eager to learn new things, and were less likely to pay close attention to the class than whites, with Hispanics midway between the other two groups (Figure 7-6). Teachers also reported that black students starting kindergarten were most likely to argue with their classmates "often" or "very often," to fight with others, and to get angry easily. To be sure, there are elements of subjectivity in all of these judgments. But evidence about disciplinary problems among older children that we review below persuades us that these differences are real and not the result of teacher bias.

If the assessments of these teachers are accurate, these racial differences in adjusting to the demands of school would seem to be strongly related to family structure. Children who live with only one parent, this study reveals, rank well behind others in their ability to persist at a task, in their eagerness to learn, and in their capacity to pay attention in school. And they are more likely to argue with others, get into fights, and get angry easily. The study also shows that single parents more often consider their own children to be hyperactive and deficient in paying attention, confirming the judgments of teachers.

In sum, black (and to some extent Hispanic) students are substantially behind their white and Asian classmates when they start kindergarten. They rank below others in tests of cognitive skills, although Latinos do catch up somewhat over the course of their first two years of schooling. Their teachers

Figure 7-6. Percentage of Kindergartners Rated by Teachers as "Never" or Only "Sometimes" Behaving in Ways Conducive to Learning, 1998

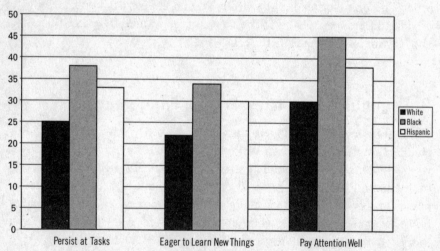

Source: National Center for Education Statistics, *America's Kindergartners*, 30, 47.

find students in both groups less eager to learn and less able to focus their energies on school tasks. In addition, African-American students appear quicker to take offense and more prone to conflict.

It's "hard to talk about [these problems] in public," Ronald Ferguson, an African-American economist at Harvard's Kennedy School of Government, has said. "Black folks don't want white folks coming into their communities and saying, 'You ought to be more like us.' " But Ferguson rightly insisted that the point had to be confronted. "The national data show an achievement gap when kids start kindergarten. So it's not that they start school equal and schools mess them up," he went on.[39]

As we noted in Chapter 4, the College Board "Task Force," as well, acknowledged the need to explore the "cultural attributes of home, community, and school," and talked at length about the attitudes toward school and toward hard work that Asian parents transmit to their children.[40] The disadvantages that African-American children bring to school right at the outset do not lend themselves to easy policy solutions; on the other hand, they are not intractable, as the schools we talked about in Chapters 3 and 4 suggest. How much could educational and other organizations accomplish if they ran truly terrific home intervention and preschool programs? That question has never been answered satisfactorily. Head Start is a large-scale program serving millions of black children, but, as Chapter 11 will argue, its returns have been meager at best.

Getting into Trouble

After kindergarten, as the NAEP evidence makes painfully clear, black students do not catch up with their classmates academically; instead, they fall further behind. Hispanics typically lag, too, but their case has much to do with a group profile strongly influenced by the continuing influx of immigrant children from uneducated homes. The difficulties of African-American children in school seem more deeply rooted and harder to remedy.

One important source of their poor performance in school is that disproportionately large numbers of black children find it hard to adjust to the demands of a well-ordered classroom. The rather modest racial differences in the incidence of behavioral problems that are visible among kindergartners do not fade away as students become more mature and more accustomed to the routines of school. To the contrary, they grow more pronounced. Those who are most resistant to the authority of the teacher are less likely to learn. And if a teacher cannot keep sufficient order, the classmates of these students will also find it hard to learn. "Why would I leave my child in a school full of unruly children who disrupt class and make the environment not conducive to learning?" a Maryland mother who put her kids in private school asked in a letter to *The Washington Post*.[41] "Unruly children," whatever their race or ethnicity, are an obstacle to learning; all good schools work hard to create order and civility, as we discussed at length in Chapter 3.

This subject (like so many others in this chapter) is obviously sensitive, but it is simply too important to duck. A wealth of evidence indicates that African-American children—and especially black boys—are far more likely than others to break school rules, disrupting their own and their classmates' education.

The extreme cases in which students have been caught doing something serious enough to result in their suspension or expulsion from school are the tip of the iceberg. Figure 7-7 summarizes the national evidence on suspensions and expulsions for 1999, using an index comparing a racial group's share of severely disciplined students to its share of the national student population.[42]

A group that is, say, 12 percent of the population and had 12 percent of the disciplinary problems would have an index of 100. As the figure indicates, however, students who are white, Hispanic, or Asian all receive less than their demographic share of punishments. African Americans are two-and-half times as likely to be disciplined as whites and fives times as likely as Asians. The Hispanic pattern is once again close to that for whites.

The NAACP and others argue that these disparities are prima facie evidence that the schools are biased against black children.[43] If true, however, then the Asian-white gap in discipline rates also suggests schools have anti-white, pro-Asian biases. As we suggested earlier, we believe that the relationship between family structure and suspensions or expulsions evident in Figure 7-7 is no coincidence. Nor is it an accident that the group with the lowest disciplinary index—Asians—also has the lowest proportion of students from single-parent families. Indeed, one can predict a group's discipline index quite reliably simply by knowing the proportion of its children living with two parents.

Black students are unjustly singled out for punishment, one scholar writes, because whites in authority are "unfamiliar and even uncomfortable with the more active and physical style of communication that characterizes African-American adolescents; the impassioned and emotive manner popular among young African Americans may be interpreted as combative or argumentative by unfamiliar listeners."[44] The Applied Research Center also asserts that "teachers' conscious or unconscious beliefs about their students of color"

Figure 7-7. Racial Differences in Rates of Suspensions or Expulsions and in Family Structure, 1999

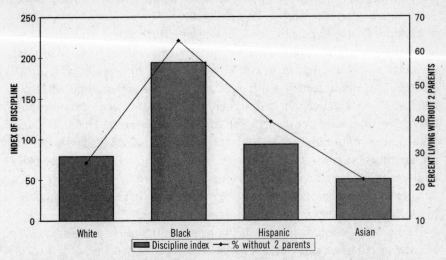

Source: The index was calculated by dividing a racial group's share of disciplinary actions by its share of the student population. It equals 100 when the proportion of students from a racial group who were disciplined matched its share of the total student population. Data on discipline from Office of Civil Rights, U.S. Department of Education, "Fall 1998 Elementary and Secondary School Civil Rights Compliance Report," unpublished document, 2000, 1. Family structure from U.S. Bureau of the Census, *American Families and Living Arrangements: March 1999*, Detailed Tables, table C2, Census Bureau Web site.

warp decision making.[45] Both analyses assume that the decision makers in these discipline cases are whites.

Such speculation may or may not seem plausible, but speculation is no substitute for evidence. The Applied Research Center studied school discipline in ten cities; in Chicago, the racial disparity in suspension rates is of the same magnitude as in other large cities, the data indicate. And yet only 49 percent of Chicago's teachers are white, while 43 percent are African American. In Miami, only 37 percent of the teachers are white, and in Los Angeles 53 percent, and yet the disparities in rates of discipline in both cities closely resemble those in systems in which a large majority of teachers are white.

We know of no large-scale studies of school discipline that take into account the race of the teacher making the complaint or of the administrator who made the decision to suspend or expel a student. But some pertinent evidence is available in work already referred to in our chapter on Asian Americans—George Farkas's survey of seventh- and eighth-graders in the Dallas Public Schools.[46] Farkas did not have evidence on suspensions or expulsions; the students were a bit young for such draconian action to occur very often. But he asked teachers to indicate which of their students they considered "disruptive." It is reasonable to think that these were the students most likely to be disciplined later in their school careers. African Americans were identified as disruptive at twice the rate for all students, and Asian Americans were only about a quarter as likely to be so labeled.

Farkas was able to take the analysis one step further and to estimate how much the race of the teacher affected these judgments. One-third of the Dallas public school teachers in his sample were African American, and it turned out that they did indeed give different average ratings than their white colleagues. White teachers only rated their black students as moderately more disruptive than white students. But African-American teachers, who certainly were not "unfamiliar" with "the more active and physical style of communication that characterizes African American adolescents," judged black students to be dramatically more disruptive than others. It was their much harsher judgment that produced the overall finding that teachers considered black pupils to be a greater threat to classroom order.

This is only one study in one city at one point in time, and its findings can be interpreted in various ways. Perhaps black teachers were especially tough on their African-American pupils, applying a higher racial double standard in their case because they were especially eager for them to succeed. Alternatively, the white teachers might have been leaning over backward to avoid appearing racist. Farkas reports that some African-American teachers in Dallas believed that white teachers "do not know how to discipline black students. They let them walk all over them."[47]

The Farkas survey asked teachers about "disruptive" kids (who may or may not have been subject to disciplinary action). Other studies throw additional light on the problem. A large-scale survey of elementary and secondary teachers in 1993–1994 included questions about what respondents thought were "serious" problems in the schools at which they worked. Figure 7-8 provides the answers about student absenteeism, verbal abuse of teachers, and disrespect for teachers, plus teachers' judgments about whether students are "unprepared to learn." Unfortunately, the categories used in tabulating the results are very crude, but we can distinguish urban from suburban schools, and those with minority enrollments of less than 20 percent from those with 20 percent or more.

The responses indicate, somewhat surprisingly, that the big differences were not between urban and suburban schools, but between schools with few and many minority students. Schools in central cities looked only a little worse than their suburban counterparts. But schools in which minority students (almost all non-Asian) constituted a fifth or more of the student body differed dramatically from those in which the minority presence was smaller.

Students in schools with high minority enrollment were considerably less likely to turn up in class at all. Additional confirming direct evidence about racial differences in absenteeism is available from other surveys as well. In 1997–1998, a startling 39 percent of San Francisco's black middle school students were absent from school for eighteen days or more (three-and-half weeks), as compared with 15 percent of whites. Even worse, in high school an appalling two out of three African Americans were absent for eighteen or more days, versus one in three whites. (The white absenteeism figures, it should be noted, are themselves shockingly high, but they are nonetheless low in comparison with blacks.)[48] Needless to say, failing to show up in school regularly severely diminishes a student's chances of doing well.

In the 1993–1994 survey, from a fifth to a sixth of teachers in central-city and suburban schools that were at least 20 percent minority described "verbal abuse" by students as a serious problem. A quarter of those teachers believed that their students did not show them proper respect. Another study based on a survey of school principals divided schools into four categories reflecting different percentages of minority students. For every type of disciplinary problem, the incidence rose as the proportion of minority students went up.[49]

Disorder in the classroom—of whatever magnitude—is educationally serious. Much media attention is focused on actual violence, but the low-level chaos that characterizes so many inner-city schools is also deeply disruptive. "Many times I have walked out of a school hanging my head in shame at the

Figure 7-8. Percentage of Teachers Who See Absenteeism, Verbal Abuse, and Disrespect as a "Serious Problem" at Their School: Central City vs. Suburban Schools, and Those with <20 Percent vs. >20 Percent Minority Enrollments, 1993–1994

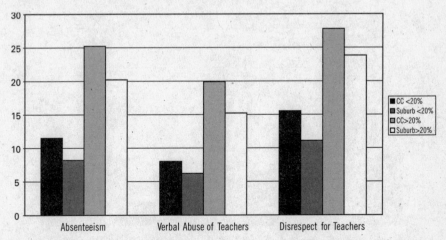

Source: National Center for Education Statistics, *Schools and Staffing in the United States: A Statistical Profile, 1993–94*, NCES 96–124 (Washington, D.C.: U.S. Department of Education, 1996), 112.

way our students behave," a longtime Washington, D.C., schoolteacher and administrator lamented in 1997. "They use abusive, derogatory language in front of adults, threaten their peers and teachers and dare you to make an issue of it. They are not only hurting themselves but all of those who want to learn."[50] Every good school attacks this problem aggressively and successfully.

Television and Homework

American students in general watch an appalling amount of television even on school days—surely another impediment to learning. But it is nonetheless stunning to find that nearly half of African-American fourth-graders spend *five hours* or more staring at a TV screen on a typical school day, about as much time as they spend in their classes at school (Figure 7-9). Add in weekend viewing, and their main "education" occurs in front of the television. Less than one-fifth of whites spend that many hours watching TV, and Hispanic children are more like whites than blacks in this respect.

Perhaps we needn't worry too much about how nine- or ten-year-olds are spending their after-school hours. We can't expect many of them to be sweating away getting ready to ace their SATs. But by the eighth grade one might

Figure 7-9. Percentage of Students Who Watch TV or Videotapes Five or More Hours on a Typical School Day, 1998–2000

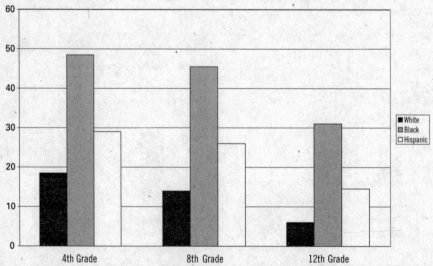

Source: NAEP Data Tool. Figures are averages of reports of students in the 1998 reading and the 2000 math assessments.

assume—or at least hope—that the academic demands of school would be more time-consuming. Thus, it is startling and dismaying to discover that close to half of all black eighth-graders watch television for what must be more than a third of their waking hours on school days.

In the twelfth grade, academic demands should be greater still, and many students spend a lot of time on sports and other extracurricular activities. Many also have part-time jobs. Nevertheless, nearly one-third of all African-American students were still watching television for five hours or more, five times the proportion among whites and more than double that for Latinos. Few racial differences in contemporary America are as sharp as these.

Does this mean these students are simply ignoring homework assignments? Not according to the students themselves. Surprisingly, the most recent NAEP evidence suggests—as Figure 5-7 in Chapter 5 shows—that Asian students alone take school seriously enough to spend a lot of time on homework. Whites, blacks, and Hispanics look pretty much identical. Indeed, in all three grades (fourth, eighth, and twelfth) the proportion of black and Hispanic students spending an hour or more a day on homework is slightly higher than for whites.

Harvard economist Ronald F. Ferguson's more detailed data on reported time spent on homework by students in the affluent Cleveland suburb of Shaker Heights found African Americans devoting an average of twenty-two minutes less on schoolwork per night than whites, a difference of only 15 percent.[51] But they were considerably less likely than whites to complete their homework. National data for 1990 tenth-graders from the National Education Longitudinal Survey also suggest a difference of modest magnitude in time spent on homework.[52]

How is it possible that black students can watch so much more television than whites and yet spend hardly any less time doing homework? Are they sleeping fewer hours? Ferguson's study found no connection between hours spent on TV and either time devoted to homework or rates of completion.[53] But he had no way of measuring the intensity of a student's concentration on schoolwork done at home. Perhaps black students manage to do nearly as much homework as their classmates—at least their non-Asian classmates—while spending an enormous amount of time before the television set by combining these two activities.

Their divided attention may explain another intriguing finding of Ferguson's, however. As Chapter 1 noted, Ferguson surveyed middle and high school students in fifteen affluent school districts (including Shaker Heights). He found that African-American students were about 20 percent less likely to complete their homework each night. They were putting the hours in, but spending the time less efficiently, evidently. Their long hours watching TV would certainly explain their reduced efficiency—their failure to actually complete their assigned work. It might also explain the disturbing finding mentioned in Chapter 1—that half of all black students reported that they didn't understand the assigned reading "very well" most of the time.

Why were African-American students so devoted to television? Ferguson reports that they regarded it as their "social homework," and felt left out of the conversation if they hadn't seen the programs all their chums had viewed the night before. One youth told him "you have to watch television to get your material to be funny." Television was thus a crucial unifying element in the culture of African-American students, a key source of group cohesion. Watching less television and devoting the time saved to "more high-yield learning activities," Ferguson observes, "would have a cost in social terms." Such deviant behavior would isolate them from their friends.

White students also watch an awful lot of television, and some may also consider it their "social homework." But they watch less of it, and most are not struggling with understanding their schoolwork to the same extent as their black classmates are.

Acting "Black"

Some scholars argue that African-American youths are embedded in an "oppositional culture" that is hostile to academic excellence. Black students, they contend, recognize the ineradicable racism of American society and conclude that educational success will not pay off. Academic achievement will not get them good jobs; there is no point in meeting the demands of school, they believe. To do so, in fact, is tantamount to "selling out," abandoning their racial identity. Resisting schools is a justifiable act of racial rebellion.[54]

The scanty evidence that has been advanced to support this theory has come chiefly from ethnographic case studies of particular schools. They may be accurate portraits of students in some big-city settings. But data from representative samples of the national population suggest that this is an overblown, highly politicized idea whose empirical foundation is extremely weak.

First of all, it cannot seriously be argued that education does not pay off handsomely for African Americans in contemporary America. Four decades ago, that was certainly the case; discrimination depressed the wages of even highly educated blacks. But evidence from a 2002 Census Bureau study indicates that black college graduates, over their working life, will today earn

$850,000 more than their peers who dropped out of high school. Those who acquire a graduate degree will earn $1.7 million more.[55] Over the past three decades, income differences between more and less educated Americans have widened in general, and educated blacks have benefited from the change.

Perhaps many black students do not know this fact. But the systematic evidence we have about their beliefs does not square with the oppositional culture theory. Several analyses of national survey data indicate that African-American youths are optimistic about the future and say that doing well in school is vital to their success.[56] Likewise, Ferguson's extremely detailed survey of Shaker Heights students in grades 7–12 provides little support for "the view that black students' peer culture . . . is more oppositional to achievement than whites.' "[57]

On the other hand, we doubt that there is much value in the responses of students to highly abstract questions about whether they think school is "important." It will be recalled from our chapter on Asian Americans that Laurence Steinberg identified clear cultural differences among high school students not by examining generalized student beliefs about such matters, but by posing an ingenious question about what students felt to be the "trouble threshold"—the level of grade that they thought would get them in trouble with their parents. The pattern did not disappear when mother's education was held constant; these are not class-based but cultural differences that follow racial lines.

Students who will settle for a C are not as likely to work as hard to succeed in school as those who regard anything less than an A– as a sign of failure. They might, however, kid themselves that they really are doing their best. An intriguing finding on this point comes from the answers given by the tenth-graders in the National Education Longitudinal Study in 1990. They were asked if they worked "as hard as they [could] almost every day" in their classes, and then were asked how much time they spent on homework each day.[58] Black students who believed that they were working just as hard as they could "almost every day" reported doing 3.9 hours of homework per week. Whites who made the same claim put in 5.4 hours, nearly 40 percent more. Asian Americans averaged 7.5 hours, about 40 percent more time than whites and nearly twice as much as blacks.

Perhaps the group differences have something to do with the special role of television in black teen culture. Perhaps black students thought that they were working as hard as they possibly could given their need to do "social homework"—keeping up with several hours' worth of television programs that more academically oriented white and Asian students regarded as luxuries.

Even if one could abolish television with the wave of a wand, however, the problem would remain. In a speech in Chicago in 1963, the Reverend Martin Luther King, Jr., offered his advice to African-American students. "When you are behind in a footrace," he said, "the only way to get ahead is to run faster than the man in front of you. So when your white roommate says he's tired and goes to sleep, you stay up and burn the midnight oil."[59]

Good advice—but largely unheeded. Black students today do not typically burn the midnight oil and run faster to catch up. Two provocative essays by Pedro Noguera of the Harvard Graduate School of Education discuss the need to "counter and transform" African-American "cultural patterns" that inhibit achievement. A "rigid connection between racial identity and school performance . . . exists in the minds of some students of color," Noguera writes. "If students regard Blackness as being equated with playing basketball and listening to rap music but not with studying geometry and chemistry, then it is unlikely that changing the school alone will do much to change achievement outcomes for students."[60]

If Noguera means that fiddling with the curriculum alone will not do much for student outcomes, we agree. But we argued in Chapters 3 and 4 that great schools alter the cultural patterns that inhibit academic accomplishment—including the disconnection from the world of reading for pleasure. We noted the paucity of books in the homes of black kindergartners earlier. Ronald Ferguson's ongoing research project on older students in fifteen affluent districts suggests that this is a continuing problem. He collected information on the number of books in the homes of teenagers. Holding parental education constant, he discovered that African-American students with parents who were college graduates had an average of 128 books in their homes. White students whose parents had never gone beyond high school had a slightly larger collection.[61] There were similar striking racial differences at every educational level.

This measure is obviously crude; one would like to know which families had nothing but mystery stories and Harlequin romances on their book shelves and which had Shakespeare, Melville, and Ellison. Nevertheless, this intriguing and depressing fact about the ownership of books is undoubtedly related to the equally depressing findings we reported at the end of Chapter 2 (see Figure 2-2). The authoritative 1992 National Adult Literacy Survey demonstrated that black college graduates had lower literacy skills than whites who had attended college only briefly, and only a little higher skills than those of whites who had no higher education at all. The racial disparity in literacy skills was equally sharp at every educational level, from high school dropouts to those with graduate degrees. Surely, these disparities have affected the academic performance of black children.

Cultural Change

Neither poverty nor culture is educational destiny, we argued at the outset. But in exploring the current racial gap in academic achievement, we cannot dismiss cultural explanations. It's tempting to ignore race and talk about social class—the disadvantages of poverty, low levels of parental education, and urban residence. But taking into account all these factors leaves roughly two-thirds of the gap in achievement unexplained.

This is a gap that appears very early in the life of black children; something about the lives of these children is limiting their intellectual development. Some risk factors have been identified by scholars: low-birth weight, single-parent households, and birth to a very young mother. There seem to be racial and ethnic differences in parenting practices as well, and the relatively small number of books in black households and the extraordinary amount of time spent watching TV appear related to those parenting practices.

African-American children tend to be less academically prepared when they first start school and are less ready, as well, to conform to behavioral demands. As a consequence, black students have disciplinary problems throughout their school careers at much higher rates than members of any other ethnic group. Although some believe that racism explains this pattern, there is no convincing evidence for that charge.

Doing well in school requires time on task and concentration, but black students spend an astonishing amount of time on their "social homework"— namely, watching television. They claim to be spending the same time on the homework assigned by their teachers as their classmates, but—given the hours devoted to TV—at best their attention is divided. That may be one reason why they are less likely to complete the school assignments. The special role of television in the life of black teen culture and the low expectations of their parents may also explain why they are willing to settle for low grades.

The process of connecting black students to the world of academic achievement isn't easy in the best of educational settings—and such settings are today few and far between. But that only means that in order to "counter and transform" African-American "cultural patterns," as Pedro Noguera calls for, fundamental change in American education will be necessary—change much more radical than that contemplated by the most visionary of today's public school officials. Recognizing the problem is the first step down that long and difficult road.

4 The Conventional Wisdom

Eight: Send Money

It's money. Money.[1]
Harold O. Levy, former chancellor, New York City Board of Education

In May 2000, the American Civil Liberties Union (ACLU) filed a class action suit against the State of California, charging that it had deprived "low-income and nonwhite" students of "basic opportunities," frustrating their "dreams of college and productive careers." These students are "consigned to a system of inadequate custodial care." The schools they attend, the ACLU claimed, "shock the conscience." They lack "trained teachers, necessary educational supplies, classrooms, even seats in classrooms, and facilities that meet basic health and safety standards."

There was more. In addition to an "underprepared and inexperienced" teaching staff, as well as a scarcity of textbooks, the buildings are "infested with vermin, including rats, mice and cockroaches," toilets are dirty and often malfunctioning, the water is sometimes unsafe to drink, classrooms are too hot or too cold, and fungus and mold threaten the students' health, the complaint for relief went on. These conditions, it concluded, "exact an enormous psychological toll"; the students "learn . . . that their State is not concerned about their education."[2]

Texas, Massachusetts, and numerous other states have made passing a statewide test a condition of high school graduation, although the requirement has been temporarily postponed in California and elsewhere. Asking minority kids to pass the same test as other students when their schools are inferior is "like saying even if you're 5-foot-8 then you're going to jam the ball," said a black parent in Cambridge, Massachusetts, in October 2001.[3] It is a frequently asserted claim.

Thus, in March 2002, *New York Times* columnist Bob Herbert described "the heart of the problem" plaguing New York City schools as "the chronic lack of resources that has condemned one generation of youngsters after another to a public school experience that is all too frequently inadequate, and in some instances little more than a joke."[4] As a consequence of underfunding, he subsequently wrote, those who attend the city's public schools "are treated the way black students were treated in the pre-*Brown* era."[5] *Education Week,* likewise, worries that "many states may be rushing to hold students and schools accountable for results without providing the essential support."[6] The "essential support" the news weekly has in mind is money.

In the past three chapters, we have stressed the role of group culture in academic achievement. Surely, however, such cultural differences do not alone explain the racial gap in school performance, readers will protest. And we agree: Schools have been falling down on their job. But the familiar list of what's wrong with schools does not explain the racial gap. The conventional wisdom sees three factors—inadequate funding, racial segregation, and too few teachers with professionally sanctioned credentials—as the major source of black and Hispanic underperformance in school. That conventional wisdom is largely wrong, we will argue in this and the next two chapters. And if the explanations are wrong, it follows that the remedies that flow from them are misguided and will not have the beneficial results that proponents claim for them.

The point we have made in the previous three chapters—culture matters—is not incompatible with other explanations, of course. A "chronic lack of resources" could further contribute to the paucity of skills that black and Hispanic students acquire in school. Perhaps the Asians in those same underfunded schools are typically better protected from the poor facilities and poor teachers by their families and the work ethic they bring to their studies. But is there, in fact, a strong causal link between school resources and disproportionately low black and Hispanic test scores? That is the central question this chapter addresses. We do not dismiss the good uses to which money can be put when used wisely, but the racial gap in academic achievement cannot be traced to inadequate school funding, we argue.

Bigger Budgets, Better Schools?

The most prominent spokesman for the view that grossly inadequate resources are to blame is Jonathan Kozol, whose 1991 *Savage Inequalities* was a best-seller.[7] The book examined a few schools in the worst neighborhoods of six cities, including Washington, D.C., New York, Chicago, and Camden, New Jersey. These dreadful schools, Kozol argued, spent a lot less per pupil than rich suburbs like Great Neck, New York; Winnetka, Illinois; and Princeton, New Jersey. He provided no evidence that these inner-city schools were typical, nor did he compare their spending with statewide averages, arguably a more reasonable baseline for judging equity. Princeton spent more than twice as much per pupil as Camden, he concluded; the funding disparities, he assumed, must have been the chief reason why its students performed so much better.

In fact, Kozol's allegations about the unfair distribution of school resources were not accurate generalizations in 1991, and in subsequent years educational spending has soared, with a disproportionate share of the additional resources going to high-minority, high-poverty schools. We welcome this trend on equity grounds. We do not think there should be large funding disparities between school districts within states. But we do not believe that money per se—additional money poured into the existing structure of public education—has either improved education overall or closed the racial gap in academic achievement.

Consider the recent historical record. Per pupil spending on America's elementary and secondary schools (in constant dollars) nearly doubled between 1970 and 2000.[8] Our educational system is not performing twice as well as a result. In fact, on the basis of the evidence NAEP has collected about what American students know, it seems safe to say that the nation's schools, overall, are no better than they were three decades ago. Black students have come a considerable distance since 1970, but the rise of a large black middle class and the end of segregated schools in the South may account entirely for that change.

Some commentators have argued that these overall spending figures are misleading, because so much of the new money that has gone to schools has been targeted at students with learning disabilities of various kinds, who qualify for expensive special education programs. It is unquestionably true that our society has been determined to expand the opportunities of students with handicaps, whatever it costs. But the best estimate suggests that special education has accounted for less than a fifth of the growth in total school spending per pupil in the recent years.[9] In sum, we have been investing a great deal of additional money in our public schools over the past generation, and yet the test scores of the students attending our increasingly well-funded schools have been essentially flat.

Their Fair Share?

Although the connection between school funding and student learning is tenuous, it is still worth asking whether black and Hispanic pupils have been deprived of their fair share of educational resources. Holding dollars constant, overall educational spending per pupil is up 91 percent over the past thirty years, but it is possible that the increases have not benefited all students equally. Perhaps the richest schools with few minority students have been getting richer, while the poor, high-minority schools have been getting poorer.

We lack good evidence for the period as a whole, but comprehensive data for the 1989–1990 school year have been compiled and analyzed by the National Center for Education Statistics (NCES) at the U.S. Department of Education. This is precisely the time period examined in Kozol's *Savage Inequalities*.[10] The investigators divided the nation's school districts into four student-population categories: less than 5 percent minority, 5–19 percent, 20–49 percent, and 50 percent or more. Then they calculated average levels of per pupil spending for each category, with surprising results (Figure 8-1).

In terms of actual dollars spent, it turned out that overwhelmingly white districts did not spend a great deal more than those with minority enrollments of 50 percent or more. The white-district expenditures were actually a bit lower. In 1989–1990, districts in which minorities were the majority spent an average of $431 a year more per pupil than those with hardly any minority students, an advantage of 8.5 percent.

These raw numbers, however, are somewhat deceptive. Minority children

Figure 8-1. School District Expenditures per Student by Percent Minority Enrollment, Actual and Adjusted for Costs and Student Needs, 1989–1990

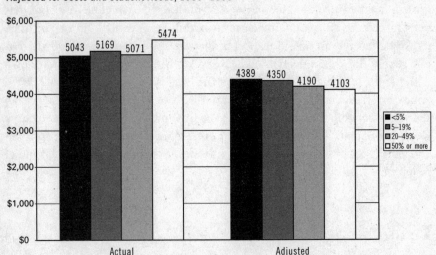

Source: National Center for Education Statistics, *Disparities in Public School District Spending, 1989–1990,* NCES 95-300 (Washington, D.C.: U.S. Department of Education, 1995), 15.

are more likely to live in big cities, where everything is expensive: transportation, janitorial and food services, housing and other living costs for teachers. Big-city students also cost more to educate because a higher proportion are classified as Limited English Proficient or as in need of "special education."[11] The right half of Figure 8-1 gives a more accurate picture. The figures there are adjusted to take into account local differences in costs and the special needs of students.

When adjustments are made for these differences, it turns out that districts with more minority students did have a little less money. But the differences were surprisingly small. Even after allowing for all the estimated extra costs, the high-minority districts spent an average of just $286 a year less than those that were nearly all-white—a discrepancy of just 6.5 percent. It is not plausible to think that such a modest deficit in funding can explain the very large racial gap in skills and knowledge.

Another surprise was that the facile contrast between "rich" suburbs and "poor" central cities so prominent in the writings of critics like Kozol turned out to be greatly overblown. In the nation as a whole, suburban per pupil spending adjusted for costs and special needs was less than $200 more per year, a mere 5 percent.

It is also noteworthy that school expenditures varied much more along economic than along racial lines. When NCES sorted out districts by income levels rather than racial composition, disparities were considerably sharper. Districts in which more than a quarter of parents lived below the poverty line spent nearly $1,200 less per pupil than did those in which no more than 5 percent of families were so impoverished, a substantial 22 percent disparity.[12] More affluent districts were able to spend more because local property taxes were the chief source of revenue to support the schools—although that reliance on the local tax base has become weaker in the last decade. Because most African Americans are not poor and many whites are, these economic differences do not correspond closely with race.

Many years have passed since this study, and unfortunately we do not have a more recent analysis that is equally comprehensive and detailed. There is no doubt, though, about the overall trend since the late 1980s. The national trend has clearly been toward a more egalitarian distribution of school dollars, a trend that disproportionately benefits blacks and Hispanics. States have assumed a larger share of responsibility for funding education, and have been particularly concerned with resources in the poorer districts. In addition, the federal government supports roughly 7 percent of the average school's budget, targeting funds for students in various disadvantaged categories. This money goes disproportionately to large urban centers with high-minority school enrollments. Federal money accounts for 14.5 percent of the school budget in New Orleans, 13.4 percent in Chicago, 12.0 percent in Baltimore, 11.7 percent in Philadelphia.[13]

The combination of state and federal aid has considerably reduced funding disparities between districts within states in recent years.[14] It is a process that has been expedited in part by litigation and threatened litigation; in more than two dozen states plaintiffs, with varying success, have brought lawsuits that assert a state constitutional right to equal educational spending. In other states—Massachusetts, for instance—legislatures have seen the handwriting on the wall and acted to create greater equality, hoping that a court would not impose remedies of its own.

Striking evidence of progress toward funding equity is contained in a 2002 report by the Council of the Great City Schools, a liberal advocacy group that describes itself as "the nation's voice for urban education." Although the Council complains that the school districts it represents are unfairly being deprived of the resources they need, the data in its report reveal that per pupil expenditures in 65 percent of all Great City school districts were higher than the average for the state in which they were located. The dismal performance of almost two-thirds of these school systems thus cannot be attributed to a lack of funds by the standards prevailing in the states in which they are located.[15]

"Overcrowded" Classes

One of the grossest signs of unfairness in our public schools, many say, is that affluent white suburban children have the advantage of small classes, while minority children are crammed into classrooms in numbers too large for the teacher to manage effectively. Differences in class size were one of the allegedly "savage inequalities" in our educational system that featured most prominently in Jonathan Kozol's account. To help the poorest children in the Chicago Public Schools learn, he suggested at one point, the "logical solution" would be to cut class size to that which could be found in posh Winnetka—seventeen students. Even a reduction from thirty to twenty-four kids, he asserted, "would be a blessing." He quotes a teacher in Camden, New Jersey, saying that "fair play" required that her classes have fifteen to eighteen students. A New York City teacher told him that "ideal class size for these kids would be 15 to 20," what "white kids in suburbs take for granted."[16]

But were Kozol's selected schools broadly representative? A close study of public schools in the years 1987–1992 found that the answer was a resounding no. (Figure 8-2) The evidence this study offers on pupil-teacher ratios at the time suggests that the average class was just about the size that the teachers quoted above called ideal.[17] Nor was it the case that black students were far more likely to be stuck in very large classes. Quite the opposite, in fact. The highest pupil-teacher ratios and the largest classes were to be found in the schools with the fewest black students, and class size went down as the proportion of African Americans increased. The pattern did reverse in the top bracket, in schools that were over 80 percent black. But even those nearly all-black schools had smaller classes than schools with the lowest proportion of blacks enrolled. When schools were classified not by their racial composition but by the proportion of students eligible for the federal lunch program, the results were again surprising. The schools with the lowest share of low-income students tended to have larger classes than those with lots of impoverished children.

This is the most recent national data we have been able to locate, but there is no reason to believe that the pattern has changed over the past decade. In 2001, the National Black Caucus of State Legislators charged that "African American and Latino students at risk of academic failure" typically attend schools in which classes are overcrowded, but it failed to cite any supporting evidence.[18] In fact, pupil-teacher ratios have continued to fall, dropping from 17.7 in 1992 to 15.1 by the 2000–2001 academic year. Over the past thirty

Figure 8-2. Pupil-Teacher Ratios in Public Schools by the Proportion of Black Students in the School, 1987–1992

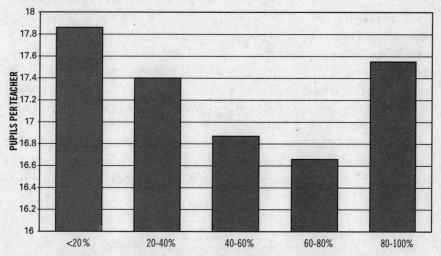

Source: Ronald F. Ferguson, "Can Schools Narrow the Test Score Gap?" in Christopher Jencks and Meredith Phillips, eds., *The Black-White Test Score Gap* (Washington, D.C.: Brookings Institution Press, 1998,) 360.

years, the number of teachers employed in our public schools has increased by 48 percent more than the number of students they have to teach, and the increase in the teaching staff has been as rapid in inner city, high-minority urban districts as elsewhere.[19]

Jonathan Kozol's contrast between the poor, largely minority schools of Camden and the affluent, largely white schools of Princeton conveyed a wildly distorted impression of the national picture a decade ago. He was right, however, that at that time there was a big difference between school resources available in those two particular communities, which he misleadingly selected as emblematic of the larger picture. But by the 2000–2001 academic year, the dismal performance of students in Camden's schools could no longer be blamed on overcrowded classes or a lack of financial resources generally. The student-teacher ratio at Princeton High School was a very low 11.8; at Camden High it had become an even lower 11.5! The number of students for each computer in the school was 5.7 in Princeton but only 3.5 in Camden. Princeton was spending a very comfortable $12,583 per pupil; Camden was spending $400 more, with no payoff in terms of student test scores.[20]

Not every inner-city, high-minority, high-poverty school today has a student-teacher ratio as low as that in Camden. But those schools typically have classes that are well below the size called "ideal" by unhappy urban teachers little more than a decade ago. Yet no one has been able to find evidence of dramatic improvements in test scores to match the dramatic declines in class size.

The idea that reducing class size will work wonders nonetheless remains widely held. What the American Federation of Teachers said in 1998 remains true today: "There's no more popular educational initiative across the country . . . than cutting class size."[21] In 2001, the NAACP outlined a five-year plan for closing racial disparities in academic achievement by at least 50 percent. It called upon the local, state, and federal governments to "aggressively target class-size reductions for the highest minority and concentrated-poverty schools." The available research, it claimed, suggested that educational gains would be "largest for black students and for those receiving free lunches."[22] In November 2002, a majority of the voters in Florida voted in favor of a referendum measure requiring major reductions in class size in all public schools in the state.

Smaller Classes in California

Teachers, of course, have long favored smaller classes. They genuinely believe students are better off with more individual attention—a conviction that seems common sense, particularly in classrooms in which learning is "cooperative," organized in small groups. Decades of research, however, have failed to establish that smaller classes have any measurable impact on student achievement. If this seems counterintuitive, it is not. If districts have to hire a great many teachers in order to reduce average class size, they are forced to be less selective in picking those teachers, with a decline in quality as a consequence. The key question, therefore, is teacher quality, not class size.

The research upon which the NAACP's 2001 "Call to Action" relied was an experiment in class-size reduction in the elementary grades in Tennessee in the mid-1980s. The Tennessee experiment was not on a scale that required massive recruitment of more teachers, so that was not a problem, and smaller classes did seem to improve student performance, especially for poor and African-American children. Critics, however, found technical problems with the study, and one concluded that, at best, it only demonstrated "possible small effects of major and costly reductions in class size" in kindergarten and first grade. Although the children studied were placed in very small classes for four years, virtually all of the observed benefits were in the first year.[23]

The Tennessee findings were nonetheless enormously cheering to the teachers and other advocates, and were used by those who persuaded the California legislature to back a huge and enormously expensive experiment with class-size reduction. California had not built new schools and hired teachers at a pace to keep up with its rapidly growing population for many years, so its classes were far larger than the national average. In 1996, the state committed itself to a $4 billion program to reduce the average size of classes by one-third, down to a maximum of twenty students in the K–3 grades. This was seen as a solution to the low levels of academic achievement among black and Hispanic students.[24]

Class-size reduction was quickly accomplished. Between the 1995–1996 and 1999–2000 school years, average class size for K–3 schoolchildren dropped from twenty-nine to nineteen. But did it help low-achieving minority students do any better? The precise impact of the program is still being debated, and can never be determined to everyone's satisfaction because California had no statewide system of standardized testing in place until 1997, making precise before-and-after comparisons impossible. The effects on test scores can be estimated by various statistical techniques, but all rest upon assumptions that can be challenged. Furthermore, other major changes were occurring in California education, most notably the abolition of bilingual education and a shift toward greater emphasis on phonics in reading instruction. Nevertheless, the broad outlines of the story are clear, and they contain important lessons.

As the California Department of Education acknowledges, the state's high expectations have not been met. This costly effort, indeed, may have done more harm than good to some categories of students. While there have been "small benefits in terms of student achievement . . . [the program's] rapid implementation may have increased underlying inequities in the state's education system," the state admitted.[25] Teacher quality has been the central problem. The year before the reforms went into effect, the state hired fewer than 4,000 new K–3 teachers. Suddenly, it needed 25,000 more to cover all the newly created smaller classes. It hired many who were inexperienced and underqualified, and they tended to end up in schools serving low-income and non-Asian minority children. Those "underprepared and inexperienced" teachers about whom the California ACLU complained were the unintended consequence of a reform that the civil rights community had fervently embraced.

The small-class mandate in California forced the hiring of many teachers who were apparently ill-qualified, especially in schools where the need for strong instruction is greatest. The sudden jump in the demand for teachers allowed those with better credentials—whether new or experienced—to move to schools in safer, more pleasant neighborhoods.[26] Reading scores rose only slightly and math scores actually declined in the most heavily black schools in the state.[27] (No comparable estimates are available for Hispanic students because so many were classified as Limited English Proficient and were not tested.)

As we noted earlier, the lack of academic progress should have been expected. The smaller the average class, the more teachers a school needs, and the harder it may be to maintain teacher quality. To cut class size by a third, the number of teachers (and thus the number of classrooms) has to go up by 50 percent.[28] Irwin Kurz, the principal of a very successful New York public school with low-income students and large classes, has said that he would rather "have one good teacher than two crummy teachers, any day."[29]

Students don't learn more unless the additional teachers are good, and good teachers—already scarce—become even harder to find when demand goes up and supply remains limited. We have serious questions about conventional measures of teacher qualification, as Chapter 10 will make clear. Nevertheless, in their desperate search for additional staff, California's high-minority, low-income schools evidently had no choice but to hire the weakest teachers in the pool. The disappointing results would seem the logical consequence.

More teachers are also extremely expensive. Teachers' salaries and benefits are the largest item in a school system's budget; California started out reimbursing schools $650 for each child in a reduced-size class, an amount that went up to $800 the following year. But those amounts did not fully cover the additional payroll costs. In addition, schools with more teachers need more space, which again adds significant and only partially covered costs.[30] Stanford University economist Edward P. Lazear has constructed a statistical model of the costs and benefits of the California reform. Reducing class size to the target of twenty students, he found, increased average educational performance by only 4 percent, while costs rose by 30 percent.[31] African Americans did not even get the 4 percent gain; those in largely minority schools ended up worse off.

Perhaps more dramatic reductions in class size would make a real difference, as many insist. But would it be the best use of the significant additional funding that such reductions would necessitate? This is medicine that we have been faithfully administering to our students for decades without great results. Suppose that the huge sums required to cut class sizes substantially were devoted instead to paying outstanding teachers higher salaries. Students learn more with good teachers, and expanding the pool of excellent teachers will take money, we will argue in Chapter 10. Some of the best schools we have observed have large classes, but the teachers are superb. Inevitably, there are trade-offs. Superb teachers would seem to be the first priority.

Filthy Bathrooms and Rodents on the Floor

Inequitable funding is the familiar complaint—the subject of numerous lawsuits across the country. But the ACLU's legal complaint against the state of California did not accuse school districts of differentiating among schools in the level of funding provided. It did not charge any school committee, superintendent, or other public official of looking at the student landscape and deciding that heavily minority schools can get along with fewer resources than others. Instead, in *Williams v. California,* plaintiffs asked the state to establish "baseline standards" that would define "a floor of minimal constitutional conditions and tools essential for education," and "provide basic educational necessities to all California public schoolchildren." Schools attended by low-income and nonwhite children, it said, often "lack the bare essentials required of a free and common school education that the majority of students throughout the State enjoy."

Many of the specifics in the ACLU bill of particulars are problematic. The complaint states, for example, that at the Luther Burbank Middle School in San Francisco a "dead rodent remained, decomposing, in a corner in the gymnasium for most of the 1999–2000 school year."[32] The source of the problem is not specified. The San Francisco Unified School District was not among the poorest-funded in the state; its per pupil expenditures, in fact, were a bit above the California average.[33] And one wonders how a dead rodent at Burbank could have remained on the gym floor for most of the year. Where were the janitors? Surely, all middle schools in the city received roughly the same money per pupil for custodial help. If the Burbank janitors were incompetent, why didn't a teacher or even the principal remove the rodent? Was there really nothing that could have been done? And would a 20 percent increase in the school budget guarantee that this would never happen again?

Textbooks are in short supply, the ACLU charged. The principal at San Francisco's Balboa High School (one of the schools named in the suit) argues that the funds are there; teachers fail to place orders on time, companies are slow to send books, and students lose them. The teachers say that Balboa "hemorrhages" textbooks.[34] The complaint also cited "bathrooms in wretched condition." But ask good teachers why that should be so, and they answer: out-of-control students trash them; the janitors watch television instead of doing their jobs; the teachers are indifferent; the administrators are apathetic.

No school should have filthy bathrooms. At Balboa High "stalls are covered with graffiti, the toilets and floors are caked with scum, and the walls are smeared with crusty, hardened spitballs made from wads of toilet paper," one reporter found.[35] Ramon Cortines came out of retirement to become interim superintendent of the Los Angeles Unified School District in 1999. Tellingly, among the goals he established was a clean bathroom for every student.[36] Surely, bathrooms should not be a matter that requires the immediate attention of a superintendent with 725,000 students, 800 principals, and 35,000 teachers to manage. Again, something is wrong beyond money. A good New York principal tells us: "I check the bathrooms several times a day because that's where the kids are likely to get into trouble. The custodian knows that the bathrooms are very important. I let him know, and they are spotless as a result."[37]

Classrooms, too, are "very important." "People are the problem, not money," a California elementary schoolteacher has told us. The ACLU found "mold," "fungus," "mildew," and "rotting organic material" in California classrooms, but her room is clean. The students scrub their homeroom. Students (rich and poor), she believes, should take some responsibility for keeping clean and orderly the "home" in which their formal learning takes place. To assume responsibility is educational. As the Los Angeles teacher noted, a gym doesn't have a rotting rodent corpse because there's no money for custodial help. Something is wrong with the culture of the school.

The ACLU made much of the number of "uncredentialed" teachers at high-minority, high-poverty schools. We're not great believers in the importance of what passes for teaching "credentials"; nevertheless, there is no doubt that high-need schools do not have the highest-quality teachers. At the time the ACLU filed suit in California, smaller classes had been mandated, making the problem particularly acute. But teacher quality is an issue everywhere. Seniority bestows choice upon teachers; when jobs open up in schools where the teaching is easy, the more experienced can grab them. Those without the same freedom to pick their school end up working in the most educationally difficult and demanding settings.

A school with a concentration of young and inexperienced teachers should be spending less on salaries, leaving extra money for other purposes. But, for accounting purposes, teachers' salaries are often averaged. Schools don't save money by having teachers who cost less; districts charge them the average teacher's salary, not their actual compensation. Thus, low salaries don't free up money in the budget that could be used to improve education. Schools that seem less appealing to the most sought-after teachers are deprived of resources to which they should be entitled. And schools that are popular with expensive teachers are free to hire whom they want, since it costs nothing extra to pay high salaries.[38]

Some schools, however, could make better use of the money they actually have, and some would make better use if they were free to do so. One high-poverty, all-minority school we visited spends thousands of dollars on noninstructional projects like Christmas decorations—nice, but a luxury. The administrative payroll, teachers told us, was padded with friends and relatives who contributed nothing important to the education of students. In their search for better teachers, distressed schools should be able to raise salaries and save money by increasing class size, for instance. But state laws and collective bargaining agreements set pupil-teacher ratios, and individual principals have little discretion over their own budgets. The schools we described in Chapters 3 and 4 use their funds in imaginative ways that are very difficult or just plain impossible in regular public schools.

A Tale of Two Cities

Contrary to conventional wisdom, the resources devoted to educating black and Hispanic students are much the same as those that go to schools serving mostly white kids, we have argued. Moreover, there is no evidence that additional funds to reduce class size, for instance, will close the racial gap unless the public system fundamentally changes—a topic to which we will return in Chapter 13.

Two stories illustrate the limits of money, per se, as an instrument for change. The first is about Kansas City, Missouri. In 2001, the city's school district lost its accreditation—a sorry end to what has been called "the longest running and most expensive experiment in the history of U.S. public education." [39]

The story begins in 1985, when in response to a desegregation suit, federal district judge Russell Clark ordered the state and the district to pour money into schools in an effort to attract white suburban students to a system that had become 75 percent black and had abysmal test scores. In response, the district created fifty-six magnet schools that had (among other things) greenhouses, lavish science labs, a planetarium, a recording studio, a 100-acre farm, and a wildlife sanctuary. Central High School, rebuilt from scratch for $32 million, boasted an Olympic-size swimming pool, a padded wrestling room, a classical Greek theater, an eight-lane indoor track, and a gymnastic center stocked with professional equipment. Fifteen years and $2 billion later, the schools were no more racially integrated than in 1985, and despite a student-teacher ratio of thirteen to one (among the lowest in the nation), test scores were just as dismal. A local attorney who had served as a court-appointed monitor for the program summed it all up: "The only things we have to show for $2 billion in new educational spending in Kansas City are beautiful buildings, highly paid, grossly inadequate teachers and a huge administrative staff that I estimate has cost us $43 million." [40]

An attorney instrumental in bringing the original suit has dismissed the test results as assessing "a very narrow range of low-level skills like vocabulary and rudimentary math." Perhaps, but if students have a very weak vocabulary and can't multiply four by seven, it is unlikely that they possess higher-level skills that will serve them well in later life. Even Professor Gary Orfield of the Harvard Graduate School of Education, one of the country's staunchest proponents of court-ordered desegregation remedies, admits that "Kansas City is a very, very sad story. They really can't show much of anything, though they spent $2 billion." [41]

What went wrong? "We have a huge social crisis, and schools can't solve it by themselves," Orfield said.[42] The poverty of the students defeated the plan. If true, this explanation has crucial implications, because the "social crisis" that Kansas City confronted is no greater than that found in any other typical large city, at least if poverty rates are the measure. Thirty percent of Kansas City children ages 5–17 live in homes with incomes below the poverty level, the same rates as in Minneapolis, and lower than that in New York, Los Angeles, Chicago, Detroit, Boston, Baltimore, Atlanta, Houston, New Orleans, Milwaukee, and a great many other large cities.[43] If practically unlimited money for the schools achieved nothing in Kansas City, it cannot be expected to be any more effective in places with even larger impoverished populations.

Poor kids can learn in good schools. We have provided portraits of such schools in Chapters 3 and 4. But having a $5 million swimming pool with an underwater viewing room and six diving boards does not make a school good. "Let me tell you something: Not all my teachers teach," a Kansas City high school senior, Sheena Williams, complained to a *Los Angeles Times* reporter in 2001. "In some classes, we watch movies every day. We watched 'Dr. Doolittle' in economics, and economics don't have nothing to do with a man talking to animals."[44]

In Cambridge, Massachusetts, the story has been much the same. Aptly described as a "famously liberal city, where 'equality' is nearly a mantra," Cambridge has substantial black and Hispanic populations, and its school authorities have long been committed to developing the talents of minority children to the fullest.[45] None of the Cambridge schools can be considered "segregated"; children are routinely bused to schools in other neighborhoods to promote racial balance. Funding is extravagant; currently, the city spends a staggering $17,000 a year per pupil, certainly among the highest in the nation.[46] It invests twice as much per child as the neighboring city of Boston. Massachusetts has an extraordinarily low average student-teacher ratio of 12.5, the second-lowest in the country. But Cambridge's is lower still, with just 9.8 students per teacher, 40 percent below the national average. Furthermore, over the past three years the city's only high school has been phasing out honors courses because they were "segregated" by race and class. Those in need of remedial work are assigned to the same classes as those already advanced enough to do college-level work. According to the interim principal, this change was "the moral thing to do."[47]

It is hard to imagine a city that has devoted more energy and resources to improving the education of minority pupils. But it has very little to show for it, at least judged by the results of the Massachusetts Comprehensive Assessment System (MCAS), a minimum-competency test in "English Language

Arts" and mathematics that, beginning in June 2003, all students must pass to receive a high school diploma. Many of Cambridge's tenth-graders in 2002 had already enjoyed the "benefit" of these new untracked, mixed-ability classes, and yet only 49 percent of the black students passed the English test on their first try, far below the statewide figure of 67 percent for African Americans.[48] In mathematics, just 35 percent of African-American students in Cambridge passed, as compared with 55 percent for the entire state. Hispanics in Cambridge do not lag behind those across the state, but they don't do any better either.

Cambridge is hardly unique, of course, in the poor performance of most of its non-Asian minority students. But it is striking that exceptionally high spending on a city's schools has had so little positive effect, especially in a city so devoted to racial equality. Black and Hispanic tenth-graders in Cambridge were less likely to pass the 2002 tests required for high school graduation than those in such communities as Somerville, Waltham, Brockton, Lowell, and Randolph. These cities with comparable demographics spend only half as much or less per pupil, and their students do not have the "benefit" of untracked, heterogeneous classes. Yet they learn significantly more.

In an August 2002 interview with the *Boston Globe*, the newly appointed principal of Cambridge's only public high school was asked why the Cambridge schools, with the highest per pupil expenditures in the state, still had an enormous racial gap in achievement. The principal hemmed and hawed, and concluded by saying that "we haven't figured it out yet, and I know we've got to, real soon."[49] Actually, the city had already attempted to reduce at least the consequences of that gap. In defiance of state law, it voted to grant diplomas to high school students who had not passed the tenth-grade MCAS exam—a decision it later reversed.[50]

Money, Money

"It's money, money," the former chancellor of the New York City schools has said. Undoubtedly, he speaks for most educators—particularly those in charge of big-city school systems where levels of student performance are abysmally low. But insufficient funding doesn't explain the racial gap in academic achievement, and money, per se, is no panacea. It does not cost more to raise academic and behavioral standards and to create a culture of learning. And when money can't be used wisely, education suffers. The people in charge of managing our public schools lack the basic tools of management every business has: the discretion to reward their best staff with higher pay, to fire those who are incompetent, to allocate funds in ways that will have a max-, imum impact on student achievement.

"It is the proper use of resources that plays the key role in outcomes," Neil F. Kreinik, the superintendent of a Queens, New York, district, has said. Gaming the system, he juggles money in creative ways, using his discretionary funds, for instance, to fund professional development one year, but using it to buy books and computer software the next year. In 2000, his district ranked twenty-ninth in spending in New York City, but his reading and math scores were in the top ten. In looking at the pattern of spending and student performance, in fact, *The New York Times* found that "across the city, the school districts that rank highest academically have, in most cases, the smallest per-student budgets."[51]

This is not to say that spending less money is a recipe for improving the schools. More money doesn't help, however, unless it is used wisely. Economists Richard Murnane and Frank Levy have reported on an interesting natural experiment that makes this point.[52] As part of a settlement in a desegregation case in the late 1980s, sixteen high-minority, high-poverty elementary schools in Austin, Texas, were given a very substantial increase of $300,000 a year for five years on top of their regular budgets. Did it promote greater student learning? Five years later, it turned out, no improvement at all was visible in fourteen of the sixteen schools.

These fourteen schools had spent the extra money reducing class size, but the teachers were simply doing what they had always done and their students were learning no more. The other two, though, did make impressive gains, because they had innovative and dynamic principals who devoted great efforts to involving parents, to reshaping the curriculum, and to training the teachers to handle their classes differently. The extra money helped to make these changes possible. But more money was no magic bullet—which the record of fourteen made clear.

That should have come as no surprise. Per pupil spending has nearly doubled in the last three decades, but American students in general are not more educated, and the rise in the knowledge and skills of black students may be due entirely to the growth of the African-American middle class and desegregation in the South. When school spending is adjusted for the extra costs associated with urban kids, districts that are overwhelmingly minority do have a little less money—but only a little. That modest difference cannot explain the racial gap in achievement. Moreover, since the 1980s, funding disparities between districts within a state have greatly lessened.

Inequity takes another form, it is often said; affluent children enjoy small classes while minority children do not. In fact, black students are not likely to be stuck in particularly large classes, and while class size has been dropping dramatically in recent years, there is no evidence that black and Hispanic children have been learning more as a result, we have argued. California mandated a reduction in class size; the result was a flood of underqualified teachers who ended up in urban schools that desperately needed strong teaching. It was a bad trade-off.

The stories of extraordinary spending in Kansas City and in Cambridge, Massachusetts, illuminate the limits of money as a cure for the racial gap. But money does matter—*sometimes*. It matters when used well, as the record of two schools in Austin, Texas, and our tales of good schools in Chapters 3 and 4 suggested. Money could help in attracting exceptionally dedicated and gifted administrators and teachers to education, for instance. But they are unlikely to come in the numbers needed without competitive salaries based on merit and other fundamental reforms.

Additional funding poured into the existing system will neither improve our schools in general nor solve the problem of underachieving black and Hispanic students specifically.

Nine: Racial Isolation

Throughout the desegregation cases, no one stopped to ask, "How are the kids doing?" What students learn is the issue. Not whether they're going to a racially identifiable school.
Robert Bartman, Missouri commissioner of education[1]

Throughout the Kansas City desegregation case, "no one stopped to ask, 'How are the kids doing?' " What a remarkable and sad statement. Two billion dollars spent to create more racially mixed schools, and, somehow, the question of student learning got lost. "Can't we at least look at whether they can read?" Justice Stephen Breyer asked when one phase of the case was argued before the U.S. Supreme Court in 1995. No, answered Missouri deputy attorney general John R. Munich. The academic achievement of the students was irrelevant.[2]

That had not been the view of the plaintiffs in the Kansas City case ten years earlier when Judge Russell G. Clark ruled that "segregation had caused a system-wide reduction in student achievement."[3] Judge Clark's order would help raise test scores to national norms within four years, predicted Arthur A. Benson II, the attorney who represented the black schoolchildren.[4] That the average school in the system was only 25 percent white explained the racial gap, in other words. Recruit more whites and the problem of disproportionately low black achievement would disappear, the attorneys assumed.

It was always a fantasy. We strongly prefer racially integrated classrooms ourselves, although we have never thought that denying parents access to neighborhood or other schools of choice was intelligent public policy. Nor have we believed that a black child must sit next to an Asian classmate in order to learn arithmetic. In the last chapter, we argued that inadequate funding does not explain the racial gap in academic achievement, and that pouring more money into schools with large enrollments of non-Asian minority students will not, in itself, accomplish any significant improvement. In this chapter, we explore the relationship between "segregation" (as it's commonly defined) and student performance. Are black and Hispanic children typically learning less than they could and should because most are attending schools in which only a minority of pupils are white?

Apartheid in Our Schools?

American elementary and secondary schools are still "segregated," it is often said. Linda Darling-Hammond, professor of education at Stanford and an important voice in scholarly debates, has complained of "apartheid in American education," suggesting an analogy to one-race schools in South Africa under white rule.[5] A 2001 report by the U.S. Department of Education echoed this complaint, although less flamboyantly. The "segregation of black and Hispanic students," it charged, has deprived these students of the "opportunity to learn."[6]

The Department of Education based its claim entirely on the work of Gary Orfield, a professor of education at Harvard, who deserves credit for having monitored trends in the racial composition of schools more closely than any other investigator. Orfield insists that attending a segregated school—which he defines as a school in which minorities are in the majority—has terrible educational and social consequences.[7] In his view, segregation is a primary, perhaps *the* primary, source of the racial gap in school achievement.

But what, in fact, is a "segregated" school? Half a century ago, the answer was simple and unambiguous. Until the Supreme Court's 1954 decision in *Brown v. Board of Education*, southern states required that black and white children attend separate schools. It was the law, and it was indeed a system of apartheid. The High Court's decision had little immediate impact. In the eleven ex-Confederate states, a mere 1.2 percent of black public school pupils attended schools that had any white students at all during the 1963–1964 school year—nine years after *Brown*.[8] But brave children, their parents and attorneys, other civil rights activists, the federal courts, Congress, and successive presidential administrations finally destroyed the Jim Crow system and ended race-based school assignments.

The courts, however, could not create schools in every community that perfectly reflected the racial mix of the population—locally or nationally— and it has become common to call schools that fail that test "segregated." It is seriously misleading, however, to confuse racial imbalance with the legally enforced separation of the races, we will argue. The two are not comparable, which is why the Supreme Court has never ruled that racial imbalance, per se, violates the equal protection clause of the Constitution. There is a constitutional obligation to remedy the deliberate separation of students on grounds of race; there is no mandate to create racially balanced schools. Racial imbalance may simply reflect residential patterns, which are beyond the purview of school authorities.

Just how racially imbalanced are schools? Figure 9-1 shows the racial composition of American public schools for 2000–2001, the most recent school year for which data are available.[9] The first group of columns, on the left of the figure, indicates the racial mix of the nation's public school population as a whole; the remaining clusters show the racial composition of the student bodies of the schools attended by the average white, black, Hispanic, or Asian student.

It's clear that whites, blacks, and Hispanics all typically attend schools in which students of their own race predominate. But there are differences. Whites are 61 percent of the nation's schoolchildren, but go to schools that are typically 80 percent white. The white concentration is disproportionately high, in other words. Blacks are 17 percent, Hispanics 16 percent, and Asians 4 percent of America's students. But these minority children are usually in much more integrated settings. Typically, around 30 percent of the classmates of both blacks and Hispanics are white. A tiny fraction are Asian-American.

Figure 9-1. Racial Composition of the Total Public School Population and of the School Attended by the Average Student from Each Racial Group, 2000–2001

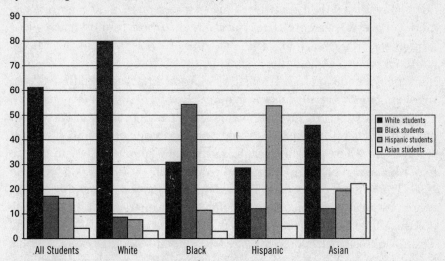

Source: Erika Frankenberg, Chungmei Lee, and Gary Orfield, *A Multiracial Society with Segregated Schools: Are We Losing the Dream?* (Cambridge, Mass.: Harvard Civil Rights Project, 2003), 24, 27.

Those are only averages, of course. Other evidence compiled by Professor Orfield and his associates reveals that a little over a third of blacks and Hispanics attend schools that are less than 10 percent white. On the other hand, close to a third of blacks and a quarter of Latinos are in schools with white majorities.[10]

Imbalance: No Surprise

Is there something wrong when so many students go to schools in which most of their classmates belong to the same racial or ethnic group? That is certainly a common assumption. If America had a racially fair and open society, it is often said, group members would not cluster either in schools or the workplace. If blacks are 17 percent of the school population, they should be 17 percent of the typical school. "Institutional racism" explains the imbalance.

That might be true if blacks were randomly distributed across the nation— 12 percent of the population in Detroit, in Salt Lake City, and in Montpelier, Vermont. But of course they're not. Like Italians, Poles, Jews, and members of every other racial or ethnic group, African Americans are more concentrated in some places than in others. This is true of virtually every group, however defined. And the local schools reflect that fact.

Take the group that the census refers to as "non-Hispanic white." These whites who do not consider themselves Hispanic are 61 percent of the country's total school enrollment. And yet in five states the student population is more than 90 percent white, while in fifteen more, there are white majorities of over 80 percent.[11] The typical school in those twenty states cannot possibly match the racial mix in the nation as a whole. In Vermont, Maine, North and South Dakota, Iowa, Indiana, Ohio, Wisconsin, and elsewhere, there are not enough black, Hispanic, and Asian school-age children to keep the white proportions down to the national average of roughly 60 percent.

Other states have relatively few whites, and a high proportion of minority children. In Hawaii, the most extreme case, barely one-fifth of public school students are white. In California, by far the most populous state in the nation, whites were only 37 percent of the public school student population in 1999. The figure is doubtless still lower by now, and if demographic change continues at its current pace, by 2010 only about a quarter of students in California's schools will be white. In Louisiana, Mississippi, New Mexico, and Texas, white schoolchildren are already a minority, and Arizona, Florida, Nevada, and New York are projected to join that list by the end of the decade.[12] In fact, about a third of America's public school students are in states in which minority kids are in the majority—or soon will be. The racial mix in schools depends in considerable part upon the racial composition of the state, and that composition varies radically.

The same is true for cities. Busing has been the standard remedy for racial and ethnic clustering in schools, but within school districts families make residential choices that result in a concentration of, say, Cambodians in one place, and Mexican Americans in another. Differences in family income also shape residential patterns. Whites have been moving into the suburbs for decades. To an increasing degree, blacks, Hispanics, and Asians are now leaving central cities as well, but they still remain much more strongly concentrated in inner-city neighborhoods. These demographic patterns have a profound effect on the racial makeup of schools and on the power of public authorities to engineer racial balance.

The high concentration of minority students in urban America is clear from the racial mix of students in the nation's twenty-six largest central-city school districts in the 2000–2001 academic year. These districts enroll about a tenth of all the public school pupils in the United States.[13] Although 61 percent of the nation's students are white, only one of these twenty-six districts (Salt Lake City) had a white majority, and just two more (Tucson and Albuquerque) were as much as 40 percent white. Seven of these giant school districts had white enrollments below 10 percent, and another ten were less than 20 percent white. In such districts, the most heroic efforts will not suffice to put the typical black or Hispanic pupil into a majority-white school. There simply aren't enough whites to go around. To transform all these central city schools to white-majority schools—avoiding allegedly harmful "segregation"—we would need to bus 1.7 million minority students out of these school districts and somehow replace them with whites.

Moreover, in many places it would not suffice to bus between the city and its nearby suburbs. In searching for whites, the net would have to be cast very widely—reaching far out into exurbia, because so many closer-in suburbs have large black and Hispanic populations. As the Kansas City case made clear, moreover, whites will not easily be persuaded to put their children voluntarily on buses heading for urban schools. "If spending a billion dollars in Kansas City does not win back the white middle class, then we will discover something very evil about America," Jonathan Kozol claimed a decade ago.[14] Actually $2 billion have now gone down the drain, and the parents who have wanted to stick with their neighborhood schools are not "evil." Suburban middle-class families—black, Hispanic, and Asian, too—make the same choice all the time: to educate their children in the communities in which they have chosen to live.

When white parents head for the lawns of suburbia, it is often said, they are attracted less by the green grass than by the color of their neighbors. This simplistic "white flight" argument does not stand up. Tens of millions of Americans have left central cities for more spacious homes in suburbia since the end of World War II. The desire to avoid contact with nonwhites can hardly have been the driving force; they were just as likely to depart from cities with few black residents as they were from those with a great many—as likely to leave Minneapolis or Seattle as Atlanta or Washington, D.C. Furthermore, African Americans, Latinos, and Asians have also been moving to green grass in very large numbers over the past three decades, and it is difficult to see how their migrations could be attributed to racial animosity.

Resegregation?

Schools today are often racially imbalanced—but not because children are assigned to schools on the basis of their race. That was once the case in the South, but that terrible chapter in the American story has closed. Nevertheless, if the public schools aren't deliberately separating the races, have minority and white students become increasingly isolated from one another? Has the situation gotten worse? After years of desegregation, the trend reversed in the 1990s, Orfield argues. Schools are becoming "resegregated." In fact, the racial gap in academic achievement, he notes, narrowed in the years in which integration was on the rise, and has widened with "resegregation"; there must be a causal relationship.[15] Further progress in closing that gap thus requires action to reverse the trend toward racial isolation.

Are schools in fact becoming "resegregated," and if so, why? Perhaps the best single measure of the level of racial imbalance in schools is an index that measures how differently black and white students are distributed among schools within each school district in the United States. If all black and white children went to school only with peers of their same race (the situation in the South before the *Brown* decision) the index would be 100—complete imbalance. If the proportion of black and white students in each school precisely reflected the racial balance in the district as a whole, the index would be zero—perfect balance. Figure 9-2 shows how the Imbalance Index has changed over the past three decades. (Similar figures are not available for Hispanics, unfortunately.)

The Imbalance Index shows that black and white students in our public schools have become much less separated over the past thirty years or so. The figure dropped by nearly half between 1968 and 1997, from 56 to 30. The de-

Figure 9-2. Imbalance Index of School Segregation, 1969–1999

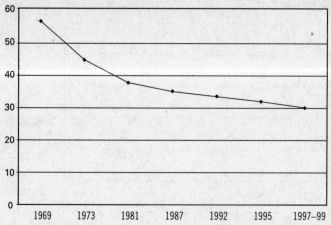

Source: Imbalance Index calculated by David Armor and Christine Rossell and supplied to us by the authors.

cline was most rapid in the 1970s, when the South's Jim Crow system was at last demolished, but it has continued steadily since then.

This Imbalance Index is a standard measure used by social scientists in studying racial separation. Orfield ignores it and thus rejects a method of assessing the racial composition of schools that finds increasing integration—not "resegregation."

Orfield employs a different measure, an Index of Exposure, which shows the proportion of whites enrolled in schools attended by the average black or Hispanic student (Figure 9-3). For blacks, he found a slight rise in exposure to whites from 1970 to 1986 and then a similar slight decline over the dozen years down to 1998. The shift does not seem large enough to justify using the dramatic term "resegregation," but this index does suggest a story different from that provided by the Imbalance Index. The Index of Exposure registers a bigger change for Hispanics, their contact with white students dropping by 11 points from 1970 to 1986, and then by another 3 points over the next dozen years.

Orfield's sole concern is minority exposure to whites—the proportion of white students who attend the same schools as minority pupils. As a result, his findings are very different than they would have been had he used the standard Imbalance Index, which measures the degree to which schools are "imbalanced" relative to the racial mix in the district. In Orfield's view, black, Hispanic, Asian, and American Indian students all belong to one undifferentiated "minority" group, and that group is "segregated" because the youngsters who belong to it are exposed to too few whites.

Figure 9-3. Exposure Index for Black and Hispanic Students, and Percent White of Total Public School Enrollments, 1970–1998

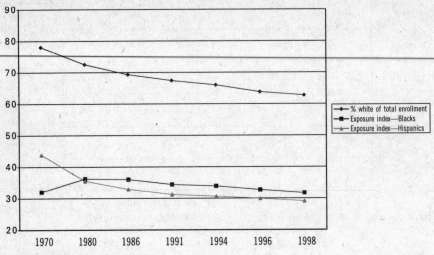

Source: Orfield, *Schools More Separate*, 37.

Figure 9-4 tries to show what this sole concern with exposure means in practice. It indicates the racial balance in two hypothetical schools. In the first, the student body is 38 percent white, 9 percent black, 41 percent Latino, 11 percent Asian American, and 1 percent American Indian. In the second, the student body is 50 percent white, 47 percent black, 1 percent Hispanic, 1 percent Asian, and 1 percent American Indian.

Most of us would think of the first school as clearly more racially integrated, more diverse, less "segregated" than the second. The second is roughly half white, half black, but it lacks the variety of cultural backgrounds and the opportunities for interracial contact contained in the first school. In the first, no one group is in the majority, and four groups are significantly represented. And yet this more diverse, ethnically rich school would register as more segregated on the Index of Exposure, because added all together, the students from the various minority groups are in the majority. And remember Orfield's sole measure of segregation is the proportion of whites in the student body, which is higher in the second school.[16]

It happens that the first hypothetical school has the same racial mix as California's public school population today, and the second exactly mirrors that of Louisiana. If every school in California and Louisiana had the same racial mix as the state's student population as a whole, Louisiana would have a higher Index of Exposure than California, simply because a slight majority of

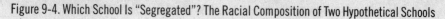

Figure 9-4. Which School Is "Segregated"? The Racial Composition of Two Hypothetical Schools

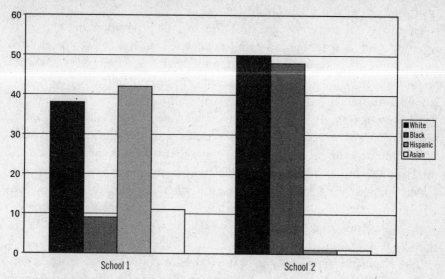

its students are white. The fact that California's schools contain a more complex racial mixture, with greater possibilities of interacting with students from several different groups, does not matter if we use Orfield's measure.

The Imbalance Index shows that over the past three decades our schools have become more racially balanced and less segregated. But the Exposure Index favored by Orfield suggests a basically unchanged level of exposure for blacks and a distinct decline for Hispanics. How can these opposed pictures be reconciled?

It is not difficult, because the two measures capture two quite different aspects of changing social reality. The Imbalance Index takes the racial composition of the public school student population of each district as a given, and asks how closely each school within it mirrors that mix. It focuses on matters that are partially within the control of local school authorities—how they assign students to particular schools within the district.

The Exposure Index, by contrast, measures the proportion of whites to be found in the school attended by the average black or Latino pupil—*without any regard to the availability of white students in the district*. If white students are only 3.9 percent of total enrollments in the Detroit Public Schools, as they are currently, then the level of exposure to whites inevitably will be close to zero. No pupil assignment policy (without somehow pulling suburban whites into city schools) can "integrate" the classrooms. The charge of "segregation" would seem to suggest a problem that has a remedy—a solution if there's good will—and yet inevitably in such cities almost all black students will be sitting next to students who are also black.

Detroit is an extreme case, but the overall proportion of whites in America's public school population has declined substantially in recent decades, and especially so in central cities. The black, Hispanic, and Asian populations have grown, and the racial and ethnic composition of the population has thus changed. The natural result of this population shift has been rising "segregation" as measured by the Exposure Index. As the top line in Figure 9-3 shows, nearly four out of five public school students in 1970 were white; today the figure is only slightly more than three out of five. Even so, the Exposure Index dropped very little for African Americans and only moderately for Hispanics. That is because the distribution of students within schools in each district became more balanced—as the Imbalance Index reveals. More students have been going to schools with a diversity that reflects their local community.

The Exposure Index, as Orfield uses it, delivers bad news—more "segregation." But that same index could be turned around with quite different results. Why not measure the proportion of minority students in the classroom of the average white student—instead of the proportion of whites learning alongside blacks and Hispanics? If we looked at the exposure of whites to minority classmates, we would find declining segregation—more whites who go to school with nonwhites. If the proportion of minority students in the total population is rising, the exposure of whites to classmates from a variety of racial and ethnic backgrounds must be rising as well. It is the opposite side of the same coin, and just as important as the side emphasized by Orfield.

Most of the decline in the Exposure Index, as previously noted, has not been for blacks but for Hispanics. The figure for African Americans in 1998 was nearly identical to what it was in 1970, but the index for Latinos registered a drop of 15 points, from 44 to 29—which means fewer whites in the schools they attend. The reason is clear: The proportion of whites in the public school population has dropped 17 percent since 1968, while that of Latinos has soared 283 percent.[17]

The explosive growth of the Hispanic population—with proportionally fewer whites and many more Latinos enrolled in the schools—has inevitably meant declining exposure of Latino pupils to whites. But that declining exposure is also the consequence of the concentration of Hispanics in just a handful of states, and in large central cities within those states.

Immigrants from Mexico, Central America, and other Latin American nations—like the Irish, Germans, Italians, Poles, and all other earlier arrivals—have not scattered randomly across the American landscape. Today, remarkably, more than half of all the Hispanics live in just two states, California and Texas. It is hardly surprising that whites are already a minority of public school students in California and Texas. Add just five more states—New York, New Jersey, Florida, Illinois, and Arizona—and we have accounted for more than three-quarters of all Latinos. By 2010, minorities in schools in Arizona, Florida, and New York as well will likely be in the majority, chiefly because of continuing Hispanic immigration and the high birth rate of these immigrants.

Given these demographic trends, it is hardly surprising that the Index of Exposure for Latino pupils has been dropping sharply. It is impossible to see what could be done to reverse the trend, however, short of a moratorium on all Latino immigration or a major effort to force most of the Hispanics living in Los Angeles to move to Salt Lake City, Fargo, or Montpelier.

The Question of Harm

If a Mexican-American child goes to a school that has mostly Mexican-American students, will he or she learn less? Is a school academically better when black and Hispanic youngsters have lots of white classmates? (Since the focus of this book is on academic achievement, we do not discuss the nonacademic benefits of racially and ethnically mixed schools.) The whole effort to measure levels of minority exposure to whites assumes that the answer is unquestionably yes. But if the racial mix in schools really matters educationally, we're in deep trouble.

In much of America, there simply isn't a great deal that can be done to change that mix. Deep demographic and economic forces shape residential decisions, and it is hard to imagine a public policy that would break up the concentration of, say, Hispanics in Los Angeles, or blacks in Detroit. In theory, it is possible to bus millions of students from central cities to suburbs and vice versa each day, although the commute would often be long. But the Supreme Court has limited the circumstances under which judges can order such busing, and a large majority of Americans are strongly opposed to it.

In any case, the strategy of busing-for-better-schools has certainly been tried, although not on the scale that some would have preferred. As part of large-scale desegregation plans in Boston and other cities, children were assigned to schools far from the neighborhoods in which they lived. These children have been studied by an army of social scientists. The result: no scholarly consensus that a school's racial mix has a clear effect on how much children learn.

Indeed, a recent assessment of the huge body of research on the subject concludes that "there is not a single example in the published literature of a comprehensive racial balance plan that has improved black achievement or that has reduced the black-white achievement gap significantly."[18] That judgment confirms an earlier study that the U.S. Department of Education called "the most comprehensive and rigorous analysis to date on the effect of desegregation on black student achievement." Moving to a racially integrated school had no significant effect on the mathematics achievement of black students, it concluded, and raised reading scores by the equivalent of two to six weeks of a school year at most.[19]

Busing plans have generally operated in cities with relatively few white school children, so the minority students who are bused for purposes of integration usually end up in schools that are still substantially nonwhite. Some of these cities—Boston among them—had a white majority in the school population when busing began but saw that majority quickly turned into a rapidly dwindling minority.

Not all black and Hispanic youngsters who attend heavily white schools in racially mixed suburbs and cities do so as a consequence of desegregation plans, of course. They live in residentially integrated neighborhoods or attend magnet schools that are predominantly white. In such settings, minority students typically do better academically, evidence suggests. And yet that does not mean that African-American and Latino pupils clearly learned more as a consequence of attending majority-white schools. The minority students whose families live in integrated communities or who have chosen magnet schools generally have parents who are relatively better educated or financially well off. They may have higher educational aspirations for their children. Those family characteristics may explain their higher levels of achievement.

Would a randomly selected cross section of black and Hispanic students show the same gains if they could be transported to heavily white schools? David Armor and Christine Rossell tried to answer the question by examining the 1992 NAEP reading and math scores of 13- and 17-year-olds and taking parental socioeconomic status into account. They adjusted the scores to reflect different levels of economic and educational advantage. By so doing, they could compare equally disadvantaged students in integrated and racially isolated settings, and were able to see how much difference the racial composition of the school makes.

Racial composition, in itself, makes almost no difference, they found. Whether African-American students attended schools that were 10 percent or 70 percent black, the racial gap remained roughly the same, as Figure 9-5 makes clear. If every school precisely mirrored the demographic profile of the nation's entire student population, the level of black and Hispanic achievement would not change.

For one small group of students, however, the results were different. The tiny fraction of 13-year-old blacks in the NAEP sample who attended schools that were over 80 percent white did dramatically better in reading. In those schools, the black-white gap in performance was cut by about two-thirds. The pattern was similar, though less pronounced, for black 17-year-olds, and for Hispanics in both age groups. It did not, however, apply to math scores. These findings are intriguing but not necessarily generalizable. The number of black and Hispanic students in overwhelmingly white schools was too small to make the results statistically significant, and the difference might have been the result of self-selection or the inadequacy of the measures of socioeconomic status—the crude definitions of who was poor and who was affluent.

Research on fourth- to seventh-grade students in the unusually rich school records of Texas in the mid-1990s by economist Eric Hanushek and two colleagues sheds important light on this issue. After applying extensive controls for other variables, the authors concluded that attending schools with a high black enrollment had a negative effect on achievement for both blacks and whites, but the impact on blacks was about twice as large as that on whites.

Figure 9-5. NAEP Reading Scores of Black and White 13-Year-Olds, Adjusted for Family Socioeconomic Status, by Percent of White Students in the School, 1992

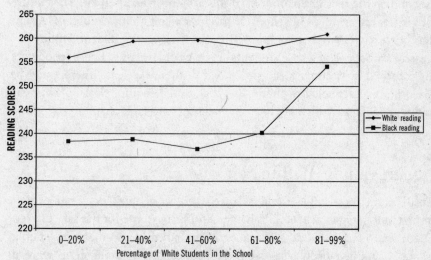

Source: David J. Armor and Christine Rossell, "Desegregation and Resegregation in the Public Schools," in Abigail Thernstrom and Stephan Thernstrom, *Beyond the Color Line: New Perspectives on Race and Ethnicity* (Stanford, Calif.: Hoover Institution Press, 2002), 243.

Furthermore, the negative effect was mainly felt by black students with above-average academic skills—those at the upper end of the black achievement distribution.[20] The lower the proportion of African Americans in their school, the better these gifted students did. The authors interpret this as a "peer effect," a view consistent with the cultural analysis we offered in Chapter 7.

If the findings of this research can be generalized beyond Texas and extended to older children, it would be a reason for creating more voluntary metropolitan school integration programs like the Boston area METCO plan, which buses inner-city black youngsters to predominantly white suburban schools.[21] However, METCO has never been subjected to a systematic evaluation that uses a control group, and we cannot be sure what such an evaluation would reveal. Shaker Heights, Cambridge, and similar suburbs, we have shown, do not have a proud record of African-American academic achievement.

In any event, there is no way to put all African-American and Latino students into schools that are more than 80 percent white. Even if every group was distributed across state and city lines in equal proportions, and we could engineer precise racial balance in every school, there just aren't enough whites in the school-age population to create an 80 percent or more white majority everywhere.

The racial composition of the school may matter, but the academic culture of the school matters more. Creating the right academic culture does not depend on the racial backgrounds of the students who attend it. The culture of greater engagement in school that we described in our chapter on Asians has been re-created, in effect, in KIPP, North Star, Amistad, and other successful schools, all of whose students are black or Hispanic. These schools are not working with a mysterious formula; in theory at least, there could be thousands of schools like them. But that would require clearing away the many roadblocks to change that we will discuss in a later chapter.

"Segregation" Within Schools

Insufficient racial and ethnic balance—the racial mix—does not explain much of the gap in academic achievement. But assume for the sake of argument that racial clustering is academically harmful, and that every public school could be racially balanced by some means. The problem of "segregation" would have been solved. Or would it?

Even within racially integrated schools, whites and Asians can be clustered in certain courses, blacks and Hispanics in others. The racial gap in academic achievement sorts students. That process becomes particularly apparent in the high school years when those who are better prepared sign up for honors and Advanced Placement (AP) courses, while the less academically skilled take easier classes. Integrated schools are not necessarily truly integrated—a problem that is arguably more depressing than that of racially identifiable schools in districts with few white students. The paucity of white kids in Boston schools is the inevitable result of demographic change; the near-absence of black and Hispanic faces in honors courses is an educational travesty that can be fixed by better preparing youngsters in the earlier grades.

Who completes AP courses and takes the exams? In 2001, 65 percent of the test-takers were non-Hispanic whites, just a shade above their share of the student population. Just 4 percent were African-American, though they comprised 17 percent of enrollments. Hispanics were 16 percent of the school population but only 9 percent of those examined. Asians were a mere 4 percent of all students but a striking 14 percent of those completing AP courses.[22] So blacks were at only one-quarter of parity in the AP competition, Hispanics just over half, and Asians had more than triple their expected share.

Is this form of "segregation" a major explanation for the racial gap in academic achievement? AP class-taking patterns look biased against blacks and Hispanics, neutral with respect to whites, and exceedingly partial to Asians. It is tempting to stare at the numbers and think they point to discrimination— to students kept out of high-level courses, which inevitably affects long-run academic success. But the discrimination argument would have to account for the seeming but implausible favoritism toward Asians.

Contemplating this pattern, the president of the school board in prosperous suburban Montgomery County, Maryland, has complained that sorting students into different classes means that "we're in effect running a segregated school system."[23] But the concentration of black and Hispanic students in less demanding classes does not seem mysterious when you recall, for example, that 35 percent of white and 41 percent of Asian eighth-graders score in NAEP's Proficient or Advanced category in mathematics, as compared with just 6 percent of African Americans and 10 percent of Hispanics. Students who don't have moderately high-level skills in the eighth grade lack the basic foundation in math to do AP work two or three years later. Again, it's a problem that needs to be addressed aggressively well before the eighth grade.

Data from large-scale national student surveys conducted by the National Center for Education Statistics reinforce the point. They reveal a clear pattern: Students with comparable academic records and tested skills, regardless of race, take the same-level courses.[24] Moreover, most tracking is self-tracking. Over 80 percent of schools today allow students to choose the level of each course they take, so long as they have had the necessary prerequisites.[25]

Civil rights groups and others often argue that black and Hispanic students rarely take AP classes because their wretched big city schools don't offer them. "California is flunking out when it comes to educating . . . students, denying them intellectually challenging courses designed to prepare them for college and holding them back by squelching their competitive chances of acceptance at colleges and universities," Mark Rosenbaum, the legal director of the ACLU's Southern California office, said at a press conference in the summer of 1999 announcing a lawsuit against the Inglewood Unified School District. The charge was a paucity of AP courses.[26]

Inglewood offered only three AP courses, while ten miles away, in Beverly Hills, there were more than a dozen offerings. But was this a story of unequal opportunity, or were there simply too few Inglewood students academically prepared to complete such courses successfully? The ACLU won its case, but ironically none of the four successful plaintiffs actually went on to enroll in the new AP courses that were provided.[27] The number of AP courses at inner-city high schools is determined to a significant degree by the low level of demand for them. If demand for such courses were higher in inner-city schools, the existing AP classes would be overcrowded, a California research institute study pointed out in 2000. In fact, the classes tend to be smaller than at places like Beverly Hills.[28]

The ACLU wanted Inglewood and other school districts to offer more AP courses. The civil rights organization was right to be angry. But inadequate education in the early grades means that doors are already closed by the time many blacks and Hispanics reach high school. Inevitably, these poorly prepared students don't sign up for advanced courses. Academic "segregation," however, is not the cause of the racial gap in skills and knowledge, but one of its tragic results.

The Slowest Track

There is no good excuse for the magnitude of the racial gap in academic performance. That fundamental assumption informs this entire book. Schools and students can do better. But, inevitably, some youngsters in every racial and ethnic group will be academically less successful than others. Schools classify those with most serious academic, emotional, and behavioral problems as eligible for "special education," a federal entitlement. Students who are so classified receive educational services tailored to address their special needs, at a per pupil cost that is at least double that of regular students.[29]

This is expensive schooling; for some students, it is also "segregated." That is, some of the children entitled to special education services are placed in autonomous classes that tend to be heavily black and Hispanic. Many of those youngsters, it is often said, have been misclassified, and that may be the case. A number of the successful charter schools we visited often ignore the label when it is attached to incoming students. Moreover, more attention to reading skills in the earliest grades might significantly reduce the number of children who later end up classified as learning-disabled. But there is a separate and important question: Do special education classes contribute to the racial gap in learning? Are they part of the explanation for the appalling disparities in skills and knowledge?

That is certainly the view of the Harvard Civil Rights Project, which held a conference in November 2000 on "Minority Issues in Special Education." "To the extent that minority children are misclassified, segregated or inadequately served," its executive summary stated, "special education can contribute to a denial of equality of opportunity, with devastating results . . ."

The Harvard Civil Rights Project referred to "minority" children, but in fact the issue is the disproportionately high number of black children in special education. In 1997, the executive summary of the conference findings noted, black children were "almost three times more likely" than those who were white "to be labeled 'mentally retarded,' " and were classified as emotionally disturbed nearly twice as often.[30]

The key statistical evidence on which the Harvard report relied is summarized in Figure 9-6. The analysis took the white share of the special education population as the baseline, and then calculated whether black, Hispanic, and Asian students were more or less likely to be classified as special education. Although the conference organizers denounced special education programs for having disproportionate numbers of "minorities," Figure 9-6 demonstrates that neither Hispanics nor Asians have more than their share of students classified as disabled. Hispanics were quite strongly underrepresented in the categories "mental retardation" and "emotional disturbance," and Asians were dramatically underrepresented across the board.

Civil rights advocacy groups, ever since the passage of the Education for All Handicapped Children Act in 1975, have been strong supporters of special education. (In 1990 it was renamed the Individuals with Disabilities Education Act.) And its steady and dramatic expansion over a quarter of a century has been welcomed by those especially concerned with the education of dis-

Figure 9-6. The Odds of Minority Students Being Classified as Learning-Disabled, 1997
(Whites = 1.0)

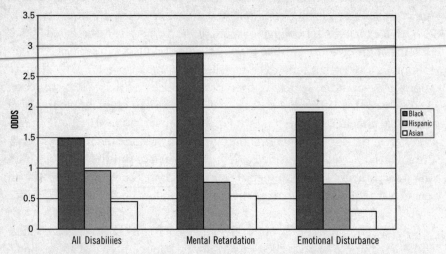

Source: Harvard Civil Rights Project, "Executive Summary: Conference on Minority Issues in Special Education," 1; available at
www.civilrightsproject.harvard.edu and at www.law.harvard.edu/civilrights. The estimate for the emotionally disturbed is from
table 2, "Odds Ratios for the U.S. and by State Across all Disabilities and for Selected Individual Disability Categories," from a
paper by Tom Parrish called "Disparities in the Identification, Funding, and Provision of Special Education."

advantaged students.[31] Nevertheless, the codirectors of the Harvard project,
Professors Gary Orfield and Christopher Edley, Jr., have been strongly critical of special education, a fact that led to the use of their research by opponents of additional federal funding—much to their dismay.[32]

In response, they refashioned a statement less sharply critical, while still
expressing considerable concern. The project's work, they said, had revealed
"serious civil rights problems in a limited number of special education programs." The central problem was the "egregious overrepresentation of
African Americans," and the "widespread underrepresentation of Asian/Pa-
cific Islanders."

Surely, they were not suggesting that Asians were being unfairly denied
access to the program. Moreover, the disparate impact argument applies
equally to Head Start, Title I, and bilingual education; they, too, are "segregated" programs in the sense that they disproportionately serve non-Asian
minority children. The important question is whether these racially identifiable classrooms are helping or hurting the children in them.

With respect to special education, specifically, that is not a question that
civil rights advocates have been willing to answer. They simultaneously object to the disparate impact of the program and seek to expand it.[33] And yet if

the program perpetuates or enlarges—and thus helps explain—the racial gap in academic achievement, its funding should be significantly reduced. We are open to the argument that special education classifications are often not in the best academic interest of black students—particularly when they contribute to racial isolation. But that is not the unequivocal message of the civil rights community.

The Conventional Wisdom

We would prefer to see less "segregation" in schools altogether. Who wouldn't? Racial clustering—in housing, in the workplace, and in schools—is not good for the fabric of American society. But the question posed in this chapter is very specific: Does racial isolation at least partly explain the racial gap in academic achievement? And conversely, would greater integration raise the level of academic achievement among non-Asian minorities?

To begin with, we have argued, minority students are not becoming more racially isolated; white students typically attend schools that are much more racially and ethnically diverse than thirty years ago, and the modest decline in the exposure of black and Hispanic students to whites is solely due to the declining share of white children in the school age population. Moreover, schools are not "segregated." They are racially imbalanced, and that imbalance reflects the fact that members of racial and ethnic groups are not randomly distributed across the nation. Latinos are about 13 percent of the nation's population, but the Los Angeles Unified School District, for instance, is 70 percent Hispanic, 13 percent black, 10 percent white, and 6 percent Asian. The district's schools will remain overwhelmingly "segregated" unless children are "bused" in by airplane. In any case, desegregation programs have historically changed the racial composition of schools without changing the academic profile of the children attending them. Who sits next to whom in a classroom does not determine how much children learn. That is, there is no evidence that a Mexican-American child attending a Los Angeles school learns less than she would in, say, Salt Lake City, all other things being equal. The racial composition of schools does not explain the racial gap in academic achievement. What matters in a school is not the racial mix, but the academic culture, and a culture that nurtures learning can be created in schools like Newark's North Star that are entirely African-American.

Even if all schools could magically become racially balanced—solving the problem of racial and ethnic clustering—different classrooms within those schools would have different demographic profiles. No one should be complacent about the disproportionately high number of non-Asian minority kids in the lowest tracks, or the high number of black children in special education. It is powerful evidence of the problem to which we are calling attention. When students lack the foundation to do the work, they cannot take AP courses; as long as a glaring racial gap in academic achievement remains, such physics classes will be dominated by whites and Asians.[34] Closing that gap, however, will take better schools, and better schools means more good teachers. That is the topic to which we turn next.

Ten: Teacher Quality

We have the wrong people in the classrooms.
Harold O. Levy, former chancellor, New York City Board of Education[1]

If they can't learn, how can they teach?
An angry Latino mother in Cicero, Illinois, after hearing the high rate of failure on
teacher licensing exams[2]

In the spring of 1994, Mark Gerson, in his senior year at Williams College, began to look for a teaching job in the urban districts of New Jersey within commuting distance from his parents' suburban home. He sent letters and résumés to eight districts; no replies. Not a flicker of interest. After a fruitless search for a public school position, he ended up in a Catholic high school in Jersey City.

That not a single public school in Jersey City contacted him is striking and telling. Five years earlier, the Jersey City school district had been taken over by the state, which described the city's schools as in a state of "total educational failure." The schools were engaged in "educational child abuse," Governor Thomas H. Kean had said.[3]

At the time Gerson started sending out letters, the students, 80 percent of whom were black and Hispanic, were still in dire educational straits. Every school door should have been thrown open to him. He was about to graduate from a very competitive college summa cum laude. He wanted to serve the urban poor, and there was a state program that allowed college graduates without education degrees to teach while taking education courses on the side. His later account of the experience he had teaching in a parochial school suggests that he would have been a gift to the system—a teacher of unusually high quality, precisely the sort of person superintendents and principals say they desperately need. His memoir of the year he spent at St. Luke High School certainly conveys an impression of extraordinary teaching talent.[4]

Perhaps no one even deigned to answer Gerson's inquiries because they assumed that anyone with his intellectual credentials was "overqualified" for the job and would never stay more than a year or two. That was an understandable concern, but one might think he would have been interviewed by some school. Given the classroom management skills that seem evident in his memoir (which usually take new teachers a while to acquire), even a year of his services might have made a difference to many students in schools in which there is already a high rate of teacher turnover.

If there is a consensus on anything in the education community, it is on the dire need of urban districts for better teachers. In fact, inadequate funding, racial isolation, and low teacher quality are the three reasons most often cited for the racial gap in academic achievement. The Education Trust publishes valuable research on the failings of our educational system. "Too little attention is paid to a devastating difference between schools serving poor and minority children and those serving other young Americans—a pervasive, almost chilling difference in the quality of their teachers," it has said.[5]

We agree that weak teachers make for weak learning. A comprehensive study of teachers in Tennessee has demonstrated that students with teachers who rank in the top quartile in effectiveness make gains over the school year that are nearly quadruple those of the students with the least effective 25 percent of teachers.[6] Studies in other states have reached similar conclusions.[7]

Better teachers are needed in the urban schools, but who qualifies as "better"? Teachers with more in the way of standard credentials and with more experience, the conventional wisdom runs. Not teachers like Mark Gerson, who lacked training from a school of education. We challenge that view in this chapter. A shortage of teachers who are "qualified" by the criteria that are now in use in every state is not the cause of the weak achievement of so many black and Hispanic pupils. Having a more abundant supply of such teachers won't solve the problem.

How Can We Identify Good Teachers?

The question of who is a good teacher is not easy to answer. In our experience, quality is usually patently obvious when you walk into a classroom, but it's hard to measure reliably. The Tennessee study showed large differences in what students learned, depending on the effectiveness of their teachers. It provided only a circular definition of teacher quality, however. The best teachers were those whose students learned the most over the course of the year, and the worst teachers were those students learned the least. Such circular reasoning gives no guidance to administrators trying to tell a promising applicant for a teaching position from one unlikely to work out.

What, then, should a principal look for in hiring a teacher? The scholarly literature provides some clues to the answer, and we will draw upon it below. But it's important to understand that the currently available evidence conflicts on many points, and debate will continue. One recent study underscored the importance of teacher quality, but found that only 3 *percent* of "the contribution teachers made to student learning was associated with teacher experience, degrees attained, and other readily observable characteristics.[8] Thus, we can be more confident about the irrelevance of the standard prescriptions for identifying good teachers than we can about the measurable traits that the schools should look for.

Minimum Competency Tests

Certainly, there are some rock-bottom demands schools should make of all teachers they hire. For instance, every applicant should have passed a minimum competency test. As of the start of 2003, thirty-nine states and the District of Columbia required applicants for a beginning teacher's license to pass a basic skills test; thirty-three states and the District of Columbia demanded a subject knowledge exam.[9] Although some of the current tests are pitched as low as the eighth- or ninth-grade level, and none of them can be considered highly rigorous, they do serve a purpose. The California Basic Educational Skills Test (CBEST) has asked teachers such questions as: "Amy drinks one-and-a-half cups of milk three times a day. At this rate, how many cups will she drink in one week?" You don't even need elementary computational skills to come up with the precise answer; it's a multiple-choice question, with five choices provided. And yet many applicants for teaching jobs in California have been unable to answer such questions correctly.

Some state teacher certification exams are considerably more rigorous. In Massachusetts, for instance, candidates are asked to write well-organized essays using correct grammar and spelling. Prospective teachers might be asked to respond to a short passage on the question of whether the "federal tax on gasoline should be raised significantly to help pay for public transportation and road improvements." They are also given sample sentences with grammatical errors that they are asked to correct, as well as passages that contain a great deal of scientific information followed by multiple-choice questions.[10]

Nevertheless, most such tests assess only basic knowledge, and a good many teachers standing in front of classrooms have taken no certification (or "licensing") exam. The demand is waived when the need for teachers is urgent, which happens to a disproportionate degree in big-city schools with largely nonwhite enrollments. As we noted in Chapter 8, it's likely that California's class-size-reduction program failed to benefit minority students in large part because so many untrained and academically weak teachers had to be hired.

A recent survey in Illinois found that the proportion of teachers who had failed at least one certification exam was five times as high in Chicago as it was in school districts with high test scores and few minority or low-income students. In the state as a whole, 8 percent of all currently employed teachers had failed at least one test of teacher competence; in five high-minority, high-poverty districts the average was 20 percent. In a dozen Chicago schools, 40 percent of the teaching staff had flunked one or more tests. The prize for incompetence went to a Chicago teacher who failed on twenty-four out of twenty-five tries, including all twelve of the tests in the subject she taught. Nevertheless, she was still teaching. These are teachers from the bottom of the barrel, and they shouldn't be in classrooms—especially classrooms with students who come to school with so few advantages, and are already struggling academically.[11]

The Chicago story is disturbing, and fragments of other evidence suggest the problem is certainly not confined to Illinois. Such failures involve only a small minority of teachers even in the high-poverty districts, however. Replacing them with people who can pass such elementary tests is thus likely to have only a marginal effect on the overall quality of teaching in the schools that most black and Hispanic students attend. If teacher quality explains the racial gap in achievement, the basic problem is not the relatively small proportion of teachers who fail state exams, but the inadequate skills of a large number of those who pass them—a problem that is not likely to be solved within the conventional public school framework, with its single salary schedule based on years of service and often irrelevant academic degrees.[12] But that is a subject to which we will return.

Teaching Experience and Degrees

The ability to pass a minimum competency test is only one possible measure of teacher quality. Experience and educational credentials beyond a bachelor's degree are arguably relevant as well. By these criteria, are black and Hispanic students shortchanged?

The available evidence was collected in the academic year 1993–1994, and offers only a crude contrast between schools in which less than 20 percent of the students are minorities (and which are thus overwhelmingly white) and those with 20 percent or more (which includes districts that are quite racially mixed). That is, it fails to compare districts that are, say, 30 percent minority with those that are 60 percent minority. The findings are nonetheless illuminating. Roughly half of the teachers in central-city schools with minority enrollments over 20 percent had a degree beyond a bachelor's, a figure not much below that for schools with white enrollments of at least 80 percent. With respect to years of experience, the difference was also small. The typical teacher in the higher-minority schools had 14.8 years of experience, not significantly below the national average of 15.2 years.[13]

This evidence—with its crude definitions of "high"- and "low"-minority schools—may conceal subtle and important disparities, but it's not worth pursuing the question further for a simple reason. Graduate degrees and years of experience, the weight of the evidence suggests, do not have a strong impact on student achievement. Students whose teachers have master's degrees do not perform at a higher level than those whose teachers have only a bachelor's. Nor do years of teaching experience seem to matter, with the minor qualification that first- and second-year teachers tend to be less effective. It does take some time to learn classroom-management skills, but after the initial break-in period, experience has little effect.[14]

A recent analysis of California public school students in the 1997–1998 academic year looked at both criteria and found only the most trivial positive effect from having either experienced teachers or those with postgraduate degrees.[15] A study of interstate differences in the NAEP scores of fourth- and eighth-graders between 1990 and 1996 also showed no positive effect at all from teaching experience of more than two years and zero effect for the possession of degrees beyond the bachelor's. Indeed, the authors suggest that the $2 billion a year currently being spent by school districts and individual teachers to obtain master's degrees in education "is arguably one of the least-efficient expenditures in education."[16]

Do They Know Their Subject?

A teacher can be certified in English and end up with a math class. Are black and Hispanic kids far more likely than whites to have instructors teaching "out of field"? The Education Trust's analysis of data from the 1999–2000 Schools and Staffing Survey found that 21 percent of classes in public secondary schools with minority enrollments of 15 percent or less were led by teachers who lacked certification in the subject of the class. In schools in which minorities made up 50 percent or more of the student body, however, the figure was 29 percent.[17]

The difference between 21 percent and 29 percent is significant, but not very dramatic. Even in the most heavily minority secondary schools, seven out of ten classes were conducted by people licensed in the subject they were teaching, as compared with eight out of ten in schools with very few minority pupils.

Unfortunately, this study does not reliably identify which teachers have mastered the "field" in which they are teaching. Middle school math teachers, in our view, should have taken college courses in mathematics, and history teachers should have studied history beyond high school. Elementary school teachers do not teach arithmetic well if they do not understand algebra. But most teachers major in education as undergraduates, and the only courses they have had in mathematics or history were in methods of teaching those subjects taught by professors in the education school or department. They have never been trained by a professional historian or mathematician.

By this much stricter criterion of teacher competence, the amount of out-of-field teaching now going on is undoubtedly much larger than it appears in the Education Trust study, which counts math education courses taught by professors of education as math training. Data showing courses taken in actual math and other arts and sciences departments might reveal sharper racial disparities than this study, with black and Hispanic children far more often stuck with inadequately prepared teachers. No one has yet found the evidence necessary to study that question.

Low Expectations

"Research clearly reveals that students rise to the expectations that are set by their teachers and school," D.C. school superintendent Paul L. Vance remarked in December 2001.[18] Low expectations depress student learning. It's a widespread conviction. "Many black students miss the joy of learning because their teachers do not think them capable of it," journalist Sam Fullwood wrote in September 2000. "Too many educators send signals—sometimes blatant and overt, but more often subtle and unconscious—to black students that they do not belong where learning is taking place," he went on.[19]

"The power of stereotypes may explain the persistent gap between black and white kids on standardized tests even when the black kids come from middle and upper socioeconomic classes," *Newsweek* reporter Sharon Begley concluded in a November 2000 story.[20] Likewise, a 2001 U.S. Department of Education report portrayed black and Hispanic students as provided with "less encouragement by teachers who may harbor doubts about their abilities and thereby contribute to a self-fulfilling prophecy of underachievement."[21] Students who pick up on the "doubts" of their teachers tune out of school.

It's a seductive theory, but does it have any basis in fact? The argument was first advanced more than three decades ago by psychologist Robert Rosenthal and a colleague, who conducted an experiment in an elementary school in San Francisco. Teachers were told at the beginning of the school year that a test had identified some of their new pupils as being "potential academic spurters." In fact, the "potential academic spurters" were randomly selected. But the students identified as having exceptional talent—those whom the teachers treated as special—actually performed significantly better than others over the course of the year, Rosenthal claimed. They lived up to the high expectations their teachers had for them, although in fact those expectations rested on no real evidence of distinctive promise. The teachers' faith had created a "Pygmalion effect," Rosenthal said—an allusion to George Bernard Shaw's play in which the hero convinces a young lady from the London slums that he can teach her to speak upper-class English, and indeed successfully does so.[22] Every student can be a Pygmalion, according to Rosenthal, provided their teachers acquire enough confidence in their potential.

The study actually found a Pygmalion effect only for first- and second-graders; the pattern did not hold for grades 3–6. Furthermore, subsequent research failed to replicate the findings consistently. Nevertheless, the study got enormous publicity; Rosenthal even appeared on the *Today* show, and his findings are still sometimes invoked as if they were well-established scientific truth. The Department of Education's recent reference to "a self-fulfilling prophecy of underachievement" is pure Rosenthal, although the original study made no mention of underperforming minority children specifically. Furthermore, the only experiment that could test the validity of the current theory as it has been applied to the racial gap would be one in which teachers were told that *all* of their minority students were "academic spurters." Would the performance of those students improve dramatically? No such study has been conducted.

The studies that can be cited in support of the theory are methodologically primitive. They ask teachers about their expectations of students, and conclude that teachers who generally expect less from blacks than whites hold negative racial stereotypes. There's an obvious problem: Typically, black students aren't doing very well in school, and their teachers have had discouraging experiences with them. In their expectations, are teachers influenced too heavily by past performance? If they don't see every student—even in, say, seventh grade—as a blank slate, are they biased?

Only one team of investigators has actually done research that adequately measures "racial stereotype bias." Lee Jussim and his collaborators, in a study of Michigan sixth- and seventh-graders, discovered that teachers' perceptions of the performance and ability of their students could be predicted from previous grades and test scores as well as from the students' own estimation of how hard they worked and how good they were in a particular subject.[23] Race turned out to play no role in teacher expectations when these characteristics were held constant.[24]

A more recent survey—a Harris poll conducted in the spring of 2001—further illuminates this issue. It found that 80 percent of teachers in schools that were at least two-thirds minority believed "all children can learn," as compared with 82 percent of those in schools with few minority pupils. There was no significant difference, in other words.[25] On the other hand, the endorsement of the innocuous platitude that "all children can learn" probably means almost nothing. A seemingly self-evident truth, it has become a mantra endlessly repeated in schools of education and by school administrators and teachers.[26]

The answers to a different but related question in the same Harris survey were more revealing. Teachers in high-minority schools registered somewhat greater pessimism when asked if their students would actually "achieve their full academic potential" in that school year. Six out of ten said yes, as compared with three-quarters of those in low-minority schools.[27] Is this evidence of bias? Or was the greater pessimism in the high-minority schools simply based on experience with these students? Either way, the difference between the two groups of teachers is not sufficiently great to lend much support to the low-expectations theory.

The theory assumes a vicious circle in which the negative perceptions of teachers influence the self-image of students, and they work less hard as a consequence. But in the 2001 Harris survey, minority students gave a surprising answer to the question "How good do your teachers expect your work to be?" A third of the white students in this national sample reported their teachers expected "excellent" work.[28] The proportion among black students, though, was significantly higher—42 percent. And it was also a bit higher for Hispanics than for whites—36 percent. The racial differences were not large, but they were the reverse of what the low-expectations theory would predict. Also illuminating were student responses to the question of whether the teacher's expectations were too low, too high, or just right. Only a sixth of all students thought they were too low; more than twice as many students said, "My teacher's expectations for me are higher than what I think I can do."[29]

Additional direct evidence about students' expectations is available in the 2001 Harris poll. When asked whether or not they had "high expectations" for their future, 81 percent of African-American students said yes, as compared with 69 percent of whites and 68 percent of Hispanics."[30] If the black students in the sample had been taught by teachers who didn't have great expectations of their futures, as is commonly assumed, the pessimism of their teachers certainly doesn't seem to have rubbed off on them.

Other questions that shed more light on the subject were asked of a national sample of public school students who were in the eighth grade in 1988. Perhaps the most striking finding from this survey, as Figure 10-1 indicates, was the overall high level of student satisfaction with their teachers, and the absence of sharp racial disparities of any kind. Black and Hispanic students certainly had not been made to feel they did not "belong" in their schools, or that they were getting a second-class education. And they were a bit more likely than whites to say their teachers were "interested in students," that they praised their efforts and "really" listened to them. All of these results contradict those we should expect if the low-expectations theory were right.

Furthermore, the researchers from the National Center for Education Statistics who conducted this study also attempted to measure the "general

Figure 10-1. Racial Differences in the Way 8th-Grade Students Perceived Their Teachers, 1988

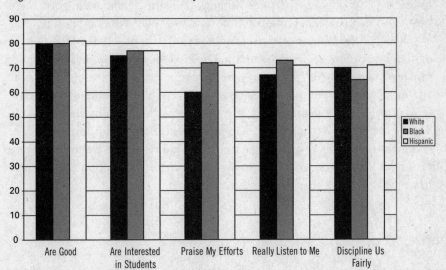

Source: National Center for Education Statistics, *A Profile of the American Eighth Grader,* National Education Longitudinal Study of 1988, NCES 90-458 (Washington, D.C.: U.S. Government Printing Office, 1990), 43.

self-concept" of these students—how much "self-esteem" they had.[31] Low expectations are alleged to take their toll by lowering self-esteem and alienating students from school. However, it turned out that just 19 percent of black students but 40 percent of whites had low self-esteem, and that 49 percent of blacks were in the top group in self-esteem, as compared with just a third of whites.

Evidence from a 1997 Public Agenda poll of 2,100 high school students generally points to the same conclusions.[32] Students were asked ten questions about their teachers. For example, did they try to make lessons fun and interesting? Were they excited about the subject they taught? Did they treat students with respect? Did they explain lessons carefully? Did they care about their students as people? On almost every question, black and Hispanic students gave their teachers ratings that were as high as, or higher than, those that whites offered.[33]

High student ratings for their own teachers suggest that the students themselves do not see low expectations as a problem that lowers the level of their own academic performance. Nevertheless, we do not entirely dismiss the "low expectations" theory—as it applies, particularly, to the culture of entire schools. Students will not learn in settings that expect nothing of them. High expectations are integral to the education provided in the No Excuses schools that we described in Chapters 3 and 4. These schools expect all students to master curricular material and conform to a behavioral code, regardless of their life circumstances. They assume that every student can listen carefully to teachers, work hard, complete homework, learn algebra, read good literature, dress neatly, get to school on time, and treat classmates as teammates.

Changing the climate of expectations is central as well to the testing, standards, and accountability movement. The No Child Left Behind Act, signed into law in January 2002, requires schools to report racial and social gaps in academic achievement and to develop programs to bring all students up to the level of proficiency. Running through the legislation is an implicit message: Teachers need to expect more, standards need to rise, and students will respond to the challenge by trying harder. In Chapter 12, we will have more to say about how much those higher expectations have accomplished in states in which they have been in place for some time.

Black Students, Black Teachers

Minority students need minority teachers who serve as "role models," it is often said. The NAACP's 2001 "Call to Action" included the complaint that

"the racial makeup" of the teaching staff at schools with black kids "very seldom matches that of the student body."[34] In November 2001, the National
Education Association (NEA) convened a national summit to address what it
termed "the critical shortage of ethnically and racially diverse teachers in
America's schools." Referring to discussions of the "teacher supply crisis," the
NEA insisted that "one essential element" was being overlooked: "the need to
recruit more teachers of color."[35]

If minority students truly need minority teachers in order to learn, the
racial gap may be impossible to close. As Figure 10-2 reveals, there are proportionally many more white teachers than white students, and many fewer
black, Hispanic, and Asian teachers than students from those racial and ethnic groups. To obtain a teaching force that perfectly mirrored the racial mix
in the student population, the number of black teachers would need to be
more than doubled, while the number of Hispanic and Asian-American
teachers would have to almost quadruple.

It is this imbalance that has led *Education Week* to call the "shortage" of minority teachers "crippling," as if the significance of the race of teachers were
self-evident.[36] White teachers (presumed to be middle-class) "bring little inter-
cultural experience from their largely suburban and small-town backgrounds," a federally funded regional educational lab has asserted.[37]

Figure 10-2. Race of Public School Teachers, 1993–1994, and of Public School Students, Fall
1999

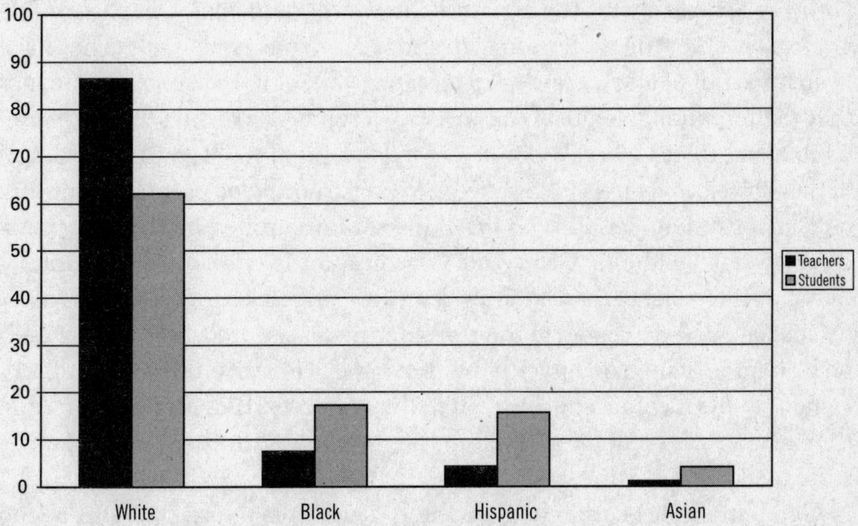

Source: National Center for Education Statistics, *Digest of Education Statistics 2001*, 58, 79.

According to the American Association of Colleges for Teacher Education, "Black, Hispanic, Asian American, and Native American role models for both minority and majority students" are essential.[38] The Applied Research Center claims that "students of color stay in school longer and achieve more when they have teachers who look like themselves." It has compiled statistics showing that in the Boston Public Schools, for example, 13 percent of the students but 61 percent of the teachers are white. In Chicago the disparity is 10 percent of the students versus 49 percent of the teachers, in Denver 24 versus 77, in Los Angeles 11 versus 53, in San Francisco 14 versus 57.[39] These numbers, the center assumes, speak for themselves, and say something very disturbing.

Concern about these disparities has spawned a cottage industry devoted to producing minority teachers. One of the nation's leading prep schools—the Phillips Academy of Andover, Massachusetts—operates an Institute for Recruitment of Teachers that minority college students attend during the summer.[40] In Belmont, Massachusetts, a nonprofit group called Recruiting New Teachers looks for minorities out of the conviction that "our teachers must look like us."[41] The DeWitt Wallace–Reader's Digest Fund's Pathways to Teaching Careers Program is a $50 million initiative aimed at turning noncertified teachers and paraprofessionals (classroom aides) into regular teachers in the hopes of expanding the number of minority instructors. As of 1997 (eight years into the program), roughly 80 percent of Pathway Scholars were black or Hispanic.[42]

The classroom aides and teachers with emergency licenses who become Pathway Scholars (with their "path" to certification completely paid for) do not usually enter the profession with strong academic credentials. They have been hired out of a desperate need for more staff, or have been placed in jobs that require minimal education. In 1997, Jerome Clark, the school superintendent in Prince George's County, Maryland, hired 1,200 new teachers, half of them black, and many uncertified. "We make no apologies for bringing into our school system people who may not be fully certified but are fully dedicated to our children," Clark said.[43] Dedication is certainly important, although white teachers can be "fully dedicated" to black students (just as black teachers may be dedicated to their white students). Moreover, certification is no guarantee of high quality. But neither is racial identity. Clark evidently assumed, as one Georgia educator put it, that minority students need exposure to teachers "who enjoy the same music, worship in the same way, eat the same food, live the same way."[44]

Good intentions certainly drive these sentiments. Nevertheless, the end result is the perpetuation of crude racial stereotypes: Blacks and Hispanics all "live" differently than whites, eat different food, have different musical and other tastes. A black teacher may be solidly middle class, while his or her students come mostly from the housing projects. Never mind, they're all black and therefore must "live the same way."

No one believes that white students need white teachers; the concern about "role models" for black youngsters is obviously a reaction to a history of too many black children seldom seeing black adults in positions of power and prestige—although, in fact, in segregated schools there were many black teachers. America has changed, and yet we don't dismiss the notion that some black and Hispanic kids—especially those in the inner city—could find a teacher with the same racial identity particularly inspiring. These are youngsters who often have no adults in their lives with much connection to school.

In making that argument, however, too many "role model" advocates not only traffic in group stereotypes; they reinforce a dangerous sense of racial isolation—a conviction that whites are foreigners with whom blacks have little in common. With respect to education, specifically, if black students believe America is "white" and doors are closed, they will see little point to working hard to acquire the skills and knowledge they need to do well. And such a strong focus on racial identity may distract from the true priority: teacher quality.

Whatever the weight one wants to assign to the "role model" argument, at the end of the day the most important question surely is: Do black students actually learn more from black teachers? Very few studies of educational achievement have examined the link to the racial identity of teachers, but until very recently, the limited research available yielded a simple conclusion: The race of teachers is irrelevant. For example, Ehrenberg, Goldhaber, and Brewer used the National Education Longitudinal Study sample of eighth-graders who were tested in 1988, and then again two years later, and found that a teacher's race or gender did "not play an important role" in how much students learned over that span of time.[45] The study did show that black, Hispanic, and female tenth-grade teachers tended to rate students of their own race or gender more highly than others on a series of questions about their performance and potential. But these more positive feelings about such students did not make any difference in student test scores.

One new study deviates from this consensus. In a paper completed in August 2001, Thomas S. Dee examined K–3 students in Tennessee in the late 1980s, where a large-scale experiment assigned both students and teachers to classes randomly.[46] He found that African-American students who had black teachers outperformed those who had white teachers in both reading and math. The advantage wasn't huge—from 4 to 5 percentile points—but it was real. Strikingly, Dee also found the same held true for white pupils. Whites learned more when they had white teachers—a gain roughly comparable to that apparent when black pupils had black teachers.

This evidence is from just one state—and not a very typical state at that. Moreover, Dee looked only at results from the earliest grades over a very few years. Much more research is needed to establish the point more generally, particularly in the light of earlier studies that reached contrary conclusions and rested on national data. Whether Dee's findings apply to Hispanic pupils is another unanswered question. But if his hypothesis could be solidly established, it would suggest the need to find many more African-American and Latino teachers—somehow. It would also suggest that the limited number of minority teachers now available should be assigned to minority classrooms—not "wasted" teaching whites or Asians. Heavily white suburban schools should not attempt to recruit a more diverse teaching staff because suburban diversity would come at the expense of draining black and Hispanic teachers from heavily minority urban districts. To have black teachers in Lincoln, Massachusetts, would be to deprive black students in Boston. We would not draw such a drastic conclusion on the basis of such slender evidence.

We are very dubious that research can ever establish the academic necessity of matching the race of teachers and students, and thus we do not believe that a paucity of black and Hispanic teachers can be shown to explain the racial gap in academic achievement. The findings of this Tennessee study are likely anomalous. And, happily, while a good many educators and civil rights activists argue that learning depends on such color-coding, their view is not widely shared by the general public. A 1994 national survey that asked Americans whether they believed that teachers and students should be matched by race or ethnicity found that only 6 percent of whites, 11 percent of Asians, and 18 percent of both black and Latino parents said yes.[47]

A Painful Trade-off

As we suggested above, of course it would be good to have more minority public school teachers, all other things being equal. That's the catch, however. At the moment, minority recruiting carries a price. Simply expanding the number of black and Hispanic teachers will do no good—indeed, it will do real harm—if those teachers have very weak academic skills.

The Applied Research Center quotes an anonymous California minority teacher in a recent publication. "They make it especially hard for teachers of color," the teacher laments. "It costs so much to go to college, and then there is the CBEST and all those other tests . . ."[48] (The CBEST is California's minimum competency test for prospective teachers.)

The young man's statement is painful, yet the pain should come as no surprise, given the racial gap in academic preparation. The supply of black and Hispanic college graduates with strong academic skills is very small, and the supply of those who choose a career teaching in elementary or secondary school is smaller still. Academically strong black college students are choosing law, medicine, and business over teaching.

The size of the pool is apparent from a study conducted by the Educational Testing Service.[49] It reveals striking racial differences in the rates at which prospective teachers pass the Praxis I and Praxis II examinations. The Praxis I is a battery of tests developed by ETS that is used by colleges to screen entry into teacher training programs. For white aspirants to the profession, it is not much of a barrier. In the years 1994–1997, 87 percent of the whites who took it received a passing score (Figure 10-3).[50] But it did screen out a very high proportion of African Americans. Nearly half of the blacks who took it failed and were not allowed to begin preparation to become teachers. (At this stage of the screening process, Hispanics did much better than blacks. No information was provided on Asians taking the exam.) Praxis I measures the same reading, writing, and math skills that NAEP assessments appraise, and the gap on NAEP scores is similarly wide.

Praxis II is a series of tests that is now part of the teacher licensure requirements in a majority of states, and is taken at or near the end of a student's teacher training. Assessing command of subject matter as well as "more generic teaching knowledge and pedagogical skill," it is the teaching profession's equivalent of the bar examinations in the states that use it—although (unlike the bar exam) it can be waived when teachers are in short supply. Despite the fact that greatly disproportionate numbers of black students are screened out by the Praxis I entrance exams and thus are no longer in the pool of potential teachers, the Praxis II tests still reveal glaring racial disparities (Figure 10-4).

The left-hand group of columns in Figure 10-4 indicates differences in failure rates in the years 1994–1997 under the standards set by the various states that used Praxis II in licensing teachers. (ETS does not establish a single passing score; each state does that for itself, and some put the bar higher than others.) In most states, the bar is certainly not very high. The late Albert Shanker, long-time head of the American Federation of Teachers, once called it "ridiculously low," serving only to screen out the "illiterates."[51] Less than a tenth of white aspirants to teaching positions failed the Praxis II in

Figure 10-3. Failure Rates on the Praxis I Exam for Entry into Teacher-Training College Programs, 1994–1997

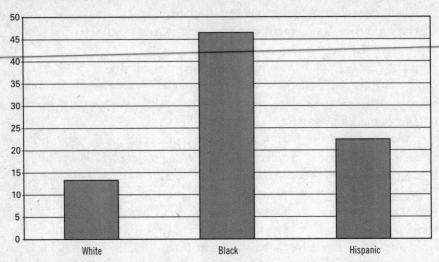

Source: Calculated from data in Educational Testing Service, *The Academic Quality of Prospective Teachers: The Impact of Admissions and Licensure Testing* (Princeton, N.J.: Educational Testing Service, 1999), 18.

1994–1997, but over a third of blacks and Hispanics did so. Again, it is important to remember that the academically stronger non-Asian minority students are now flocking to other professions.

There are good grounds for suspecting that many of the black and Hispanic teaching applicants who failed the Praxis II test nonetheless managed to get hired as teachers. The Illinois stories we referred to earlier in this chapter studiously refrained from providing any information about the race of the teachers who were working without having passed the certification exam, obviously a very touchy subject for a newspaper to examine. But we know that greatly disproportionate numbers of these underqualified teachers were employed by the Chicago Public Schools, where half the teachers are African-American or Hispanic. These facts, plus the disparities shown in Figure 10-4, make it very likely that most of those to whom Chicago gave emergency licenses were black or Latino.

The columns in the center of the figure reveal the effect of lowering standards for entry into the teaching profession, setting the passing score well below the point at which most states place it today. If selection standards for teachers were significantly relaxed, the white failure rate would drop only slightly, since few whites fail as it is. The black and Hispanic failure rate would fall by 10 to 15 points, moderately expanding the supply of minority

Figure 10-4. Failure Rates of Prospective Teachers on Praxis II Exams, Under Current State Standards, a Lower Standard, and a Higher Standard, 1994–1997

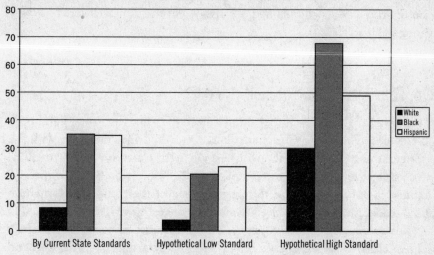

Source: Calculated from data in ETS, *Academic Quality,* 35.

teachers who qualify for teaching licenses. But the downside would be a drop in standards at a time when many knowledgeable observers think that we already have too many teachers with marginal academic qualifications.

On the far right side of Figure 10-4, we see the impact of raising the Praxis II passing score, as some educational reformers have been recommending for a generation. The academic skills of the average new teacher would be significantly stronger, but the failure rate of whites and Hispanics would go up by 15 to 20 points, and the impact on blacks would be even bigger. Today one out of three African Americans who prepare to become teachers fail Praxis II; if the standard were higher, the number would become two out of three.

Thus, we face a stark and painful trade-off—although only in the short run, we hope. Schools can hire more minority teachers, but must lower academic standards to do so. Or they can raise the standards for entering the profession, with fewer black and Hispanic teachers as a result. Albert Shanker of the AFT did not see it as a difficult choice. "Ask the parents in the Asian or Hispanic or African-American communities whether they want role models for their children who can't read and write English at a high school level," he said. "Ask them where their children will be in 20 years if they have not learned these skills because their teachers didn't have them."[52] The successful charter schools we describe in Chapters 3 and 4 hire many white teachers, although the students—with the exception of only one school—are all non-Asian minorities. But when we asked the principals whether the parents complained, we always got the same answer. They just want good teachers.

Do Teacher Test Scores Matter?

It can be argued, however, that standardized tests like the Praxis I and II do not accurately measure a teacher's skills. Or even if they do, those with the strongest test results may not do the best job in the classroom. Unfortunately, we do not have a rich literature exploring the connection between the academic skills of teachers and the performance of their pupils. Information about teacher test scores is rarely available to investigators, who are forced to rely upon such crude measures as courses taken and possession of a master's degree. Thus, we lack adequate evidence on a crucial question: Are scores on such tests as Praxis I and II all that meaningful?

Some useful clues are to be found in the pioneering research of James S. Coleman, published nearly forty years ago, about which we will write more in the next chapter. Coleman, a sociologist at Johns Hopkins University, not only administered achievement tests to hundreds of thousands of schoolchildren. He also gave a brief vocabulary test to their teachers. It turned out that the verbal skills of teachers distinctly influenced the achievement of their pupils, and that the effect was strongest for black students.[53] The Coleman Report, as it came to be known, appeared at a time when the racial integration of schools was the burning issue in education, and this finding received no attention in the public debate that the work provoked. However, a reanalysis of the Coleman data three decades later confirmed the finding that students whose teachers had rich vocabularies performed markedly better than those whose teachers did not.[54]

A study of North Carolina school districts in 1977–1978 also found that teacher scores on a national teacher test developed by the Educational Testing Service were strongly related to the reading and math skills of high school juniors.[55] The authors concluded that improving teacher quality, defined by test performance, would do much more to help at-risk students than reducing class size or any other single reform under discussion. Later studies of teachers in Texas, Alabama, and Tennessee yielded similar conclusions.[56] Several investigators have also found a positive relationship between the selectivity or prestige of the college a teacher attended and the test score gains of their students.[57] Not surprisingly, teachers with the strongest academic skills tend to do more to foster the intellectual development of their students.

Public Schools, Private Schools

High-need children need high-quality teachers. But the argument about inadequate teachers as a major source of the racial gap in achievement, as it is commonly framed, cannot withstand critical scrutiny. There is, to begin with, the problem of who qualifies as an excellent teacher. The standard measures of excellence do not tell us much, and by those standard measures black and Hispanic students are not notably disadvantaged.

Minority kids are about as likely to have teachers with degrees beyond a bachelor's, as well as teachers with considerable classroom experience—characteristics that do not have a clear effect on achievement in any case. Racial differences in exposure to out-of-field teaching do exist, but those differences are quite modest and the available data do not adequately measure true mastery of a teaching field. The standard arguments about the contribution of low teacher expectations to the racial gap in academic performance are not supported by the evidence.

Having more black teachers in our public schools would be desirable—all other things being equal. But all children learn most from those with the most to teach, it appears. Skills and knowledge matter, and an all-out effort to recruit more minority teachers will not close the racial gap in student performance if teacher selection standards are thereby lowered. At the moment, that is the trade-off, largely because successful African-American students have an abundance of other career choices.

Without question, better teachers are needed in urban schools. The unusually rich Texas data to which we referred at the end of the last section confirm the Education Trust's point: African-American students are much less likely than whites to have teachers with high scores on the state teacher exams. The heavier concentration of black teachers in big-city districts is part of the explanation; the average black teacher in Texas scores in the bottom one-sixth of all test-takers. In addition, white teachers in those same schools tend to have relatively low scores. We strongly suspect that there is nothing unusual about Texas. Black children, so heavily concentrated in large urban districts, have weak teachers (both black and white), and their inadequate skills and knowledge reflect that fact.

The Education Trust argues that "disproportionately large numbers of our weakest teachers" have been "systematically assigned" to minority and poor children.[58] But American public school teachers are not conscripts in the Army, who are "assigned" to duty where they are most needed. Teachers choose where they work. They may have to settle for a school they find unattractive when first starting out. With increasing seniority, however, they acquire the power to move to a school of their choice.

Some very gifted teachers will want to work in troubled inner-city schools out of a sense of mission. But many leave. In Chapter 7, we presented evidence showing that a great many teachers in such schools complain of having experienced "verbal abuse" from their students and feel that their students are "unprepared to learn." Jacqueline Goldwyn Kingon took a job teaching in the New York City system in 1999 and two years later told the story of her "year in the trenches." "The system and internal politics wear you down—not with intellectual challenges but with emotional and physical demands out of proportion to the job, creating fear, frustration and a sense of futility," she wrote. "The children, too, import a host of problems into the classroom."[59]

How can New York and other cities keep their best teachers? Much would have to change. North Star's Norman Atkins, readers might recall, wanted to "capture within the public sector the magic of the small, mission-driven private schools [he had] seen in Harlem and the Lower East Side." Those small, mission-driven private schools (many of them church-affiliated) often find highly qualified teachers who want to stay, although in general their salaries are half of those paid in public schools.[60]

They can hire whom they want—young college graduates who have never been near an education school, although they may have gone through an alternative learn-the-basics program like Teach for America. Perhaps more important, their teachers find themselves in an orderly setting in which students are eager to learn and prepared to do so. Figure 10-5 sums up some of the key contrasts, and they could hardly be sharper. We used information from this survey earlier, in Chapter 7 (see Figure 7-8), to show that problems of student absenteeism, disrespect for teachers, and verbal abuse of teachers were far more prevalent in schools with strong concentrations of minority pupils. Here we see that private and parochial schools, many of which have substantial minority enrollments, have very few troubles of this sort. It is in traditional public schools that teachers are surrounded by students who get pregnant, treat them with contempt, and convey a sense of apathy and indifference to learning.

The same survey revealed that private school teachers were also much more likely to feel that they are "recognized for a job well done," that they "take part in making most of the important education decisions" in their schools, that they receive "a great deal of support from parents for the work" they do. And they are far less likely to believe that "routine duties and paper-work interfere" with their teaching and to "sometimes" have the despairing feeling that "it is a waste of time to try to do my best as a teacher."[61] Overall, the level of job satisfaction is much higher in private schools because teachers feel a common sense of mission. We assume that the findings would be much the same for teachers in charter schools, were the data available.

Teachers make large financial sacrifices to work in private schools, and low-income parents strain their budgets to send their children to them. Other parents pray their kids win a lottery that would admit them to a charter school or provide the tuition for a private or parochial education though a voucher. Christina Asquith spent a year teaching in a public school in what she described as a "a heroin-ravaged Puerto Rican neighborhood" in North Philadelphia. "A significant handful of teachers were so incompetent that it was dangerous. They screamed at the students all day and created a climate of fear, abuse, and violence," she recalled.[62] Such teachers lose their jobs in private, parochial, and good charter schools. They do not have tenure.

The racial gap today would be narrower if more black and Hispanic parents were free to choose such schools. The fact that the schools we described in Chapters 3 and 4 have been chosen by the families in itself makes a difference in their atmosphere, we noted. But the teachers, too, have made a choice. Parents have signed up their children for schools with teachers who

Figure 10-5. The Private School Difference: Percent of Public and Private Secondary School Teachers Rating Student Behaviors a "Serious Problem" at Their School, 1993–1994

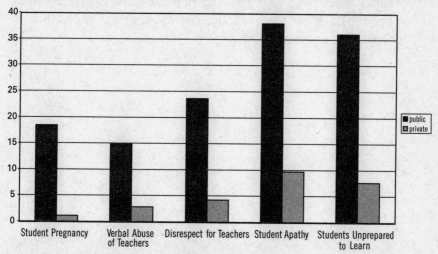

Source: National Center for Education Statistics, *Schools and Staffing in the United States: A Statistical Profile, 1993–94*, NCES 96-124 (Washington, D.C.: U.S. Government Printing Office, 1996), 112–113.

want to be there; no one screams at kids all day. Teacher quality is higher because the criteria for selection do not include irrelevant requirements that exclude idealistic and academically strong applicants.

The issue of school choice is a complicated one and we will return to it. In the next chapter, however, we turn to a discussion of two major federal programs: Title I of the Elementary and Secondary Education Act (ESEA) and Head Start. Both date back to 1965 and aimed to help disadvantaged kids catch up academically. What have they accomplished? The answer is essential to an understanding of what still needs to be done.

The discussion of federal programs in Chapter 11 is followed by a chapter that evaluates state educational reforms—specifically the academic standards and systems of accountability put in place in the 1990s. What do we know about their impact—or likely impact—on the racial gap? The 2001 No Child Left Behind Act has mandated annual testing in grades 3–8, as well as consequences for "low-performing" schools that receive Title I funds. Looking at the difference that state reforms have made should allow us to assess the likely effect of the new federal legislation in the coming years.

Finally, in Chapter 13 we confront a depressing question. Although we have suggested that differences in group culture have a significant impact on school performance, we have also argued that good schools can do much to overcome cultural and other disadvantages. We have described a few terrific schools. Why aren't there many more of them? In fact, why aren't they the norm? And can they become so? Chapter 13 attempts to provide an answer, by examining the formidable obstacles that stand in the way of real educational change. Among the most important of those obstacles are the barriers to changing the rules that govern who teaches and what they're paid. Schools without good teachers are not good schools.

5 Serious Effort, Limited Results

Eleven: Congress Strikes Out

What happened to the children? Do you mean you spent a billion dollars and you don't know whether they can read or not?
Senator Robert F. Kennedy, 1966[1]

After spending $125 billion of Title I money over 25 years, we have virtually nothing to show for it.
Secretary of Education Roderick R. Paige, 2001[2]

Visiting North Star, KIPP, and other wonderful schools is like a trip to a foreign and magical land. Can the extraordinary become the usual—what we expect to see when we walk through the door of the typical urban school? Most of the best schools are the inspiration of young idealists who want to work with the disadvantaged. They are missionaries with a sense of calling. But if good schools depend on such exceptional people, there won't be many of them. And thus the question becomes: If we can't spread magic into every classroom, can we take steps that will make a real difference? For if not, good schools are a hopeless project.

The dream of expanding the educational opportunities open to children disadvantaged by race or poverty is hardly a new one. Indeed, the desire to level the playing field was a major reason for the creation of our public school system in the first place. Education would no longer be reserved to children whose parents were well enough off to pay for it. It would be available to all, regardless of their family's ability to pay, because it was supported by taxes paid by all citizens.

Although that was a great step forward, it hardly erased all of the disadvantages that children brought with them to school. Many subsequent educational innovations were prompted by the same democratic concern—to make schools places to promote the upward social mobility of youths who were not born to privilege.

In the turbulent 1960s, this traditional impulse took a new form. Until then, elementary and secondary education was the responsibility of local communities and, to a limited extent, state governments. But during President Lyndon B. Johnson's War on Poverty, the federal government stepped in. Its two most important programs were Title I of the Elementary and Secondary Education Act, which provided federal funds for compensatory education in high-poverty schools, and Head Start. Although the focus of both was on overcoming economic deprivation, the connection between race and poverty was so strong that these can be considered efforts to overcome racial gaps in educational opportunity.

A "Passport" out of Poverty

We start the story in 1965, when the federal government first became a major educational player. That was the year in which the Elementary and Secondary Education Act (ESEA) was passed. Title I, which provided extra resources to high-poverty schools, was its most important provision.

ESEA was integral to President Lyndon B. Johnson's War on Poverty. "Today, we reach out to five and a half million children held behind their more fortunate schoolmates by the dragging anchor of poverty," the president said in announcing the legislation.[3] The act would provide the one sure "passport" to a better life for children in poverty—their means of escape.[4]

In order to "reach out" to "educationally deprived children," Congress appropriated a billion dollars (a staggering sum at the time), 80 percent of which went to Title I. The money was distributed on the basis of need—as determined by a complicated formula involving both federal and state calculations. But, since that formula gave a slice of the federal pie to 94 percent of the nation's school districts, it was a political gift to almost every member of the House of Representatives. And indeed, that ongoing desire to spread the money so broadly arguably undermined the program's effectiveness.

Although passed at the crest of the civil rights revolution, ESEA was not a civil rights measure per se. But it disproportionately affected black children, half of whom lived in poverty in 1965. In subsequent decades, the Hispanic population exploded, and by now, six out of ten students eligible for Title I assistance are either African American or Latino.[5] Has the money been well spent? That is, have the academic skills of the targeted children improved as a consequence of federal aid—the only true measure of effectiveness? Certainly, compared to 1965, there are far fewer black families living in poverty. And scores on NAEP did go up in the 1970s and much of the 1980s. But there is no convincing evidence that either change can be traced to the federal antipoverty program; the children exposed to Title I programs have shown no distinctive progress in school, numerous studies indicate.

ESEA did more than augment school budgets. It spurred racial integration. Under the 1964 Civil Rights Act, states that engaged in discriminatory practices were prohibited from receiving federal funds. The federal government, however, did not provide substantial aid for state and local education until the passage of the 1965 act. The money became a big stick, finally beginning the process of serious desegregation in the Deep South. The region could no longer afford to maintain Jim Crow schools. As a consequence, more than a decade after the Supreme Court's decision in *Brown v. Board of Education*, black and white children began to attend the same schools.[6]

ESEA was an important change, but less than its framers had hoped for. Neither the dollars themselves, nor the desegregation forced upon the South by the availability of federal funds, leveled the playing field. In retrospect, that's not too surprising. States and local school districts could use their new money as they chose, within only very loose guidelines. Congress unwisely assumed they would make wise educational choices.

But Can They Read?

The federal government had never run schools, and it was not about to begin doing so. But for the first time Congress did express an interest in knowing whether its money for an ambitious public project had been well spent.[7] Title I, in its final form, contained a provision mandating an evaluation of the program—a last-minute addition demanded by Senator Robert F. Kennedy. Senator Kennedy insisted on evidence of actual "educational achievement"—not because he was concerned about taxpayers' dollars per se but because he worried about impoverished children. "What I want to make sure of is not just that the money is not wasted, because you can find more money," he said, "but the fact that the lives of these children are not wasted."[8]

Prior to the passage of the final bill, Kennedy turned to Francis Keppel, U.S. commissioner of education, and said, "Look, I want to change this bill because it doesn't have any way of measuring those damn educators like you, Frank, and we really ought to have some evaluation in there. . . ."[9] Kennedy got the change he demanded, but in fact, the provision mandating Title I evaluations was vague and innocuous. The act required only that local or state educational agencies receiving federal funds file a "report" on their programs each year.

These documents were dutifully submitted, but they contained no hard evidence of the "educational achievement" that Kennedy had wanted in order to empower the parents of low-income children who "really don't have a lobby speaking for them."[10] Most of the reports, as one scholar describes them, were essentially "travel brochures, with extensive anecdotes and little objective data to support claims of 'success.'" They contained photographs and testimony promoting the local districts that produced them, but nothing parents could use to force educational change. Moreover, no one in the Office of Education was even assigned the task of reading them, much less of analyzing them to judge which projects had actually achieved something. The reports piled up unread in cartons, until they had to be warehoused to make room for the next year's crop. "The whole thing is done for appearances," said one education official. They were never read, said another, because education officials knew that they were "garbage."[11]

The absence of anything resembling objective evidence of educational achievement allowed extravagant claims to be made about the success of Title I without fear of contradiction. One state claimed ecstatically that ESEA was "bringing about an educational revolution." The Office of Education itself waxed eloquent about "the creative energies" released by the legislation, and the "new approaches" that could "break through the apathy and intellectual inertia which often surround the child from poverty areas."[12]

At a Senate hearing following the first annual Office of Education report on ESEA, Senator Kennedy gave President Johnson's new commissioner of education, Harold Howe II, a hard time. Having been told by constituents from Harlem and other low-income neighborhoods that they had seen no "educational revolution" in their children's schools, Kennedy asked Howe, "What have you accomplished with the billion dollars you got for elementary and secondary education last year?" Howe responded by listing the number of books that had been purchased with federal funds, the amount of money expended on teachers, equipment, and materials. Books were fine, but Kennedy wanted to know whether the children could actually read them.

Title I was just a year old, Howe replied. "It is just like planting a tree; you don't plant it one day and then pull it up every week and look at the roots to see if it's growing."[13] Kennedy did not bother to make the obvious rejoinder. You don't figure out whether a tree is growing by tearing it out of the ground to examine its roots; you simply measure its height. What Kennedy wanted, and could not obtain from Howe, were similar measurements demonstrating that Title I children were learning to read better than they had before.

The Coleman Report

Title I reports were public relations spin. But another evaluation of schooling for disadvantaged children was in the works, and this one would contain much data—although not of the sort that was welcome in either education or government circles. In the summer of 1966, James S. Coleman released the results of the massive survey of nearly 600,000 schoolchildren and 60,000 teachers to which we referred earlier. The Coleman Report was prompted by an obscure provision of the Civil Rights Act of 1964 that directed the U.S. Office of Education to measure "the lack of availability of equal educational opportunity for individuals by reason of race, color, religion, or national origin" in the nation's public schools.[14]

Coleman's boldest innovation was to break from the traditional approach of educational researchers, who had always focused their attention on "inputs" into the educational system—school funding, the quality of the facilities, average class size, the educational degrees and experience of teachers, and so forth. Coleman gathered lots of data on such inputs, but he was also determined to measure "outputs"—the level of knowledge students could demonstrate on standardized tests in major subjects. He expected to find "striking" differences in the quality of the schools that black and white children generally attended, which in turn would result in marked differences in academic performance.[15] Black kids in overcrowded, dilapidated schools with only marginally qualified teachers, he assumed, had less opportunity to learn than white kids attending more affluent suburban schools, and that inequality would mean lower test scores for African-American children.

That assumption, it turned out, was not supported by the data Coleman gathered. His massive report demonstrated, first of all, that school "inputs" were surprisingly similar across the nation. In 1965, black and white children generally went to separate schools, but the resources available were pretty equal. Even more astonishing, where "inputs" differed, those differences didn't bear much relation to "outputs"—pupil performance. Students with similar backgrounds had similar test scores, whether they came from a "good" or a "bad" school.

In other words, it was a student's family—parental education, occupation, income, and race—that made the real difference. Compared to these huge influences, none of the school-related variables counted for very much. Asked for a brief summary of Coleman's findings, a Harvard sociologist said: "It's all family."[16]

These results were acutely embarrassing to the Office of Education, the federal agency that sponsored the research.[17] Its job was to make schools bet-

ter, but Coleman's work suggested that schools didn't make much of a difference. If it was "all family," then surely a few hundred bucks a year of ESEA
money for each low-income pupil was not likely to produce notable educational gains.

Coleman, of course, had not established this proposition as an iron law of
sociology, true for all times and places. At most, his findings suggested that
spending more money per pupil, reducing class size, obtaining more teachers
with master's degrees and the like were not likely to improve student test
scores significantly in public schools as they were constituted in 1965, when
the data were collected. But that was a point too subtle to convey to the press
and to Congress, and the Office of Education dealt with the problem by producing a summary of the Coleman report that ignored its most important and
most unsettling results. It then released the full report in circumstances designed to generate a minimum of press coverage—which is what it got.[18]

Nevertheless, word about Coleman's massive study did get around, even
though the volume itself was almost impossible to read for anyone without
graduate training in the social sciences. The Harvard statistician Frederick
Mosteller and Daniel Patrick Moynihan summed up the revolution Coleman
had wrought in a 1972 collection of essays reanalyzing the data. "Henceforth," Mosteller and Moynihan said, "no study of the quality of education or
the equality of educational opportunities can hope to be taken seriously unless it deals with educational achievement . . . as the principal measure of educational quality."[19] In other words, educational innovations justified as
measures to expand opportunity would have to provide an answer to Senator
Kennedy's probing question: Did the beneficiaries of the program actually
learn to read better?

Hard Looks at ESEA

If schools had more money to spend on low-income children, their test scores
would go up, the framers of Title I assumed. But the Coleman Report suggested otherwise. Another federally sponsored statistical study released a
year later raised similar doubts. In its 1967 report, *Racial Isolation in the Public Schools*, the U.S. Commission on Civil Rights provided a lengthy appraisal
of the academic performance of black children enrolled in compensatory education programs—programs for the disadvantaged—in a wide range of
cities, and offered a scathing verdict. There was no evidence that children
were actually learning more as a result of these compensatory efforts.[20]

These concerns led Congress to amend ESEA in 1967, requiring evaluations of the program that had some intellectual weight. The results of the first serious study of the Title I program, the two-volume TEMPO report issued in 1968, were devastating. Even though this study focused on a sample of school districts that were thought to have been unusually successful, the results revealed that "none of the programs appear to have raised significantly the achievement of participating pupils, as a group, within the period evaluated." If anything, average achievement in the Title I schools sampled was *declining* slightly. None of these "successful" districts showed statistically significant achievement gains attributable to Title I funds.[21]

The researchers responsible for the TEMPO study had found their task exceedingly difficult and insisted no definitive conclusions could be drawn from their work. The biggest problem was that districts had used Title I funds in such a variety of ways that "in practice there seemed to be no real Title I program to evaluate."[22] Instead, there were thousands of different programs in the fifty states, and the districts provided no precise information on the nature of their intervention or on student achievement. Nevertheless, the bottom line was that none of the programs identified as successful was generating measurable gains in student achievement.

Because the TEMPO study was open to criticism on technical grounds and yielded extremely disturbing, unwelcome results, the Office of Education conducted other evaluations—many others, as it turned out. The main result of the initial disappointing evaluations, one scholar observed in 1975, was merely "the spawning of more evaluations." By then, some $52 million had been spent on assessments of program effects, with few positive results.[23] Education officials seem to have thought that they could find good news *somewhere,* if only they looked for it long enough.

Writing in 1982, after several more years had passed, Carl Kaestle and Marshall Smith noted that more recent studies had yielded more cheering results—slightly more cheering. But "at best," they said, the results were "only relatively promising."[24] Nothing that has been uncovered in subsequent decades compels a more positive conclusion.

Nevertheless, funding for the program continued to grow substantially. Neither presidents nor members of Congress were eager to take on the politically powerful education establishment. No evidence suggested that Title I had narrowed the achievement gap between poor and affluent children, but that was not news politicians were eager to deliver. Voters who learned the disconcerting facts might even wonder about the judgment of those responsible for spending taxpayers' money in such large amounts when the results were so meager.

It was thus a rare departure from the norm when President Richard Nixon boldly set forth some unwelcome truths in his March 1970 Message on Education Reform. Warning of the tendency to "let wishes color our judgment about the educational effectiveness of many special compensatory programs," he noted the "growing evidence that most of them are not yet measurably improving the success of poor children in school."[25] But when Nixon tried to push cuts in the education budget through Congress, he met with overwhelming resistance and was eventually forced to sign what *The New York Times* called "the most expensive education legislation ever passed by Congress."[26]

By fiscal year 2001, the $1 billion program had become a $10 billion program. Adjusting for inflation, expenditures were approximately double what they had been at the outset. Starting in 1988, amendments to the legislation attempted to ensure that students were actually learning and required more accountability. Little actually changed. Schools whose pupils showed no progress were henceforth designated as needing "program improvement." That meant they were required to develop plans that promised future progress. But funds were never withheld if the progress failed to materialize—which usually proved to be the case.

In January 2001—in the waning days of the Clinton administration—the Department of Education quietly issued a report that assessed "progress and challenges" in the Title I program since 1994. *High Standards for All Students*, however, received little press coverage, perhaps because it offered more bad news. It found a few tiny shreds of encouraging evidence that the achievement gap between students in high-poverty and low-poverty schools had narrowed a bit over the preceding few years in six of nine states that had recently conducted their own assessments. But the gap had widened a bit in the other three.

Furthermore, the report noted, tests devised by states tended to be less demanding than those used by the National Assessment of Educational Progress, and the NAEP results did not provide any indication of general progress across the nation. Indeed, the NAEP findings suggested that the national gap between poor and affluent children had widened quite substantially. For example, the reading achievement gap among nine-year-olds had grown from 27 points in 1988 to 40 points in 1999; in math the gap had jumped from 20 points in 1986 to 29 points in 1999. Both of these represented increases of roughly 50 percent.[27] This unfortunate trend, of course, mirrored the trend in the racial gap specifically. Thirty-five years of Title I had failed to put education on the right track.

The latest evidence thus suggests precisely what the first evaluations of Title I indicated more than three decades ago: Money must be well spent.

Just giving another billion or $10 billion to the schools will not, in itself, improve the reading and math skills of their most disadvantaged students. Welcome as it is, extra money is not the secret to good schools, as we have already seen.

The Sad Story of Head Start

The War on Poverty generated another federal educational program aimed at disadvantaged children: Head Start. Launched in 1965, it sought to provide a "head start" to preschoolers growing up in impoverished households. The program would not only "rescue" children from poverty; it would "put them on an even footing with their classmates as they enter school," President Johnson declared.[28]

Since 1965, some 20 million children have been through a Head Start program at a cost to the public of $60 billion. Currently, nearly a million children are enrolled, with expenditures averaging $6,600 a year per child. At the outset, Head Start drew mostly black children, but the mix changed over time. In 1980, only 42 percent of the participants were African-American; on the other hand, a third of all black children in the age group were in Head Start, as compared with just 7 percent of white children. Today, a third of Head Start recipients are black, and another 30 percent are Hispanic.[29] Had the program put these non-Asian minority children on an "even footing with their classmates," as envisioned, the racial gap in skills and knowledge would have disappeared by kindergarten or first grade. In fact, as we have seen, it didn't. And it looks like Head Start has had no lasting impact on the academic performance of the minority children it has served.

The first efforts at evaluating Head Start were extraordinarily encouraging. A few preliminary small-scale studies suggested, as we believe, that IQ is strongly influenced by environment. Even six to eight weeks of a Head Start summer session seemed to produce IQ gains that averaged ten points. Two other studies found that Head Start had completely eliminated the racial gap in IQ scores.[30] Sargent Shriver, director of the Office of Economic Opportunity, could thus point to scientific evidence when he testified before the House of Representatives that the federal program could raise the IQs of poor children by an average of 8 to 10 points.

Shriver's optimism was justified by the information he had on hand. Regrettably, though, better studies soon yielded a very different impression. Needless to say, that different impression with respect to one federal program does not speak to the larger question of the link between environment

and IQ. On the question of Head Start specifically, however, Shriver was relying upon a few flawed pilot investigations of individual programs. These
were studies in which the last observation of the children was made at the
end of their participation, before they had entered regular public school. The
studies raised two questions: Were these programs representative of Head
Start in general? And did the gains observed at the end of the program hold
up over time, or were they transitory?

In 1969, the Westinghouse Learning Corporation released the first comprehensive national study of the effects of Head Start, based on a large, representative sample of students exposed to the program, with a matched
control group of non–Head Start students living in the same neighborhoods
and attending the same schools. The results were dismaying. The study revealed that the very impressive cognitive gains reported by earlier investigators were inflated. Even more devastating, the study found that students who
had made gains did not maintain them through the early grades of regular
school. The apparent benefits faded away with the passage of time. On the
average, Head Start alumni performed no better than students in a control
group from similar backgrounds who had never been in the program. Looking at their schoolwork in the third grade, you couldn't tell who had gone
through Head Start and who had not.

The dismal results were not altogether surprising. The originators of Head
Start wanted to begin with a pilot program for 2,500 students, but President
Johnson insisted on a massive effort that would reach 500,000 children in the
first summer. Not enough trained teachers could be found, and thus many
Head Start staffers were parents or other neighborhood residents with no
teaching experience and often with no college degree. Head Start became an
important jobs program for the parents of the pupils; over a third of the staff,
according to one study, were parents of current or former participants.[31]

The Office of Economic Opportunity was so dismayed by the Westinghouse findings that it contemplated abolishing Head Start. But, as was the
case with Title I, mere evidence that a costly, much-ballyhooed educational
program was not improving the cognitive skills of the students was not sufficient to put an end to it. President Richard Nixon was disturbed at the bad
news, but concluded that Head Start should be expanded. "Preliminary evaluations of this program," he said, "indicate that Head Start must begin earlier
in life, and last longer, to achieve lasting benefits."[32]

Put on the defensive by the Westinghouse study, supporters of the program denied that the study measured success by the right criteria. Imparting
measurable academic skills to preschoolers was not the rationale for the program, they argued, conveniently forgetting the initial claims that Head Start

would level the academic playing field. The aim, they now said, was to promote the "social and emotional growth" of disadvantaged children—to nurture "the whole child." Skills and knowledge that could be tested were not particularly important. Indeed, they were not "developmentally appropriate." In other words, preschoolers were too young to learn their numbers, letters, and other cognitive skills.[33]

By 1987, not even Yale psychologist Edward F. Zigler, a cofounder of Head Start, was willing to defend the general idea of preschooling as providing an academic lift. Advocates of preschool education, he said, were peddling an illusion: that early intervention "would reduce school failure, lower drop-out rates, increase test scores, and produce a generation of more competent high school graduates." In fact, "preschool education [would] achieve none of these results." Zigler didn't see these programs as a "waste of time and money"; he simply urged policy-makers to lower their expectations.[34]

It was undoubtedly wise advice, but politicians don't generally promote programs with a keep-expectations-down message. Moreover, many members of Congress who voted to spend billions on Head Start genuinely believed that the funds would significantly improve the academic performance of black, Hispanic, and other disadvantaged children. They turned a blind eye to the evidence that the returns were, at best, meager. Head Start, like Title I, was a politically appealing, feel-good program. Everyone could agree that poverty was hard on blameless children, so any federal effort purporting to help them was difficult to attack without seeming mean-spirited.

The Latest Research

Having admitted in 1987 that Head Start had not produced the desired academic results in young children, Zigler was nevertheless still calling Head Start "America's Most Successful Educational Experiment" five years later. As its cofounder, he was unwilling to abandon his creation.[35] But recent scholarly research—although generally ignored in the media—has raised further doubts about the program's efficacy, considerably advancing our understanding of its impact.

A 1995 study by economists Janet Currie and Duncan Thomas, for instance, compared children who had attended Head Start with their siblings who had not, thus obtaining a control group that was better than that employed in the 1969 Westinghouse study.[36] Currie and Thomas discovered modest cognitive benefits for whites exposed to the program, though their measures were tests taken not long after the children had left Head Start and could not address the question of whether the gains faded away in a few years. At the age of ten, whites who had gone through Head Start scored 5 percentile points higher on standardized tests than their siblings, not insignificant, but nothing to celebrate. Perhaps more significant, they were 47 percent less likely to be forced to repeat a grade in the early school years.

Head Start children who were African-American, though, showed no educational benefits at all. Their test scores were no better, and they were just as likely to be held back a grade in school as black children from similar socioeconomic backgrounds who did not participate in the program. Only one discernible gain was found for black children: those in Head Start were more likely to have been immunized against measles. The health care benefits of the program, though, came at a very steep price. The annual cost of Head Start, the authors note, is more than seven times the average cost of providing outpatient services to a child in a family on welfare covered by Medicaid.

In a subsequent paper, Currie and Thomas took another look at the impact of Head Start on African-American children. Those who had been in Head Start experienced no sustained gains, they concluded, because they went on to inferior public schools.[37] Perhaps. But Head Start veterans were attending the same elementary schools as their siblings, presumably. Leaving aside the question of whether the schools these students attended were uniformly terrible, and by what criteria, shouldn't the greater skills they acquired in the preschool program have prepared them better? Or were the schools really so damaging as to cancel out all early gains? If so, then the rationale for Head Start is out the window.

A 2000 study of another data set by Eliana Garces, Thomas, and Currie yields somewhat better news about the impact of Head Start upon whites, but the results for African-Americans are nearly as disappointing as before.[38] Earlier work had examined the program's impact on the academic success of children in elementary school. This study, however, examined adults (under 30) in 1995, and sought to determine whether those who been in a Head Start program enjoyed greater "economic and social success" than those of similar socioeconomic background who had not. It found that whites who had gone through Head Start were 20 percentage points more likely to have graduated from high school, and 28 points more likely to have attended college. Those findings suggest that Professor Zigler in 1987 was too pessimistic about the long-term educational payoff of preschool education—with respect to whites.

Unfortunately, Zigler's pessimism was justified when it came to blacks. Head Start increased neither high school graduation nor college attendance rates.[39] Black children who had been in Head Start were, however, 12 percent less likely to have been charged with a criminal offense later in life. That was the only good news. The 12-percentage-point difference between the Head Start graduates and others, however, could have been due to selection bias; the mothers who chose to enroll their children in the program and stick with it may have been particularly attentive parents.[40]

Head Start thus seems to have some educational benefits for white children. But the evidence of this study points to the same conclusion as many others: It does not seem to have improved the educational achievement of African-American children in any substantial and lasting way.

Less is known about the long-term effects of Head Start participation by Hispanic children. The studies discussed above provide no details on them, because there were too few Latino pupils in the samples. Another study by Janet Currie and Duncan Thomas, "Does Head Start Help Hispanic Children?" is the only one to look at the question, and the positive answer it provides is based only on short-term measures. The authors find that Latino Head Start participants scored better on three standardized tests than their peers who had never been exposed to the program.[41] But all of these tests were given at a very young age, and thus it is impossible to know whether the gains faded away as the child progressed through school, as they did with African Americans. The study contained one measure of more long-term effects: grade retention. And on that score, the results of Head Start participation seem strongly positive. But the average child in the sample was only about nine when the data were collected.[42]

Little Accomplished

The two largest and most expensive federal programs that serve a largely minority constituency appear to have accomplished very little for their intended beneficiaries. Possibly a reformed Head Start could do more to overcome the handicaps that many minority and poor children have when they start kindergarten or first grade. A better-trained teaching staff that makes cognitive development an important goal, in addition to "social and emotional growth," might produce different results. The concept of Head Start remains attractive, but whether it can be translated into programs that are truly effective remains uncertain.

Title I, by contrast, channeled substantial amounts of federal money into almost 15,000 separate school districts, on the assumption that local school authorities and teachers knew what to do to improve the performance of disadvantaged children. Only a lack of resources stopped them from taking the necessary steps, they believed. Even in the very early years of the program,

Senator Robert Kennedy wanted schools to be held accountable for the results of their efforts, but no mechanism was created to ensure that the beneficiaries of Title I actually learned more. Funds were withheld from southern school districts that were resisting the mandate to achieve racial integration, and compliance followed. But no school district was ever denied a penny when it was discovered that a high proportion of its black fourth-graders had not yet learned to read. The result has been, as the current secretary of education, Rod Paige, has put it, an expenditure of $125 billion with "virtually nothing to show for it."

The No Child Left Behind Act, the 2001 revision of ESEA, fundamentally reformed Title I. It is obviously too soon to reach any conclusions about the effectiveness of those legislative changes. But some valuable clues are available in the record of educational reform in a few states that served as models for No Child Left Behind, and these will be explored in Chapter 12.

Twelve: Raising the Bar

I have parents coming in and telling me, "Oh, my God. At dinner, my kids were talking about parts of speech! We never heard that before. And to see people get excited about adjectives and adverbs—and to hear kids saying to me, "Can we read more?"—that's really something.
Sharon Morell, principal, Severna Park Middle School,
Anne Arundel County, Maryland[1]

With all due respect, the prevailing attitude among too many politicians and policy-makers is something right out of the movie "Field of Dreams": "If we set the high standards, the students will achieve." It is folly—no, it is fraudulent. . . .
Bob Chase, president, National Education Association[2]

Title I has been altered by the No Child Left Behind Act, the 2001 revision of the omnibus Elementary and Secondary Education Act. Head Start is also undergoing reform as we write. The returns from these long-established programs, we have argued, have been exceedingly disappointing, but neither the federal government nor the states have abandoned their commitment to educational programs aimed at helping disadvantaged children, a great many of whom are African American and Hispanic. This time, however, the focus is on educational outcomes. Will these newer efforts have a significant impact on the academic achievement of these non-Asian minority students? If the current drive for educational reform does not improve black and Hispanic test scores, it will have failed.

The War on Poverty aimed to help children from low-income families. Improving schools in general was not its point. But the 1970s brought a loss of confidence in the overall quality of America's public schools. A plethora of negative reports on the state of education culminated in *A Nation at Risk* in 1983. Prepared by the National Commission on Excellence in Education at the request of the U.S. Secretary of Education, the report concluded that "the educational foundations of our society [were] presently being eroded by a rising tide of mediocrity that threatens our future as a Nation and a people."[3]

The result was an enormous amount of activity at the state level, particularly in the South, where teachers' salaries went up, class size was cut, and tougher high school graduation requirements were introduced. A consensus developed among education reformers: Students must learn more and states must set higher academic standards. The existing standards in many states were laughably low, and many had none at all. Education was becoming a national issue, and in his 1990 State of the Union address, the first President George Bush announced specific education goals to be met in the year 2000—just a decade hence. Within ten years, he pledged, our students would be "first in the world in science and mathematics achievement"; all would leave grades 4, 8, and 12 "having demonstrated competency in challenging subject matter. . . ."[4]

It was a dream; it didn't happen. Among the listed goals was a significant increase in "the academic performance of all students . . . in every quartile, with the distribution of minority students in each quartile . . . more closely reflect[ing] the student population as a whole."[5] The top quarter of African-American students, in other words, should perform about as well as the top quarter of white or Asian students. Although the scores of black students on the National Assessment of Educational Progress tests did rise more rapidly than those of whites in the 1970s and 1980s, as we've seen, that progress was not sustained in subsequent years.

Nor was there any hope that American students were on their way to becoming "first in the world" in science and math. A 1999 test of the math and science skills of eighth-graders around the globe put American students well behind students in Singapore, Taiwan, Russia, Canada, Finland, Hungary, the Netherlands, and Australia. Only countries such as Iran, Jordan, and Chile did worse. Although Secretary of Education Richard Riley tried to put the best possible face on the news, his reaction was hardly reassuring. "American children continue to learn," Riley said, "but their peers in other countries are learning at a higher rate."[6]

Standards and Accountability

Those other countries in which children "are learning at a higher rate" generally have a national curriculum. We do not, and probably never will. Local control over education is a cherished tradition. As journalist James Traub points out in a *New York Times Magazine* article on testing, "the most straightforward solution to poor academic achievement might well have been the same kind of national curriculum that seems to work well elsewhere in the world. . . ." But early on, it became plain "that our own answer would be neither national nor curricular."[7] It was clear, however, that 15,000 school districts, each acting alone, could not make America "first in the world" academically. If the power of the federal government was limited, states would have to drive reform.

By now, in part to address the yawning racial gap in academic achievement, forty-nine states (Iowa is the exception) have some semblance of statewide standards in the core subjects of language arts and math, and all fifty test their students.[8] More than half have school accountability systems, rating the performance of all of their schools or identifying those that are low-performing, and an increasing number are demanding a passing score on tests as a condition of grade promotion and high school graduation. Some of these exams are ridiculously easy; others, like those in Massachusetts, set challenging expectations at each grade level in which students are assessed. All are works in progress, with the standards and systems of accountability still being refined.

The theory behind the unprecedented commitment to standards and accountability is quite simple. Most students will learn less than they should unless they and their teachers understand precisely what is expected, and tests are integral to measuring academic progress. In addition, those tests must have consequences. Raising the bar—insisting that students demonstrate a certain level of proficiency—will be meaningless unless failing to clear it makes a difference. Without consequences, neither the district administrators, nor the schools, nor the students themselves will be motivated to do better.[9]

All three elements of this package of reforms—standards, testing, and accountability—are fraught with complexity. Academic standards (frameworks specifying what students should know in each subject) are buffeted by cultural and political winds; conflicts rage over what to emphasize in the teaching of American history, which books children should read, how math should be taught. There are good tests and bad tests, and the good tests aren't good unless they are aligned with the standards a state adopts. Most off-the-shelf tests won't do, because they are not aligned with state standards and fail to provide detailed information on an individual student's performance. The process of working effectively with testing contractors and getting the assessment right requires both substantial funding and a high level of technical expertise. But, most important, administrators and teachers must be trained to use the test data well. The response to the tests is more important than the tests themselves.

It is the accountability piece, however, that is the hardest to implement. Accountability means that educators and students alike will be held responsible for student performance on standards-based tests. High stakes will be attached to test scores; the scores will trigger consequences. And consequences, in turn, will drive academic improvement.

That is the theory. It's a pipe dream, critics say. NEA president Bob Chase, whose epigraph opens this chapter, labels as "folly" the conviction that students will learn more if high standards are set and consequences instituted for not meeting them. Student learning will not improve, he maintains, until the problem of "savage inequalities" (he borrows Jonathan Kozol's term) is addressed—until disadvantaged kids are no longer "likely to attend schools with crumbling facilities, overcrowded classrooms and inadequate resources."[10] Other skeptics of high-stakes testing make somewhat different, although related arguments.

Richard Elmore, professor of education at Harvard, is among the most thoughtful of these skeptics. His is also a resource argument, but the resource he has in mind is the capacity of teachers to meet the new expectations imposed upon them by the state. "Low-performing schools, and the people who work in them, don't know what to do," he argues. "If they did, they would be doing it already."[11]

Better education, Elmore argues, requires expanding the knowledge and skills of teachers in general—training them "to engage in sustained improvement of their practice," a demand for which they are ill prepared. Teachers and administrators have traditionally been solo practitioners; teachers work in isolation, delivering content to students without input from their peers or administrators. The result: Schools "are hostile to the learning of adults and, because of this . . . are necessarily hostile to the learning of students."[12] Test results given "to an incoherent, atomized, badly run school [will not] automatically make it a better school."[13]

These are contentions that cannot be lightly dismissed. But, in settings that are "hostile to the learning of adults," will change occur without strong incentives—without the pressure that test scores provide? At the heart of the disagreement between accountability proponents and their critics lies this question of incentives. If teachers are not used to subjecting themselves "to the discipline of measuring their success by the metric of students' academic performance," as Elmore notes, are they likely to impose new demands upon themselves without external pressure?

The organization and culture of schools has not altered significantly over the last century. And yet Elmore envisions teachers, without the external pressure that statewide testing generates, suddenly deciding to embrace change and create a shared, "coherent, explicit set of norms and expectations about what a good school looks like."[14] Superintendents, principals, and other administrators must "rebuild the organization of schooling around a different way of doing the work."[15] In the absence of low test scores and public discontent, however, what are the levers of reform? Necessity is usually the mother of institutional reform. Organizations (and the people who work for them) are seldom eager for change absent a crisis.[16]

The same basic point holds for students. The evidence we presented in Chapter 5 on how much time they spent on homework strongly suggested that relatively few non-Asian pupils place a very high priority on academic accomplishment. Employers seldom ask for the high school transcripts of students who head directly into the workplace. Most colleges are basically nonselective. It seems unlikely that many students will devote much more time to schoolwork without real consequences attached to inadequate learning. Well-designed statewide assessments provide the equity of one minimum standard for all students, wherever they live.

Sanctions in Existing State Reforms

States have imposed a variety of sanctions upon low-performing students and schools. Students who fall behind are going to summer school and repeating grades; states are beginning to deny diplomas to those whose scores on standards-based tests are labeled inadequate. Efforts aimed at turning around failing schools have taken a variety of forms, which are usefully summarized in a report written by Ronald C. Brady for the Fordham Foundation.[17]

Brady groups school intervention strategies into three categories: mild, moderate, and strong. Mild interventions consist of minimally intrusive measures such as identifying failing schools (subjecting them to "sunlight'), mandating a school improvement plan, supplying technical assistance, providing additional professional development for teachers and tutoring for students.[18] At the next level up, districts might add instructional time, alter staff assignments or the decision-making process, change the principal, or implement what is called Comprehensive School Reform, which usually involves substantial curricular and other changes.

The most intrusive interventions consist of reconstituting schools (removing and replacing staff), closing schools, offering vouchers to students trapped in schools that fail to improve, imposing curriculum changes, and state takeovers that may involve turning to profit or nonprofit providers to take charge. As Brady says, however, these strong interventions are rarely tried; they are always politically, and sometimes legally, difficult. Vouchers, of course, are likely to trigger the greatest opposition, and only Florida has tried them as a sanction for chronically failing schools. Florida's A-Plus Program was designed to allow students to escape to a better private or public school when the one they were in received two F's over a four-year period, but in August 2002, it was struck down on state constitutional grounds, although the state is appealing the ruling.[19] Making such strong interventions happen more often was one of the objectives of NCLB, Brady argues, although its school choice component (unlike that in Florida) is confined to other public schools within the same district.

The stronger sanctions were written into NCLB as mandatory steps when schools were shown to be chronically failing. The track record of success with milder interventions has been judged inadequate. How successful, however, have been the more draconian measures undertaken by states? Not very, Brady concludes. "While there have been successful turn-arounds, the intervention experience is marked more by valiant effort than by notable success," he writes.[20]

The standards, testing, and accountability measures that states have put in place are all steps in the right direction; in the right setting, with the right leadership, they force some change. But they have not leveled the educational playing field, equalizing opportunity for black and Hispanic kids, which is the central concern of this book. The stories of educational reform in Texas and North Carolina illustrate the point.

The Texas and North Carolina Models

The state standards and accountability systems are works in progress, but we do have some data to evaluate their success in improving the school performance of black and Hispanic pupils and in reducing the gap in academic achievement. We know from the national NAEP results that the overall racial gap has not narrowed over the past dozen years or more. Perhaps, however, these average, nationwide scores conceal impressive success in a handful of pioneering states—states that have instituted standards, tests, and systems of accountability with particular effectiveness.

The evidence on this matter is less than ideal. NAEP administers several different kinds of tests, as Chapter 1 explained; some are given within states (allowing us to compare one against another), but only in the fourth and eighth grades. Thus we lack state-level information about the skills of students at the end of their secondary schooling. Their final high school year is obviously the most important single point at which to judge how much students have learned, which is why, in earlier chapters, we relied so heavily on twelfth-grade scores on the regular NAEP assessments—those given to a national sample of the student population. That no state-level data are available for students about to graduate from secondary school severely limits our ability to appraise the effects of reform. Some states may have done wonders with youngsters in the last third of their K–12 careers; we simply don't know from the NAEP evidence available.[21]

A further limitation of the evidence is that a number of states in the past have chosen not to participate in the NAEP state testing program, which was purely voluntary until the passage of the No Child Left Behind Act. In addition, some states have participated in the state NAEP assessment only erratically, and in some subjects but not others. Nevertheless, we have enough data from state NAEPs to judge whether at least a few model states have achieved major reductions in the black-white or Hispanic-white achievement gaps by the eighth grade.

In the national effort to reform schools, Texas and North Carolina unquestionably stand out. Both have been called "models" for the No Child Left Behind Act. In the case of Texas, this is based in part on the experience of George W. Bush as governor from 1994 to 2000.[22] Bush not only made improving schools his major focus as governor, but went on to make the issue a centerpiece of his successful presidential campaign.

Texas has set clear minimum academic standards in reading, writing, and mathematics, and requires that each public school pupil in grades 3–10 be tested each year. It assigns ratings to all schools, provides assistance to the low performers, and has a system of accountability that includes school closure, reconstitution, and the option of transferring to another school. Not only is each school expected to make overall progress; scores must be reported for each racial subgroup and for economically disadvantaged children, and they too must show progress.

Judged by the state's own tests, the schools of Texas have improved dramatically. When the results of the Texas Assessment of Academic Skills (TAAS) were first reported in 1994, only 52 percent of fourth-graders passed the reading, writing, and math tests; by 2001, the figure was up to 81 percent. The gains of black and Hispanic pupils have been especially impressive. The passing rate for African-American tenth-graders in math has risen from 32 to 79 percent, and for Latinos from 40 to 83 percent.[23] In 2000, Jim Nelson, the Texas education commissioner, said proudly that "one of the things we talk about a great deal is . . . the fact that we've been able to close the gap in achievement between our minority youngsters and our majority youngsters. . . ."[24]

North Carolina has also been widely praised for its efforts to upgrade its public schools.[25] Over the five years in which the state has administered its standardized tests, the ABCs of Public Education, scores have risen substantially, and minority pupils have shown particular improvement. It, too, provides assistance to low-performing schools, and has a system of sanctions that includes reconstitution and student transfers.

Arguably, North Carolina leads the nation in the intensity of its concern about the achievement gap. The state's first annual *State of the State Report* in 1989 began a tradition of publishing detailed school achievement data for racial and ethnic subgroups, and in 2001 the state released its first annual *Minority Achievement Report,* with several dozen pages of statistics detailing minority scores. In 1999, the two houses of the North Carolina General Assembly created a joint commission devoted exclusively to monitoring the achievement gap. Two years later, the state's strenuous efforts to improve minority achievement were recognized by the NAACP, which gave North Carolina its Educational Advocacy Award for a State Governmental Agency.

The most glowing accounts of educational progress in Texas, North Carolina, and other states rest heavily upon scores on the state's own unique assessments. Comparisons between states on the basis of those tests is impossible. The proportion of students with passing grades in the various states will differ depending on the difficulty of the tests given. A 90 percent passing rate on a statewide exam that demands a knowledge of nothing more than rudimentary arithmetic may signify less real progress than a 70 percent passing rate on a more challenging exam in another state. To judge which one is doing better, we need the common yardstick that NAEP—and only NAEP—provides.

When we measure Texas and North Carolina by that yardstick, we can see why those states are correctly considered to be at the forefront of the current national reform effort. Fourth-grade NAEP math scores in North Carolina rose by an average of 20 points between 1992 and 2000, more than double the gain in the United States as a whole. Texas ranked number two in the nation in its progress, with a jump of 15 points. In eighth-grade math, North Carolina again led the nation, with a gain of 30 points, and Texas ranked third, with a 17-point gain. In fourth-grade reading, North Carolina ranked second in the U.S. and Texas sixth in their rates of gain between 1992 and 1998. And Texas had the fourth-highest scores in the 1998 writing assessment.[26]

These results are all the more impressive when we consider the fact that they cannot be attributed to unusually favorable economic or demographic circumstances in those two states. Although Texas and North Carolina are in the booming Sunbelt, they nonetheless fall a little below the national average in the educational level of their adult populations and in per capita income levels.[27] Furthermore, per pupil spending in both states is significantly below the national average.[28]

The demography of neither state is particularly conducive to high academic achievement. North Carolina has few Hispanic residents but a very large African-American population, so the minority share of total enrollments slightly exceeds the national average. Texas has nearly as many black students as the typical state and two-and-a-half times as many Hispanics; whites make up a mere 43 percent of its student population, 20 points below the national average.[29]

When all the variations in the characteristics of parents are taken into account, the record of Texas (though not that of North Carolina) looks even better. An elaborate analysis of state differences in NAEP scores in the years 1990–1996 found that Texas ranked number one in the nation in educational progress when the influence of these variables was held constant.[30]

In short, Texas and North Carolina—especially Texas—deserve their reputations as models of what can be achieved by raising the bar: setting clear standards, measuring student progress in meeting them, and holding accountable students and schools when they do not meet expectations.

The Persistent Racial Gap

Texas and North Carolina have raised student scores on the nation's most reliable assessment, NAEP, as well as on their own systems of tests. In some other states, as well, there are signs that testing and accountability are forcing real academic change that could result in similar academic gains. Students are beginning to take school more seriously and to work harder. Teachers are putting their heads together to come up with new strategies. Expectations are rising. Students in Anne Arundel County, Maryland, and elsewhere are even getting "excited about adjectives and adverbs."

This is heartening, but an overall rise in NAEP scores in a state does not mean that the racial gap is closing. If the average performance of all groups— white, Asian, black, Hispanic—improves, that is certainly welcome news. But we also want to see group differences dramatically diminished. It can't be said too often: Closing the skills gap is the key to real racial equality in American society. Only when the average black graduate of the nation's high schools knows as much calculus as the average white student will black incomes match those of whites.

Looking at the showcase states of Texas and North Carolina is a good way to find out whether overall educational progress necessarily means a narrowing of the racial gap. Figure 12-1 examines how the black-white achievement gap in math and reading changed in Texas, North Carolina, and the country as a whole over the 1990s. Figure 12-2 provides the same information about the performance of Hispanic students.

What do the NAEP numbers tell us? Figure 12-1 reveals discouraging answers about the progress of African Americans. In 1992, before either Texas or North Carolina had done much to establish systems of standards and accountability, the black-white gap in fourth-grade math in those states was a few points narrower than in the United States as a whole. By 1996, when those students were in the eighth grade, it had widened nationally and had widened in Texas as well.[31] In North Carolina it did not increase enough to be statistically significant; on the other hand, it didn't close at all.

The experience of a second group of students tested in math, those who were in the fourth grade in 1996 and the eighth grade in 2000, should be more relevant to the issue at hand, because the state reforms had been in place for more of their school careers. The results, unfortunately, are even less cheering. The black-white gap nationally increased by 7 points over the four years. In both Texas and North Carolina, which led the nation in *overall* math gains, the distance between whites and African Americans widened by an almost identical 6 points.

In reading, the black-white gap in the U.S. dropped by 8 points between

Figure 12-1. The Black-White Score Gap in Mathematics, 1992–1996 and 1996–2000, and in Reading 1994–1998, 4th- and 8th-Graders, U.S., Texas, and North Carolina

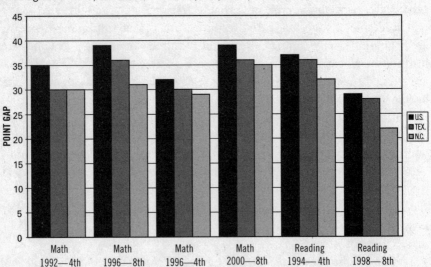

Source: NAEP Data Tool.

1994 and 1998. But, again, neither Texas nor North Carolina was unusually successful by national standards, despite their energetic and highly publicized reform efforts. In Texas, the gap fell at exactly the national rate, 8 points; in North Carolina it declined by a trivial 2 points more than that. The black-white gap, in short, continued as if reform had never occurred. The NAEP scores of African-American students went up in both states, but those of whites rose as rapidly or more rapidly.

For Hispanics, the Texas and North Carolina results are a little better, Figure 12-2 indicates, although not in math for the first group of students—those tested in 1992 and 1996. The national gap for those youngsters widened by a substantial 5 points. In Texas, it increased even more, by 9 points. In North Carolina, it grew by 3 points less than the national average, but the change, although less dramatic, was still in the wrong direction. The 1996–2000 math figures show improvement, however. The national gap for this group of Hispanic students increased by 7 points, while it declined by 4 points in Texas and by 6 points in North Carolina. Reform was thus followed by a limited but not insignificant narrowing of the math gap between Latino and white pupils.

In reading, the Hispanic-white gap in Texas narrowed by 8 points between 1994 and 1998, slightly greater than the national drop of 5 points. Latino students in North Carolina, however, made fewer gains (relative to whites), and

Figure 12-2. The Hispanic-White Score Gap in Mathematics, 1992–1996 and 1996–2000, and in Reading 1994–1998, 4th- and 8th-Graders, U.S., Texas, and North Carolina

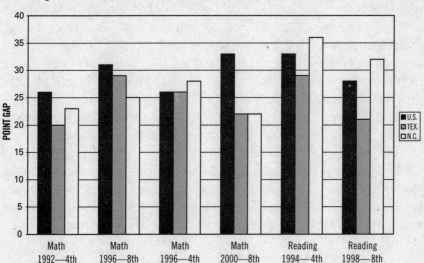

Source: NAEP Data Tool.

in 1998 the reading gap was still 4 points wider than the national average. Thus, the Texas results for Hispanics in reading were moderately impressive, while in North Carolina they were quite disappointing.

State NAEP scores are also available in science and in writing. In science, the black-white and Hispanic-white gaps are just as large in Texas and North Carolina as elsewhere in the country—very large indeed. The reforms in those two model states have done nothing whatever to close the glaring racial gap in command of basic science.

Both states—but especially Texas—did unusually well in teaching writing skills to minority pupils, however. On the 1998 NAEP writing assessment, Texas white students were a little above national average, but blacks and Hispanics were well above the national average for their groups. As a result, the black-white gap and the Hispanic-white gap in writing was a third smaller in Texas than in the United States as a whole. But in North Carolina the gap between blacks and whites in writing skills looks roughly the same as the national one. With respect to the writing skills of Hispanics, however, the state looks good.

Texas and North Carolina, as already discussed, both have their own elaborate testing system, and those results are positive. But the results of the NAEP exams in those states are less impressive. In 2000, only 19 percent of black eighth-graders in Texas did badly enough to flunk the TAAS math exam, and yet the NAEP math test that same year revealed that 60 percent of African Americans had skills that were Below Basic. Likewise, only 15 percent of Hispanic eighth-graders failed the TAAS math exam, while 40 percent were Below Basic on NAEP. It is possible, of course, that NAEP has an unduly demanding definition of what constitutes "basic" knowledge at a particular grade level, but the knowledge and skills needed to achieve a Basic grade on an NAEP assessment are pretty minimal. Indeed, both Texas and North Carolina recognize that they set the bar very low in the first phase of their reform effort, and are now introducing tests that are considerably more demanding. In the 2002–2003 school year, Texas replaced the TAAS exams with the more rigorous Texas Assessment of Knowledge and Skills (TAKS).

Thus, for all of their heartening achievements, neither Texas nor North Carolina has yet hit upon the formula necessary to close substantially the black-white achievement gap in reading, math, and science, although they have made impressive progress in writing. They are doing somewhat better with Hispanics, but the progress certainly cannot be called extraordinary.

A Broader Look at the Racial Gap in State NAEP Assessments

Perhaps other model states have accomplished far more without having gotten much publicity for it. We wish it were true. We've reviewed the data from all the state NAEP assessments and have not found any secret successes. It would be too cumbersome to present the evidence for three dozen or more states, but the general pattern is clear from Figure 12-3. It plots the 1998 reading scores and the 2000 math scores of fourth- and eighth-graders in ten states. The ten include several that have been most often identified as leaders in the standards and accountability movement (Texas, North Carolina, Massachusetts, New York, Maryland, and Virginia), and a few others that have not been pioneers in the reform movement (Arkansas, Alabama, California, and Missouri).

Scores do vary somewhat from state to state, largely because their populations differ considerably in their average educational attainment, income, and other social characteristics that influence school achievement.[32] In addition, some states have school systems that do a better job than others. Thus, the range for white eighth-graders on the NAEP reading assessment, for example, goes from a high of 277 in New York (5 points above the white national average) to a low of 263 in Arkansas (9 points below it). This 14-point

Figure 12-3. 4th- and 8th-Grade Reading Scores by Race for the U.S. and Selected States, 1998

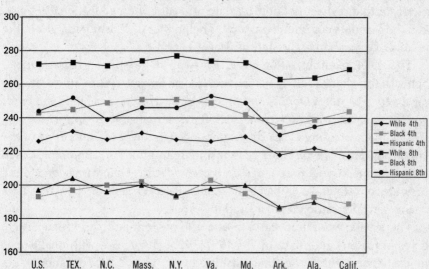

Source: NAEP Data Tool.

difference is the equivalent of a little more than one grade level, so in reading white eighth-graders in Arkansas are roughly a year behind their age group in New York.

States like New York and Arkansas are very different—in their economies, their demography, and their history. Across the nation, states vary. And yet what stands out most from this graph is the remarkable constancy of the racial gap. Where black or Hispanic reading scores are above the national average, those of whites in the state also tend to be. Where minority students perform below average, the typical white score is also low. The lines on the chart thus tend strongly to move in the same direction. The scores of blacks and Hispanics are indeed a little better in the educationally celebrated states. The racial gap, however, remains very wide because the tide of reform lifts all students—white, black, and Hispanic. Precisely the same pattern appears in a chart of fourth- and eighth-grade math results for the same states (not given here).

No Child Left Behind

The standards and testing movement began in the states, but the federal government has played an important role as well. The U.S. Department of Education has long been reluctant to withhold funds from recalcitrant jurisdictions; its bark has been worse than its bite. Nevertheless, laws passed by Congress and embodied in departmental regulations deliver important messages that register not only on state officials but on educational activists and the business community as well. The politics of Washington affect the politics of education at the state and local level.[33]

The 1994 reauthorization of ESEA—called the Improving America's Schools Act—had precisely that state and local impact. At the time of its passage, very few states were in the process of developing academic standards and tests aligned with those standards. It's true that state governors were instrumental in creating Goals 2000, announced in the president's State of the Union address in 1990. Those goals inspired thousands of community-based organizations to work for changes in the schools, which in turn added to the pressure on states to implement standards-based reform. But the 1994 changes in ESEA also played an important part.[34]

The 1994 law required states to establish content and performance standards in reading and math by the 1997–1998 school year, with final assessments aligned with those standards three years later. Many questions were left unanswered. What can states realistically expect all students—regardless of family income or racial and ethnic identity—to know by, say, eighth grade? Does the answer to that question depend on the percentage of students likely to pass? What, precisely, should the assessments look like? Implementing the law was more difficult than Congress envisioned. As a consequence, the Department of Education was forced to grant waivers to over thirty states that did not meet the initial deadline. No state lost funds as a consequence of non-compliance.

In theory, at least, the last waivers have been granted.[35] With the passage of the latest revision of ESEA—the 2001 No Child Left Behind Act—Congress demonstrated a new level of seriousness about standards, assessment and accountability. The commitment was central to achieving the act's primary aim: closing the achievement gap between the advantaged and disadvantaged. Congress gave schools a dozen years (starting with the end of the 2001–2002 school year) to bring every student up to the level of "proficiency." By 2005, all states will be required to administer high-quality tests annually to all students in grades 3–8. These tests must be aligned with solid academic standards, and the results must be made publicly available, broken down by race, ethnicity, and other student characteristics. Schools whose high-performing whites and Asians make the overall average look good will still be classified as low-performing if their black and Hispanic students are "left behind." NCLB demands a break with the unacceptable performance patterns of the past.

It's a remarkable turn of events. The racial gap—hidden from public view until so recently—has suddenly acquired top billing in the national educational agenda. In 1965, ESEA was the product of concern about poverty; it was part of President Johnson's War on Poverty. By 2001, the White House, members of Congress in both parties, and important players in the business and educational communities had come to view the academic performance of black and Hispanic students as a distinct—and distinctively urgent—problem. Many minority children, yes, live in poverty. But more than a third of black families are middle class, a third live in suburbia, and even in upscale communities like Shaker Heights, Ohio, black children are not faring well academically.[36] The No Child Left Behind Act broadcasts that long-unacknowledged truth, and says, in effect, forget the excuses. Teachers, administrators, parents, and students: Get to work. The racial gap—in cities and suburbs—is a national crisis.

Every student must be academically "proficient" by the end of the 2013–2014 school year, the NCLB legislation states, and every school must demonstrate "adequate yearly progress" toward that goal.[37] They cannot get their white, Asian, and more affluent students up to proficiency first, and then start working on their "at risk" youngsters; those students too must show "continuous and substantial improvement" in reading and math. Schools—and whole districts—that receive Title I funds (58 percent of the country's public schools) and do not make adequate progress are subject to sanctions spelled out in the law.

For instance, Title I schools that have failed to improve for two years are required to develop intervention plans that may consist of strategies such as professional development for the staff or additional instructional time. Parents have the right to transfer their child to a school that is not on the "in need of improvement" list, and districts cannot use school overcrowding as an excuse to avoid the requirement. Parents must be offered the option of at least two schools, although their choice is limited to public schools within the same district.

After another year of inadequate progress, students become entitled to use some of the school's federal money for tutoring, weekend classes, and other private or public help. Ultimately, Title I schools that cannot meet state standards are vulnerable to "restructuring"—staff replacements, reconstitution as a charter school, state or private management takeovers. None of these sanctions is entirely new; each can be found in one state reform or another. But NCLB has gathered them up, created a timetable, and made them mandatory nationwide. States can ignore the mandates, but they risk losing Title I funds.

Dreaming Away, Again

Our summary of some of the main provisions of No Child Left Behind obviously touches on only a few of its main points. It's a huge legislative package—containing much that is good and much that is potentially problematic. Just for starters, there are huge definitional questions built into the legislation—what one scholar has called a "squishiness in terms".[38] For instance, all children must be academically "proficient" in twelve years. What does the term mean?

It comes from NAEP, and has a clear definition there. Yet the definition that education authorities in Michigan and Mississippi give to the term may vary enormously and differ substantially from the NAEP definition. In 2000, 84 percent of North Carolina fourth-graders scored at the proficient level on the state mathematics test; according to the NAEP assessment in North Carolina the same year, only 28 percent of those students were Proficient. According to the Arkansas state tests, 41 percent of fourth-graders were proficient at math in 2000; by the NAEP standard, the figure was just 12 percent. For Connecticut, it was 60 versus 32; for Michigan, 75 versus 29.[39]

Not all states fit this pattern. In Massachusetts, where one of us serves on the state board of education, the definition of "proficiency" corresponds roughly to that used by NAEP. That is the case in Louisiana as well. In both states, only a small minority of students had reached proficiency by 2002. Louisiana's goal, before NCLB was passed, was to get all students to the level of "basic" by 2009—regarded as a difficult task. In Massachusetts, too, the immediate goal has been to get a high percentage of students in every group into (or above) the minimum-skills category that the state labels "Needs Improvement." That, in itself, is considered an accomplishment.

NCLB mandates that all students reach "proficiency" by 2014, and in incremental steps show "adequate yearly progress" (AYP). That seems a rather straightforward demand; in fact, it is not. As we write, "yearly" progress doesn't literally mean yearly, but gains at least every three years—the cumulative effect being "proficiency" after twelve years. Moreover, Ohio and Indiana are already gaming the system with approval from the federal Department of Education. The AYP steps they have proposed assume much bigger student achievement gains will occur in the final three years than in the nine preceding years. Taking advantage of a technical loophole in the law, these two states have built procrastination (or realism?) into the implementation of NCLB.[40]

However the AYP steps are laid out, the only way to make all American students "proficient" by 2014 will be to define "proficiency" as an accomplishment far below the traditional NAEP standard. As Chapter 1 noted, in the most recent NAEP math and reading assessments, only 32 percent of all American students scored at the Proficient or Advanced level in fourth-grade reading. For blacks, the figure was just 12 percent, and for Hispanics 16 percent. The results in math were even worse, with only 5 percent of blacks, 10 percent of Hispanics, and 26 percent of all students rated Proficient or Advanced in fourth grade. By the twelfth grade, even fewer non-Asian minority students reached the top NAEP categories. Within our present educational structure, getting all of our students to anything close to what NAEP defines as Proficient within NCLB's time frame is not possible. It's not possible in Massachusetts, or in any other state.

The framers of NCLB could not have meant to require "proficiency" as NAEP defines it. In fact, some argue that "proficiency" in NCLB is best understood as the level NAEP calls Basic. If so, why the legislation used the NAEP term is a mystery. But, in any case, getting everyone up to Basic is utopian enough. White scores are discouraging, those of non-Asian minori-

ties far more so. At the end of twelve years of education, seven out of ten
African Americans lack even a Basic command of math, as NAEP defines it.
That is the case for more than half of Hispanics too. Reading scores are some-
what better, but still terrible. Even these devastating figures are too opti-
mistic, since most special education and LEP students were not assessed by
NAEP.

The country has put a great deal of money and effort into reforming education with almost no progress in diminishing the racial gap. NCLB, many
hope, will usher in a new era of rapid progress. Recent trends—even in a
showcase state like Texas—do not suggest much reason for optimism.

Are Really Tough Standards Politically Feasible?

Educators in many states are arguing that the goals of No Child Left Behind
are impossible to meet. "The whole point of this [law] is school improvement,
not a theater of the absurd where all schools get on the [low performing] list
and no one can ever get off," the director of strategic planning and implementation in St. Paul, Minnesota, has said.[41] "All schools" ending up on the
list is not likely, but as of June 2002, even officials in the showcase state of
North Carolina were projecting more than 70 percent of schools failing to
meet adequate yearly progress goals.[42] In much-celebrated Texas, as well,
state officials in January 2003 were anticipating a high number of schools failing to meet tough new testing standards, and federal sanctions as a consequence.[43] Across the nation, the level of alarm has been rising. Faced with
long lists of failing schools, Congress and the U.S. Department of Education
will "either have to make some amendments in the act or write creatively in
the regulations," Connecticut's Education Commissioner warned in June
2002.[44]

In Massachusetts, the level of alarm and political opposition has remained
relatively low as a result of both generous education funding and a state testing system that, as of the spring of 2003, seems to be working. (Whether that
will remain the case when it becomes clear that not all students can reach the
level of "proficiency" by 2014—as NCLB demands—is another question.)

The Commonwealth began pouring money into education when a major
reform bill was enacted in 1993. Most of the new money went to high-need
communities like Boston, Springfield, Lawrence, and Lowell. The state Department of Education developed rigorous academic standards and established a comprehensive system of tests (MCAS). Starting with the class of
2003, passing the tenth-grade tests in English Language Arts (ELA) and math
became a requirement for high school graduation.

As noted earlier, passing MCAS with a grade of "Needs Improvement" is the equivalent of scoring at the Basic level on a NAEP exam. Remember that Chapter 1 (Figure 1-2) showed that 69 percent of African-American twelfth-graders in the nation and 56 percent of their Hispanic classmates do not meet that standard; they lack a Basic command in mathematics. In reading, 43 percent of blacks and 36 percent of Latinos fall below Basic. Thus, Massachusetts was gambling that its reforms could result in a level of skills and knowledge dramatically at odds with the national picture. If the state failed to meet its extraordinarily ambitious goal—involving remarkable advances in learning for a very high proportion of its minority students—it would find itself denying high school diplomas to half or more of its black and Hispanic students.

When the tenth-grade MCAS started to count, scores began to climb dramatically. Just 48 percent of tenth-graders in the class slated to graduate in 2002 passed both the English Language Arts and mathematics MCAS tests on their first try when it was not part of the graduation requirement. In the next year's tenth-grade class, covered by the requirement, the proportion jumped to 68 percent. Consequences, in other words, changed the level of student effort; students could do better, we learned. And so could educators. Effort—inspired by sanctions connected to a statewide test—paid off.

Nearly a third of the members of the class of 2003, though, did not pass both tests the first time around. The figure was predictably much higher for black and Hispanic students—60 percent and 67 percent respectively. The chief reason for their failure, a pilot study of four urban high schools revealed, was recognized even by the students themselves. Seventy-four percent of failing students thought that missing school "a lot" was a "big reason," and 64 percent admitted that they had not put "enough effort into school and homework."[45] Flunking had a salutary effect on their behavior; 67 percent said that they were now working harder at their studies. Without the MCAS graduation requirement there is every reason to believe that students without even minimal math and literacy skills would have been ignored—a long and dishonorable tradition in American public education.

In addition, Massachusetts is providing these students with a great deal of extra help to lift them over the bar. In the 2002–2003 academic year, the state put $50 million into remediation, $30 million of which went to high schools—a remarkable and unprecedented commitment. Students began receiving support, attention, and resources that simply didn't exist before. With each retest, as a result, thousands of previously failing students in the class of 2003 were making it over the bar.

When the results came in from the December 2002 retest, an amazing 90 percent of all the members of the class of 2003 had met the MCAS standard, although for African Americans, the figure was a still-sobering 75 percent, and for Hispanics 70 percent. By contrast, 94 percent of whites and 90 percent of Asians had passed.[46]

With another retest to come (as we write), the number still failing will be cut further. And students who have not passed before leaving high school will be eligible for remedial classes at community colleges, where they can prepare for another attempt on the MCAS. Other help will be available from a variety of sources.[47] In addition, Massachusetts provides waivers for some students who have failed MCAS. These students must have taken the exam three times and scored within four points of the cutoff score. The superintendents in their districts must also file an appeal that includes teacher recommendations, evidence of a solid attendance record, and grades comparable to those of their classmates who passed the exam.[48]

In November 2002, the state board of education also softened the impact of failure somewhat by allowing local districts to issue "certificates of attainment" to students who have failed to meet the MCAS requirement after three tries, but who had passed their courses and attended school 90 percent of the time.

The rise in passing rates on MCAS, the waivers, and the "certificates of attainment" have at least temporarily undercut the opposition to high-stakes testing in Massachusetts that has been led by organizations like FairTest. Opponents have also been handicapped by the failure of most urban superintendents, the business community, and any of the major political actors to join them. In other states, however, the political opposition has been stronger.

In the 2002 elections, at least five Democratic gubernatorial candidates ran on platforms pledging less reliance on the use of standardized tests. Three won: Janet Napolitano in Arizona, Jennifer Granholm in Michigan, and Jim Doyle in Wisconsin.[49] Arizona had already delayed its exit exam (in the face of massive numbers of students expected to fail the math test). Numerous other states as well have either postponed the graduation requirement or lowered the level of academic expectations.

Leveling the Playing Field

"If you don't assess where you are, what the students have learned or not learned, you're teaching in the dark. That's analogous to driving at night without headlights," Secretary of Education Rod Paige said in 2001.[50] Most people concur. A September 2000 Public Agenda survey of parents found 75 percent agreeing that "students pay more attention and study harder if they know they must pass a test to get promoted or to graduate."

Nevertheless, a slightly higher percentage said it was "wrong to use the results of just one test" to decide a student's fate.[51] The reliance on one test for purposes of grade promotion or as an exit exam from high school (although with multiple opportunities to pass it) remains far from settled in most states. Indeed, it seems safe to predict increasing conflict over high-stakes testing in the coming years. Under the best of circumstances, confidence in the reliability of test results would be controversial, but the racial gap in scores makes their use particularly painful.

Starting in the late 1980s, a movement for testing, standards, and accountability began to sweep the states, and in January 2002 the president signed into law the No Child Left Behind Act, passed by Congress the previous month. Closing the racial gap is its central aim. Will mandatory testing, scores broken down by race and ethnicity, an insistence on "adequate yearly progress," and various sanctions for poor performance finally level the academic playing field? If the record of two model states, Texas and North Carolina, is any measure, the prospects are not good. The much-celebrated effort in those two states did improve the knowledge and skills of students in general, but the racial gap did not narrow. White scores went up; black scores went up. But the difference between them remained about as wide.

The acid test of education reform is its ability to level the playing field. "In education, the time we waste today can mean a lifetime wasted tomorrow," Lyndon B. Johnson said in introducing Title I in 1965. "Wasted" was a bit of hyperbole, but as long as the typical black or Hispanic student knows much less than the average white or Asian, racial and ethnic equality will remain an elusive goal.

At various points in this book, we have briefly alluded to the steps that need to be taken on the road to real change, and we will say more about that question in the conclusion. Before taking up that issue, however, we must consider the various barriers to reform that are built into the traditional public school system—the subject of the next chapter.

Thirteen: Roadblocks
to Change

It's easier to continue to do the things that we've always done. It always is. [But if]
we do the things we've done, we'll get the same results that we've got[ten] before.
Anthony Alvarado, former chancellor of Instruction in San Diego[1]

Most Americans today agree with Anthony Alvarado: Schools need to change.[2] That's not a new perception. In education, as in all walks of life, Americans have long believed that things can be made better. Educational enthusiasms of one sort or another have appeared and disappeared throughout the last century.[3] And yet, fundamental problems with the school system remain—foremost among them, the racial gap in academic achievement that warps the fabric of American life.

Moreover, *plus ça change* . . . At least that has been the American educational story so far. More often than not, what appears to be a break in continuity simply perpetuates the fundamentals of the status quo, with predictable results. Appearances aside, reforms have been superficial, leaving the fundamental structure unaltered. The centralized, highly bureaucratic public school systems in our large cities today reflect the balance of forces among the many players who have an interest in schools. Parents and their children are players, but far from the most powerful. Their interests are often not well served by the system.

We have described some wonderful public schools where youngsters living in distressed communities thrive. But it is no accident that none of them is a traditional public school. They are charter schools, freed from most of the constraints under which regular schools operate. (Rafe Esquith's classroom in the Hobart Elementary School is the one exception, but Esquith's fame and outside funding allows him to break almost all of the usually crippling rules.) The principals in these charter schools have real power—over their budgets, their discipline policies, and their staffing—and have used it to replicate the strengths of the best inner-city private and parochial schools. There are good charter schools and bad ones.[4] But no entire urban school district has been able to achieve results comparable to those we found in the best charter schools, and we doubt that any ever will without fundamental reform in the structure of public education.

Wanted: More Good Teachers

Almost everyone agrees that good teaching makes an enormous difference, and this is especially true for black and Hispanic students, who typically arrive in school already behind. San Diego superintendent Alan D. Bersin made improving the quality of instruction his central aim. Approximately 54 percent of San Diego's school population is non-Asian minority, and the racial gap is characteristically large. In 2001, for instance, just 30 percent of Latino ninth-graders passed the math portion of a new high school exit exam on their first try (a shade better than the percentage for blacks), while more than two-thirds of Asians and whites got passing scores.[5]

Bersin and Alvarado (who stepped down as chancellor in February 2003) arrived together in the summer of 1998, and designed a "Blueprint for Student Success" that raised the district's annual budget for the "professional development" of teachers from approximately $1 million to $55 million in the academic year 2002–2003. With a network of trained, highly qualified teachers in place—at least one for each school—they aimed to create a culture of learning and to improve teaching across the board. (Perhaps it was only realistic, but it seems telling that the initial goal was just *one* good teacher per school.)

Alvarado came from District 2 in New York City, where (among other changes) he worked hard to upgrade the skills of teachers. He gained a national reputation as a reformer on the basis of his New York experience. But his critics contend that the reading and other curricular material he introduced were a disaster—a classic case of misplaced enthusiasm for progressive education. As of 2000, 45 percent of District 2's students did not meet the minimum state standard, and only 10 percent exceeded it.[6]

In San Diego as well, the promised results of a plan that put teacher training at its center had not materialized by the time Alvarado departed. Reading and math scores actually fell from 2001 to 2002; the district was said to be "awash in textbooks that emphasize pleasant problem-solving exercises" at the expense of demanding content. Scores on the California Standards Test in Physics, reported in August 2002, put San Diego eighth from the bottom among the 232 districts in the state. Alvarado had purchased skateboards to demonstrate Newton's Third Law of Motion and other such equipment for a district that lacked the material necessary to do complex and challenging scientific experiments. Critics also charged that social promotions to high school had become the norm.[7]

The San Diego story raises several questions. Can reformers focus on one part of the problem of poor schooling—in this case, weak teachers—and turn a district around, closing the racial gap in academic performance? And can a handful of trained teachers create a culture of learning and inspire better instruction throughout the system? San Diego has been investing an extraordinary $55 million a year—over $7,000 per teacher—in professional development; how much impact is such a program likely to have?

No is the answer to the first two questions, we suspect. Piecemeal reform will not work; teachers need to be better, but they also need a good curriculum—not watered-down science and undemanding math. Schools need a critical mass of good teachers, not one or two. Moreover, Bersin and Alvarado were relying on professional development to turn weak teachers into the sort of strong instructors whose skills might have compensated for the inadequate textbooks and other material the district was offering.

We opened Chapter 10 with a remark by the former schools chancellor in New York who contended that "the wrong people [were] in the classrooms." He was not bemoaning the lack of professional development in the New York City schools. He was brooding about the high numbers of teachers in the city who were having great difficulty passing what Levy called "a simple, easy test" of their professional competence and subject-matter knowledge. Many had taken the exam numerous times. In the lowest-performing school districts, the failure rate for uncertified teachers was almost 40 percent.[8] Can "Instructional Leaders" of the sort that the San Diego team identified transform such teachers?

The New York failure rate on the licensing exam has been high, but certification is no guarantee of quality. As the Education Trust has observed, most licensing exams currently in use exclude only the "weakest of the weak" from the classrooms.[9] That leaves plenty of teachers who are still pretty ineffective. In February 2001, the president of the District of Columbia Board of Education, Peggy Cooper Cafritz, charged that about half of the district's public school teachers were unqualified or incompetent.[10] The basis of her judgment is not clear, but the consistently awful performance of D.C. students on the NAEP exams certainly lends plausibility to the charge.[11] Some teachers are of course terrific; others are good enough; but too many are not up to the tough job they face—especially in urban schools. Teachers with tenure, however, are well protected against dismissals. And the structure and culture of public education drive away those who might serve young kids best.

Saints, Masochists, and Low-Aspiring Civil Servants

Teaching in a regular public school is a profession for saints, masochists, or low-aspiring civil servants. To do the job splendidly asks too much in the way of sacrifice; simply to meet minimum standards asks too little in terms of skills, knowledge, imagination, and dedication. Moreover, those who do it splendidly tend to be educational isolates, while those who could be better are resistant to significant change.

The country will need an estimated two million new teachers over the next decade, and the pool of saints and masochists is obviously extremely limited.[12] Urban school systems, particularly, must find a way of attracting more smart, articulate, hardworking people, eager to teach the kids who most need academic nurturing. And they must make the job attractive to those who demand a safe, orderly, educationally committed environment in which they can actually teach, as well as time for a life outside of school. Potential teachers do not need an Ivy League degree—overrated, in any case. But they do need academic skills, a talent for communicating ideas, and some sense of calling.

Strong students don't generally become public school teachers, and those who do so are more likely than others to leave the profession.[13] That's no secret. Sandra Feldman, the president of the American Federation of Teachers, has said as much. "You have in the schools right now, among . . . the teachers who are going to be retiring, very smart people," she noted, referring especially to the many women who went into teaching in the days when other professions were less welcoming. But "we're not getting in now the same kinds of people," she acknowledged.[14] It is rather stunning to see the leader of one of the two national teachers unions tacitly admitting that many of her members are not "very smart people."

The process of entering the profession is bound to discourage many of the "very smart people" to whom the AFT president referred, now that they have broader options open to them.[15] The education schools that offer the requisite courses are the first problem. The vast majority are basically nonselective.[16] Much of the curriculum is intellectually undemanding, at best— deadening, at worst. Although he is a professor at the Harvard Graduate School of Education, Richard Elmore has offered the acid judgment that education schools "actively promote mediocrity and incompetence."[17] The best and the brightest aren't drawn to training for mediocrity or incompetence.

Why do we require college students who hope to become public school teachers to do most of their course work in an education school or department? Those who hope to teach chemistry in college study chemistry in graduate school, not methods of teaching it. Wouldn't aspiring elementary and secondary school teachers be better off mastering a subject in the context of a broad liberal education? Some training in how to teach and in developmental psychology would undoubtedly be useful, but such courses do not require an entirely separate school of education. Our private and parochial schools are filled with uncertified teachers without an education degree who do an excellent job.

The issue of reforming teacher training was raised in a September 2002 report by the Carnegie Corporation, which recommended that schools of education "should start training teachers the same way medical schools train doctors" with a teaching residency comparable to a medical residency.[18] The analogy with medical school seems strained. Before they enter medical school, students spend four years in college studying biology, chemistry, and other disciplines necessary to their later medical education. But most teachers receive all of their training while in college. The question is whether specializing in education properly prepares them for the profession.

The argument for an education degree rests on the questionable assumption that there is a large and complex body of pedagogical knowledge that all teachers must have—knowledge equivalent to that which states demand of future doctors and lawyers. Stanford University education professor Linda Darling-Hammond and other defenders of the status quo insist that strong subject-matter knowledge is far from sufficient. "People who go through teacher education learn how to look at kids, how to understand what's going to be appropriate for different kids at different ages, how people learn and how to construct a curriculum that builds on the way people learn well and easily."[19] These seem important things for teachers to know, but is it really necessary to devote most of a college career—or even a full year of graduate study—to learn them?

In fact, there is no consensus on what teachers need to know, aside from the subject matter they teach. Demanding all those courses in pedagogy keeps a person like Richard McGowan out of the profession. With twenty years' experience teaching college-level history and philosophy, he found himself ineligible to teach in the Indiana public schools.[20] Although some states have created alternative paths to certification to make room for teachers like him, such stories are legion. "Too many potential teachers are turned away because of the cumbersome process that requires them to jump through hoops and lots of them," Secretary of Education Richard Riley noted in 1999.[21] The truly talented thus look to other professions.

To eliminate this "cumbersome process" that deters outstanding young people from becoming teachers will require a change in the criteria that generally govern the award of teaching licenses, however. As we shall see below, the political forces that can be mobilized to prevent such a change are formidable.

Academically talented and visionary college students are discouraged from public school teaching by other aspects of the profession as well. Most jobs in the private sector are rungs on a ladder of opportunity: Do well, and your pay goes up; do badly and you risk unemployment. In marked contrast to most Europeans, only a minority of Americans prefer to be paid a fixed salary without incentives for higher pay.[22] Those attracted to teaching, however, are in that minority. They have to be. The profession offers almost total security but very little in the way of economic opportunity.

The pay scale in almost every school district in the United States is radically egalitarian. It is determined not by performance, not by any bottom line (the academic success of the students), but solely by higher-education degrees (which may be unrelated to the teacher's subject area) and years of service—"endurance, not excellence," as one observer has put it.[23] Moreover, for purposes of compensation, master's degrees in physical education and mathematics are equivalent, although the latter is far more difficult to achieve and likely to contribute far more to students' intellectual development.

Risk-takers who thrive on the opportunities created by change are not likely to choose public school teaching, although there is no survey data that confirms this speculative point. There are no incentives to try something daringly new, and strong incentives not to. Those who dream of building a better mousetrap, starting a business, floating a new legal argument, or even fixing an inefficient government agency don't generally end up in the classroom. Many teachers care deeply about kids; they want to do good. But the nature of the job and the trade-offs involved are built-in roadblocks to change. Public schools are not environments in which innovators thrive. Indeed, innovators are seldom welcome. The Rafe Esquiths and Jaime Escalantes are ignored at best, or, more often, harassed. They do not become role models; almost no one tries to emulate them.

If the teaching profession does not reward imaginative, ambitious, competitive innovators, it's not surprising that talented and ambitious college students are more likely to choose other careers, ones that reward high performance with rapid promotion, higher pay, and greater freedom to experiment. The reward structure of the profession and the quality of those most likely to enter it, in other words, are closely linked. As it is, the intrinsic satisfactions of teaching are inadequately reinforced by the external rewards commonplace in other professions. Excellence in teaching is assumed to be its own reward, although doctors, lawyers, and even university professors typically expect higher status and pay as part of a package of professional recognition.

Thus, a career ladder and pay differentials (based on qualifications and performance) are necessary steps toward attracting much better teachers to the large urban districts where most black and Hispanic children go to school. Ambitious public school teachers today generally have nowhere to go—except into administration, a quite different job. Math and science teachers are in short supply everywhere, and the problem is particularly acute in the high-minority schools that have a hard time attracting and keeping teachers in high demand. The reason for the short supply is obvious: College graduates with solid training in mathematics or science have many attractive career options; if schools want them, they need to compete in the market. That would mean a higher salary for promising or proven math teachers than for those who teach English, of whom there is an abundance.

A rigidly egalitarian and bureaucratic pay scale also precludes the award of higher pay for the jobs that teachers are most likely to abandon. Teachers who are idealistic and potentially excellent may start their careers in high-poverty, high-minority inner-city schools, but will move on rather quickly to jobs in more comfortable settings, often closer to their homes. How many would stay if given a salary incentive to do so? Surely, some would. It seems ironic that the highly egalitarian reward structure for teachers works to the disadvantage of students who attend schools in inner-city neighborhoods.

The Milken Family Foundation is currently investing heavily in a promising experiment focused on precisely this problem.[24] Its Teacher Advancement Program (TAP), now operating in a few dozen schools in six states, offers a strategy to "attract, retain and motivate talented people to the teaching profession—and keep them there." Participating schools reward teachers "for how well they teach their students," and use the TAP's comprehensive system for teacher evaluation. They create "multiple career paths" for teachers, allowing them to move up to positions of greater responsibility as mentors of other teachers and as master teachers. It is much too early to look for results, but this is clearly the direction in which our schools should be moving.

Hands-Tied Administrators

"These days, the greatest obstacle to making schools successful is inertia. Administrators lack the energy and ambition to change the habits, procedures and cultures with which their staffs are comfortable, even if their students haven't been learning much," Jay Mathews, the *Washington Post* education reporter, has written.[25]

True, and no surprise. The structure of the profession nurtures a culture of inertia. Once a principal has taken the job, John E. Chubb and Terry M. Moe have noted, "the incentives promote behavior that is classically bureaucratic. Doing a good job, and thus doing what is necessary to get ahead, requires playing by the rules, implementing them as faithfully and effectively as possible—and staying out of trouble." Innovative actions "are bound to be threatening to the interests of someone, somewhere, in a position of political power."[26]

In addition, most states require superintendents and principals to become licensed, which involves a specified number of years teaching and a degree in educational administration. In some states there are also exams. These are careers, as political scientist Frederick M. Hess puts it, that "emphasize procedures rather than performance, allow credentials to insulate practitioners from accountability, and offer little room for entrepreneurial individuals . . ." As a result, they attract "candidates more concerned about security than success."[27] And because success takes a back seat to security, almost half of principals surveyed in 2001 thought it a "bad idea" to hold them responsible for student test scores.[28]

In New York, Los Angeles, and a few other big cities, the licensing process has been waived and superintendents brought in from outside the field of education, with much media fanfare. These are appointments meant to rattle the system—to break the culture of inertia. The power of the appointees to do so, however, is very limited. In fact, in a Public Agenda nationwide survey of principals and superintendents conducted in the summer of 2001, more than half of the superintendents complained they had to "work around the system to get things done." Both principals and superintendents complained that their hands were tied—that they lacked essential "authority and autonomy."[29]

In July 2002, New York City's new mayor, Michael Bloomberg, reached outside the field of education to name as chancellor of instruction Joel I. Klein, a former Justice Department lawyer best known for leading the antitrust prosecution of Microsoft. Both Bloomberg and Klein became whirlwinds of reform activity. Five months after his appointment, Klein announced, as part of a package of change, the creation of a "leadership academy" to train school principals. And yet, as Diane Ravitch has noted, "it is hard to see how it will help to train principals to be leaders when they have so little control over their staff, resources, or discipline policy."[30] Districts like

New York are "burdened not only with the enormous educational challenges of poverty and despair but by the tensions and rigidities of large bureaucracies," John E. Chubb has written in an essay titled "The System."[31]

That bureaucracy determines the school budget, how it's to be used, the size of the teaching staff and the pay scale, as well as a multitude of other aspects of schooling within the district. Principals are most often stuck with hiring the teachers that the central office has sent; it's extraordinarily difficult to fire anyone, as we will discuss below; and teacher shortages mean that principals are often grateful for warm bodies. With respect to salaries, the culture of teaching compounds the problem of collectively bargained contracts and district regulations, as Frederick Hess points out.[32] Proposals tying pay to student performance are at odds with the culture of the profession.

"Of course, the system does not really expect principals to succeed by being innovative," Chubb has noted. "The system gives principals almost no financial discretion. The principal is expected less to lead the school in creative directions than to manage the school according to the rules set out by the local board and the state. The only leader in the public system expected truly to lead is the superintendent."[33]

Superintendents are expected to lead; most do not succeed in doing so. Roy Romer, appointed superintendent of the Los Angeles Unified School District (LAUSD) in June 2000, had been a three-term governor of Colorado before he arrived in the City of Angels, and (like Klein) he certainly came ready to make things happen. Journalist Matthew Miller watched Romer closely for months. "I'm convinced that his experience, skills, and intellect make him the most talented person ever to hold the superintendent's job in Los Angeles, and perhaps in the nation," he wrote. "I also believe Romer is almost certain to fail, if by success we mean moving the needle on poor student achievement in a meaningful, lasting way," he concluded.[34] The test-score evidence available at the time of this writing confirms Miller's judgment. The "needle" has barely moved in the Los Angeles Unified School District.

The job is impossible, Miller came to believe. "A big-city superintendent ... operates in a straitjacket ..." The LAUSD is a $9 billion corporation; it serves more than 700,000 schoolchildren and contains 800 principals and 35,000 teachers. In that unmanageable behemoth, if Romer moves that "needle on poor student achievement in a meaningful, lasting way," it will be a first. Big-city superintendents last an average of 2.5 years. High expectations and quickly dashed hopes have made the job "a keep-your-bags-packed kind of career," as Michael Casserly, executive director of the Council of the Great City Schools, has described it.[35]

Rudy Crew became chancellor in the New York City school system in

1995; he was the tenth to be hired in a dozen years. He did manage to last four years, but it took the entire time to accomplish just one of his initial aims: abolishing tenure for principals. It was an essential step. If superintendents can't fire administrators who don't perform and replace them with people who do, how can they possibly improve the system? Other changes Crew wanted were not accomplished. "If I want to get things done, like instituting a longer school day," Crew told a *Time* reporter, "I have to go get the Governor's signature, the mayor's signature, the commissioner's signature, the board of regents' signature. Do you understand how much of my life I could spend here just getting those stars in alignment?"[36] No superintendent gets "those stars in alignment" very often, and, in any case, most don't keep their jobs long. Principals and teachers can thus afford to mark time—ignoring most attempts at reform, waiting until the day a new superintendent appears and assuming he or she will also soon disappear.

Crew's dependence on the collective consensus among all those players illuminates another major roadblock to reform: the political web in which all of them are enmeshed. "Schools are in the middle of the political arena," Donald R. McAdams, a former member of the Houston Board of Education, has noted.[37] "School reform is not reasoned debate about children, curriculum, teaching, and learning. It is political combat. Everyone is for school reform. But nearly everyone has another agenda."[38] What the governor was willing to give Rudy Crew, the mayor might object to. The state commissioner of education and the members of the board of regents also had their own agendas, which may or may not have had much relationship to better education.

For most political actors, the first item on their agenda is holding on to the power they have. That means maintaining the existing balance of political forces that created the status quo. Whenever a fundamental change is made, there will be winners and losers. The governor, the mayor, and other political players each have constituent groups upon whom they depend; a real reform that appeals to one is not likely to appeal to all.

In a big-city school system with a majority of students belonging to one minority group or another, a civil rights protest is among the scariest of threats. Exit exams determining high school graduation, changes in admissions criteria to magnet school programs or in other aspects of student assignment policy, new discipline policies, new hiring criteria, reductions in the food services workforce, a switch from one construction or maintenance subcontractor to another, or from one vendor to another—all such changes have possible racial dimensions that can spell political trouble. Better safe than sorry, most superintendents and other administrators surely believe.

So do many other players. The business community is usually engaged in the politics of school reform; elected and appointed officials cannot ignore those who pay most of the property taxes and keep a city economically afloat. But business leaders are rarely comfortable on the front lines in a battle for social change. They often want to do good; many see better schools as in their interest. Their business is business, however, and safety lies in sticking very close to the center on all politically charged issues.

Controversial stands are bad public relations. It is no accident that the favorite reforms of business titans like Walter Annenberg and Bill Gates, who have given $500 million and $350 million respectively to the public schools, are totally mainstream. Their programs have posed no challenge to the system itself.[39] Such philanthropists are not interested in disturbing the status quo, and given the magnitude of their grants—a gesture of trust in the system—their involvement in education becomes, in itself, a roadblock to change. By subsidizing the status quo, they strengthen it.

Roy Romer, a savvy former governor, probably never imagined how hard it would be to change the LAUSD—a mere school district. But from the superintendent on down, administrators in a public school system are constrained by rules, politics, and culture. All three constraints are intimately bound up with the power of the teachers unions—the most formidable roadblock of all.

Unions

Unions are "the preeminent power in American education," political scientist Terry M. Moe has written in an article that canvasses the landscape of teachers' unions and public schools.[40] As Moe points out, their extraordinary power derives in part from the fact that, in effect, they sit on both sides of the negotiating table. When management at General Motors squares off against the United Automobile Workers, each side has much at stake in the outcome of the negotiations. GM wants to keep its costs down; the union wants higher wages and other benefits. A CEO must protect the company's bottom line; caving in to excessive union demands erodes make-or-break profits. The union's desire to get more for its members is constrained by recognition that the company needs to make enough profit to stay afloat. If it goes under, or moves production to Mexico, the jobs will disappear.

Public education is very different. It's not a competitive business. Indeed, it is a near-monopoly. There is no equivalent bottom line; certainly, the amount that students have learned is not an analogue to the profit margin of a company. If students leave the system to attend private schools, their parents still pay the same taxes to support public schools. Union negotiators do not confront management representatives who are responsible to a completely different constituency; union power influences the makeup of the management team itself, a point to which we will return below.

More than four out of five of the nation's elementary and secondary school teachers belong to one of two unions: the National Education Association (NEA) or the American Federation of Teachers (AFT). Outside the South, wages, hours, and much else are settled through collective bargaining.[41] Even in the South—in a right-to-work state like Texas—school boards cannot ignore groups representing employees. Although unions do not technically have collective bargaining rights, the Texas Education Code, for instance, provides for formal "consultation" with the Houston Federation of Teachers and other employee organizations. The political power of those organizations gives them enormous leverage when issues involving wages and other working conditions are on the table.[42]

Collective bargaining settles the obvious bread-and-butter issues. As already noted, across the nation those settlements deprive superintendents and principals of the flexibility that every manager of a successful business takes for granted. In the fall of 2000, New York chancellor Harold O. Levy complained that the city tolerated "inadequate teacher education, noncompetitive pay, inflexible work rules and regulations denying bright people in other professions a chance to switch into teaching."[43] With the partial exception of inadequate teacher education, these are problems created by the power of unions.[44] "In a typical union contract," Moe writes, "there are so many rules about so many subjects, and the rules themselves can be so complicated, that it may take more than a hundred pages to spell them out." In the large urban districts, contracts actually can run to three hundred pages. Every provision in them reduces the discretion—and thus the innovative power—of principals and other administrators.

The "inflexible work rules and regulations" to which Levy referred cover almost every aspect of a teacher's professional life. There are rules about such obvious matters as pay, fringe benefits, hiring, firing, and promotion. But the contracts also regulate class preparation time, the school calendar, lunch duty, hall duty, after-school activities, student disciplinary procedures, class schedules, class size, professional development, professional meetings, and so forth. Even a curriculum change that eliminates a teaching position is a matter of union concern. In the spring of 2002, the California Teachers Association tried (unsuccessfully) to extend its power to curricular decisions and the selection of textbooks and instructional material—one of the few corners of education not already controlled by the unions.

The job of unions is to protect the interests of teachers. The job of schools is to educate the students. Many well-meaning reformers—Walter Annenberg, for example—fail to understand the difference between the two objectives. Most teachers, of course, genuinely care for their students and try hard to shape their development in positive ways. They want them to learn. On the other hand, the organizations that teachers form to speak for them collectively have a different, not always complementary, objective. Teachers unions seek higher wages, shorter hours, smaller classes, and a host of other things they perceive as better for their members. They want job control, and to limit the power of school administrators—management—over their members. One principal told us he had wanted a lunchtime meeting to discuss the school's failing students, but the teachers said it was not in their union contract.

What's good for unions is not necessarily good for kids, in other words. The point becomes excruciatingly clear in contemplating the rules that often govern jobs. When there's a vacancy, the most senior applicant gets the position. And when a teacher with seniority wants a job in a particular school, a beginning teacher without tenure is out of luck. Quality is irrelevant. In 1990, Cathy Nelson was named Minnesota's "teacher of the year." But by the time the award was announced, she was no longer working as a teacher; she had been laid off as a result of her district's last-hired, first-fired policy. After finding herself repeatedly bumped by teachers with greater seniority in a series of schools, she left the profession.[45]

Many a principal wishes that other teachers would depart—not the Cathy Nelsons, obviously, but those who either aren't any good or simply don't fit in that particular school. Getting rid of an unwanted teacher, however, can be an expensive nightmare. After three years in most systems, teachers have tenure and are protected not only by union contracts, but by state laws and regulations. William Coats is an education attorney in the state of Washington. "There are so many layers of regulation," he says, that in cases brought against incompetent teachers, the volume of documentation he handles "is comparable to the O. J. Simpson trial."[46]

Three months into his tenure as superintendent of schools in Milwaukee, Howard Fuller attempted to terminate three teachers and a principal for misconduct. He had a video of one teacher reading a newspaper while his students were shooting craps, and other equally incriminating evidence. His staff told him that it was not enough to fire them. "I was under the illusion that I was the damn superintendent, and that I could actually do something," he later said. He was wrong; his staff was right. The teachers kept their jobs.[47]

As the new principal of P.S. 86 in New York City, Sheldon Benardo tried to remove "one of the worst teachers" he'd ever seen from his school. Litigation dragged on for three and half years, during which time the teacher collected her full salary. A settlement was finally negotiated, but was the whole process worth it? "I'd have to think hard before trying it again," Mr. Benardo told a *Christian Science Monitor* reporter.[48] Firing a teacher protected by tenure is so difficult that, in many cases, administrators don't even try. In a practice known as "the dance of the lemons" or "passing the trash," administrators make deals with the unions, giving bad teachers satisfactory evaluations in exchange for union cooperation in shifting them to another school or into make-work positions outside the classroom.

Teachers unions are organizations dedicated to improving the working conditions of employees and are thus resistant to any change that would elevate the interests of students over those of teachers. That fact is obviously a serious roadblock to change. The principal in a regular public school who wants to pick a philosophically compatible teaching team as the best charter schools do—or to hold on to a wonderful teacher with little seniority, like Cathy Nelson—can't do it. On the other hand, tenured teachers who can't teach, can't control a class, and behave in manifestly unacceptable ways are in the system as long as they want to stay, with rare exceptions. Moreover, a superintendent who would like to compete against, say, General Electric in the open market for mathematicians is out of luck. The laws of supply and demand don't apply in the public schools; wages do not increase when the demand for a particular kind of teacher outstrips the supply.

The current system would not be as bad if school boards negotiating contracts with the unions put a high priority on protecting students from rules and regulations that make no educational sense. But to a large extent, as alluded to earlier, management and labor in a public school system are on the same side of the table—especially in strong union states. Whether elected or appointed, serving on a school board is a political job. Members are either directly elected or owe their position to elected officials. And it happens that unions are usually powerhouses in local, state, and national politics.

Often working short days and enjoying long vacations, union members have the time to lick envelopes, man the phone banks, ring doorbells, and in general mobilize support for sympathetic candidates in political contests. The substantial funds that the union can contribute to a campaign further magnify the value of a union endorsement. School board elections are low-profile, low-turnout affairs that often attract less than a tenth of eligible voters. But union members, their families, and a high number of those whom the unions have reached with their message are sure to turn out. Parents seldom perceive a conflict between their interests and those of the teachers.

Rarely are there any visible groups that convey a different message. Even if many parents are unhappy about the schooling their children are receiving, few will see the remedy as involving political action—unless union opposition is also politically well organized. The result is often a management team that is, in large part, a creation of the union itself. It is thus not likely to spearhead change—biting the hand that feeds it.

At the state and national level, too, the teachers unions are politically active—investing in the candidates of their choice, mobilizing voters, "researching" issues, lobbying legislators and executive branch appointees, monitoring their record in office, keeping the press informed, and so forth. They are arguably the single most important interest group in the Democratic Party—and a very powerful interest group in many states. Their power shapes the education agenda of the Democrats, and in that way affects all state and federal education policy. Perhaps most important, as Moe notes, they can use that power to veto change—to protect the rigid bureaucratic rules that protect educators at the expense of the students whose interests they are supposed to serve.

Unions have not been able to get everything they want, of course. They desperately wanted to defeat Florida governor Jeb Bush in his reelection bid in 2002; they failed to do so. They can ask for much higher teachers' salaries, but in fact schools must make do with the money that taxpayers are willing to provide. Some reforms that unions find unwelcome cannot be stopped altogether, although they usually can be trimmed to a significant degree. As Chapter 2 indicated, the NEA initially opposed statewide testing, for instance. Unlike the AFT, it refused to endorse No Child Left Behind. But while it lost the fight against testing, it has continued to argue for "more flexible" portfolios and against the use of "high-stakes" assessments.

Union reaction to the decade-old charter school movement fits this pattern.[49] Although Albert Shanker, longtime head of the American Federation of Teachers, was an early supporter, unions were and are generally hostile to the charter idea. The problem, from their point of view, is that (in most states) charter school teachers need not be union members, and that teachers at these schools lack many of the job protections that unions typically secure in their contracts with school districts. Once it became clear that the charter concept had broad appeal, unions switched to damage control. While professing to be supporters of the basic idea, they have fought to place strict caps on the number of charter schools in a state, pushed for requirements that charters be unionized, and sought to keep them enmeshed in the web of regulations so as to make them as much like regular public schools as possible.[50]

Union opposition, overt or covert, has not killed the charter drive; in the 2002–2003 school year there were approximately 2,700 charter schools in thirty-six states and the District of Columbia, a remarkable growth in a period of just a decade.[51] But they are still only a tiny fraction of the more than 90,000 public schools in the country. Because charter schools tend to be small, they represent an even smaller fraction of total enrollments—a shade above 1 percent. Few parents today have the option of choosing a charter school for their children. Moreover, at the rate the movement has been growing, Frederick Hess has calculated, 2,000 new charter schools would have to be started each year through 2015 for the total enrollment to approach 10 percent of the public school population."[52] Nevertheless, we will argue below, their very presence—and the stunning success of some—is a long-term threat to union power, and the unions know it. Hence the fight they are putting up.

Standards, Testing, and Accountability

Many supporters of standards, testing, and accountability see these reforms—which have swept the states and are now embodied in federal law—as a means of circumventing the roadblocks to change created by rules and regulations for which unions are in great part responsible. Tenured teachers can't be fired, except under the most extraordinary circumstances. Principals can't offer higher salaries to the best and brightest in order to lure them into teaching inner-city students who desperately need high-powered and deeply committed help. But now, at last, there are consequences for falling down on the job. Schools can find themselves invaded by state department of education teams established to intervene in failing schools; the state itself or private management companies like Edison Schools can start running local schools; students have the right to leave a persistently "failing" public school for a more successful one; federal funds can be withdrawn.

In other words, schools are now accountable to an unprecedented degree, at least in theory. The No Child Left Behind Act demands that black and Hispanic students, as well as those who are white and Asian, become "proficient" in core subjects by the end of the school year 2013–2014. Will this new system of accountability be sufficient to bring real change? Both the federal government and the states have pointed a finger at public schools and said, in effect, you have a responsibility to educate every child. You cannot shirk that responsibility. And yet a brave school administrator might ask in response, "Where is the freedom to meet that responsibility? We can never meet the visionary goal of universal proficiency without changing many things over which we have no power."

In fact, that is the one rejoinder that public school authorities are unlikely to offer. They have continued (and will continue) to say, send more money. They may complain about kids in poverty, families in disarray. But they are too embedded in the system to force a look at the real issue; the roadblocks to change that ensure too much educational mediocrity.

Standards, testing, and accountability are a long-overdue and much-needed reform. In Massachusetts, school systems are responding positively to the new expectations, as we noted in the previous chapter. But can states across the nation institute and retain tough tests with real consequences for those who fail? Many eighth-graders do not have eighth-grade skills, at least if we accept the NAEP standard of what Basic achievement is. How many students can schools refuse to promote to the ninth grade? How many youngsters can be kept from graduating from high school on the basis of their performance on a statewide test? The question becomes particularly difficult when greatly disproportionate numbers of the failing students are black or Hispanic. The racial gap in academic achievement is, in this sense, itself a roadblock to change.

In addition, under the best of circumstances, federal and state mandates have limited power to force change. As Chester E. Finn, Jr., former assistant secretary of education and current president of the Thomas B. Fordham Foundation, has noted, "Washington has remarkably little clout. . . . Beyond jawboning and sun-lighting, there's not a lot the feds can do" if states resist No Child Left Behind.[53] The federal government has never actually withheld funds from schools with students in poverty; to do so punishes the kids for the sins of the adults.

States can set standards and impose testing, which may be of mixed quality—a fact the federal government can't fix. In any case, those standards must be implemented by the schools and the teachers within them, who can make or break the state's reforms. Departments of education can take charge of failing school districts, but experience in New Jersey and elsewhere suggests such takeovers do not work well; states don't know how to run local school systems effectively. State authorities can send intervention teams to help weak schools, but such teams are outsiders, there today and gone tomorrow, and are only as good as the people assigned to them.

No Child Left Behind gives parents an unprecedented right to transfer their children out of schools that fail to make "adequate yearly progress" over a two-year period. That entitlement promises more than it can deliver. What does such a "right" mean in districts in which most schools are mediocre or worse, and those that parents prefer are full?

As of early 2003, school authorities have shown themselves to be extremely reluctant to meet their legal obligation to provide the parents of children in failing schools information about better alternatives. Class action suits have already been filed by angry parents in New York City and Albany, and similar criticisms have been made of the Boston School Department.[54] "The idea that choice should be limited by a lack of capacity runs counter to the intent of this law," officials at the U.S. Department of Education have stated. School authorities "cannot say that all the good schools are full and deny parents access."[55] Will the department (in an unprecedented move) actually deny Title I schools federal funds and deprive kids of services when the school districts ignore the law? Tough talk is easy, but punitive action has always been politically difficult. In addition, there are obvious limits to how much and how quickly it is possible to expand enrollments at the better schools.

Choice

It is no accident that all of the wonderful schools we describe in Chapters 3 and 4 are charter schools, as we noted at the outset of this chapter. They are free from most of the constraints under which regular schools operate. The principals in these charter schools control their budgets, choose their teachers, ignore the usual credentials that determine who can be hired, establish the length of the school day, and so forth.[56]

In addition, choice—that exercised by teachers, parents, and students—is integral to their success. Only teachers for whom the school is right join the staff and stay. Principals and teachers gain leverage from the simple fact that students who come willingly can be told: "If you don't like it here, go elsewhere. The academic and behavioral demands are not as high in most schools; you will be able to spend more hours watching television and fewer engaged in schoolwork. But, it's your choice. We open doors; you must choose to walk through them."

Unless more schools are freed from the constraints of the traditional public school system, the racial gap in academic achievement will not significantly narrow, we suspect. Indeed, every urban school should become a charter. States must insist that schools meet rigorous academic standards, and student results on statewide standards-based tests should be the most important measure of success. Many will be educationally disappointing, some will be corrupt, but unlike the traditional public schools, those that fall down on the job can be closed—and have already been closed in substantial numbers.[57] Within the public school system, they are uniquely accountable, and they provide a setting in which good education at least has the potential to flourish.

We're a long way off from urban districts charterizing all schools. In the foreseeable future, those who want to run charter schools will have to start from scratch—overcoming numerous roadblocks to change in this respect as well. Getting started is very difficult, and some state charter laws make it particularly difficult.[58] But regardless of the details of a particular state law, a charter school is, in part, a business, requiring a level of entrepreneurship that those who want to dedicate their lives to rescuing inner-city kids do not generally have. The founders need to design a school and make their way through a lengthy and sometimes politically difficult application process, secure start-up capital, find a facility, negotiate a lease, buy books, computers, and supplies, locate vendors who will provide cafeteria and other services, solve transportation problems, meet a payroll before the school even officially opens, gain trust in the community, fend off well-organized anticharter attacks, and recruit students.

If the KIPP replication project works, and the network includes two hundred schools by 2010, as planned, some of the start-up problems for this relatively small number of schools may be mitigated. For-profit companies (and other "education management organizations") can also solve capital and some of the other problems—provided they demonstrate more success than they have to date. But the larger problems will remain: the political, union, and other opposition that discourages would-be founders and limits the scale of the entire effort; the difficulty of finding superb and effective principals and teachers who are willing to stick with a job that's relentlessly hard.[59]

The roadblocks to creating charter schools are substantial; those standing in the way of using public money to send low-income students to private and parochial schools are even greater, of course. As Terry M. Moe notes, "a genuine victory by the voucher movement would have far-reaching consequences for the 'system,' affecting, possibly in big ways, the number of people it employs, the amount of money it controls, the distribution of power, the prospects for collective bargaining, and much more."[60] A great many people have a powerful vested interest in maintaining the educational status quo, and anything that would rock the boat—perhaps even capsize the boat—will be bitterly resisted.

Furthermore, the general public is ambivalent about voucher plans. Some widely publicized surveys have found that roughly two out of three Americans oppose the idea, but these surveys are based on poorly framed questions that stack the deck against vouchers.[61] When parents are asked about their interest in private schools if cost were no barrier, their response is much more positive.[62] Those more favorable attitudes, however, do not translate into significant political pressure for school choice. Even in inner cities, where support for the idea of vouchers is particularly high, Moe observes that "there is little overt demand. The support is there, but it is latent."[63] Opinion in favor of drastic change in the system will have to be mobilized at a much higher level than it is now to overcome the enormously powerful forces that buttress the status quo.[64]

A 2002 Supreme Court decision lowered one major barrier in the way of the voucher movement. In *Zelman v. Simmons-Harris,* the justices rejected the argument that using public funds for tuition at religious schools violated the establishment clause of the First Amendment. However, many state constitutions today include so-called Blaine amendments that mandate stricter separation of church and state than the U.S. Constitution does, and it will require further legal or political victories to overcome that obstacle.

Cracks in the Edifice

The obstacles to true reform—to creating quality education that would enable schools to close the racial gap—are formidable. We have run through some of them in this chapter. The process of becoming a teacher is, with few exceptions, cumbersome and mind-numbing, with the result that talented young people choose other professions. For the most part, principals cannot select their own teaching team and the pay scale is rigidly egalitarian. Schools have been given the responsibility of educating every child without the freedom essential to doing so. The profession does not reward imaginative, ambitious, competitive innovators. Educators are enmeshed in a political web, which means school reform is often not about children, but about power. Rules, regulations, politics, and a culture hostile to reform all constrain those who want change. Unions have enormous power, and yet what's good for the unions is not necessarily good for kids. And so forth.

More than a decade ago, in *Politics, Markets, and American Schools,* John Chubb and Terry Moe wrote: "We believe existing institutions cannot solve the problem [of low-performing students], because they *are* the problem. . . ."[65] Those in charge of the current system—those with vested interests in the status quo—have the power to prevent fundamental change. In fact, preventing change is precisely the point of the elaborate school bureaucracy (of which reformers all complain), Chubb and Moe argue. Policy decisions are made by a wide range of constituent groups, but those decisions are never self-implementing. Noncompliance is always a danger, hence the need for hierarchies of authority and formal rules to limit discretion and insulate policies from the power of new political actors with new agendas.

No Child Left Behind, as we already noted, was envisioned as a means of circumventing the many obstacles to change. The standards, tests, and accountability built into the law have the potential to raise overall student performance in the context of encouraging educational change. Whether they will succeed in substantially closing the racial gap—getting every student up to proficiency, as the law also requires—is a separate question. An attempt has been made to lighten the bureaucratic hand—to allow "unprecedented flexibility in the use of Federal education funds in exchange for strong accountability for results." But that flexibility is confined to state and district decisions involving federally funded programs, which means primarily Title I.

Closing the racial gap will demand more than existing reforms can promise; the charter schools we admire would not have succeeded without the freedom to set salaries, school hours, curricular and other matters. It has been equally important that parents, students, and teachers have chosen to be there; the academic engagement of the students, their willingness to adhere to the established norms of behavior, and the extraordinary commitment of their principals and teachers all depend on choice. That choice and the considerable (but not unlimited) freedom that charter schools enjoy are essential ingredients in any serious effort to close the gap.

"Defenders of the status quo have faced . . . little in the way of concerted opposition. . . . No powerful political groups with a stake in public education—business groups, civil rights groups, civic groups, religious groups—have dedicated themselves to reforming the institutions of educational governance," Chubb and Moe noted in 1990. Today, that solidarity in defense of the status quo may be starting to erode. Schools like KIPP and North Star tell a story about potential—the sort of academic achievement that might result from fundamental educational change. They provide a window on another landscape, a glimpse of a different future for black and Hispanic kids.

In addition, important voices in the African-American political and educational community are beginning to throw their support behind vouchers. They include the Rev. Floyd Flake, a former member of the U.S. House of Representatives; former Milwaukee schools superintendent Howard L. Fuller, J. Kenneth Blackwell, Ohio secretary of state; and civil rights hero and former congressman Andrew Young, among others. It is perhaps only a matter of time before these distinguished men are widely perceived as the voice of civil rights, speaking for black parents and their children. Organizations such as the Black Alliance for Educational Options—with Fuller as chairman of the board—have already begun the process of grass-roots organizing in the inner city.

Moe's survey data, which we discussed earlier, suggest that latent support for vouchers in inner cities is already strong. The lure of charter schools and even vouchers may prove irresistible if No Child Left Behind fails to close the racial gap in academic achievement, as we predict it will. Closing that gap requires fundamental change in the structure of American education. Today the roadblocks to real reform are still in place, but NCLB, charter schools, and the small voucher experiments already up and running are the first cracks in the edifice—a heartening harbinger, perhaps, of better things to come.

Conclusion

When you fail, when everybody fails my child, what happens? Nothing. Nobody gets fired. Nothing happens to nobody, except my child.
Parent at a New York City School Board meeting[1]

Do you think American education needs to be restructured or reformed? One hundred percent.
Question posed to Jaime Escalante and his answer[2]

We opened this book with a devastating portrait of the racial gap in academic achievement. An employer hiring the typical black high school graduate, or the college that admits the average black student, is choosing a youngster who has only an eighth-grade education. In most subjects, the majority of black students by twelfth grade do not have even a "partial mastery" of the skills and knowledge that the authoritative National Assessment of Educational Progress says are "fundamental for proficient work" at their grade. In math, only 0.2 percent of blacks score at the Advanced level, the very top of the scale; the figure for whites is 11 times higher, and for Asians 37 times higher. Hispanic scores on the nation's educational report card are not significantly different from those of blacks. African Americans have made tremendous gains since the days when most sat in classrooms in legally segregated schools. But they have made no further progress in the past fifteen years, and have fallen back in some subjects.

These numbers make us furious. More than a third of blacks today are in the middle class; a third live in suburbia. Racial progress on many fronts has been enormously heartening. But in a society committed to equal opportunity, we still have a racially identifiable group of educational have-nots—young African Americans and Latinos whose opportunities in life will almost inevitably be limited by their inadequate education. There is no good excuse for this racial gap in skills and knowledge. "If white kids were being paralyzed by a system the way minority kids are, the system would change, the attitudes even of the union members would change," the Reverend Floyd Flake has charged.[3] Plenty of white and Asian kids are also being shortchanged, but it is the black and Hispanic numbers that suggest appalling indifference.

In part, however, the gap has been ignored because the numbers are painful and frightening, we suspect. But if we shut our eyes to a painful reality, the problem will never be fixed. Ignorance is often comfortable ground on which to stand, and yet this is a problem that requires the sort of radical reform that only discomfort and anger will inspire. Anger is already long overdue. These are our children. Ongoing racial inequality is not only morally unacceptable; it corrupts the fabric of American society and endangers our future.

The racial gap is evident in suburban as well as inner-city schools, but it is the high-need kids from distressed neighborhoods who are most in danger of reaching adulthood without the basic skills and knowledge they need to prosper. The origins of the problem of inadequate schooling do not lie with the children themselves. They are only kids, after all—kids who come into kindergarten already behind. But the solution does lie in part with them and with their parents. Schools cannot level the playing field without help. They need families and students to meet them halfway.

Families must help their children to the best of their ability, and agree that unacceptable behavior is a family affair. Students must take responsibility for their decisions. Schools cannot do their job unless students get to school on time, attend classes faithfully, work hard, finish their homework, pay attention to their teachers, and honor the rules governing civility and decorum.

Meeting the demands of schools is harder for members of some racial and ethnic groups than for others. Some group cultures are more academically advantageous than others. Asian parents typically expect their children to work extraordinarily hard in school—and the children do so, cutting classes less often than their peers, enrolling in AP classes at triple the white rate, spending twice as much time on homework as their non-Asian classmates. As a result, on some math tests, the white-Asian gap is actually larger than the black-white gap. But whites can learn to work as hard as Asian students do, and so, obviously, can blacks and Hispanics. The values, habits, and skills that we call "culture" are not impervious to change. Indeed, they are shaped and reshaped by the social environment, and schools can play an invaluable part in that process.

Group cultural differences thus mean that schools have to work harder and smarter, particularly with highly disadvantaged non-Asian minority students. The best inner-city schools have greatly extended instructional time and created safe environments. They focus relentlessly on the core academic subjects, insisting that their students learn the times tables, basic historical facts, spelling, punctuation, and the rules of grammar. But they also aim to transform the culture of their students, as that culture affects academic achievement.

Recall the rhetorical question of Gregory Hodge, the head of the Frederick Douglass Academy in New York's Harlem. "Are we conservative here?" he asked us. "Of course we are," he answered. "We teach middle-class values like responsibility." KIPP's David Levin echoed Hodge. "We are fighting a battle involving skills and values. We are not afraid to set social norms," he said. The best schools work hard to instill "desire, discipline, and dedication"—KIPP watchwords. Disciplined behavior and disciplined work go hand-in-hand. But these educators also believe, as Rafe Esquith has put it, that their "job is to open a lot of doors. . . . [The students'] job is to choose which ones to walk through." They make choices, and choices have consequences. "It's not my job to save your souls," he tells his class. "It's my job to give you an opportunity to save your own soul."

Excellent schools deliver a clear message to their students: No Excuses. No excuses for failing to do your homework, failing to work hard in general; no excuses for fighting with other students, running in the hallways, dressing inappropriately, and so forth. Americans need to say to their schools as well: No Excuses. Given the challenges urban students face, more money well spent could improve education. But it does not cost more to set high academic and behavioral standards, and inadequate funding and overcrowded classes do not explain the racial gap. Neither does racial isolation. Family poverty is no excuse for failing to teach kids.

It's true that too many teachers and too many principals are not up to the job. Even Sandra Feldman, president of the American Federation of Teachers, has admitted as much. But the unions have contributed substantially to the problem. Their insistence on traditional teaching credentials, their opposition to market-based and merit pay, and their rigid rules about hiring and firing and other aspects of the job are major obstacles to attracting academically gifted and ambitious college graduates into the profession.

The American educational system is a recipe for mediocrity. Many good people work in schools and in school administration. But the teaching profession does not reward imaginative, ambitious, competitive innovators. Nor does it reward dedication or (for the most part) impressive student results. Big-city superintendents and principals operate in a bureaucratic and political straitjacket. Indeed, the nature of their jobs encourages inertia. Doing a good job, doing what's necessary to get ahead, requires playing by the rules and staying out of trouble. Even the best superintendents say they have to work around the system to get the job done. That system is in great part a creation of the teachers' unions, with their enormous power to set rigid rules and regulations that determine even such matters as class preparation time, the school calendar, class schedules, lunch and hall duty, and after-school activities. Without incentives for excellence and innovation, and the discretionary power to meet the needs of students, no wonder so many schools are so disappointing.

No Child Left Behind, with its standards, tests, and system of accountability, was conceived as a way around some of the obstacles to change that ensure continuing mediocrity. With its emphasis on student results as measured by test scores (outputs instead of inputs like money) and its consequences for inadequate progress, it's a big step in the right direction. It should be enforced strenuously—within the grave limits of federal power over schools.

But there has been much tinkering with the existing public school system since 1965, and the results have been too meager. The two largest federal programs serving a largely minority constituency—Title I and Head Start—have accomplished very little. The standards, tests, and accountability measures that states have put in place have not leveled the playing field, and No Child Left Behind will not suffice to close the racial gap. KIPP, North Star, Amistad and other such schools are radically different from ordinary public schools. At a minimum, principals need what these charter schools have: control over their budgets, the power to hire unlicensed but academically strong teachers, the authority to restructure the school day, the freedom to shape the curriculum and to turn their schools into ones that students choose to attend.

As we indicated in the last chapter, we are also voucher advocates for low-income urban families. We noted that survey data indicate that latent support for vouchers in inner cities is already strong. In speaking to the National Education Association in August 2002, Secretary of Education Rod Paige noted that "competition is here to stay, and it is growing. If we don't bring real reform to public schools, . . . families will leave the system in droves."[4] We believe that's true, but they need someplace to go, of course. If the Black Alliance for Educational Options (BAEO), the Institute for Justice, and other organizations committed to school choice succeed, however, parents will have private and parochial, as well as public, options.

Vouchers are a matter of basic equity. The term "middle class" is slippery, but here's one good definition: Middle-class parents are people who can choose where their children go to school by choosing where they live. Choice should not be a class-based privilege.[5] Howard Fuller, head of the BAEO, has put the point well: "This is a debate about power . . . about whether parents of low-income, mostly African American children should obtain a power that many critics of the choice movement exercise every day on behalf of their own children."[6]

African Americans today can serve as secretary of state, CEO of a major corporation, president of an Ivy League university, chief surgeon at a major hospital. But their access to positions of power and prestige—and to well-paying jobs in general—will be limited if they typically leave high school with an eighth-grade education. Americans with equal skills and knowledge have equal earnings today—whatever their race or ethnicity. But those equal skills and knowledge are the unfinished business of the civil rights revolution of the last forty years.

The racial gap is thus the most important civil rights issue of our time. If Americans care about racial equality (and they do, all surveys of public opinion suggest), they must demand more than the current reform movement is offering—standards, tests, some consequences for educational failure, and limited public school choice. The nation's system of education must be fundamentally altered, with real educational choice as part of the package.

The alternative to a radical overhaul is an appallingly large number of black and Hispanic youngsters continuing to leave high school without the skills and knowledge to do well in life; doors closed to too many non-Asian minorities; the perpetuation of ancient inequalities. Is that acceptable? What decent American will say yes?

Notes

Introduction

1. Alan Richard, "California School Sets Own Path on Achievement Gaps, *Education Week,* May 8, 2002, 1.

2. Dale Mezzacappa, "Facing an Issue Few Want to Touch," *Philadelphia Inquirer,* June 17, 2001, A1.

3. National Center for Education Statistics, *Digest of Education Statistics 2001,* NCES 2002-130, (Washington, D.C.: U.S. Department of Education 2002), 17, and NCES, *The Condition of Education 2001,* NCES 2001-072 (Washington, D.C.: U.S. Department of Education, 2002), 145.

4. Robert P. Moses and Charles E. Cobb, Jr., *Radical Equations: Math Literacy and Civil Rights* (Boston: Beacon Press, 2001), 5, 14.

5. Lawrence E. Gladieux and Watson Scott Swail, "Financial Aid Is Not Enough," *College Board Review,* no. 185 (Summer 1998), 6; "Reading and Mathematics Achievement: Growth in High School," Washington, D.C.: U.S. Department of Education, National Center for Education Statistics, December 1997.

6. Michael A. Fletcher, "Ind. Schools Shrink Black-White Divide: A Focus on Attitudes Raises Altitudes in Scores," *Washington Post,* February 21, 2002, A3.

7. We use the terms "Hispanic" and "Latino" interchangeably here; likewise the terms "black" and "African American." The latest available enrollment figures are for 1999; National Center for Education Statistics, *The Condition of Education 2001,* 110. In 1972, only 20.6 percent of public school students were black or Hispanic. Since then, the black share has risen by less than 2 percentage points, from 14.8 percent to 16.5 percent. The figure for Hispanics has nearly tripled, rising from 5.8 percent to 16.2 percent, due to both continuing heavy immigration from Latin American countries and the high fertility rates of Hispanic women.

8. Annual meeting of the Education Leaders Council, September 26–28, 1992, Denver, Colorado.

9. Quoted in Michael Kelly, " 'F' for School Reform," *Washington Post,* April 11, 2001, A27.

10. Hugh Davis Graham, *The Uncertain Triumph: Federal Education Policy in the Kennedy and Johnson Years* (Chapel Hill: University of North Carolina Press, 1984), 79.

11. Herb Peyser, letter to *The New York Times,* June 1, 2002, A14.

12. Sarah Tantillo, "Culture Formation in Charter Schools: Two Case Studies," unpublished dissertation, Graduate School of Education, Rutgers, The State University of New Jersey, January 2001, 72.

One: Left Behind

1. "Views over the Gap," *Education Week,* March 15, 2000, 19.

2. Michael A. Fletcher, "Ind. Schools Shrink Black-White Divide: A Focus on Attitudes Raises Altitudes in Scores," *Washington Post,* February 21, 2002, A3.

3. Liz Seymour, "Too Few Make Cut as Fairfax's Gifted," *Washington Post,* April 28, 2002, C8.

4. There are three types of NAEP assessments. The Trend NAEP is an exam devised to be comparable over the three decades that NAEP has been operating. It tests students at ages 9, 13, and 17. We use some of its findings—in fig. 1-4, 1-5, and 1-6 later in this chapter, for example—but rely more heavily on the Main NAEP, an assessment based on much larger samples of students in the fourth, eighth, and twelfth grades. It is supposed to be more responsive to changes in the curriculum, since its purpose is not to gauge long-term trends. But it appears to have changed little since 1990, and those are the findings we use here. A further advantage of the Main NAEP is that data since 1990 may be obtained by using the remarkable and convenient NAEP Data Tool, available at http://nces.ed.gov/ nationsreportcard/naepdata. The Data Tool not only supplies the results of all Main NAEP assessments since 1990; it allows researchers to cross-tabulate results by a great many variables, permitting much more analysis than is possible using the published volumes reporting assessment results. The third type of NAEP assessment is the state assessments, conducted in about two-thirds of the states since 1990. We analyze some of the findings in chap. 12. The 2001 No Child Left Behind Act makes it mandatory for all states to participate in the state NAEP exams henceforth. All references to NAEP results in the text are based on data gathered through the NAEP Data Tool unless otherwise indicated.

5. The average performance of American Indians on NAEP tests is also very poor. This book does not deal with them, both because their numbers are small and because the situation of American Indians is unique in a number of ways.

6. We cannot provide similar evidence on performance in science, writing, and civics in the same year because the Main NAEP data were not reported in a form to allow comparisons across grade levels. But it is quite clear from other evidence that the racial gap is as wide or even wider in other subjects. See fig. 1-6. On the 1999 Trend NAEP, 90 percent of whites scored higher than the average black in science, and 78 percent of whites scored above the average for Hispanics.

7. Blacks in the twelfth grade were 12 points behind white eighth-graders in mathematics and 13 points behind in geography. We do not have comparable tests of whites in the seventh grade, but we know their scores in the fourth grade, and can calculate the average gain they made each year between the fourth and eighth grades. On that basis, we can conclude that in both subjects black students scored about the same as whites in the seventh grade. There are problems with this method, as discussed in Christopher Jencks and Meredith Phillips, eds., *The Black-White Test Score Gap* (Washington, D.C.: Brookings Institution Press, 1998), 26–29 and chap. 7. Nonetheless, it is a useful way of illustrating the dimensions of the problem, in our view.

8. A note about terminology. We will use "racial" here to include Hispanics, though they are not officially a "racial" but an "ethnic" group. In fact, the federal government treats them as a quasi-racial group in everything but name, and it will be simpler to use the adjective "racial" rather than "racial or ethnic." Likewise, we use the term "white" to refer to non-Hispanic whites, to avoid sprinkling the text with that odd and cumbersome term. For a critical discussion of how these categories have been defined by federal agencies, see Stephan Thernstrom, "The Demography of Racial and Ethnic Groups," in Abigail Thernstrom and Stephan Thernstrom, eds., *Beyond the Color Line: New Perspectives on Race and Ethnicity in America* (Stanford, Calif.: Hoover Institution Press, 2002), 13–36. For more on this complex and often bizarre story, see Peter Skerry, *Counting on the Census? Race, Group Identity, and the Evasion of Politics* (Washington, D.C.: Brookings Institution Press, 2000).

9. These definitions are provided in all NAEP publications reporting results by achievement levels. See, for example, National Center for Education Statistics, *NAEP 1998 Reading Report Card for the Nation and the States*, NCES 1999-500 (Washington, D.C.: U.S. Department of Education, 1999), 9.

10. Critical reviews of the NAEP levels by the General Accounting Office and the National Academy of Sciences have suggested that the standards are unrealistically high. Recent NAEP reports preface discussions of achievement levels by calling them "provisional"

and subject to future revision; see, for example, the *NAEP 1998 Reading Report Card*, 8–12.

11. These precise ratios should not be taken too seriously, because all the NAEP tests are based on samples, and even very large samples have some margin of error. The math figures given are for 1996, because the 2000 mathematics assessment did not report the proportion of students rating as Advanced to the decimal point level. Although the ratios are speciously precise, they vividly illustrate the unquestionable fact that the alarmingly large differences between average students of different races are even greater when you look only at those at the very top of the distribution. Note the very similar ratios among students who scored in the top bracket (750 or better) on the 1999 SAT test in mathematical reasoning. Just 168 black students in the country, 0.14 percent of all African-American test-takers, had 750 or better, as compared with 1.84 percent of whites and 6.29 of Asian Americans. The white-black disparity was 13 to 1; the Asian-black disparity was 45 to 1. SAT data from College Entrance Examination Board, "1999 National Ethnic/Sex Data," unpublished, unpaginated document, 2000.

12. See Stephan Thernstrom and Abigail Thernstrom, "Racial Preferences in Higher Education: An Assessment of the Evidence," in Stanley A. Renshon, ed., *One America? Political Leadership, National Identity, and the Dilemmas of Diversity* (Washington, D.C.: Georgetown University Press, 2001), 169–231.

13. National Center for Education Statistics, *Digest of Education Statistics 2001*, NCES 2001-072 (Washington, D.C.: U.S. Department of Education, 2002), 17. The white high school completion rate for that age group was 56 percent.

14. U.S. Bureau of the Census, Current Population Reports, Special Studies, P-23-80, *The Social and Economic Status of the Black Population in the United States: An Historical View, 1790–1978* (Washington, D.C.: U.S. Government Printing Office, 1979), 94–95. In the North and West, the gap between blacks and whites in the number of years of school completed was much narrower.

15. According to the most recent official estimates by the National Center of Education Statistics, 91.8 percent of non-Hispanic whites aged 18–24, 83.7 percent of blacks, 64.1 percent of Hispanics, and 94.6 percent of Asian/Pacific Islanders were high school graduates in 2000; National Center for Education Statistics, *Dropout Rates in the United States, 2000*, NCES 2002-114 (Washington, D.C.: U.S. Department of Education, 2002), 20. Jay Greene of the Manhattan Institute has employed different methods to study the question, and they indicate much lower high school completion rates, especially for non-Asian minority students. Greene estimates that just 76 percent of whites in the relevant age group actually received a public school diploma in 2000, 79 percent of Asians, and only 55 percent of blacks and 53 percent of Hispanics; Jay Greene, *Public School Graduation Rates in the United States*, Civic Report no. 31 (New York: Manhattan Institute, 2002), 3. Greene's research is the source of the figures on state-level high school graduation rates by race given in the widely consulted "Quality Counts" special issue of *Education Week*, January 9, 2003, 83. Some of the difference between the Greene and NCES numbers is due to the fact that Greene does not count students who earn GEDs or other high school equivalency certificates as high school graduates, while NCES does. Nor does Greene have information on graduates of private schools who were attending public school in the ninth grade and then transferred to a private institution. But there remains a large discrepancy after allowing for these factors. Greene's findings are important, and may be of particular relevance to anyone appraising the success of state educational policies. It would be a mistake, though, to conclude from Greene's work that little more than half of blacks and Hispanics today finish high school, and that even fewer thus could be going on to higher education. His failure to include students who passed high school equivalency exams seems misguided to us. Although some studies have suggested that students with GEDs are not much better off than high school dropouts without them, the most recent evidence points in the opposite direction. Thus a large-scale NCES national survey of eighth-graders in 1988 that traced them to 2000 found that students with GEDs or other equivalency certificates had median earnings

28 percent higher than high-school dropouts without a certificate in 2000, and were far more likely to have obtained some postsecondary education; National Center for Education Statistics, *Coming of Age in the 1990s: The Eighth-Grade Class of 1988 12 Years Later,* NCES 2002-321 (Washington, D.C.: U.S. Department of Education, 2002), 22, 40. Acquiring a GED thus paid off very significantly. Greene's estimates indicate that a bare majority of black and Hispanic students finish high school, and it is logical to conclude from that that much less than a majority receives any postsecondary education. But this NCES survey found that a striking 76.5 percent of the black students had obtained some postsecondary educational training, identical to the white figure; Hispanics were only slightly behind, at 69.7 percent (21). (The data are displayed in Fig. 2-1 in the next chapter.) It should be noted that estimates of high school graduation and dropout rates for Hispanics are especially problematic. As we shall show in chap. 6, lumping together immigrant and native-born Latino children gives a very misleading picture.

16. Frank D. Bean and Marta Tienda, *The Hispanic Population of the United States* (New York: Russell Sage Foundation, 1987), 234.

17. Ronald F. Ferguson, "Responses from Middle School, Junior High, and High School Students in Districts of the Minority Student Achievement Network," Weiner Center for Public Policy, John F. Kennedy School of Government, Harvard University, November 18, 2002.

Two: Tests Matter

1. *The NewsHour with Jim Lehrer* (PBS), January 24, 2001.

2. Remarks at the NAACP Daisy Bates Education Summit, May 18, 2001.

3. Scott Greenberger, "Five Lives/One Test: For the Class of 2003, MCAS Is a Moment of Truth," *Boston Globe,* September 9, 2001, A1.

4. Richard Rothstein, "Attention to Scores Comes at a Price," *New York Times,* November 24, 1999, B11.

5. Deborah Meier, *Will Standards Save Public Education?* (Boston: Beacon Press, 2000), 85.

6. Theodore Sizer, "A Sense of Place," commenting on Meier's essay in *Will Standards Save Public Education?* 72.

7. Jonathan Kozol, introduction to Meier, *Will Standards Save Public Education?* xi.

8. Lynn Olson, "Test-Makers Poll Finds Parents Value Testing," *Education Week,* August 2, 2000, 16. The official name of FairTest is the National Center for Fair and Open Testing.

9. Public Agenda, "Survey Finds Little Sign of Backlash Against Academic Standards or Standardized Tests," October 5, 2000.

10. Business Roundtable, "Assessing and Addressing the 'Testing Backlash,'" Spring 2001, downloaded from the BRT Web site.

11. Steve Farkas and Jean Johnson, "Time to Move On: African-American and White Parents Set an Agenda for Public Schools," a Report from Public Agenda, 1998, 17.

12. Ron Rude, "Isn't that Interesting! Do Kids Really Have to Like What They Learn?" *Education Week,* August 8, 2001, 47.

13. Peter Sacks, *Standardized Minds: The High Price of America's Testing Culture and What We Can Do About It* (Cambridge, Mass.: Perseus Books, 1999), 3, 7, 9, 15, 46, 110.

14. Gail Russell Chaddock, "Adverse impact?" *Christian Science Monitor,* November 30, 1999, 14.

15. *The NewsHour with Jim Lehrer* (PBS), February 15, 2001.

16. "What's Wrong with Standardized Tests," FairTest Web site, no date. We found it posted in September 2001.

17. "The Full Measure," Report of the National Association of State Boards of Education, Study Group on Statewide Assessment Systems, October 1997.

18. The court found that that "while the TAAS test does adversely affect minority students in significant numbers, the TEA (Texas Education Agency) has demonstrated an ed-

ucational necessity for the test, and the Plaintiffs have failed to identify equally effective alternatives"; *GI Forum v. Texas Education Agency*, 87 F. Supp.2d 667 (2000).

19. NAACP, National Education Department, Call to Action: From Access to Accountability, From the Courts to the Community," NAACP Web site, undated, but posted in September 2001, when we read it.

20. R. A. Dyer, "Most Latinos Back TAAS Exit Exam Despite Bias Fears," *Fort Worth Star-Telegram*, July 24, 2000, 11. The survey was conducted May 26 to June 15; the court's decision in the MALDEF case had come down in mid-January, five months earlier.

21. See the discussion of Asian achievement in chap. 5.

22. *Almost* everyone understands the point, but the plaintiffs in their suit against MCAS did initially make a Fourteenth Amendment argument relying solely on disparate impact. The First Amended Class Action Complaint filed in the U.S. District Court for the District of Massachusetts on October 10, 2002, 67, states: "Before the State Defendants finalized the MCAS exam, they knew as a result of their field testing and studies that the use of the MCAS exam as a graduation requirement would have a disproportionate, adverse impact on Black/African-American students, Hispanic students, and students with limited English proficiency."

23. Claude M. Steele and Joshua Aronson, "Stereotype Threat and the Test Performance of Academically Successful African Americans," in Christopher Jencks and Meredith Phillips, eds., *The Black-White Test Score Gap* (Washington, D.C.: Brookings Institution Press, 1998), chap. 11. Although the authors note at the outset (402–403) that black college students underperform in their courses as well as on standardized tests, they fail to see that this undermines their arguments about tests. These opening pages come dangerously close to saying that black students are incapable of displaying the intellectual skills they have acquired in any possible setting because they live in a hostile, racist society. This essay goes on to describe experiments in which black students were given some tests in a context designed to heighten their racial awareness and others not, and reports that black students performed better when race was not salient. The authors never pause to consider the obvious implication for college admissions policies. When students think that they have been admitted to Stanford on the basis of their race rather than their other qualifications, because Stanford boasts of its undying commitment to affirmative action in admissions, does that not give great salience to race in their mind and heighten their "stereotype vulnerability"? Likewise, doesn't allowing black undergraduates to live in a "Malcolm X House" or other racially defined setting, as Stanford and other schools do, increase their "stereotype vulnerability?"

24. One review of the literature estimates that the grade point average of African-American college students is no better than that of whites with SAT scores that are 240 points lower; Robert Klitgaard, *Choosing Elites* (New York: Basic Books, 1985), 164. Even a volume that amounts to a brief in defense of racial preferences in admissions to higher education—William G. Bowen and Derek Bok, *The Shape of the River: Long-term Consequences of Considering Race in College and University Admissions* (Princeton, N.J.: Princeton University Press, 1998)—concedes this point, and devotes several pages to a discussion of black "underperformance," defined as performing less well in courses than could be expected from their SAT scores (see 72–86). If there is "racial bias" in the SATs, it is a bias *in favor of blacks*.

25. Christopher Jencks, "Racial Bias in Testing," chap. 2 of Jencks and Phillips, *The Black-White Test Score Gap*; see esp. 56, 67, and 83.

26. FairTest, "What's Wrong with Standardized Tests?" FairTest Web site, no date.

27. Delegates to the annual convention in July 2001 took a vote on whether to support proposed federal legislation that would allow a parental opt-out. "NEA seeks Opt-Out of Mandatory Testing" *Washington Post*, July 7, 2001, A7.

28. Business Roundtable, "Assessing and Addressing the 'Testing Backlash.'"

29. Anand Vaishnav, "For Now, State Drops Plan to Put MCAS on Records," *Boston Globe*, May 28, 2002, B4.

30. "Testing Plus: Real Accountability with Real Results," NEA statement posted on its Web site, no date, read by authors in September 2001. In July 2002, the NEA Assembly voted to "support development of new systems to measure student performance." Tracey Wong Briggs, "New Leader, Challenges for NEA," *USA Today*, July 8, 2002, 7D.

31. Theodore R. Sizer, *Horace's Hope: What Works for the American High School* (Boston: Houghton Mifflin, 1996), 84.

32. Sizer, *Horace's Hope*, 154.

33. There was much New York press devoted to Mills's conversion to testing. See, e.g., Michael Winerip, "Never Mind the Inventive Curriculum: One Test Fits All," *New York Times*, November 18, 2001, 31.

34. Richard Matthews, "Students Are Happy: Survey Shows Teens Blind to Failure of Their Schools," *Atlanta Journal-Constitution*, August 9, 2001, 24A.

35. The *College Board News*, 2000–2001, table 7, "Rising Grades and Falling Test Scores May Indicate Grade Inflation." This reports a rise to 40 percent in 2000. The 2001 figure has just been released, and it is 41 percent; see the editorial, "High Schools Inflate Grades, and Parents Are Fooled," *USA Today*, August 30, 2001. The combination of grade inflation and subjectivity makes data on GPAs useless in answering questions about racial and ethnic group differences in knowledge and skills, and perhaps for that reason such data are not systematically gathered.

36. Siobhan Gorman, "Bush's Big Test," *National Journal*, February 24, 2001, 549.

37. Tara H. Arden-Smith, "Struggling Students GEAR Up," *Boston Globe*, September 2, 2001, B10.

38. National Center for Education Statistics, *Coming of Age in the 1990s: The Eighth-Grade Class of 1988 12 Years Later*, NCES 2002-321 (Washington, D.C.: U.S. Department of Education, 2002), 21. Possibly, these figures are higher than most of those discussed in footnote 39 because the study defined "postsecondary education" to include "any college, university, vocational, technical, or trade school designed for those who have completed high school" (19). A skeptic might think that a great many of the black and Hispanic students reporting some higher education had merely received a little vocational training. Although the study provides no information on this point, data from the October 2000 Current Population Survey reveal that only 3.7 percent of black students enrolled in institutions of higher education were attending vocational schools, and just 3.9 percent of Hispanics; U.S. Census Bureau, "Enrollment and Employment Status of Recent High School Graduates 16–24 Years Old: October 2000," Census Bureau Web site. Thus, this could have only a trivial impact on the overall educational attainment of either group.

39. The estimates from the National Education Longitudinal Study indicate somewhat higher rates of college attendance than the standard Current Population Survey figures available in *The Condition of Education 2001*, 151–152. The CPS estimates that 61 percent of the 25–29-year-old black high school graduates in 2000 had attended college, as compared with 68 percent of whites and 52 percent of Hispanics. Blacks were thus 11 percent less likely than whites to have gone on to college, and Hispanics 26 percent less likely. The Hispanic college attendance figures are distorted downward because they include recent immigrants who had completed high school before immigrating to the United States and went to work directly when they arrived. For further discussion of this point, see chap. 6 below. A recent National Center for Education Statistics analysis of four national samples of youths graduating from high school in the 1970s and 1980s found that African Americans were an average of only 9 percent less likely to go on to college than their white classmates; National Center for Education Statistics, *Educational Achievement and Black-White Inequality*, NCES 2001-061 (Washington, D.C.: U.S. Department of Education, 2001), 28. Unfortunately, the number of Latinos in these particular samples was too small to permit generalizations about them.

40. Susan Nielsen, "Back from College, Dream Deferred," *Oregonian*, July 15, 2001, F1.

41. NCES, *Educational Achievement and Black-White Inequality*. This evidence has a unique feature: It includes a measure of each sample member's academic skills at the end

of high school, based on standardized tests given to all of them. Given the magnitude of the white-Hispanic gap on NAEP tests given at age 17 or in the twelfth grade, it is very likely that the same patterns hold for Latinos, though there were not enough of them in the samples to make the calculation.

42. National Center for Education Statistics, *Descriptive Summary of 1995–96 Beginning Postsecondary Students: Six Years Later,* NCES 2003–151 (Washington, D.C.: U.S. Department of Education, 2003), 23–24.

43. Kenneth R. Weiss, "Cal State Expels 2,009 Students for Lack of Skills," *Los Angeles Times,* January 24, 2001, A3. Even after a full year of remedial work, this story reports, Cal State had to drop more than 6 percent of its freshmen because they still had such a limited grasp of English and mathematics. These students were advised to attend a community college until they could pass the CSU placement tests. We have no comparable evidence for the nation as a whole, but a 1995 NCES national survey found that 29 percent of all freshmen were enrolled in at least one remedial course. No racial breakdown was provided, but the rate was dramatically higher in colleges whose enrollment was less than 50 percent white. NCES, *Remedial Education at Higher Education Institutions in Fall 1995* (Washington, D.C.: U.S. Department of Education, 1996). At schools with high minority enrollments, 43 percent of freshmen had to take one or more remedial courses, as compared with 26 percent at those with low minority enrollments. Asians counted as minorities in these figures, and thus the figures may underestimate the proportion of blacks and Hispanics in the remedial courses.

44. Clifford Adelman, *Answers in the Tool Box: Academic Intensity, Attendance Patterns, and Bachelor's Degree Attainment* (Washington, D.C.: U.S. Department of Education, 1999), 74. The central argument of this impressive study is that whether or not you took lots of difficult courses in high school—in math and science in particular—is more predictive of college success than GPAs or scores on standardized tests. The study offers little information on racial differences in courses taken, nor is such information available in many other places, so we cannot pursue the issue here. However, we are dubious about the causal weight Adelman gives to the pattern of course selection. It may be true that most students who enter college today with four years of Latin in secondary school do very well in college. It does not follow that requiring four years of Latin of all high school students would dramatically improve the intellectual level of the college student body. If students who currently choose to do so much Latin are atypical in other ways—as seems highly likely—a dramatic increase in Latin enrollments in high school might have little effect on college performance.

45. Jim Castro, quoted in the Education Leaders Council "Weekly Policy Update," April 12, 2002. Source: e-mail exchange with ELC.

46. Christopher Jencks, "Racial Biases in Testing," in Christopher Jencks and Meredith Phillips, eds., *The Black-White Test Score Gap* (Washington, D.C.: Brookings Institution Press, 1998), 73.

47. National Center for Education Statistics, *Adult Literacy in America: A First Look at the Results of the National Adult Literacy Survey* (Washington, D.C.: U.S. Department of Education, 1993). The study also estimated levels of "document literacy," but the results correspond so closely to those for prose literacy that we ignore them here.

48. National Center for Education Statistics, *Adult Literacy,* 18, 34. Thirty-eight percent of blacks, but only 14 percent of whites, fell into the lowest prose literacy level. In quantitative literacy, the precise percentage of blacks in the bottom level was 46.

49. Paul Siegel, "On the Cost of Being a Negro," *Sociological Inquiry,* 35 (1965), 41–57. Many subsequent studies make the same assumption. Two dozen studies of this issue published before 1987 are listed in Reynolds Farley and Walter Allen, *The Color Line and the Quality of Life* (New York: Russell Sage Foundation, 1987), 322–325.

50. The complicating factors include regional differences in wage levels, for instance; 55 percent of blacks but only a quarter of whites live in the South, where wages tend to be lower. Incomes are also related to age, and the average age of Hispanics is younger than

that of whites; their lower earnings reflect fewer years in the labor force. In addition, these educational categories are very broad, and it is probable that within each one whites have more education. Among those with less than nine years of schooling, for example, most whites would have had at least eight, but Latinos perhaps only six.

51. George Farkas and Keven Vicknair, "Appropriate Tests of Racial Wage Discrimination Require Controls for Cognitive Skills: Comment on Cancio, Evans, and Maume," *American Sociological Review* 61 (August 1996), 557–560. Another study, by Derek Neal and William R. Johnson, found that controlling for education as measured by test scores reduced the black-white wage gap for males by three-quarters, to 27 cents per hour, and reversed it for black females, who earned 3 cents an hour more than white females. Derek A. Neal and William R. Johnson, "The Role of Pre-Market Factors in Black-White Wage Differences," *Journal of Political Economy* 104 (October 1996), 869–896. For further evidence, see Stephan Thernstrom and Abigail Thernstrom, *America in Black and White: One Nation, Indivisible* (New York: Simon & Schuster, 1997), 443–447.

52. Gretchen Hoff, letter to *The New York Times*, December 13, 1999, 32.

Three: Building Academic Skills

1. Bill Hirschman, "Seeking Level Ground; Educators and Parents Wonder: Is It Fair to Hold All Kids to the Same FCAT Standard?" *Sun-Sentinel* (Fort Lauderdale, Fla.), September 24, 2000, 1H.

2. Samuel Casey Carter, *No Excuses: Lessons from 21 High-Performing, High-Poverty Schools* (Washington, D.C.: Heritage Foundation, 2000), was our starting point in looking for great schools.

3. Norman Atkins, "Charter Schools Are Public Schools," *New York Times Magazine*, June 14, 1998, 48.

4. Quoted in William Bunch, "Making Schools Work," *Brown Alumni Magazine*, July–August 2000, 53.

5. For evidence supporting Atkins's belief that after-school programs that attempt "mop-up duty" are far less effective than a longer school day, see U.S. Department of Education, *When Schools Stay Open Late: The National Evaluation of the 21st-Century Learning Centers; First-Year Findings* (Washington, D.C.: U.S. Department of Education, 2003). This is a report of a study of sixty-two federally funded after-school centers by Mathematica Policy Research, Inc. It found that these programs had little impact on the students who attended them, academically or in any other way.

6. Quotations from principals and teachers at the schools we have visited are from observations in the course of school visits or individual conversations between the authors and the principals/teachers, unless otherwise indicated.

7. A certain number of children do choose to leave the KIPP academies. In the 2001–2002 academic year, 7 percent of the students left KIPP-Houston, mostly from the fifth grade. The attrition rate at KIPP-Bronx is about 2 percent. Eric Hubler, " 'No Shortcuts to Academic Excellence," *Denver Post*, July 31, 2002, B1. These are very low rates, of course, for urban schools with high-poverty students.

8. On the educational importance of choice in general, see Caroline M. Hoxby, "If Families Matter Most, Where Do Schools Come In?" in Terry M. Moe, ed., *A Primer on American Schools* (Stanford, Calif.: Hoover Institution Press, 2001), 89–126.

9. Sarah Tantillo, "Culture Formation in Charter Schools: Two Case Studies," unpublished Ph.D. dissertation, Rutgers Graduate School of Education, January 2001, 72. In an important book published in 1987, James S. Coleman and Thomas Hoffer argue that in previous generations "children were surrounded by functional communities," which were a "critical resource" for parents and schools in their effort to shape the lives of the young. As a consequence, the parents may have had little money and little education, but their children generally "showed the middle-class virtues of hard work, diligence, respect for the teacher, and good behavior in school: qualities that served them well in preparing them for further education and the mobility it brought." *Public and Private High Schools: The Impact of Communities* (New York: Basic Books, 1987), 8. It's a speculative point, but if, in fact,

schools can no longer count on the values of a functional community to support them, at a minimum they must have parents who have signed on.

10. Tantillo, "Culture Formation," 130, 132–133.

11. These scores come from the Web sites of the schools: www.kipp.org; www. amistadacademy.org; www.northstaracademy.org.

12. Luncheon talk, Mass Insight, Boston, October 17, 2000.

13. Tantillo, "Culture Formation," 55–57.

14. Anemona Hartocollis, "In School," *New York Times*, February 24, 1999, A21.

15. James W. Stigler and James Hiebert, *The Teaching Gap: Best Ideas from the World's Teachers for Improving Education in the Classroom* (New York: Free Press, 1999), 110–120.

16. Jeff Lemberg, "Program Helps Teachers Share Lesson Plans," *Boston Globe*, July 28, 2002, C6. The history teacher was Rob McGreevey (leaving teaching and heading into a doctoral program) and the science teacher was Dana Lehman.

17. Lisa Coryell, "School's Success Rooted in Order," *Trenton Times*, May 20, 2001.

18. Tantillo, "Culture Formation," 132–133.

19. Bunch, "Making Schools Work," 53.

20. That parents who take their children out of the public system are looking, at least in part, for a more disciplined atmosphere is a point frequently made in journalistic accounts. See, e.g., Cindy Rodriguez, "Minority Students Treading Path to Private Schools," *Boston Globe*, February 16, 2002, B1. Rodriguez quotes the principal of a Boston Catholic school that is 33 percent Vietnamese and 11 percent black. "What I'm hearing from parents is that they want strong discipline," she said. Parents want students to be taught in a moral atmosphere, Rodriquez reports. National survey data on private and parochial versus public schools are also illuminating. On the question of safety, 55 percent of Americans think nonpublic schools are superior. The figure jumps to 64 percent when the issue is discipline, and 63 percent when the survey asked about "teaching moral values"; Terry M. Moe, *Schools, Vouchers, and the American Public* (Washington, D.C.: Brookings Institution Press, 2001), table 2-4. The survey was conducted in 1995.

21. Tantillo, "Culture Formation," 96.

22. National Center for Education Statistics, *Digest of Educational Statistics 2001* (Washington, D.C.: U.S. Department of Education, 2002), 167.

23. *Los Angeles Times* poll, November 18–December 12, 1997, reported in the *Los Angeles Times*, special series on "Public Education: California's Perilous Slide," pt. 1, "Why Our Schools Are Failing," May 17, 1998, S8.

24. Emily Sachar, *Shut Up and Let the Lady Teach: A Teacher's Year in a Public School* (New York: Simon & Schuster, 1991), 150.

25. Sachar, *Shut Up*, 67, 69, 75, 98, 148.

26. *Los Angeles Times*, "Why Our Schools Are Failing," S7.

27. Steve Farkas and Jean Johnson, "Time to Move On: African-American and White Parents Set an Agenda for Public Schools," Public Agenda report, 1998, 33.

28. Paul E. Barton, Richard J. Cly, and Harold Winglinsky, *Order in the Classroom: Violence, Discipline, and Student Achievement* (Princeton, N.J.: Educational Testing Service, 1998).

29. Farkas and Johnson, "Time to Move On." Blacks in the survey were slightly less concerned than whites about school discipline, suggesting that some may worry that their children will be unfairly singled out for harsh treatment.

30. Tantillo, "Culture Formation," 66.

31. Tom Loveless, ed., *The Great Curriculum Debate: How Should We Teach Reading and Math* (Washington, D.C.: Brookings Institution Press, 2001) is the best single source for a discussion of the contemporary war. The essential history to read on this century-old conflict is Diane Ravitch, *Left Back: A Century of Battles over School Reform* (New York: Simon & Schuster, 2000). For the math wars specifically, see David Klein's long essay "A Brief History of American K-12 Mathematics Education," available at *www.mathematicallycorrect.com*.

32. Klein, "A Brief History," 33–34.

33. The statement to which Riordan was referring was the "Open Letter to United States Secretary of Education, Richard Riley" that had the title "Mr. Secretary, We Ask That You Withdraw Your Premature Recommendations for Mathematics Instruction." It appeared in the *Washington Post*, November 18, 1999, A5, and is also available at *www.mathematicallycorrect.com/riley.htm*. The Riordan endorsement was in Richard Riordan, "School Board Should Stick with Tradition: The LAUSD Must Return to the Basics and Hold Each Teacher Accountable," *Los Angeles Times*, May 2, 2000, B9.

34. For an abundance of material from this point of view, see *www.mathematicallycorrect.com*. Useful stories in the press include Kiran Randhawa, "District Calls on Book Salesmen to Defend 'Fuzzy Math' to Parents," *Riverdale Review*, January 31–February 6, 2002, and Mark Clayon, "If This Is Math, Then We're at War," *Christian Science Monitor*, May 16, 2000, 16. Loveless, *The Great Curriculum Debate* contains a number of references to parental rebellion.

35. Anemona Hartocollis, "The New, Flexible Math Meets Parental Rebellion," *New York Times*, April 27, 2000, 1.

36. Hartocollis, "The New, Flexible Math," 1.

37. Testimony at the Massachusetts Board of Education monthly meeting, July 25, 2000, transcript, 77.

38. Gail Russell Chaddock, "Reinventing Our Public Schools," *Christian Science Monitor*, April 13, 1999, 15.

39. Samuel Casey Carter, "No Excuses: Seven Principals of Low-Income Schools Who Set the Standard for High Achievement," Heritage Foundation, undated, 14.

40. Janet Bingham, "CSAP Focused Schools Can Bridge Learning Gaps, Experts Say," *Denver Post*, July 26, 2001, A1.

41. Courtland Milloy, "Homework That Parents Need to Do," *Washington Post*, February 19, 1997, B1.

Four: Not by Math Alone

1. Jonathan Coleman, *Long Way to Go: Black and White in America* (New York: Atlantic Monthly Press, 1997), 227.

2. William Bunch, "Making Schools Work," *Brown Alumni Magazine*, July-August 2000, 53. Atkins was referring specifically to the point of the trips the North Star students take to the Florida Everglades and other places that affluent kids go to "as a matter of course." But the vision he articulated runs through the entire education North Star offers.

3. www.amistadacademy.org/about.modelschool.behavior.html, July 2, 2002.

4. College Board, *Reaching the Top: A Report of the National Task Force on Minority High Achievement* (New York: College Board Publications, October 1999).

5. College Board, *Reaching the Top*, 7, 14, 17, 18.

6. Laurence Steinberg, *Beyond the Classroom: Why School Reform Has Failed and What Parents Need to Do* (New York: Simon & Schuster, 1996), 86.

7. George Farkas, *Human Capital or Cultural Capital? Ethnicity and Poverty Groups in an Urban School District* (New York: Aldine de Gruyter, 1996), 11–13, summarizes the views of another sociologist, Anne Swidler, and applies them to schools. The first quotation is Farkas, the second is Swidler as quoted by Farkas.

8. Lisa Coryell, "School's Success Rooted in Order," *Trenton Times*, May 20, 2001.

9. Carol Novak, Interview with Jaime Escalante, *Technos Quarterly*, 2, no. 1 (Spring 1993), www.technos.net/tq_02/1escalante.htm. Escalante is best known from the 1988 feature film *Stand and Deliver*, which told the remarkable story of the academic success of his math students in a predominantly Latino East Los Angeles public school with an abysmal academic record.

10. The Dacia Toll quotation is from Jodi Wilgoren, "In a Society of Their Own, Children Are Learning," *New York Times*, February 7, 2001, B9.

11. Reynolds Farley, Sheldon Danziger, and Harry J. Holzer, *Detroit Divided* (New York: Russell Sage Foundation, 2000), 142.

12. Levin told the "I'm the boss" story at a forum at the Massachusetts Department of Education, October 17, 2000.

13. Samuel Casey Carter, "No Excuses: Seven Principals of Low-Income Schools Who Set the Standard for High Achievement," Heritage Foundation, undated, 18.

14. Unpublished transcript, Brookings Papers on Educational Policy, Conference on National Standards, May 15–16, 2000; Brown Center on Education Policy, Brookings Institution, Washington, D.C.

15. An alternative peer culture has the additional benefit of steering students away from neighborhood gangs. For a good recent description of the hazards of gang life for young black males, see Orlando Patterson, *Rituals of Blood: Consequences of Slavery in Two American Centuries* (New York: Basic *Civitas* Books, 1998), 137–145.

16. Farley et al., *Detroit Divided*, 142.

17. Wilgoren, "In a Society of Their Own," B9. See also the Amistad Web site.

18. Marcos Maldonado, quoted on the KIPP Web site, www.KIPP.org., viewed in May 2002.

19. Sandy Banks, "Disney Awards Teacher with a Touch of Class," *Los Angeles Times*, December 6, 1992, B1.

20. Carter, "No Excuses: Seven Principals," 15.

21. In a 1990 study, Roslyn Mickelson found that black students do believe that "achievement and effort in school lead to job success later on." But they were more doubtful when asked about the likelihood of fair treatment in the workplace; cited in Ronald F. Ferguson, "Teachers' Perceptions and Expectations and the Black-White Test Score Gap," in Christopher Jencks and Meredith Phillips, eds., *The Black-White Test Score Gap* (Washington, D.C.: Brookings Institution Press, 1998), 292–293.

22. Quoted in Richard Rothstein, "The Growing Revolt Against the Testers," *New York Times*, May 30, 2001, p. A19.

23. Steinberg, *Beyond the Classroom*, passim.

24. Ralph Ellison, "The World and the Jug," in John F. Callahan, ed., *The Collected Essays of Ralph Ellison* (New York: in Modern Library, 1995), 164.

25. Ellison, "The Shadow and the Act," in *Collected Essays*, 299.

26. Terry M. Moe, *Schools, Vouchers, and the American Public* (Washington, D.C.: Brookings Institution Press, 2001), table 2-6. The survey was conducted in 1995. The black percentage was 57, the Hispanic 54, but (mysteriously) only 35 percent of whites signed on to the notion.

27. The Web site of the Millwood public school district in Oklahoma City, www.millwood.k12.ok.us/Students.htm, which we visited on March 22, 2002, contained "The Black Pledge of Allegiance," labeled as possibly "pertinent or relevant." That Pledge speaks of "One nation of Black people . . . Totally united in the struggle for Black Love, Black Freedom, and Black Determination."

28. Robin Dougherty, "The Browning of America: Interview with Richard Rodgriquez," *Boston Globe*, April 14, 2002, E4.

29. Lawrence Jackson, *Ralph Ellison: The Emergence of Genius* (New York: Wiley, 2002), 151.

30. Dougherty, "The Browning of America," E4.

31. Ellison, "The Shadow and the Act," 57.

32. Ellison, "Indivisible Man," first published in 1970, in *Collected Essays*, p. 394; and " 'A Completion of Personality': A Talk with Ralph Ellison," in *Collected Essays*, 799.

33. Novak, interview with Jaime Escalante.

34. Jonathan Rauch, "Courting Danger: The Rise of Anti-Social Law," Bradley Lecture, American Enterprise Institute, December 11, 2000.

35. "Never Let Them See You Sleep," interview with Karin Chenoweth, *Washington Post Magazine*, April 7, 2002, 14.

36. Megan Tench, "Straight Talk: Urban Teens Advised on What It Takes to Get Ahead," *Boston Globe*, August 5, 2002, B1.

37. DeNeen L. Brown, "A Good Word for Grammar: Pr. George's Schools Urged to Get Tough," *Washington Post,* March 16, 1998, 1.

38. Ellison attended Tuskegee from 1933 to 1936. According to Lawrence Jackson's biography of the great writer, the students were taught that their "ability to transcend jim crow would operate in proportion to their use of 'Good English,' "; *Ralph Ellison,* 110. Much of the education Tuskegee offered was relentlessly hostile to black culture, but this message regarding language was invaluable to Ellison. The 1996 fight in Oakland, California, over the school board's recognition of "Ebonics" as the primary language of African-American children was precisely about the legitimacy of insisting that black children learn to switch to standard English, when appropriate, of course. For a balanced discussion of the issue, see John H. McWhorter, *The Word on the Street: Fact and Fable about American English* (New York: Plenum Publishing Co., 1998), chaps. 6–8.

39. Orlando Patterson, "What to Do When Busing Becomes Irrelevant," *New York Times,* July 18, 1999, 17. Patterson is right to say the problem crosses class lines, but obviously it is more true of some African Americans than others. In an article on life in the Robert Taylor Homes in Chicago, the *Wall Street Journal* (December 19, 2000, 1) described the special isolation of the underclass: "Unemployment and a sense of alienation from mainstream society grew more pronounced until public housing life became like life nowhere else."

Five: Asians

1. Margaret Gibson, *Accommodation Without Assimilation: Sikh Immigrants in an American High School* (Ithaca, N.Y.: Cornell University Press, 1988), 132.

2. Richard Rothstein, "On Culture and Learning," *New York Times,* October 11, 2000, B10. No scholar has contributed more than Thomas Sowell to an understanding of "cultural influences on achievement." Among his many books, see particularly *Ethnic America: A History* (New York: Basic Books, 1981) and *Race and Culture: A World View; Migrations and Culture: A World View;* and *Conquests and Cultures: A World View* (New York: Basic Books, 1994, 1996, 1998).

3. Julian Guthrie, "Not Geeks, Gangsters at Schools; Asian American Parents, Students meet in S.F. to Find Solutions, End Myths About Their Culture," *San Francisco Examiner,* May 14, 2000, C1.

4. Guthrie, "Not Geeks."

5. It is very rare to find distinctions among the various Asian groups made in the data we have to work with. An exception is Heather Kim, *Diversity Among Asian American High School Students* (Princeton, N.J.: Educational Testing Service, 1997), which provides data on educational achievement for Chinese, Japanese, Korean, Filipino, South Asian (Indian or Pakistan), and Southeast Asian students.

6. Julian Weissglass, "Racism and the Achievement Gap," *Education Week,* August 8, 2001, 72.

7. Data from the 1982 High School and Beyond survey, as given in Clifford Adelman, "The Rest of the River," *University Business,* January–February 1999, 42–45.

8. Figures are from the Asian-American Politics Web site, www.asianam.org.

9. U.S. Bureau of the Census, *Educational Attainment in the United States: March 2000,* Detailed Tables (Washington, D.C.: U.S. Department of Commerce, 2001), table 1A. Some of the young Asians included in these figures were recent immigrants who had completed college before coming to the United States. But we have seen no evidence that native-born Asian Americans are lagging behind their parents in rates of college graduation.

10. Lily May I. Johnson, ed., *Minority Student Opportunities in United States Medical Schools, 15th Edition* (Washington, D.C.: Association of American Medical Colleges, 2000), 303.

11. Elizabeth Chambliss, *Miles to Go 2000: Progress of Minorities in the Legal Profession,* American Bar Association Committee on Racial and Ethnic Diversity in the Profession (Chicago: American Bar Association, 2000), 3.

12. Available at www.asianam.org.

13. This happened in the fourth-grade mathematics and science assessments in 2000 and in the eighth-grade math assessment in 1996. See National Center for Education Statistics, *NAEP 1996 Mathematics: Report Card for the Nation and the States* (Washington, D.C.: U.S. Department of Education, 1997), app. E; The *Nation's Report Card: Mathematics 2000* (Washington, D.C.: U.S. Department of Education, 2001), 212–213; and "Overview of Procedures Used for the NAEP 2000 Science Assessment," NAEP Web site, 15.

14. On two of the four math exams given in the past decade (in 1992 and 2000), the difference was statistically significant, and they probably would have been on the other two as well if the number of Asian students included in the sample had been larger.

15. Calculated from data given in Emory Curtis, "Another View: We Need Radical Changes in K–3 School," *Ethnic NewsWatch*, March 9, 2000. Although a great deal of information is provided on the University of California Web site, www.ucop.edu, it does not include data on the racial composition of the UC-eligible population.

16. Gerald W. Bracey, "The Secret to Those High Asian Test Scores: Affluent, Well Educated Daddies, Mommies, Too," column, February 11, 1998, on America Now Web site, www.america-tomorrow.com/ati/gb80211.htm.

17. Laurence Steinberg, *Beyond the Classroom: Why School Reform Has Failed and What Parents Need to Do* (New York: Simon & Schuster, 1996), 86.

18. Bracey, "The Secret."

19. Richard J. Herrnstein and Charles Murray, *The Bell Curve: Intelligence and Class Structure in American Life* (New York: Free Press, 1994), argues the case for the genetic view of IQ—unconvincingly to us. The pages devoted to the question "Do Asians Have Higher IQs than Whites?" leave the answer uncertain. Few studies of the issue have been done and their results conflict. See pages 272–276, 299–301. Stanley Sue and Sumie Okazaki, "Asian-American Educational Achievement: A Phenomenon in Search of an Explanation," *American Psychologist*, 45 (1990), 913–920, rejects IQ explanations of Asian school success; see 915. However, see Richard Lynn's rejoinder in defense of the IQ hypothesis in the same journal, August 1991, 875–876.

20. Steinberg, *Beyond the Classroom*, 87.

21. Steinberg, *Beyond the Classroom*, 180–181.

22. Steinberg, *Beyond the Classroom*, 91, 161.

23. Steinberg, *Beyond the Classroom*, 91–94.

24. Steinberg, *Beyond the Classroom*, 96–100. Steinberg's book is aimed at a popular audience and includes hardly any of the statistical data he compiled. One reason to doubt that Steinberg had enough Asians of the third or prior generations is that an analysis of the very large National Education Longitudinal Study sample of 1988 eighth-graders found too few cases of Asian students in this category for meaningful analysis; Lingxin Hao and Melissa Bonstead-Bruns, "Parent-Child Differences in Educational Expectations and the Academic Achievement of Immigrant and Native Students," *Sociology of Education*, 71 (1998), 175–198.

25. The leading figure in the "new second generation" school is Alejandro Portes. For recent summaries of the large body of scholarship in this vein, see Alejandro Portes and Ruben G. Rumbaut, eds., *Legacies: The Story of the Immigrant Second Generation* (Berkeley, Calif.: University of California Press, 2001), and Ruben G. Rumbaut and Alejandro Portes, *Ethnicities: Children of Immigrants in America* (Berkeley, Calif.: University of California Press, 2001).

26. U.S. Bureau of the Census, *School Enrollment in the United States—Social and Economic Characteristics of Students: October 1999*, Current Population Report P20-533 (Washington, D.C.: U.S. Department of Commerce, 2001), table B.

27. Kim, *Diversity Among Asian American High School Students*, 21.

28. The census data on the earlier history of Asian educational achievement in the U.S. is usefully reviewed in Charles Hirschman and Morrison G. Wong, "The Extraordinary Ed-

ucational Attainment of Asian Americans: A Search for Historical Evidence and Explanations," *Social Forces*, 65 (1986), 10–12. Chinese and Japanese born before World War I obtained less education than native-born whites. In the 1915–1924 birth cohort and all
subsequent ones, the opposite was the case. Both groups were acquiring more schooling
than native whites.

29. For a searching and subtle analysis of the educational achievement of Jews in Prov-
idence, Rhode Island, in the first third of the twentieth century, see Joel Perlmann, *Ethnic*
Differences: Schooling and Social Structure Among the Irish, Italians, Jews, and Blacks in an
American City, 1880–1935 (New York: Cambridge University Press, 1988), chap. 4. Perlmann analyzes group differences with the most elaborate controls for social and economic
background, and finds large residual variations that can only be explained by what he terms
"pre-migration cultural attributes."

Six: Hispanics

1. Quoted in Michael Barone, *The New Americans: How the Melting Pot Can Work*
Again (Chicago: Regnery, 2001), 131.

2. Jill Levy, "How College Can Tear at a Family Soul," *Los Angeles Times*, January 23,
2000, A1.

3. Michael Barone develops the comparison between Italians and Hispanics in chaps.
3 and 4 of *The New Americans*, and we are indebted to his insights. However, he devotes
very little attention to education.

4. Richard D. Alba, *Italian Americans: Into the Twilight of Ethnicity* (Englewood
Cliffs, N.J.: Prentice-Hall, 1985), 59.

5. Alba, *Italian Americans*, 54. For a useful table on group differences in rates of naturalization from 1910 to 1970, see Reed Ueda, "Naturalization and Citizenship," in Stephan
Thernstrom, ed., *Harvard Encyclopedia of American Ethnic Groups* (Cambridge, Mass.:
Harvard University Press, 1980), 747. In 1910, only 18 percent of Italian immigrants had
taken out American citizenship, one of the lowest rates of any group at the time. Mexicans
had an even lower naturalization rate of just 11 percent in 1910.

6. Joel Perlmann, *Ethnic Differences: Schooling and Social Structure Among the Irish,*
Italians, Jews, and Blacks in an American City, 1880–1935 (New York: Cambridge University Press, 1988), chap. 3.

7. George Farkas, *Human Capital or Cultural Capital? Ethnicity and Poverty Groups*
in an Urban School District (New York: Aldine de Gruyter, 1996), 13.

8. Alba, *Italian Americans*, 120–121. The Italian advantage in the third generation
came about largely because they were more concentrated in places with higher overall levels of educational attainment—Northeastern metropolitan areas—and few resided in the
South. When place of residence was held constant, WASPs still had a lead of 0.9 of a year in
median years of school completed. But that still represented a huge generational advance
for Italians.

9. Alba, *Italian Americans*, 120–121.

10. Frank D. Bean and Marta Tienda, *The Hispanic Population of the United States*
(New York: Russell Sage Foundation, 1987), 398. For similar cautions about both of the
current umbrella labels, "Hispanic" and "Asian-American," see Alejandro Portes and Ruben
G. Rumbaut, *Immigrant America: A Portrait* (Berkeley, Calif.: University of California
Press, 1990), 138–139.

11. U.S. Bureau of the Census, *The Hispanic Population in the United States: Popula-*
tion Characteristics, March 2000, Current Population Report P20-535 (Washington, D.C.:
U.S. Department of Commerce, 2001), fig. 1.

12. Min Zhou, "Growing Up American: The Challenge Confronting Immigrant Children and Children of Immigrants," *Annual Review of Sociology*, 23 (1997), 63–95.

13. The 2000 Census reported that 48 percent of Hispanics reported their race as
white, and 42 percent as "other," with most of the remainder identifying as multiracial; U.S.
Census Bureau, "Overview of Race and Hispanic Origin, 2000," *Census 2000 Brief*,

CENBR/01-1 (Washington, D.C.: U.S. Department of Commerce, 2001), 10. But the census race question is poorly constructed, and many of those who chose "other" probably did not regard themselves as nonwhite. For a critique, see Stephan Thernstrom, "The Demography of Racial and Ethnic Groups," in Abigail Thernstrom and Stephan Thernstrom, eds., *Beyond the Color Line: New Perspectives on Race and Ethnicity* (Stanford, Calif.: Hoover Institution Press, 2002), 23–25. As noted there, a 1991 Current Population Survey that posed the question of race differently found that 95.7 percent of Hispanics identified as white, 2.2 percent as black, 0.4 percent as American Indian, and only 1.5 percent as "other." An equally important question is how non–Hispanic Americans would classify Hispanics racially. Unfortunately, we have no evidence at all on that point.

14. The best review of the demographic history of Mexicans in the United States is A. J. Jaffe, Ruth M. Cullen, and Thomas D. Boswell, *The Changing Demography of Spanish Americans* (New York: Academic Press, 1980), chap. 6 and app. B.

15. Manuel Gamio, *Mexican Immigration to the United States: A Study of Human Migration and Adjustment* (Chicago: University of Chicago Press, 1930), 71.

16. For a vivid and penetrating contemporary account, see Paul S. Taylor, *Mexican Labor in the United States: Imperial Valley,* University of California Publications in Economics (Berkeley, Calif.: University of California Press), vol. VI, no. 5 (1930).

17. Leo Grebler, Joan W. Moore, and Ralph C. Guzman, *The Mexican-American People: The Nation's Second Largest Minority* (New York: Free Press, 1970), 149–150.

18. Grebler et al., *Mexican-American People,* 149

19. Jaffe et al., *Changing Demography of Spanish Americans,* 166. In 1960, second-generation urban Mexican males aged 35–44 and living in the Southwest, for example, had median incomes 27 percent higher than their immigrant counterparts; Grebler et al., *Mexican-American People,* 192.

20. Estimates of the number of illegal Mexican immigrants living in the U.S. vary widely. One that probably errs on the high side is that, in the period 1965–1986, 28 million Mexicans entered the U.S. illegally, more than twenty times the number of legal migrants from Mexico. According to the same estimate, 23 million of these illegals returned to Mexico, so the net increase was only around 5 million. Even the 5 million figure is quadruple that for legal migrants; Douglas S. Massey, Jorge Durand, and Nolan J. Malone, *Beyond Smoke and Mirrors: Mexican Immigration in an Era of Economic Integration* (New York: Russell Sage Foundation, 2002), 45.

21. Gallup News Service, "Majority of Americans Identify Themselves as Third Generation Americans," July 10, 2001.

22. Jaffe, *Changing Demography,* 22.

23. Jaffe, *Changing Demography,* 18.

24. Jaffe, *Changing Demography,* 182.

25. National Center for Education Statistics, *The Condition of Education 2001,* NCES 2001-072 (Washington, D.C.: U.S. Department of Education, 2001), 110.

26. National Center for Education Statistics, *Digest of Education Statistics 2001,* NCES 2002-130 (Washington, D.C.: U.S. Department of Education, 2002), 58.

27. U.S. Bureau of the Census, *School Enrollment in the U.S., October 1999,* P20-533 (Washington, D.C.: U.S. Department of Commerce, 2001), table B.

28. Gregory Rodriguez, *The Emerging Latino Middle Class* (Los Angeles: Pepperdine University Institute for Public Policy, 1996), examines Hispanics in Southern California over the 1980–1990 decade, and shows that immigrants were twice as likely to be poor as the native-born. Moreover, the poverty rate for the foreign-born fell sharply with length of residence in the U.S., ranging from 25 percent for the most recent arrivals to just 10 percent for those present 25 years or more (7–8). Similarly, an analysis of Current Population Survey data for 1996–1999 by Jeffrey Grogger and Stephen J. Trejo finds that Mexican Americans' earnings rose sharply with longer residence in the U.S. and between the first and second generations; *Falling Behind or Moving Up? The Intergenerational Progress of Mexican Americans* (San Francisco: Public Policy Institute of California, 2002), 22.

29. U.S. Census Bureau, *Profile of the Foreign-Born Population in the United States: 1997*, Current Population Report P23–195 (Washington, D.C.: U.S. Bureau of the Census, 1999), 20–21. It might be thought that this reflects the more recent arrival of Mexican immigrants. But standardizing the figures by the length of residence for all foreign-born persons—calculating what the Mexican rate would be if they had been resident as long as immigrants in general—only increases the Mexican figure from 15 percent to 17 percent, a trivial amount. It is impossible to resist the conclusion that immigrants from Mexico appear to be less interested in becoming American citizens than members of any other national group.

30. President's Advisory Commission on Educational Excellence for Hispanic Americans, *Creating the Will: Hispanics Achieving Educational Excellence* (Washington, D.C.: President's Advisory Commission on Educational Excellence for Hispanic Americans, 2000). The sole reference to Hispanic immigrants is app. C, 68. The only other allusion to immigration in the entire document is a sentence stating that "some Hispanic families have been here since before the United States was a nation, and many others arrive here daily" (6). The vital distinction between the newcomers and those long resident in the United States is never made in the analysis that follows.

31. President's Avisory Commission, *Creating the Will*, 13.

32. President's Advisory Commission on Educational Excellence for Hispanic Americans, *Testing Hispanic Students in the United States: Technical and Policy Issues; Executive Summary* (Washington, D.C.: President's Advisory Commission on Educational Excellence for Hispanic Americans, 2000), 4.

33. National Center for Education Statistics, *Dropout Rates in the United States: 2000*, NCES 2002-114 (Washington, D.C.: U.S. Department of Education, 2002), 13. George Vernez and Allan Abrahamse, *How Immigrants Fare in U.S. Education* (Santa Monica, Calif.: RAND Corporation, 1996), 22, concludes that "the main reason for the low in-school participation rates among Mexican immigrant youths of high school age is that they do not enter the U.S. school system in the first place." By the age of 15, the authors note, the typical Mexican youth has been out of school for two years. These immigrants do not "drop out" of American schools; they never "drop in" in the first place.

34. Grogger and Trejo, *Falling Behind or Moving Up?* 12.

35. National Center for Education Statistics, *Coming of Age in the 1990s: The Eighth-Grade Class of 1988 12 Years Later*, NCES 2002-321 (Washington, D.C.: U.S. Department of Education, 2002), 14, 21. The high level of Hispanic educational attainment is especially striking because some Latinos in the sample must have been born outside the U.S. But the sample universe was of eighth-graders attending an American school in 1988, so immigrants who arrived at a later age were not included.

36. Bean and Tienda, *Hispanic Population*, 234; U.S. Bureau of the Census, *Statistical Abstract of the United States, 1976* (Washington, D.C.: U.S. Government Printing Office, 1976), 123.

37. Traditionally, such students have been excluded from the assessments, and we know from recent efforts to test them that they have substantially lower reading scores—7 points lower than the Hispanic average in the 2000 assessment of fourth-grade reading skills, for example. National Center for Education Statistics, *The Nation's Report Card: 4th-Grade Reading, 2000* (Washington, D.C.: U.S. Department of Education, 2002), Table C32. The 7 points were equal to one-quarter of the overall white-Hispanic gap on that test. Including the LEP students in the math assessment, however, made little difference; see National Center for Education Statistics, *The Nation's Report Card: 2000 Mathematics* (Washington, D.C.: U.S. Department of Education, 2002), Table B60.

38. Rodriguez, *Emerging Latino Middle Class*, 13. It should be noted, though, that the educational systems of most Latin American countries have been improving of late, and that very recent Hispanic immigrants typically have considerably more schooling than they did a generation ago. The evidence is assembled in B. Lindsay and Roberto Suro, *The Improving Educational Profile of Latino Immigrants* (Washington, D.C.: Pew Hispanic Cen-

ter, 2002). Immigrants from Mexico are still the least educated, with those from Central America slightly ahead; those from the Caribbean and from South America are substantially ahead.

39. U.S. Bureau of the Census, *1990 Census of Population: Persons of Hispanic Origin in the United States,* 1900 CP-3-3 (Washington, D.C.: U.S. Government Printing Office, 1993), table 3.

40. Ofelia Garcia and Ricardo Otheguy, quoted in *Testing Hispanic Students in the United States,* 5–6.

41. For evidence that oral English skills are even more important to employers than reading skills, see Barry R. Chiswick, "Speaking, Reading, and Earnings Among Low-Skilled Immigrants," *Journal of Labor Economics,* 9 (1991), 149–170.

42. Bean and Tienda, *Hispanic Population,* 272.

43. The same pattern shows up in analysis of Current Population Survey data for 1994–2000; see Joel Perlmann, "Young Mexican Americans, Blacks, and Whites in Recent Years: Schooling and Teen Motherhood as Indicators of Strengths and Weaknesses," Working Paper No. 335, Jerome Levy Institute, Bard College, 2001. Perlmann reports that 33 percent of Mexican immigrants aged 19–24 were high school graduates, as compared with 72 percent of those in the second generation. The figure for the third or higher generations was 77 percent—progress, but only very modest progress.

44. Richard Alba et al., "Only English by the Third Generation? Loss and Preservation of the Mother Tongue Among the Grandchildren of Contemporary Immigrants," *Demography,* 39 (August 2002), 467–484. These findings are from table 1.

45. The parallel we have drawn between Latinos and Italians, though, is strengthened by what Alba et al. found in their 1940 census sample. Second-generation Italian children in 1940 were far less likely to report English as their mother tongue than those from other European immigrant groups. But, by 1970, third-generation Italians were indistinguishable from the others; Alba et al., "Only English by the Third Generation?" table 3.

46. Christine Rossell, *Dismantling Bilingual Education: Implementing English Immersion: The California Initiative* (San Francisco: Public Policy Institute of California, 2002), i, 105.

47. Christine Rossell and Keith Baker, "The Educational Effectiveness of Bilingual Education," *Research in the Teaching of English,* 30 (1996), 7–74, reviews the results of 300 studies of the issue, and sums up the results of the 72 that they found methodologically acceptable. In tests of reading skills, 22 percent of these studies found bilingual education superior to "sink or swim" methods, 33 percent found it inferior, and 45 percent found no difference between the two. In grammar, only 7 percent of the studies found bilingual education superior and 64 percent rated it inferior. In math, bilingual education was superior in just 9 percent of the studies and inferior in 44 percent. Even this comparison is unduly favorable to bilingual education, because it is being compared with "sink or swim," and few people advocate that approach. Presumably bilingual education would appear even less effective if compared with "structured immersion" programs that do not teach Spanish literacy and use English as the main basis for instruction. The President's Advisory Commission on Educational Excellence for Hispanic Americans strongly supports bilingual education but makes no argument beyond citing the saying that "we don't stop walking when we learn to swim. We shouldn't stop speaking Spanish when we learn English" (25). It never mentions any of the conflicting research evidence about its efficacy.

48. Rossell, *Dismantling Bilingual Education,* 50.

49. Students were placed in a bilingual class when they came from a home in which a language other than English was spoken and *also* had low scores on a series of tests. In California, it was those who scored no higher than the 36th percentile. This regulation assumed that these students must have performed poorly because of their language background. But approximately 36 percent of students from English-speaking homes could be expected to score at the 36th percentile or below. And we could expect a considerably higher proportion than that of these Hispanic students to have low scores because of the

low educational level and low incomes of their families; Rossell, *Dismantling Bilingual Education*, 29–31.

50. Rossell, *Dismantling Bilingual Education*, 100.

51. Carola Suárez-Orozco and Marcelo Suárez-Orozco, *Transformations: Immigration, Family Life, and Achievement Motivation Among Latino Adolescents* (Stanford, Calif.: Stanford University Press, 1995), 58.

52. Garcia and Otheguy, quoted in *Testing Hispanic Students in the United States*, 8.

53. Vernez and Abrahamse, *How Immigrants Fare in U.S. Education*, 22.

54. Suárez-Orozco, *Transformations*, 165. Equally striking, the families of these students in Mexico had an average score of 8.23 on an index of socioeconomic status, compared with just 4.92 for the first-generation Mexican immigrant students in the Southern California sample and 5.45 for those in the second generation (table A.4, 204). It is hard to understand why a cross-national study designed to refute the theory that the cultural background of Mexican immigrants impedes the adjustment of their children to American schools failed to examine Mexican children from the same social strata as the blue-collar and agricultural workers who actually dominate the migration stream from Mexico to the United States.

55. Marcelo Suárez-Orozco and Carola Suárez-Orozco, *Children of Immigration* (Cambridge, Mass.: Harvard University Press, 2001), 125–128; *Transformations*, 57–58.

Seven: Blacks

1. Michael A. Fletcher, "A Good-School, Bad-Grade Mystery: Educators Striving to Close Racial Gap in Affluent Ohio Suburb," *Washington Post*, October 23, 1998, A1.

2. Debra J. Dickerson, *An American Story* (New York: Anchor Books, 2000), 132.

3. Dickerson, *An American Story*, 64.

4. Dickerson, *An American Story*, xiii.

5. John McWhorter, *Losing the Race: Self-Sabotage in Black America* (New York: Free Press, 2000), 126. Chap. 3 of this book develops the theme that "the actual determining factor" of the poor average school performance of African Americans is "a culture-internal legacy." For other insights into the cultural dimensions of contemporary racial issues, see Shelby Steele, *The Content of Our Character: A New Vision of Race in America* (New York: St. Martin's Press, 1990), and *A Dream Deferred: The Second Betrayal of Black Freedom in America* (New York: HarperCollins, 1998).

6. Orlando Patterson, "Taking Culture Seriously: A Framework and an Afro-American Illustration," chap. 15 of Lawrence E. Harrison and Samuel P. Huntington, eds., *Culture Matters: How Values Shape Human Progress* (New York: Basic Books, 2000), 206. Patterson explores the cultural issue more fully in *Rituals of Blood: Consequences of Slavery in Two American Centuries* (New York: Basic Civitas Books, 1998).

7. This history is reviewed in Stephan Thernstrom and Abigail Thernstrom, *America in Black and White* (New York: Simon & Schuster, 1997), chap. 1. For evidence of the glaring disparities in educational achievement as recently as the 1940s and 1950s, see 84–86.

8. Fletcher, "A Good-School, Bad-Grade Mystery," A1; Debra Viadero, "Even in Well-Off Suburbs, Minority Achievement Less," *Education Week*, March 15, 2000, 22. John U. Ogbu has written a detailed analysis of the racial gap in the Shaker Heights public schools, *Black American Students in an Affluent Suburb: A Study of Academic Disengagement* (Mahwah, N.J.: Lawrence Erlbaum Associates, 2003), which appeared too late for us to incorporate in the text. His perspective, though, is very close to ours. An eminent black scholar with strong credentials as a civil rights advocate, Ogbu was invited to do his research by black parents in the community who hoped that he could identify hidden biases in the schools that were holding their children back. He was unable to find such biases and concluded that the family and peer culture of African-American schoolchildren was the central problem. A few of his sponsors agreed, but many attacked him for "blaming the victim." See Susan Goldsmith, "Rich, Black, Flunking: Cap Professor John Ogbu Thinks He Knows Why Rich Black Kids are Failing in School. Nobody Wants to Hear It," *East Bay Express*, May 21, 2003.

9. For example, both parents are graduates in nine of ten white Shaker Heights families but only 45 percent of black ones. These differences, though, are not nearly as sharp as those in the academic performance of children in the Shaker Heights Schools; Ronald F. Ferguson, "A Diagnostic Analysis of Black-White GPA Disparities in Shaker Heights, Ohio," *Brookings Papers on Education Policy: 2001* (Washington, D.C.: Brookings Institution Press, 2001), 356.

10. This effort is described in Pedro A. Noguera, "Racial Politics and the Elusive Quest for Excellence and Equity in Education," *Education and Urban Society,* 34 November 2001), 18–41. Nearly three years after the network was founded, the author concedes that "there is still no sign that the districts in MSAN have discovered ways to close the achievement gap." Data compiled by Ronald F. Ferguson on the fifteen districts in the network do not challenge this gloomy assessment; see "Responses from Middle School, Junior High, and High School Students in Districts of the Minority Student Achievement Network," Weiner Center for Public Policy, John F. Kennedy School of Government, Harvard University, November 18, 2002. We present evidence on the dismal record of the Cambridge, Massachusetts, public schools in chap. 8.

11. Ferguson, "A Diagnostic Analysis," 381. Ferguson suggests that black students, especially males, shy away from fast-track courses out of fear of becoming isolated and losing their "connectedness to the African American community" (381–385).

12. "Results by Gender and Ethnic Group, Shaker Heights City School District, Cuyahoga County," 1999–2000 school year, available on the Ohio Department of Education Web site: www.ode.state.oh.us. The pattern was not confined to the twelfth grade. Just 21 percent of black fourth-graders passed all the state tests, as compared with 81 percent of whites.

13. U.S. Census Bureau, *Black Population in the United States: March 2000,* PPL-142 (Washington, D.C.: U.S. Government Printing Office, 2001), table 21.

14. U.S. Census Bureau, *Black Population,* table 15.

15. Brigid Schulte and Dan Keating, "Pupils' Poverty Drives Achievement Gap," *Washington Post,* September 2, 2001, A1.

16. Richard Kahlenberg, *All Together Now: Creating Middle-Class Schools Through Public School Choice* (Washington, D.C.: Brookings Institution Press, 2001).

17. Poverty, family income, and residential data from *Black Population.* Educational attainment of mothers of children 6–18 in 1999 from National Center for Education Statistics, *The Condition of Education, 2000* (Washington, D.C.: U.S. Government Printing Office, 2000), table 5-1.

18. The NAEP residential category is "fringe," which means suburbia plus large towns not part of a metropolitan area. The vast majority of people in it are suburban residents.

19. Meredith Phillips, "Understanding Ethnic Differences in Academic Achievement: Empirical Lessons from National Data," in David W. Grissmer and J. Michael Ross, eds., *Analytic Essays in the Assessment of Student Achievement,* NCES 2000-050 (Washington, D.C.: U.S. Department of Education, 2000), 112. Phillips's findings on the role of social-class differences in explaining the black-white gap are very close to ours on other points as well. Looking only at children whose parents had no more than a high school diploma cut the gap in the Phillips study by 31 percent, as compared with 38 percent in our analysis. Among the children of college graduates, Phillips found the gap was wider by 6 percent; our figure is 12 percent. For children living in suburbia, the racial gap was 6 percent less in the Phillips study and 15 percent less in ours. In short, she also found that applying controls for family background narrowed the gap significantly but not dramatically. The bottom line of both studies is the same: even among families with roughly comparable levels of education, similar incomes, and similar places of residence, the black-white gap in educational achievement remains very large.

20. See, for example, Larry V. Hedges and Amy Nowell, "Black-White Test Score Convergence Since 1965," chap. 5 of Christopher Jencks and Meredith Phillips, eds., *The Black-White Test Score Gap* (Washington, D.C.: Brookings Institution Press, 1998). In chap. 4

of the same volume, Meredith Phillips and collaborators explain a much higher fraction of the cognitive skills gap in 5- and 6-year-olds by considering many other measures. Some of these, though, include estimates of variations in parenting practices that we would call race-based cultural differences, not socioeconomic differences, as will be clear from our discussion in the section of the chapter called "Preschoolers." The authors see positive effects of what they term "middle-class parenting practices." But if black parents with incomes and education that would rank them as middle class do not follow those practices, then the differences are not really rooted in social class per se. It seems particularly questionable that Phillips included having a maternal grandparent who was born in the South among the variables controlled. Since as recently as World War II four out of five African Americans were residing in the South but only one in four whites, blacks today are far more likely than whites to have a grandparent of southern origins. The effect of using this variable is to smuggle race in by the back door.

21. Very little information is available about the distribution of wealth in American society, and we have been unable to locate any studies that examine racial differences controlled for age, education, income, and family composition. For a brief summary of the scanty evidence on racial differences in wealth, see Thernstrom and Thernstrom, *America in Black and White,* 197–198.

22. National Center for Education Statistics, *America's Kindergartners: Findings from the Early Childhood Longitudinal Study, Kindergarten Class of 1998–99, Fall 1998,* NCES 2000-070 (Washington, D.C.: U.S. Department of Education, 2000), 18–19.

23. National Center for Education Statistics, *Children's Reading and Mathematics Achievement in Kindergarten and First Grade,* NCES 2002-125 (Washington, D.C.: U.S. Department of Education, 2002), 41–42.

24. It should be noted, though, that 29 percent of the Hispanic children in the original sample of beginning kindergartners were excluded from study because their English was too poor for reliable testing; *America's Kindergartners,* 12. Generalizations about Latino children as a whole on the basis of this study thus need to be qualified. Apparently, the students excluded will be the subject of a separate study in the future.

25. Meredith Phillips et al., "Family Background, Parenting Practices, and the Black-White Test Score Gap," Jencks and Phillips, *The Black-White Test Score Gap,* 108. The study of 1998 kindergartners, by contrast, showed an initial gap of .638 standard deviations in math and .401 standard deviations in reading. This may be hopeful evidence of recent change, but it may reflect some peculiarity in the sample, and one would like further confirmation of the point from other sources.

26. U.S. Department of Labor, *The Negro Family: The Case for National Action* (Washington, D.C.: U.S. Government Printing Office, 1965).

27. The College Board, *Reaching the Top: A Report of the National Task Force on Minority Achievement* (Washington, D.C.: U.S. Department of Labor, 1999); Jencks and Phillips, *The Black-White Test Score Gap.*

28. The information in this and the next several paragraphs is drawn from David J. Armor, *Maximizing Intelligence* (New Brunswick, N.J.: Transaction Publishers, 2003), chap. 4, "Race, Family, and Intelligence." Armor analyzes data from the Youth Study, which followed a group of 9,000 children born to a representative sample of 5,000 women who were first surveyed in 1979 between the ages of 16 and 21. Armor makes use of IQ scores, among other measures. Particularly since the publication of Richard Herrnstein and Charles Murray's *The Bell Curve* (1994), many have mistakenly understood IQ as a trait determined by genes and fixed at birth, impervious to environmental influences. That is only one conception of IQ, and it would be unwise to throw out the baby with the bath water. Armor takes a radically different approach. His entire book is a sustained argument about the importance of environmental and cultural factors in the intellectual growth of young children. The right combination of factors, he demonstrates, can do much to "maximize" IQ, and the wrong combination much to depress it.

29. It is not clear why black mothers have so many more low-birth-weight babies, but

poverty is not a sufficient explanation. The Hispanic poverty rate is about as high as that of blacks, but there are many fewer low-birth-weight Latino infants. A demographer argues that the remarkably high black out-of-wedlock birth rate is responsible; Nicholas Eberstadt, *The Tyranny of Numbers; Mismeasurement and Misrule* (Washington, D.C.: AEI Press, 1995), 54–60.

30. For brief summaries of the evidence, see Orlando Patterson, *Rituals of Blood*, 132–145, and Sara McLanahan, "Parent Absence or Poverty: Which Matters Most?" in Greg Duncan and Jeanne Brooks-Gunn, eds., *Consequences of Growing Up Poor* (New York: Russell Sage Foundation, 1997). For more extended discussion of the evidence, see Sara McLanahan and Gary Sandefur, *Growing Up with a Single Parent: What Hurts, What Helps* (Cambridge, Mass.: Harvard University Press, 1994).

31. In the 1998 kindergarten study, 40 percent of black children were living with two parents, versus 83 percent of white children.

32. For an attempt to show that economic factors explain these demographic differences, see William Julius Wilson, *The Truly Disadvantaged: The Inner City, the Underclass, and Public Policy* (Chicago: University of Chicago Press, 1987), 84–89. The evidence to the contrary seems overwhelming to us. See David Ellwood and Jonathan Crane, "Family Change Among Black Americans: What Do We Know?" *Journal of Economic Perspectives*, 4 (Fall 1990), 65–84; and Robert D. Mare and Christopher Winship, "Socioeconomic Change and the Decline of Marriage for Blacks and Whites," in Christopher Jencks and Paul E. Peterson, eds., *The Urban Underclass* (Washington, D.C.: Brookings Institution, 1991), 175–203.

33. Jencks and Phillips, *The Black-White Test Score Gap*, 24, 45–46.

34. Jencks and Phillips, *The Black-White Test Score Gap*, 43.

35. Meredith Phillips et al., "Family Background, Parenting Practices, and the Black-White Test Score Gap," in Jencks and Phillips, *The Black-White Test Score Gap*, 127.

36. George Farkas, *Human Capital or Cultural Capital? Ethnicity and Poverty Groups in an Urban School District* (New York: Aldine de Gruyter, 1996). Chap. 3 offers a fascinating discussion of racial differences in the "auditory processing" ability of young children, their ability to "comprehend patterns among auditory stimuli," which he relates to "differences between their family linguistic culture and standard English." This depresses the reading skills of Hispanic children and those with relatively uneducated mothers. But it has its most powerful effect on black children. Analyzing a national sample tested in 1986–1988, Farkas found that "the lower reading skills of African-American children are essentially completely explained by their deficits in auditory processing" (22). This, however, cannot explain the sharp racial gap among children from college-educated homes in Shaker Heights. We doubt that many of the African-American students there were exposed to much "black English" in their early years.

37. Phillips, "Family Background," 129, n. 42.

38. Roland G. Fryer and Steven D. Levitt, "Understanding the Black-White Test Score Gap in the First Two Years of School," NBER Working Paper 8975, June 2002.

39. Reginald Fields, "Academic Disparity Hits Suburbs as Well," *Akron Beacon Journal*, March 7, 2002, A1.

40. College Board, *Reaching the Top*, 14, 17–18.

41. Letter to the editor from Elizabeth Camesi, *Washington Post*, September 14, 2002, A20.

42. Discipline data from Office of Civil Rights, U.S. Department of Education, "Fall 1998 Elementary and Secondary School Civil Rights Compliance Report," unpublished document, 2000, 1. Family structure as given in U.S. Bureau of the Census, *American Families and Living Arrangements: March 1999*, P20-537 (Washington, D.C.: U.S. Government Printing Office, 2000), table C2.

43. NAACP, "Call to Action in Education," report released by the organization's Education Department, November 2001. The logic here is the same as that of critics who claim that black-white differences in crime rates do not reflect real differences in the be-

havior of the groups but rather the bias of law enforcement authorities. For a critique of such arguments, see Thernstrom and Thernstrom, *America in Black and White*, chap. 10.

44. Russell J. Skiba, Robert S. Michael, Abra C. Nardo, and Reece L. Peterson, *The Color of Discipline: Sources of Racial and Gender Disproportionality in School Punishment*, Policy Research Report #5RSI (Bloomington, Ind.: Indiana Education Policy Center, 2000), 17.

45. Applied Research Center, *Facing the Consequences: An Examination of Racial Discrimination in the Public Schools* (Oakland, Calif.: Applied Research Center, 2000), 2.

46. Farkas, *Human Capital*, 102–104. The data were collected in the fall of 1986.

47. Farkas, *Human Capital*, 100.

48. Dr. Stuart Biegel, *SFUSD Desegregation Paragraph 44 Independent Review, Report No. 15, 1997–1998* (San Francisco: San Francisco Unified School District, 1999), 95. Similar data for the Seattle public schools are tabulated in a somewhat different way, but the pattern is the same. On a typical day in the 1995–1996 school year, 29 percent of black high school students were absent without excuse, double the white average. Attendance has improved considerably since then, By 2000–2001, the black truancy rate was down to 17 percent, but the white rate had fallen to 7 percent, so the racial disparity remained very large. Data available at www.seattleschools.org. In the state of Florida, 27 percent of black students in grades 9–12 were absent without excuse for at least 10 percent of their classes, 26 percent of Hispanics, 20 percent of whites, and 12 percent of Asians in the 1999–2000 academic year. See www.myfloridaeducation.com.

49. The answers were broken down by schools whose student bodies were less than 5 percent minority, 5–19 percent, 20–49 percent, and 50 percent or more. National Center for Education Statistics, *Violence and Discipline Problems in U.S. Public Schools: 1996–1997*, NCES 98-030 (Washington, D.C.: U.S. Department of Education, 1998). More recent information about all of these problems was gathered in the U.S. Department of Education's 1999–2000 Schools and Staffing Survey. The only results available thus far, unfortunately, are from a brief analysis conducted by *Education Week*; see Jennifer Park, "Deciding Factors" in the paper's "Quality Counts 2003" special issue, January 9, 2003, 17–18. This sketchy story includes the information that teachers in high-minority schools were far more likely than others to report that student misbehavior interfered with learning at their school, that tardiness was a serious problem, and that student disrespect for teachers was widespread.

50. Eugene Williams, Sr., quoted in Courtland Milloy, "Homework That Parents Need to Do," *Washington Post*, February 19, 1997, B1.

51. Ferguson, "A Diagnostic Analysis," 388. Ferguson notes that the difference was attributable to the fact that whites were far more likely to be taking academically demanding courses that required more homework.

52. Philip J. Cook and Jens Ludwig, "The Burden of 'Acting White': Do Black Adolescents Disparage Academic Achievement?" in Jencks and Phillips, *The Black-White Test Score Gap*, 383–384.

53. Ferguson, "A Diagnostic Analysis," 366–369.

54. John U. Ogbu has written extensively elaborating and defending this theory; see, for example, *Minority Education and Caste: The American System in Cross-Cultural Perspective* (New York: Academic Press, 1978). Ogbu even extends this theory to Latinos, on the grounds that Mexicans were the victims of America's imperialistic expansion in the 1840s and were deeply alienated from American society because of that bitter historical memory. We argued in the previous chapter that almost all Hispanic children in our schools today derive from voluntary immigration in the twentieth century, which makes this line of argument highly implausible. For a case study of black students in a Washington, D.C., high school from this perspective, see Signithia Fordham, *Blacked Out: Dilemmas of Race, Identity, and Success at Capital High* (Chicago: University of Chicago Press, 1996).

55. U.S. Census Bureau, "The Big Payoff: Educational Attainment and Synthetic Esti-

mates of Work-Life Earnings," *Current Population Reports*, P23–210 (July 2002). Whites obtained even greater payoffs to education. But that is because, as we have demonstrated, at each level of education completed, whites are more literate and numerate, on the average, and it is those cognitive skills that the labor market rewards.

56. See Daniel G. Solorzano, "Mobility Aspirations Among Racial Minorities, Controlling for SES," *Sociology and Social Research*, 75 (July 1991), 182–187. National Center for Education Statistics, *Student Peer Groups in High School: The Pattern and Relationship to Academic Outcomes*, NCES 97-055 (Washington, D.C.: U.S. Department of Education, 1997), 6. For similar further analysis, see Cook and Ludwig, "The Burden of 'Acting White,'" and James W. Ainsworth-Darnell and Douglas B. Downey, "Assessing the Oppositional Culture Explanation for Racial/Ethnic Differences in School Performance," *American Sociological Review*, 63 (1998) 536–553. Ainsworth-Darnell and Downey's excellent critique of the Ogbu theory is marred by the authors' persistent attempts to reduce the cultural differences they find to differences in "material conditions." Material conditions are far from a sufficient explanation for many cultural differences relevant to educational achievement, starting with the stark black-white difference in the prevalence of low-birthweight babies.

57. Ferguson, "A Diagnostic Analysis," 364.

58. Ainsworth-Darnell and Downey, "Assessing the Oppositional Culture Explanation."

59. Speech by the Reverend Martin Luther King, Jr., in Chicago, 1963, as quoted in Shelby Steele, *The Content of Our Character: A New Vision of Race in America* (New York: St. Martin's Press, 1990), 138. Ronald Ferguson has used the same metaphor: "After all, no runner ever came from behind by running the same speed as race leaders"; see his essay "Addressing Racial Disparities in High-Achieving Suburban Schools," *Policy Issues* (North Central Regional Educational Laboratory), issue 13 (November 2002), 4.

60. Pedro A. Noguera, "Racial Politics and the Elusive Quest for Excellence and Equity in Education," *Education and Urban Society*, 34 (November 2001), 18–41, and "The Trouble with Black Boys," *Harvard Journal of African Americans and Public Policy*, 3 (Fall 2001), 23–46.

61. Ferguson's oral presentation at the Seminar on Social Inequality, John F. Kennedy School of Government, Harvard University, December 9, 2002.

Eight: Send Money

1. Edward Wyatt, "Success of City School Pupils Isn't Simply a Money Matter," *New York Times*, June 14, 2000, A1.

2. *Williams et al. v. State of California et al.*, Superior Court of the State of California, County of San Francisco, First Amended Complaint for Injunctive and Declaratory Relief, August 14, 2000.

3. John McElhenny, "Minority Students Improve on MCAS Test, but Gap with Whites Widens," AP News wire story, October 24, 2001.

4. Bob Herbert, "In Search of Magic," *New York Times*, March 21, 2002, A37.

5. Bob Herbert, "An Unequal Education," *New York Times*, May 20, 2002, A23.

6. "A Better Balance: Standards, Tests, and the Tools to Succeed," *Quality Counts 2001, Education Week* special issue, January 11, 2001, 8.

7. Jonathan Kozol, *Savage Inequalities: Children in America's Schools* (New York: Crown, 1991). For more recent expressions of this view, see Jonathan Kozol, "Malign Neglect: Children in New York City's Public Schools Are Being Shortchanged—Again," *The Nation*, June 10, 2002, 20. In the same vein, see the *New York Times* editorial "A Visionary School Plan in Maryland," April 30, 2002, A28.

8. National Center for Education Statistics, *Digest of Education Statistics 2001*, NCES 2002-130 (Washington, D.C.: U.S. Department of Education, 2002), 191.

9. Eric A. Hanushek, "Spending on Schools," in Terry Moe, ed., *A Primer on America's Schools* (Stanford, Calif.: Hoover Institution Press, 2001), 79–81. This calculation is for the

1980–1990 period, and is based on the standard estimate that special education costs 2.3 times as much as regular education. Richard Rothstein and K. H. Miles present a higher estimate for special education in *Where's the Money Gone? Changes in the Level and Composition of Education Spending* (Washington, D.C.: Economic Policy Institute, 1995), but the authors still cannot deny that the money schools have available for regular students has increased very substantially since the 1960s.

10. National Center for Education Statistics, *Disparities in Public School District Spending, 1989–1990*, NCES 95-300 (Washington, D.C.: U.S. Department of Education, 1995). We use the adjusted bivariate results rather than the multivariate ones, which are also provided. The purpose of the multivariate analysis was to isolate the effects of race per se from that of other variables that are correlated with race, such as the median value of owner-occupied homes in the district. This analysis may be preferable for some purposes, but we are not interested in "pure" racial differences controlled for a long list of other characteristics correlated with race. The actual disparities, controlled only for cost of living and special-needs students, seemed more important. It might be noted that the effect of controlling for all these additional variables is an estimate that minority-majority districts spent 15 percent *more* per pupil than low-minority districts. The bivariate estimate that such districts spent 6.5 percent *less* is more meaningful, we think.

11. The study adjusted for student needs on the assumptions that special education students cost 2.3 times as much as regular students and both compensatory education and Limited English Proficient students cost 20 percent more.

12. *Disparities in Public School Spending*, 17.

13. *Digest of Educational Statistics 2001*, table 93. It should be noted that the valuable investigations that the Education Trust has conducted on these equity issues are badly marred by its curious decision to compile school district spending data without including any federal funds. This is true, for example, of all its interesting "state summary" reports that it makes available on-line. Since most federal funds are targeted toward lower-income and higher-minority districts, this decision gives a distorted picture of the money available to them. The rationale for this strange exclusion is given in Education Trust, "The Other Gap: Poor Students Receive Fewer Dollars," *Education Trust Data Bulletin*, March 6, 2001, 2. The method employed, it states, "recognizes that federal education dollars are intended to supplement rather than supplant tax revenues raised from state and local sources," and that "federal law forbids states from using" such funds "to equalize basic education." This strikes us as a questionable reading of the law, and we note that the federal government has never taken any steps that would confirm this interpretation by denying funds to a state on the grounds that it wasn't doing enough on its own to equalize expenditures. But even if this interpretation were correct, it seems irrelevant to the citizen thinking about the problem. If we want to know whether increasing per pupil expenditures can improve the performance of poor and minority children, surely what matters is the total spent on them, not just the total coming from local and state sources. At the very least, the Education Trust should give total per pupil expenditure figures as well as those for local and state funds alone, which would reveal much less inequality than the Education Trust suggests.

14. The authors of one study that examined funding disparities within states calculated seven different measures of disparity, and found that in the years 1980–1994 inequality declined on at least five of the seven measures in over three-quarters of all the states. National Center for Education Statistics, *Trends in Disparities in School District Level Expenditures per Pupil*, NCES 2000-020 (Washington, D.C.: U.S. Department of Education, 2000). William N. Evans, Sheila Murray, and Robert Schwab, "School Houses, Court Houses, and State Houses After *Serrano*," *Journal of Policy Analysis and Management*, 16 (January 1997) studied data from 16,000 school districts for the years 1972–1992, and found a similar movement toward greater equality in spending. The authors estimate that state revenues for local schools reduced inequality by 20 percent in 1972; by 1992, state funding had the effect of cutting inequality by more than half (19). James E. Ryan collected data from seventy-four urban school districts in the 1993–1994 academic year. After adjusting for differ-

ences in cost of living and student needs, he found that forty-five of the seventy-four spent more per pupil than the statewide average. Of the fifty-nine districts with more than 50 percent minority enrollments, thirty-six spent above the state average; see "The Influence of Race on School Finance Reform," *Michigan Law Review*, 98 (May 1999), 437–441.

15. Council of the Great City Schools, *Beating the Odds II: A City-by-City Analysis of Student Performance and Achievement Gaps on State Assessments* (Washington, D.C.: Council of the Great City Schools, 2002), 35. That expenditures in these cities were comparable to those in the suburbs might have seemed surprising good news. But the Council argued that the one-third of instances in which this was not the case was "disturbingly high," and a number whose significance was "hard to overstate" (41). The Council's rhetoric about alleged unfairness, though, would lead us to expect that big-city schools would have less money than others in the great majority of cases, and the facts show that not to be the case.

16. Kozol, *Savage Inequalities*, 89, 135–36, 143.

17. In fact, pupil-teacher ratios are not precise measures of the number of students in the average class, because teachers normally do not teach every hour. The average class is thus somewhat larger than these figures suggest. Jay Greene has shown that the dramatic drop in the pupil-teacher ratio in recent decades has not produced an equally sharp drop in average class size. Using survey data gathered by the NEA, Greene found that the total number of students taught by the average secondary school teacher dropped 28 percent between 1971 and 1996, from 134 to 97. But the size of the average secondary school class did not fall correspondingly in these years, because teachers reduced the number of class hours they taught instead of the size of their average class, giving themselves more free periods each day; Jay P. Greene and Greg Forster, "Widespread Exploitation: How the Teachers' Unions Take Advantage of Their Own Members," *National Review Online*, February 10, 2000. This complication, though, should not distort the pattern revealed in the table. There is no reason to think that teachers in schools with large numbers of black students teach fewer and thus larger classes than those in low-minority schools. Unfortunately, direct evidence on the size of classes is much harder to find than pupil-teacher ratio data.

18. National Black Caucus of State Legislators, Committee on Elementary and Secondary Education, "Closing the Achievement Gap," report, November 2001, 6 (available at www.nbcsl.com).

19. Greene and Forster, "Widespread Exploitation"; National Center for Education Statistics, *Projections of Education Statistics to 2011*, NCES 2001-083 (Washington, D.C.: U.S. Department of Education, 2001), table 32; National Center for Education Statistics, *Characteristics of the 100 Largest Public Elementary and Secondary School Districts in the United States, 2000–2001*, NCES 2001-346 (Washington, D.C.: U.S. Department of Education, 2001), table 71.

20. Figures from the "school report cards" provided on the New Jersey Department of Education Web site.

21. "Class Size Counts: The Research Shows Us Why," *American Teacher* (the official magazine of the AFT), April 1998.

22. NAACP, "Call for Action in Education," report released by the organization's Education Department, November 2001, 11.

23. The positive results of the Tennessee STAR experiment are emphasized in Alan B. Krueger, "An Economist's View of Class Size Research," in Lawrence Mishel and Richard Rothstein, eds., *The Class Size Debate* (Washington, D.C.: Economic Policy Institute, 2002), For criticism, see Eric Hanushek, "Evidence, Politics, and the Class Size Debate," in the same volume.

24. Brian M. Stecher and George W. Bohrnstedt, eds., *Class Size Reduction in California: The 1998–99 Evaluation Findings*, executive summary (Sacramento, Calif.: California Department of Education, 2000). This is a report put together by a consortium that includes the American Institutes for Research and the RAND Corporation, and is available at www.classize.org.

25. Stecher and Bohrnstedt, *Class Size Reduction in California*. For an analysis of more recent data that draws the same broad conclusions, see Christopher Jepson and Steven Rivkin, *Class Size Reduction, Teacher Quality, and Academic Achievement in California Public Schools* (San Francisco: Public Policy Institute of California, 2002).

26. As of December 2001, the *Los Angeles Times* reported, 14 percent of California teachers lacked credentials, and most were in the lowest-performing schools. Duke Helfand, "Lack of Qualified Teachers Undermines State Reforms," *Los Angeles Times*, December 12, 2001, A1.

27. Jepson and Rivkin, *Class Size Reduction*.

28. Assume that a school has 20 teachers, 20 classrooms, and 600 students, 30 per class. Cut class size by a third, to 20, and the school will need 30 teachers and 30 classrooms, an increase of 50 percent in both.

29. Editorial, *Las Vegas Review-Journal*, June 28, 2000, 8B.

30. The estimated cost of a current Arizona proposal to reduce class size from 22 to 17 students per teacher in grades K–3 is $117 million in salaries for additional teachers and nearly three times that—$302 million—on additional classrooms; Pat Flannery, "Smaller Classes Come at High Cost," *Arizona Republic*, October 1, 2001. Moreover, space can't be manufactured quickly.

31. Edward P. Lazear, "Smaller Class Size Isn't a Magic Bullet," *Los Angeles Times*, September 2, 1999, B9.

32. The Luther Burbank Middle School in San Francisco allegedly had the dead rodent in the gym for most of the academic year. *Williams et al. v. State of California et al.*, Superior Court of the State of California, County of San Francisco, First Amended Complaint for Injunctive and Declaratory Relief, August 14, 2000.

33. *Digest of Educational Statistics 2001*, tables 93 and 169.

34. Bernice Yeung, "Hard Lessons," *San Francisco Weekly* (New Times, Inc.), October 11, 2000, unpaginated.

35. Yeung, "Hard Lessons."

36. Matthew Miller, "The Super," *Washington Monthly*, 33, no. 6 (June 2001), 35.

37. Personal communication to the authors.

38. On the problem of districts averaging teacher salaries, see Paul T. Hill, "Fairer Pay for All Teachers," *Christian Science Monitor*, November 20, 2000, 9; Paul T. Hill, "A Better Way to Allocate Pay for Teachers," *The Record* (Bergen County, N.J.), November 27, 2000, L3; Marguerite Roza, "Policy Inadvertently Robs Poor Schools to Benefit the Rich," *Seattle Post-Intelligencer*, September 24, 2000, F1; and Marguerite Roza, "The Challenge for Title I," *Education Week*, April 4, 2001, 38, 56.

39. Blake Hurst, "End of an Illusion," *American Enterprise*, 11, no. 4 (June 2000), 44–45.

40. Sharon Churcher and Alison George, "In Kansas [City] They Spent $2 Billion on Schools. Now They Have Greek Statues and the Pupils Can't Read," *Mail on Sunday* (London), July 21, 2002, 58.

41. Stephanie Simon, "Schools a $2 Billion Study in Failure," *Chicago Tribune*, May 30, 2001, 8.

42. Simon, "Schools," 8

43. *Digest of Education Statistics 2001*, table 93.

44. Stephanie Simon, "High Cost for Low Grades," *Los Angeles Times*, May 18, 2001, A1.

45. Scott Greenberger, "Cambridge Eyes Income, Not Race, for Desegregation," *Boston Globe*, December 16, 2001, A1. See also Pedro A. Noguera, "Racial Politics and the Elusive Quest for Excellence and Equity in Education," *Education and Urban Society*, on the discouraging lack of results from the efforts of the Minority Student Achievement Network, an association of fifteen liberal communities (including Cambridge) that seeks to increase minority achievement.

46. Mary Hurley, "Cambridge Notes: School Budget OK'd, but Critics Speak Out," *Boston Globe*, May 13, 2001, 11.

47. The dropping of honors classes is described in Mary Hurley, "Rindge Becoming a Bore for Brightest?," *Boston Globe,* July 7, 2002, 9.

48. MCAS results from the Massachusetts Department of Education Web site, www.doe.mass.edu.

49. "Jury Out on Change at Rindge," *Boston Globe,* August 25, 2002, B8.

50. Agnes Blum, "Cambridge Votes to Defy State on MCAS," *Boston Globe,* April 24, 2002, B5.

51. Edward Wyatt, "Success of City School Pupils Isn't Simply a Money Matter," *New York Times,* June 14, 2000, 1.

52. Richard J. Murnane and Frank Levy, "Why Money Matters Sometimes," *Education Week,* September 11, 1996. The authors further develop their analysis of the changes needed in our schools in their book *Teaching the New Basic Skills: Principles for Educating Children to Thrive in a Changing Economy* (New York: Free Press, 1996).

Nine: Racial Isolation

1. Tanika White and Kate Beem, "The School Test: A Focus on Instruction, Not Integration," *Kansas City Star,* August 22, 1999, A1.

2. William H. Freivogel, "Missouri Argues to End Desegregation Plan," *St. Louis Post-Dispatch,* January 12, 1995, 1A.

3. Freivogel, "Missouri Argues."

4. Lynn Horsley, "KC Schools' Stress on Test Scores Called Excessive," *Kansas City Star,* June 5, 1995, A1.

5. Linda Darling-Hammond, "Apartheid in American Education: How Opportunity Is Rationed to Children of Color in the United States," in Tammy Johnson, Jennifer Emiko Boyden, and William J. Pittz, *Racial Profiling and Punishment in American Schools* (Oakland, Calif.: Applied Research Center, 2001), 39–44. Jonathan Kozol has described New York City, arguably the most liberal community in America, as "the nation's largest and now uncontested bastion of apartheid education." See his "Malign Neglect: Children in New York City's Public Schools Are Being Shortchanged—Again," *The Nation,* June 10, 2002, 20.

6. National Center for Education Statistics, *Paving the Way to Postsecondary Education: K–12 Intervention Programs for Underrepresented Youth,* NCES 2001-205 (Washington, D.C.: U.S. Department of Education, 2001), 8.

7. Appendix A of *Paving the Way to Postsecondary Education* provides a "Review of the Literature on Opportunities to Learn." The only citations it gives to work on segregation trends are to publications by Orfield. The most recent publication on this subject from Orfield and his associates is Erika Frankenberg, Chungmei Lee, and Gary Orfield, *A Multiracial Society with Segregated Schools: Are We Losing the Dream?* (Cambridge, Mass.: Harvard Civil Rights Project, 2003.) This volume seems to be this year's version of an annual report on the subject by Orfield and collaborators. For other specimens, see Gary Orfield, *Schools More Separate: Consequences of a Decade of Resegregation* (Cambridge, Mass.: Civil Rights Project, Harvard University, 2001), and Gary Orfield and John T. Yun, *Resegregation in American Schools* (Cambridge, Mass.: Civil Rights Project, Harvard University, 1999).

8. Gerald N. Rosenberg, *The Hollow Hope: Can Courts Bring About Social Change?* (Chicago: University of Chicago Press, 1991), 50.

9. Frankenberg et al., *A Multiracial Society,* 27.

10. Frankenberg et al., *A Multiracial Society,* 28, 33.

11. Figures in this and the next paragraph are from the National Center for Education Statistics, *Digest of Education Statistics 2001* (Washington, D.C.: U.S. Government Printing Office, 2002), 58.

12. U.S. Bureau of the Census, *The Hispanic Population: 2000 Census Brief,* C2KBR/01-3 (Washington, D.C.: U.S. Department of Commerce, 2002), 3.

13. Frankenberg et al., *A Multiracial Society,* 54.

14. Mary Jordan, "Kansas City's Costly Integration Strategy," *Washington Post,* April 11, 1992, A1.

15. Orfield, *Schools More Separate*, 12–13.

16. Orfield's single-minded emphasis on exposure to whites is especially curious because he does call attention to the dramatic decline in the white share of school enrollments and the growth of the Hispanic and Latino student populations over the past three decades, and even declares that it indicates "the need for new ways of thinking about race relations." Despite that sound observation, his conception of how best to measure school segregation hasn't changed a bit.

17. Frankenberg et al., *A Multiracial Society*, 23.

18. David J. Armor and Christine Rossell, "Desegregation and Resegregation in the Public Schools," in Abigail Thernstrom and Stephan Thernstrom, *Beyond the Color Line: New Perspectives on Race and Ethnicity* (Stanford, Calif.: Hoover Institution Press, 2002), 239. This essay reviews the literature and presents new evidence. For a full-scale treatment of the issue from this point of view, see David J. Armor, *Forced Justice: School Desegregation and the Law* (New York: Oxford University Press, 1995).

19. Thomas Cook et al., *School Desegregation and Black Achievement* (Washington, D.C.: National Institute of Education, U.S. Department of Education, 1984), 6–42. Cook also found the estimated effects of desegregation varying so widely that it was hard to place much weight on any measure of central tendency.

20. Eric A. Hanushek, John F. Kain, and Steven G. Rivkin, "New Evidence about *Brown v. Board of Education:* The Complex Effects of School Racial Composition on Achievement," Working Paper no. W8741 (Cambridge, Mass.: National Bureau of Economic Research, 2002).

21. Although METCO has been in operation for nearly four decades now, at the cost of many tens of millions of dollars, its educational effects have never been systematically assessed.

22. Data from the College Board Web site, www.collegeboard.com. Totals do not add up to 100 percent because of students classified as "other" or "unknown."

23. Brigid Schulte, "Montgomery Failing Its Students, Audit Finds," *Washington Post*, September 24, 2000, C1.

24. Tom Loveless, *The Tracking and Ability Grouping Debate* (Washington, D.C.: Thomas B. Fordham Foundation, 1998), 18. In fact, the study found black students were 10 percent more likely to be assigned to top-track classes than whites with similar skills. However, that advantage disappeared when the racial composition of schools was controlled; see p. 18 and n. 41. This suggests that black students with low scores were getting into top-track classes in heavily minority schools where the competition was easier.

25. Ronald F. Ferguson, "Why America's Black-White School Gap Persists," unpublished paper, Weiner Center for Public Policy, John F. Kennedy School of Government, Harvard University, July 13, 2001, n. 13: "Currently, the standard arrangement is that no student is officially forbidden from entering a class at any level."

26. David Hill, "Test Case: A California Lawsuit Challenges Widespread Inequities in the Availability of Advanced Placement Courses, *Education Week*, March 1, 2000, 34.

27. Hill, "Test Case," 34.

28. Julian R. Betts, Kim S. Rueben, and Anne Danenberg, *Equal Resources, Equal Outcomes? The Distribution of School Resources and Student Achievement in California* (San Francisco: Public Policy Institute of California, 2000), 132–140.

29. See a 2002 study by the United States General Accounting Office, *Per Pupil Spending Differences Between Selected Inner City and Suburban Schools Varied by Metropolitan Area*, GAO-03-234 (Washington, D.C.: U.S. General Accounting Office, 2002), 37, for the estimate that special students cost school districts twice as much on average as regular students.

30. Harvard Civil Rights Project, Executive Summary: Conference on Minority Issues in Special Education," 1; available at www.civilrightsproject.harvard.edu. The estimate for the emotionally disturbed is from table 2, "Odds Ratios for the U.S. and by State Across all Disabilities and for Selected Individual Disability Categories," from a paper by Tom Parrish called "Disparities in the Identification, Funding, and Provision of Special Education."

31. Between 1976 and 2000, the proportion of students found eligible increased 65 percent—from 8 percent of the student population to 13 percent; *Digest of Education Statistics, 2001,* 66. The cost has gone up even more; Wade Horn and Douglas Tynan, "Revamping Special Education," *Public Interest,* Summer 2001.

32. In September 2001, they felt compelled to write to the chairman of the Senate Committee on Labor, Health and Human Services, and Education, arguing that the "use of our research to oppose federal special education funding guarantees or increases is a clear distortion of our intent and findings." Gary Orfield and Christopher Edley, Jr., to Senator Tom Harkin, September 28, 2001, available on the Harvard Civil Rights Project Web site (see n. 30 above).

33. A similar incoherence may be found in the NAACP's recent summary of its position on educational issues: NAACP, National Education Department, "Call to Action: From Access to Accountability." This document simultaneously complained that "students of color" are overrepresented in special education and that "many minority students who do in fact have special behavioral needs are nonetheless disciplined harshly without consideration of their disability." Is the NAACP not advocating that fewer minority children be placed in special education, with the result that schools could discipline disruptive children more freely—without respect to their "disability"?

34. The results of the 2000 science assessment were not tabulated in a form that allows comparisons across grade levels or age groups. But the 1999 NAEP Trend Assessment did allow such comparisons. On that exam, the mean science score of black 17-year-olds was 254. White 13-year-olds averaged 266, 12 points better, while whites who were only 9 scored 240. The black 17-year-old score was almost exactly halfway between that of whites who were 9 and 13, and thus about what whites who were 11 would likely have scored had the test been administered at that age.

Ten: Teacher Quality

1. Yilu Zhao, "Many Teachers Keep Failing Test for Certification," *New York Times,* April 29, 2002, B1.

2. Kate N. Grossman, Becky Beaupre, and Rosalind Rossi, "Poorest Kids Often End Up with the Weakest Teachers," *Chicago Sun-Times,* September 7, 2001.

3. Robert Hanley, "New Jersey Seizes School District in Jersey City, Citing Total Failure," *New York Times,* October 5, 1989, A1.

4. Mark Gerson, *In the Classroom: Dispatches from an Inner-City School That Works* (New York: Free Press, 1997). He tells the story of his search for a teaching job in the Introduction.

5. Education Trust, "Honor in the Boxcar," *Thinking K–16,* 4, no. 1 (Spring 2000), 3.

6. S. Paul Wright, Sandra P. Horn, and William L. Saunders, "Teacher and Classroom Context Effects on Student Achievement: Implications for Teacher Evaluation," *Journal of Personnel Evaluation in Education,* 11 (1997), 57–67.

7. For an excellent recent example of the large literature on this, see Steven G. Rivkin, Erich A. Hanushek, and John F. Kain, "Teachers, Schools, and Academic Achievement," unpublished paper, July 2002.

8. Dan D. Goldhaber, "The Mystery of Good Teaching," *Education Next,* Spring 2002, 50.

9. "Quality Counts 2003: If I Can't Learn from You," a special issue of *Education Week,* January 9, 2003, 90. Texas, Arizona, and Ohio have subject knowledge tests but not a basic skills assessment.

10. These examples are from the Massachusetts Department of Education Web site, viewed on February 2, 2001: www.doe.mass.edu/teachertest.

11. Grossman et al., "Poorest Kids." For additional detail, see Rosiland Rossi and Dave McKinney, "Why Are Teacher Tests Secret?" *Chicago Sun-Times,* September 7, 2001.

12. Economist Dan D. Goldhaber, a leading researcher on this subject, estimates that over 95 percent of school districts today pay teachers according to a single salary schedule based on years of experience and degrees held; see "Teacher Pay Structure and Teacher

Quality: The Crucial Role of Teacher Compensation in Shaping the Teacher Workforce," address at the Consortium for Policy Research in Education's November 2002 National Conference on Teacher Compensation and Evaluation, Chicago, 37.

13. National Center for Education Statistics, *Schools and Staffing in the United States: A Statistical Profile, 1993–94*, NCES 96-124 (Washington, D.C.: U.S. Department of Education, 1996), 54.

14. See, for example, Harold Wenglinksy, *How Teaching Matters: Bringing the Classroom Back into Discussions of Teacher Quality* (Princeton, N.J.: Educational Testing Service and Milken Family Foundation, 2000), 21–25, which shows that neither years of teaching experience nor having a teacher with a master's or higher degree had any effect on eighth-grade math and science scores on the 1996 NAEP tests. Using the exceptionally rich data available for Texas, Rivkin, Hanushek, and Kain, "Teachers, Schools, and Academic Achievement," reach the same conclusion. For a defense of the conventional criteria, see Linda Darling-Hammond, *Teacher Quality and Student Achievement: A Review of State Policy Evidence* (Seattle: Center for the Study of Teaching and Policy, University of Washington, 1999). Although the focus is on the effects of teacher certification, there is much pertinent evidence in a literature assessment by the Abell Foundation, *Teacher Certification Reconsidered: Stumbling for Quality* (Baltimore: Abell Foundation, 2001). For Darling-Hammond's response, see "The Research and Rhetoric on Teacher Certification: A Response to 'Teacher Certification Reconsidered,' " available at www.nctaf.org. For a rejoinder to that, see the Abell Foundation's *Teacher Certification Reconsidered: Stumbling for Quality: A Rejoinder.*

15. Julian R. Betts, Kim S. Rueben, and Anne Danenberg, *Equal Resources, Equal Outcomes? The Distribution of School Resources and Student Achievement in California* (San Francisco: Public Policy Institute of California, 2000), 194–202.

16. David W. Grissmer, Ann Flanagan, Jennifer Kawata, and Stephanie Williamsons, *Improving Student Achievement: What State NAEP Test Scores Tell Us*, MR-924-EDU (Santa Monica, Calif.: RAND Corporation, 2000), 105.

17. Education Trust, *All Talk, No Action*, August 2002. The study examined only secondary schools, because teachers in elementary schools don't have specialized certificates in a particular subject. Usually, they teach all subjects in one class for the entire day.

18. Jay Mathews, "More of City's Students Take Advanced Classes, Participation in AP, IB Courses Grows," *Washington Post*, December 6, 2001, T3.

19. Sam Fullwood III, "Low Expectations Hurt Black Students," *Plain Dealer*, September 4, 2000, 1B.

20. Sharon Begley, "The Stereotype Trap," *Newsweek*, November 6, 2000, 66.

21. National Center for Education Statistics, *Paving the Way to Postsecondary Education: K–12 Intervention Programs for Underrepresented Youth*, NCES 2001-205 (Washington, D.C.: U.S. Department of Education, 2001), 9.

22. Robert Rosenthal and Lenore F. Jacobson, *Pygmalion in the Classroom: Teacher Expectation and Pupils' Intellectual Development* (New York: Holt, Rinehart & Winston, 1968). For a fascinating and devastatingly critical history of the influence of this work, see Samuel S. Wineburg, "The Self-Fulfillment of the Self-Fulfilling Prophecy," *Educational Researcher*, 16 (December 1987), 28–37. Shaw's *Pygmalion* was subsequently turned into the musical *My Fair Lady*, which is how it is best known.

23. Lee Jussim, Jacquelynne Eccles, and Stephanie Madon, "Social Perception, Social Stereotypes, and Teacher Expectations: Accuracy and the Quest for the Powerful Self-Fulfilling Prophecy," *Advances in Experimental Social Psychology*, v. 28 (1996), 281–388. The key findings on race are reported on 333–335. The only evidence of bias found was a problack bias in a school district that was 97 percent African-American; teachers there viewed the performance of their black students as favorably as they did other students, even though the other students had higher grades and test scores. Another illuminating study by the same authors is "The Accuracy and Power of Sex, Social Class, and Ethnic Stereotypes: A Naturalistic Study in Person Perception," *Personality and Social Psychology*

Bulletin, v. 24. For a valuable review of the literature, see Ronald F. Ferguson, "Teachers' Perceptions and Expectations and the Black-White Test Score Gap," in Christopher Jencks and Meredith Phillips, eds., *The Black-White Test Score Gap* (Washington, D.C.: Brookings Institution Press, 1998), 273–317.

24. Teachers in the study by Jussim et al. did have lower expectations of black students, on the average. But these judgments were not racially biased, because they reflected the poorer performance of these students in the past. Ronald Ferguson argues that teachers should display a different form of race neutrality—one in which expectations of students are based not only on their measurable past performance but on their "unobserved potential." But, as he notes, if "potential" differs from past performance, "it is difficult to prove"; Ferguson in *The Black-White Test Score Gap*, 275–276, 281–283. This standard thus seems too vague to be usable in any empirical study.

25. MetLife, *The MetLife Survey of the American Teacher 2001: Key Elements of Quality Schools*, a report on a poll conducted by Harris Interactive, Inc., www.metlife.com, 67.

26. That teacher experience can alter expectations negatively is strongly suggested by the fact that an earlier MetLife survey, in 1992, found that 93 percent of teachers said that "all children can learn" before they began teaching, but that after two years in the classroom, the figure dropped to 86 percent. This time, they found that 86 percent of teachers with 0–5 years of experience endorsed that statement, but that the figure dropped to 81 percent for those with 6–25 years of experience, and fell to 73 percent for those with 26 or more years of teaching; *MetLife Survey*, 64.

27. *MetLife Survey*, 70.

28. *MetLife Survey*, 75. Unfortunately, no information was provided about how many said "good," "fair," etc., in the report of the study.

29. In addition, half of all students from low-income families and more than 60 percent of those getting D's and F's said teachers expected too much of them. Unfortunately, no racial breakdowns are provided. But since African Americans and Latinos are strongly overrepresented in both of these categories, there must have been a sharp racial difference as well. More minority students, it seems clear, believe their teachers expect too much—not too little—of them. *MetLife Survey*, 76.

30. *MetLife Survey*, 77.

31. National Center for Education Statistics, *A Profile of the American Eighth Grader*, National Education Longitudinal Study of 1988, NCES 90-458 (Washington, D.C.: U.S. Department of Education, 1990), 17.

32. Ronald Ferguson presents three tables of results from this survey, and we use his numbers; see "Test-Score Trends Along Racial Lines, 1971 to 1996: Popular Culture and Community Academic Standards," in Neil J. Smelser, William Julius Wilson, and Faith Mitchell, eds., *America's Becoming: Racial Trends and Their Consequences*, vol. 1 (Washington, D.C.: National Academy Press, 2000), 381–383

33. On the other hand, mysteriously, 56 percent of black students thought it was a "somewhat serious" or "serious" problem at their school that too many teachers were "doing a bad job." The figure was only 36 percent for whites and 45 percent for Hispanics. Many black students who were extremely satisfied with their own teachers nonetheless had a poor impression of the teachers at their school in general. We have no explanation, except to note that this resembles a puzzling national pattern among adults, who give poor marks to the public school system in general but at the same time rate the schools their children attend as very good.

34. NAACP, National Education Department, "Call to Action: From Access to Accountability, From the Courts to the Community," NAACP Web site, November 2001.

35. National Education Association, "Diversity in the Teaching Force Collaborative and National Summit," available at www.nea.org, visited February 20, 2002.

36. Karla Scoon Reid, "Prep-School Program Opens Doors for Minority Teachers," *Education Week*, August 8, 2001, 6.

37. "Critical Issue: Educating Teachers for Diversity," NCREL (North Central Re-

gional Educational Laboratory), undated, on web site www.ncrel.org, visited January 21, 2001.

38. Quoted in Mark S. Lewis, "Supply and Demand of Teachers of Color," Digest Number 94-8, ERIC (Educational Resources Information Center), undated, on the ERIC Web site, www.ericsp.org/pages/digests/supply_demand_teacher_94-8.html, visited January 21, 2001.

39. Applied Research Center, *Facing the Consequences: An Examination of Racial Discrimination in the Public Schools* (Oakland, Calif.: Applied Research Center, 2000), 19.

40. Reid, "Prep-School Program Opens Doors."

41. Reid, "Prep-School Program Opens Doors."

42. DeWitt Wallace–Reader's Digest Fund, "Recruiting, Preparing and Retaining Teachers for America's Schools: Progress Report, Pathways to Teaching Careers" (August 1997), at www.wallacefunds.org/publications/pdf/dwpathways.pdf.

43. Charles Babington and Liza Frazier, "Improving Marks in Prince George's Schools Do Not Sway Skeptics," *Washington Post*, October 15, 1997, B4.

44. Marjorie Coeyman, "Like Student, Like Teacher," *Christian Science Monitor*, November 21, 2000, 15.

45. Ronald G. Ehrenberg, Daniel D. Goldhaber, and Dominic J. Brewer, "Do Teachers' Race, Gender, and Ethnicity Matter? Evidence from *NELS88*," Working Paper no. 4669 (Cambridge, Mass.: National Bureau of Economic Research, 1994).

46. Thomas S. Dee, "Teachers, Race and Student Achievement in a Randomized Experiment," Working Paper no. 8432 (Cambridge, Mass.: National Bureau of Economic Research, 2001).

47. Data are from the National Opinion Research Center's 1994 General Social Survey, as reported in Jack Citrin, "The End of American Identity?" in Stanley Renshon, ed., *One America? Political Leadership, National Identity, and the Dilemmas of Diversity* (Washington, D.C.: Georgetown University Press, 2001), 298.

48. Applied Research Center, *Facing the Consequences*, 19.

49. Educational Testing Service, *The Academic Quality of Prospective Teachers: The Impact of Admissions and Licensure Testing* (Princeton, N.J.: Educational Testing Service, 1999).

50. Calculated from data in table 4, p. 18.

51. Albert Shanker, "Quality Assurance: What Must be Done to Strengthen the Teaching Profession," *Phi Delta Kappan*, 78 (November 1996), 220–224.

52. Albert Shanker, "Will CBEST Survive?" *New York Times*, March 7, 1996, E7 (paid advertisement for American Federation of Teachers).

53. U.S. Department of Health, Education, and Welfare, *Equality of Educational Opportunity* (Washington, D.C.: U.S. Government Printing Office, 1996), 316–319.

54. Ronald G. Ehrenberg and Dominic J. Brewer, "Did Teachers' Verbal Ability and Race Matter in the 1960s? *Coleman* Revisited," *Economics of Education Review*, 14 (1995), 1–21.

55. Robert P. Strauss and Elizabeth A. Sawyer, "Some New Evidence on Teacher and Student Competencies," *Economics of Education Review*, 5 (1986), 41–48.

56. For Ferguson's study of Texas elementary and secondary schools in the late 1980s, see his essay "Can Schools Narrow the Test Score Gap?" in Christopher Jencks and Meredith Phillips, eds., *The Black-White Test Score Gap* (Washington, D.C.: Brookings Institution Press, 1998,) 354–356. For Texas elementary schools in the years 1990–1994, see John F. Kain and Kraig Singleton, "Equality of Educational Opportunity Revisited," *New England Economic Review*, May-June 1996, 81. Data from Alabama are analyzed in Ronald F. Ferguson and Helen F. Ladd, "How and Why Money Matters: An Analysis of Alabama Schools," in Helen F. Ladd, ed., *Holding Schools Accountable: Performance-Based Reform in Education* (Washington, D.C.: Brookings Institution Press, 1996). For Tennessee, see S. Paul Wright, Sandra P. Horn, and William L. Saunders, "Teacher and Classroom Context Effects on Student Achievement: Implications for Teacher Evaluation," *Journal of Personnel Evaluation in Education*, 11 (1997), 57–67.

57. Donald R. Winkler, "Educational Achievement and School Peer Group Composition," *Journal of Human Resources*, 10 (1975), 189–204; Anita A. Summers and Barbara L. Wolfe, "Do Schools Make a Difference?" *American Economic Review*, 67 (1977), 639–652; Ronald G. Ehrenberg and Dominic J. Brewer, "Do School and Teacher Characteristics Matters? Evidence from High School and Beyond," *Economics of Education Review*, 13 (1994), 1–17.

58. Education Trust, "Honor in the Boxcar."

59. Jacqueline Goldwyn Kingon, "A View From the Trenches," *New York Times*, April 8, 2001, Section 4A (Education Life supplement) 30.

60. Salary differentials are given in *Digest of Education Statistics: 2001*, 85. On qualifications, see Dale Ballou and Michael Podgursky, *Teacher Pay and Teacher Quality* (Kalamazoo, Mich.: W. E. Upjohn Institute for Economic Research, 1997), 130–131.

61. *Digest of Education Statistics 2001*, 83. The classic statement on the private school advantage is James S. Coleman and Thomas Hoffer, *Public, Catholic, and Private Schools: The Importance of Community* (New York: Basic Books, 1987). For an excellent, more up-to-date review of this issue, see Joseph Viteritti, *Choosing Equality: School Choice, the Constitution, and Civil Society* (Washington, D.C.: Brookings Institution Press, 1999), chap. 4.

62. Christina Asquith, "A Real Education," *Columbia Journalism Review*, March-April 2002, 14.

Eleven: Congress Strikes Out

1. Milbrey Wallin McLaughlin, *Evaluation and Reform: The Elementary and Secondary Education Act of 1965, Title I* (Cambridge, Mass.: Ballinger Publishing Co., 1975), 21.

2. Quoted in Michael Kelly, " 'F' for School Reform," *Washington Post*, April 11, 2001, A27.

3. Quoted in "Guidelines: Special Programs for Educationally Deprived Children," Department of Health and Human Services, 1966.

4. Hugh Davis Graham, *The Uncertain Triumph: Federal Education Policy in the Kennedy and Johnson Years* (Chapel Hill: University of North Carolina Press, 1984), 208.

5. U.S. Department of Education, Planning and Evaluation Service, *High Standards for All Students: A Report from the National Assessment of Title I on Progress and Challenges Since the 1994 Reauthorization* (Washington, D.C.: U.S. Department of Education, 2001), 6.

6. Harvey Kantor and Robert Lowe, "Class, Race, and the Emergence of Federal Education Policy," *Educational Researcher*, 24 (April 1994), 9, deny this, claiming that termination of federal funding was "a hollow threat," and attributing the sudden success of the desegregation drive to court actions. This seems doubtful: Between 1965 and 1968, there were about two hundred terminations of federal funding because of failure to comply with the antidiscrimination provisions, which represented 7 percent of the 2,800 school districts in the South; Gerald N. Rosenberg, *The Hollow Hope: Can Courts Bring About Social Change?* (Chicago: University of Chicago Press, 1991), 49. The cutoff provision had sharper teeth than might be thought, because federal funds quickly became quite significant to the budgets of the southern states. By the 1971–1972 school year, federal dollars amounted to 28 percent of elementary and secondary school expenditures in Mississippi and 22 percent in Alabama. They meant about $90 million a year in new money in each state; Rosenberg, *The Hollow Hope*, 98–99.

7. McLaughlin, *Evaluation and Reform*, vii.

8. McLaughlin, *Evaluation and Reform*, 2.

9. Graham, *The Uncertain Triumph*, 79.

10. McLaughlin, *Education and Reform*, 1.

11. McLaughlin, *Education and Reform*, 22–24.

12. McLaughlin, *Education and Reform*, 22–24.

13. McLaughlin, *Education and Reform*, 21.

14. U.S. Department of Health, Education, and Welfare, *Equality of Educational Opportunity* (Washington, D.C.: U.S. Government Printing Office, 1996), iii.

15. Gerald Grant, "Shaping Social Policy: The Politics of the Coleman Report," *Teachers College Record*, 75 (September 1973), 22.

16. Ellen Condit Lagemann, *An Elusive Science: The Troubling History of Educational Research* (Chicago: University of Chicago Press, 2000), 195.

17. Only one major finding of the Coleman Report meshed at all with the agenda of the Office of Education, and then only partly so. At a time when OE officials were pushing for school desegregation, it was helpful that Coleman concluded that black children were still highly segregated in the nation's schools, and that this was educationally harmful to them. But he found that the core problem was not racial segregation, but social-class segregation. Integrating poor black children with poor white children—which is mainly what happened when court-ordered busing to achieve racial balance began on a large scale a few years later—would not enhance the learning of either group. According to Coleman's analysis, students from low-income homes, whether black or white, do better in schools with middle-class majorities. In fact, this part of the analysis was open to serious question. Some of the reported differences were in the wrong direction and others were very small, and Coleman was unable to control for selection bias. It is doubtful that lower-class black children attending largely white, middle-class schools were typical of the lower-class black population at the time.

18. The political considerations that led to the release of the sanitized "summary" document are described in Grant, "Shaping Social Policy," 22–32.

19. Frederick Mosteller and Daniel P. Moynihan, eds., *On Equality of Educational Opportunity* (New York: Random House, 1972).

20. United States Commission on Civil Rights, *Racial Isolation in the Public Schools* (Washington, D.C.: U.S. Government Printing Office, 1967), 115–140.

21. McLaughlin, *Education and Reform*, 34–39.

22. McLaughlin, *Education and Reform*, 37.

23. McLaughlin, *Education and Reform*, vii, 118.

24. Carl F. Kaestle and Marshall S. Smith, "The Federal Role in Elementary and Secondary Education, 1940–1980," *Harvard Educational Review* 52 (November 1982), 396–400.

25. Grant, "Shaping Social Policy," 33. Grant notes that Daniel Patrick Moynihan, then serving as Nixon's chief domestic policy advisor, was "the principal architect" of this message, and that Moynihan did a great deal to promote Coleman's message in both the federal government and the academy.

26. Robert B. Semple, Jr., "Nixon Signs Education Bill with Reluctance," *New York Times*, April 14, 1971, as quoted in Grant, "Shaping Social Policy," 36.

27. U.S. Department of Education, *High Standards for All Students*, 17.

28. Diane Ravitch, *The Troubled Crusade: American Education, 1945–1980* (New York: Basic Books, 1983), 159.

29. United States Department of Health and Human Services, *2002 Head Start Fact Sheet*; Eliana Garces, Duncan Thomas, and Janet Currie, "Longer Term Effects of Head Start," National Bureau of Economic Research Working Paper 8054, December 2000, 8.

30. Research and Evaluation Office, Project Head Start, Office of Economic Opportunity, *Review of Research: 1965 to 1969* (Washington, D.C., June 1969), 39.

31. Edward Zigler and S. Muenchow, *Head Start: The Inside Story of America's Most Successful Educational Experiment* (New York: Basic Books, 1992), 231–232.

32. Zigler and Muenchow, *Head Start*, 74.

33. Michael David Shumsky, "Can Head Start Help Narrow the Racial Gap in Educational Performance? A Critical Review of the Literature and a Blueprint for the Future of Head Start," unpublished paper, Harvard University, June 1999, 22–26; Ravitch, *The Troubled Crusade*, 159.

34. Edward F. Zigler, "Formal Schooling for Four-Year-Olds? No," in Zigler and Sharon L. Kagan eds., *Early Schooling: The National Debate*, 36–37, quoted in Darcy Ann

Olsen, "Universal Preschool Is No Golden Ticket," CATO Institute Policy Analysis, No. 333, February 9, 1999, www.cato.org.

35. This is the subtitle of Zigler and Muenchow's *Head Start.*

36. Janet Currie and Duncan Thomas, "Does Head Start Make a Difference?" *American Economic Review,* 85 (1995), 341–364.

37. Janet Currie and Duncan Thomas, "School Quality and the Longer-Term Effects of Head Start," NBER Working Paper 6362, January 1998.

38. Garces, Thomas, and Currie, "Longer Term Effects of Head Start."

39. The authors say in the text of their article that black males who were veterans of Head Start were more likely to have graduated from high school. But since this did not hold for blacks as a group, that suggests that the reverse was the case for black females.

40. In other words, selection bias rather than exposure to Head Start may be involved, because the mothers were a distinctive group. They may have had greater concern for their children's development than other poverty mothers who did not choose to enroll their youngsters in Head Start. That concern might also have led them to be more effective as mothers, and to raise children who were somewhat less likely to fall afoul of the law in later life. It is possible that a similar mechanism could explain the positive educational effects found for whites. We lack the data to rule out that possibility with any certainty.

41. Janet Currie and Duncan Thomas, "Does Head Start Help Hispanic Children?" *Journal of Public Economics,* 74 (1999), 235–262.

42. This information is not given in the article. But Currie and Thomas, "Does Head Start Make a Difference?" is based on the same data. Table 2 of that paper gives the mean age of whites in the sample as 8.3 years, and that of African Americans as 9.0 years, so nine seems a safe maximum for Hispanics.

Twelve: Raising the Bar

1. Darragh A. Johnson, "Md., Va. Standardized Tests Score High on Parent Anger," *Washington Post,* November 11, 2001, C1.

2. Bob Chase, "Another 'Field of Dreams' Education Summit?" *Knight Ridder/ Tribune,* September 27, 1999.

3. National Commission on Excellence in Education, A *Nation at Risk: The Imperative for Education Reform* (Washington, D.C.: National Commission on Excellence in Education, 1983).

4. This history is summarized in Diane Ravitch, *National Standards in American Education: A Citizen's Guide* (Washington, D.C.: Brookings Institution Press, 1995), chap. 2. The goals are listed in an appendix, 187–192.

5. Ravitch, *National Standards,* 188.

6. Diana Jean Schemo, "U.S. Students Fail to Keep Up in Global Science and Math Tests," *New York Times,* December 6, 2000, A1.

7. James Traub, "The Test Mess," *New York Times Magazine,* April 7, 2002, 46.

8. For a thoughtful overview of these developments, see Williamson M. Evers, "Standards and Accountability," in Terry Moe, ed., A *Primer on America's Schools* (Stanford, Calif.: Hoover Institution Press, 2001), chap. 9, and a collection of essays edited by Evers and Herbert J. Walberg, *School Accountability* (Stanford Calif.: Hoover Institution Press, 2002).

9. The theory is spelled out and defended in Julian R. Betts and Robert M. Costrell, "Incentives and Equity Under Standards-Based Reform," in Diane Ravitch, ed., *Brookings Papers on Educational Policy: 2001* (Washington, D.C.: Brookings Institution Press, 2001), 9–61.

10. Bob Chase, "Another 'Field of Dreams' Education Summit?"

11. Richard F. Elmore, "Unwarranted Intrusion," *Education Next,* Spring 2000, 31.

12. Richard F. Elmore, "Bridging the Gap Between Standards and Achievement: The Imperative for Professional Development in Education," Albert Shanker Institute, www.ashankerinst.org.

13. Elmore, "Unwarranted Intrusion," 31.

14. Elmore, "Unwarranted Intrusion," 31.

15. Elmore, "Bridging the Gap."

16. James Traub tells the story of Ronald Ross, hired as the new superintendent in Mount Vernon, New York, who looked at the test scores in that largely black district and used the abysmal picture to force change on recalcitrant teachers. But the scores were essential to the leverage he had. (Traub, "The Test Mess," 46.) And even in that district in desperate shape, after five years of conflict, Ross left for a job outside the educational system.

17. Ronald C. Brady, "Can Failing Schools Be Fixed?," report of the Fordham Foundation, January 2003, www.edexcellence.net.

18. Anecdotal evidence suggests that sunlight can become a leverage for at least limited change. In Texas, for instance, the release of the latest results on the statewide test receives saturation coverage in the media, and school ratings matter. When the Texas Education Agency issued its annual school accountability ratings in 2002 and Berkner High School in Dallas was labeled "Low Performing," principal Dave Casey felt he had "let down the kids, parents, teachers, everyone." Scott Parks, "How Ratings Touch Schools," *Dallas Morning News*, September 22, 2002, 33A.

19. For a discussion of the benefits of the program, see Jay Greene, "An Evaluation of the Florida A-Plus Accountability and School Choice Program" (New York: Manhattan Institute, 2001). Opponents of vouchers include most professional educators. For a critique of the Greene analysis, specifically, see Gregory Camilli and Katrina Bulkley "Critique of 'An Evaluation of the Florida A-Plus Accountability and School Choice Program,' " *Education Policy Analysis Archives*, 9, no. 7 (March 4, 2001), http://epaa.asu.edu/epaa/v9n7.

20. Brady, "Can Failing Schools Be Fixed?" 30.

21. This lack of data raises questions about the interpretation in a recent report by the Council of Chief State School Officers: Rolf K. Blank and Doreen Langesen, *State Indicators of Science and Mathematics Education, 2001: State-by-State Trends and New Indicators from the 1999–2000 School Year* (Washington, D.C.: Council of Chief State School Officers, 2002). The authors present depressing state-level data on racial gaps in student achievement in the fourth and eighth grades in chap. 1 of the report. The remaining chapters provide a highly optimistic spin by discussing improvements in the rate at which minority students are enrolled in advanced courses, in teacher qualifications, etc. Most of these changes, though, involve students at the end of middle school or in high school. A more candid report would have acknowledged that we have no NAEP data demonstrating that they have led to improved student performance.

22. June Kronholtz, "What Constitutes Failure? Education Bills Ponder Answer," *Wall Street Journal*, May 21, 2001, A24.

23. See the Texas education Web site, www.tea.state.tx.us/student.assessment.

24. Connie Mabin, "State: Students Score Record High on TAAS Tests," AP wire, May 17, 2000.

25. Tyce Palmaffy, "The Gold Star State," *Policy Review*, March-April 1998, 12–17.

26. For a more skeptical view of the Texas record, see Stephen P. Klein, et al., "What Do Test Scores in Texas Tell Us?" Rand Issue Paper no. 202 (Santa Monica, Calif.: RAND Corporation, 2000). We agree with the authors' point that the educational progress evident from rising TAAS scores needs to be checked against another yardstick, and that state NAEP scores are the best yardstick. But the NAEP record of Texas is quite impressive when one considers levels of parental education, per capita incomes, and the proportion of minority and/or low-income students in the state. None of these factors would lead us to expect Texas to be anywhere near the top of the list on the NAEP assessments. Klein and his colleagues, though, are correct in stressing how little the racial gap in NAEP scores has narrowed in Texas.

27. National Center for Education Statistics, *Digest of Education Statistics 2001*, NCES 2002-130 (Washington, D.C.: U.S. Department of Education, 2002), 21; U.S. Census Bureau, *Statistical Abstract of the United States: 2001* (Washington, D.C.: U.S. Government Printing Office, 2002), 426.

28. *Digest of Education Statistics 2001*, 192. In 1998–1999, the latest year for which the data are available, Texas spent $6,161 per public school pupil, 12 percent below the national average. North Carolina spent 13 percent less per pupil than the U.S. average.

29. *Digest of Education Statistics 2001*, 58.

30. David W. Grissmer et al., *Improving Student Achievement: What State NAEP Test Scores Tell Us*, MR-924-EDU (Santa Monica, Calif.: RAND Corporation, 2000), 68–73.

31. Strictly speaking, these are not all the "same" students. Some of the public school fourth-graders of 1992 and 1996 were not eighth-graders in Texas public schools four years later, because they had left the state, had not been promoted with their class each year, or had transferred to a private school. And some of the eighth-graders of 1996 and 2000 had not been fourth-graders in Texas four years earlier because they had been living in another state, had been fifth-graders who were held back a year before they reached the eighth grade, or were enrolled in a private school in the fourth grade. It is impossible to say if this affects the results significantly, but it is hard to see how it would bias the major conclusions.

32. Grissmer's comparison of state NAEP scores found that most of the variation in scores from state to state was due to differences in family characteristics; his measures were race, parental education, family income, the teenage birth rate, the proportion of single mothers, the percentage of mothers who were employed, and the proportion of families that had moved within the past two years; Grissmer, *Improving Student Achievement*, 15–16, 69.

33. Michael Cohen, "Implementing Title I Standards: Assessments and Accountability: Lessons from the Past, Challenges for the Future," unpublished paper for the Fordham Foundation Conference, "Will No Child Truly Be Left Behind? Challenges of Making This Law Work," Washington, D.C., February 13, 2002.

34. Ravitch, *National Standards*; Cohen, "Implementing Title I Standards."

35. In April 2002, the Department of Education signed binding compliance agreements with four states and the District of Columbia, giving them an extra three years to comply with the 1994 act. Twenty-seven states and Puerto Rico, as of that date, were already operating under waivers giving them extra time, ranging from one to three years. If they fail to meet current timetables, states may—for the first time—lose federal funding; Erik W. Robelen, "State, Ed. Dept. Reach Accords on 1994 ESEA," *Education Week*, April 17, 2002, 1, 28–29.

36. For evidence on the size of the black middle class under various definitions, see Thernstrom and Thernstrom, *America in Black and White*, chap. 7.

37. It is not only racial and ethnic groups that must show "adequate yearly progress"; students with disabilities, those with limited English proficiency, and the economically disadvantaged must also display gains.

38. Dan Goldhaber, "What Might Go Wrong with the Accountability Measures in the 'No Child Left Behind Act'?" unpublished paper for the Thomas B. Fordham Foundation Conference on "Will No Child Truly Be Left Behind? Challenges of Making this Law Work," Washington, D.C., February 13, 2002.

39. These disparities are reviewed in Lynn Olson, "A 'Proficient' Score Depends on Geography," *Education Week*, February 20, 2002, 1, 14–15. The magnitude of the problem is vividly illustrated in the charts of fourth-grade and eighth-grade math scores for two dozen states included in this article.

40. Chester E. Finn, Jr., reviews this picture in his editorial comment in *Gadfly* (Fordham Foundation), January 30, 2003.

41. Norman Draper, "Task Force Shapes State's No Child Left Behind Plan; Some Educators Say Standards Impossible to Achieve," *Star Tribune* (Minneapolis), January 9, 2003, B1.

42. Robert A. Frahm, "Too Many Schools to Be Left Behind?" *Hartford Courant*, June 9, 2002, A1.

43. Joshua Benton, "Big Test Lies Ahead for Texas Schools," *Dallas Morning News*, January 31, 2003, 1A.

44. Frahm, "Too Many Schools," A1.

45. Mass Insight Education, *Taking Charge: Urban High School Students Speak Out About MCAS, Academics, and Extra-Help Programs* (Boston: Mass Insight, 2002), 6, 12.

46. It is not as easy as might be thought to arrive at precise figures. It would be simple if all the tenth-graders of 2000–2001 were still living in Massachusetts and still enrolled in public school, and if all the twelfth-graders in 2002–2003 had been enrolled in the tenth-grade of a Massachusetts school two years before. But neither is the case. Some students have moved away or dropped out; others have moved into the schools since then. The passing rates given in the text are the percentages of students enrolled in Massachusetts high schools who had met the requirement after the November 2002 retest. Estimating the passing rates of particular groups is further complicated by the fact that many students who initially reported themselves as of "mixed" race subsequently identified with a specific racial group, with most of them switching to the African-American category. Hence the number of black students in the 2003 class increased by 22 percent between the spring of 2001 and the fall of 2002, while the number of white students rose by just 1 percent.

47. See the Massachusetts Department of Education Web site for remediation details. Michele Kurtz, "MCAS Results Treated with Care by Educators," *Boston Globe*, February 26, 2003, B1, summarizes the options.

48. Michele Kurtz, "110 More to Graduate Without Passing Exam," *Boston Globe*, February 6, 2003, B3.

49. Ronald Brownstein, "School Testing Backlash in Five Governor's Races," *Los Angeles Times*, October 27, 2002, A26.

50. Quoted in Mike Bowler, "Education Boss Wants Texas-Style Reading," *Baltimore Sun*, April 11, 2001, 1A.

51. "Survey Finds Little Sign of Backlash Against Academic Standards or Standardized Tests," Public Agenda, results released October 5, 2000.

Thirteen: Roadblocks to Change

1. Quoted in Amy M. Hightower, "San Diego's Big Boom: District Bureaucracy Supports Culture of Learning," Report no. R-02-2, Center for the Study of Teaching and Policy, University of Washington, January 2002,

2. Public Agenda, which collects survey data, has a number of polls relevant to this issue on its Web site, www.publicagenda.org. For instance, in January 2002 an ABC News/Washington Post survey found that 83 percent of the public thought that "improving education and the schools" should be a high priority for the president and Congress, with more than half giving it the highest priority. In May 2000, an ICR/Washington Post/Kaiser/Harvard poll found that 64 percent of Americans believed the public school system needed "major changes." And in August of that year, 61 percent of the public said they were "somewhat dissatisfied" or "completely dissatisfied" with the quality of education in the U.S. We do not have similar survey data that goes back to the beginning of the twentieth century, obviously, but infer the long-standing interest in change from the uninterrupted history of reform movements. On the other hand, it is equally true and equally important that the public tends to be considerably more satisfied with its own local public schools. Thus, a 1995 national survey that is analyzed in detail in Terry M. Moe's *Schools, Vouchers, and the American Public* (Washington, D.C.: Brookings Institution Press, 2001) found that only 26 percent of American adults and 20 percent of the parents of public school children believed that the schools *in their districts* needed "major changes" (47). When the question was shifted to the schools in their "state as a whole," the proportion thinking major changes were needed jumped by 9 points. The evidence cited above suggests that views of the schools become markedly more critical when the question is framed in terms of schools in the nation as a whole.

3. The invaluable book on the history of educational reform in the twentieth century is Diane Ravitch, *Left Back: A Century of Battles over School Reform* (New York: Simon & Schuster, 2000). In *Spinning Wheels: The Politics of Urban School Reform* (Washington, D.C.: Brookings Institution Press, 1999), Frederick M. Hess looks at the educational land-

scape in the mid-1990s, and concludes that urban districts ceaselessly spin the wheels of re-form in an effort that doesn't go anywhere. New policies are adopted and abandoned with amazing rapidity.

4. Charter schools are a relatively new addition to the educational scene, and few have been subjected to careful scholarly evaluation. None, in fact, has been examined with the use of control groups as in the voucher studies discussed in the next chapter. For an interesting but very brief and tentative assessment of the achievements of 376 charter schools in ten states, see Tom Loveless, *How Well Are American Students Learning?: The 2002 Brown Center Report on American Education* (Washington, D.C.: Brookings Institution, 2002), 30–36. The average overall level of student achievement at these schools, Loveless found, was disappointing. On the other hand, he suggests that the reason may be that such schools attract many students "who are struggling academically in public schools before ever setting foot on a charter school campus." Thus, the schools may be "doing an excellent job" with a relatively low-achieving population (32). Loveless also found that urban charters perform better than those in suburban or rural areas, and that new charter schools tend to do poorly in the first two years. Obviously, it will take a great deal of further research to make more definitive judgments. But certainly a great advantage of charter schools is that those that fail to meet the performance goals specified by the chartering authority are closed down. Thus, the Lynn Community Charter School in Massachusetts was closed by the state board of education in 2002 both because of the stagnant test scores of its students and because of its chaotic administration. To our knowledge, no regular public school in the entire state of Massachusetts has ever been shut down because it was doing a poor job educationally. Indeed, until the standards and accountability movement in the various states and No Child Left Behind, even the most dreadful public schools were allowed to go on doing what they had always been doing without interference from anyone.

5. Chris Moran, "Report Evaluates Education Progress Among Local Latinos," *San Diego Union-Tribune*, October 3, 2001, B1.

6. Louisa C. Spencer, "Progressivism's Hidden Failure," *Education Week*, February 28, 2001, 29.

7. Paul Clopton, letter to the *San Diego Union-Tribune*, September 4, 2002; Steve Kleinstuber, letter to the *San Diego Union-Tribune*, September 4, 2002; John de Beck, San Diego School District Board member, letter to *La Prensa–San Diego*, July 13, 2001.

8. Yilu Zhao, "Many Teachers Keep Failing Test for Certification," *New York Times*, April 29, 2002, B1.

9. Frederick M. Hess, "Break the Link," *Education Next*, Spring 2002, 22.

10. Justin Blum, "Half of District Teachers Weak, Board Chief Says," *Washington Post*, February 22, 2001, 1.

11. Black students in the District of Columbia consistently score well below the national average for blacks—indeed, at the bottom of the heap. In the 1998 NAEP reading assessments, D.C.'s eighth-grade black students scored 6 points—the equivalent of half a year's schooling—behind African Americans in Mississippi, the poorest of the fifty states. They were nearly as far behind them in math achievement as well. Although there are many impoverished neighborhoods in the District of Columbia, there also is a large and prosperous black middle class, much of it employed by the federal government. Furthermore, the per pupil spending figure for D.C. was $10,611 in 1998–1999, 51 percent above the national average and more than double the figure for Mississippi, the lowest in the nation; National Center for Education Statistics, *Digest of Education Statistics 2001* (Washington, D.C.: U.S. Government Printing Office, 2002), 193. D.C. also has fewer uncertified teachers and fewer who are teaching "out-of-field" than most American communities today. If half of its teachers are indeed not qualified, which seems quite plausible to us, it is not because they fail to meet the criteria the educational establishment thinks are important.

12. National Center for Education Statistics, *Predicting the Need for Newly Hired Teachers in the United States* to 2000–09, NCES 1999-026 (Washington, D.C.: U.S. Department of Education, 1999).

13. According to the National Center for Education Statistics Baccalaureate and Be-

yond Longitudinal Study of college graduates in 1992–1993, public school teachers had average combined SAT scores that were 58 points lower than those of college graduates entering all other professions (948 vs. 1006); Dan D. Goldhaber, "Teacher Pay Structure and Teacher Quality: The Crucial Role of Teacher Compensation in Shaping the Teacher Workforce," data for an address at the Consortium for Policy Research in Education's November 2002 National Conference on Teacher Compensation and Evaluation, Chicago, 5. In 2000, *Education Week* analyzed federal data on beginning teachers and found that "novice teachers who had scored in the top quartile on college-entrance exams were nearly twice as likely to leave the profession (26 percent) as those who scored below the top quartile (14 percent)." "Who Should Teach? Quality Counts 2000," special issue of *Education Week*, January 13, 2000, 17.

14. Matthew Miller, "Rethinking & Relearning About How to Teach Teachers," *Orlando Sentinel*, June 25, 2000, G1.

15. The widening of options for both women and African Americans is apparent from figures on the proportion of college graduates employed in K–12 education. In the years 1967–1971, 48 percent of white females with a college diploma were teachers, and 59 percent of black females; by 1992–1996, the percentages had dropped to 21 and 20 percent. Equally striking, 23 percent of black men with a college diploma were teachers in the late 1960s; by the early 1990s the figure had plunged to just 7 percent; Finis Welch, "Half Full or Half Empty? The Changing Economic Status of African Americans, 1967–1996," in Abigail Thernstrom and Stephan Thernstrom, eds., *Beyond the Color Line: New Perspectives on Race and Ethnicity* (Stanford, Calif.: Hoover Institution Press, 2002), 194.

16. Sam Minner, in "Our Own Worst Enemy," *Education Week*, May 30, 2001, 33, tells the tale of a meeting to screen applicants for admission into a teacher education program. The committee interviewed a young man nearing the end of his college career who wanted to teach science at the middle or high school level, but didn't know how many planets there were in our solar system or what a phylum was. He was admitted. Other evidence suggests this is not a unique story.

17. Quoted in "Reporter's Notebook," *Education Week*, September 27, 2000, 12.

18. Paige Akin, "Rigorous Teacher Training Proposed," *Richmond Times-Dispatch*, September 19, 2002, B1.

19. Kate Zernike, "Less Training, More Teachers: New Math for Staffing Classes," *New York Times*, August 24, 2000, 1.

20. Editorial, "Attracting the Best," *Indianapolis Star*, June 14, 1999, A10.

21. Quoted in Marci Kanstoroom and Chester E. Finn, Jr., eds., *Better Teachers, Better Schools* (Washington, D.C.: Thomas B. Fordham Foundation, July 1999), 7.

22. Everett Carll Ladd and Karlyn H. Bowman, *Attitudes Toward Economic Inequality* (Washington, D.C.: AEI Press, 1998), 118–123.

23. Ronald Brownstein, "Make the Buck Stop with Teachers by Linking Raises to Student Results," *Los Angeles Times*, February 5, 2001, 5. More than 95 percent of school districts have a single salary schedule for teachers, with differentials only for seniority and degrees held; Dan Goldhaber, "Teacher Pay Structure and Teacher Quality: The Crucial Role of Teacher Compensation in Shaping the Teacher Workforce," address at the Consortium for Policy Research in Education's November 2002 National Conference on Teacher Compensation and Evaluation, 37. A bit of experimentation with merit pay is occurring in a few districts—Cincinnati and Denver among them.

24. Information on the program was drawn from the Milken Family Foundation Web site at www.mff.org/tap/tap.taf.

25. Jay Mathews, "The Best Thing About Reform: It Won't Matter," *Washington Post*, February 17, 2002, B5.

26. John E. Chubb and Terry M. Moe, *Politics, Markets, and America's Schools* (Washington, D.C.: Brookings Institution Press, 1990), 56–57.

27. Frederick M. Hess, "A License to Lead? A New Leadership Agenda for America's Schools," Progressive Policy Institute, 21st Century Schools Project, January 2003, 12.

28. Hess, "A License to Lead?" 4.

29. Public Agenda, "Trying to Stay Ahead of the Game: Superintendents and Principals Talk About School Leadership," 2001.

30. Diane Ravitch, "Guest Editorial," *Gadfly*, January 23, 2003.

31. John E. Chubb, "The System," in Terry M. Moe, ed., *A Primer on America's Schools* (Stanford, Calif.: Hoover Institution Press, 2001), 34. For a much fuller statement of this perspective, see Chubb and Moe, *Politics, Markets, and America's Schools,* especially chap. 2.

32. Frederick M. Hess, *Revolution at the Margins: The Impact of Competition in Urban School Systems* (Washington, D.C.: Brookings Institution Press, 2002) For a good summary of the arguments see Hess, "The Work Ahead," *Education Next,* Winter 2001, 8.

33. Chubb, "The System," 39.

34. Matthew Miller, "The Super," *Washington Monthly*, 33, no. 6 (June 2001), 35.

35. Rebecca Winters, "Is Superintendent . . . a Job for a Super Hero?," *Time,* February 7, 2000, 70.

36. Winters, "Is Superintendent . . . a Job for a Super Hero?," 70.

37. Donald R. McAdams, "Lessons from Houston," *Brookings Papers on Education Policy 1999* (Washington D.C.: Brookings Institution Press, 1999), 129.

38. Donald R. McAdams, *Fighting to Save Our Urban Schools . . . and Winning!: Lessons from Houston* (New York: Teachers College Press, 2000), xvi.

39. See Chester E. Finn, Jr., and Kelly Amis, *Making It Count: A Guide to High-Impact Education Philanthropy* (Washington D.C.: Thomas B. Fordham Foundation, September 2001); and *Can Philanthrophy Fix Our Schools? Appraising Walter Annenberg's $500 Million Gift to Public Education* (Washington D.C.: Thomas B. Fordham Foundation, April 2000).

40. Terry M. Moe, "Teachers Unions and the Public Schools," in Moe, *A Primer on American Schools,* 151–183. We have relied heavily on Moe in this discussion of teachers unions.

41. Moe, "Teachers Unions," 152–155, discusses the difficulties in getting precise figures about current union membership.

42. Donald R. McAdams, *Fighting to Save Our Urban Schools,* 86.

43. Harold O. Levy, "Why the Best Don't Teach," *New York Times,* September 9, 2000, 15.

44. Teacher education is only a partial exception because, in fact, the unions care where teachers are trained. The National Council for Accreditation of Teacher Education is heavily influenced by the priorities of the unions, and thus the education schools accredited by NCATE are likely to turn out teachers who become loyal union members.

45. Thomas Toch, "Why Teachers Don't Teach," *U.S. News & World Report,* February 26, 1996, 62.

46. Marjorie Coeyman "It's Not Always So Easy to Say 'You're Fired!' Removing a Bad Teacher Can be Lengthy and Costly—Discouraging Schools from Taking Action," *Christian Science Monitor,* February 22, 2000, A13.

47. Hess, *Revolution at the Margins,* 93–94 and 58.

48. Coeyman, "It's Not Always So Easy to Say 'You're Fired!' "

49. The history is reviewed in Chester E. Finn, Bruno V. Manno, and Greg Vanourk, *Charter Schools in Action* (Princeton, N.J.: Princeton University Press, 2000). Subsequent developments up to the present may be tracked on two valuable Web sites: www.uscharterschools.org and www.edexcellence.net.

50. Moe, "Teachers Unions," 179–181; Bess Keller, "Unions Turn Cold Shoulder on Charters," *Education Week,* March 27, 2002, 1.

51. The best source of data on the growth of charter schools, the picture in each state, the number closed, and so forth is the Center for Education Reform; see www.edreform.com. CER has issued a *National Charter School Directory 2002–2003,* which profiles the almost 2,700 charter schools serving students in 36 states and Washington, D.C., as

of that school year. Another CER publication, *Charter School Laws Across the States*, offers in-depth analysis of the nation's forty charter laws.

52. Hess, "Break the Link," 22.

53. Chester E. Finn Jr., "Editorial Comment," *Gadfly*, January 9, 2003.

54. Chris Sheridan, "Some Accountability, Lots of Confusion," *Cleveland Plain Dealer*, February 2, 2003, H2; Megan Tench, "Opportunity Knocks: Woman Details Bureaucracy Fights on School Change," *Boston Globe*, February 4, 2003, B1.

55. Stephanie Banchero, "It's Time to Implement School Reform Law, U.S. Official Says," *Los Angeles Times*, November 27, 2002, A15; Tench, "Opportunity Knocks."

56. There are some district schools that have all the characteristics of charters but are not officially in the charter category. For example, in Worcester, Massachusetts, the University Park Campus School is a small neighborhood school that shows what can be done to bring quality education to at-risk children who arrive in seventh grade underprepared for a serious academic program. The school is a collaboration between the district and Clark University, and the university promises a tuition-free college education to every student who can meet the entrance requirements after receiving a University Park diploma. It is a much-celebrated school in Massachusetts but would not have had the success it has enjoyed if it were not, in all but name, a charter school.

57. Bruno V. Manno, "Yellow Flag," *Education Matters*, 3, no. 1 (Winter 2003), 18, reports that more than two hundred charter schools have gone out of business thus far because of educational or fiscal failures.

58. A good summary of the difficulties is contained in Bryan C. Hassel, "Friendly Competition," *Education Next*, 3, no. 3 (Winter 2003), 8.

59. On the political opposition to charter schools, see, for instance, Manno, "Yellow Flag," 16.

60. Moe, *Schools, Vouchers, and the American Public*, 2.

61. Thus, the annual Phi Delta Kappa poll on attitudes about education asked the same question about vouchers from 1970 to 1991, and found rising levels of support. In 1991, when the question was last posed that way, 50 percent of Americans favored vouchers and 39 percent opposed them. Then the question was rewritten so as to imply that the purpose of vouchers was to subsidize "at public expense" parents whose children were already attending private schools. That cut the level of support in half, to a mere 24 percent. This dramatic change was not a change in public attitudes; it was purely the result of framing the question in a radically different way. A 1992 Gallup poll that used a version of the original PDK poll found that 70 percent of the public favored vouchers, at the same time that the new PDK question put the figure at a mere 24 percent. For this evidence and much more on the intricacies of the polling data, see Moe, *Schools, Vouchers, and the American Public*, chap. 7.

62. Moe, *Schools, Vouchers, and the American Public*, 130.

63. Moe, *Schools, Vouchers, and the American Public*, 373.

64. Not many Americans are even informed enough about the issue to have strong opinions; in a 1995 survey, 65 percent said that they had never heard of vouchers. Moe, *Schools, Vouchers, and the American Public*, 191. The evidence we have of the results of a very few voucher experiments is promising. The most careful and sophisticated analysis available at present is William G. Howell and Paul E. Peterson, *The Education Gap: Vouchers and Urban Schools* (Washington, D.C.: Brookings Institution Press, 2002). It shows that children who received vouchers financed by private donors that allowed them to attend private schools in New York City, Washington, D.C., and Dayton, Ohio, performed better than a control group of identical children in the public schools. The most striking finding was the racial difference in the effects of choice. Black students, two-thirds of the total, made significantly greater gains in private school than their counterparts in the public schools. Whites and others—the authors lump them all together in the "all other ethnic groups" category—failed to show statistically significant improvement. Why African Americans should benefit from private schools more than others was not explained, but we sus-

pect that these schools are more like families than regular public schools, and more effective in transforming the culture these children brought with them from home. A debate over the validity of this study was going on when this book went to press.

65. Chubb and Moe, *Politics, Markets, and America's Schools*, 3.

Conclusion

1. Quoted in Nat Hentoff, "Low Budget, High Achievers," *Washington Times*, June 11, 2001, op-ed, A17.

2. Carole Novak, interview with Jaime Escalante, *Technos Quarterly*, 2, no. 1 (Spring 1993). (www.technos.net/02/1escalante.htm)

3. Russ Baker, "The Ecumenist Is the Growing Alliance Between Inner-City Preachers and Right-Wing Local Politicians. A Bargain with the Devil? The Reverend Floyd Flake Thinks Not," *American Prospect*, January 17, 2000, 26.

4. Quoted in William J. Bennett, "Staying on the Same Page," *Washington Times*, August 7, 2001, A15.

5. For the best argument for vouchers on grounds of equity, see Joseph P. Viteritti, *Choosing Equality: School Choice, the Constitution, and Civil Society* (Washington, D.C.: Brookings Institution Press, 1999).

6. Center for Education Reform Web site, http://edreform.com/school_choice/fuller_choice.htm.

Index

Page numbers in *italics* refer to figures.